NATIONAL GEOGRAPHIC

TRAVELER
Cuba

![National Geographic logo]

NATIONAL GEOGRAPHIC
TRAVELER
Cuba

Christopher P. Baker
Photography by Pablo Corral Vega
and Cristobal Corral Vega

Contents

Page 1: A friendly Havana
welcome
Pages 2–3: Parque Martí,
Cienfuegos, at sunset
Left: Sun, sand, and reef-fringed
waters are some of Cuba's
allures.

How to use this guide

See back flap for keys to text and map symbols

The *National Geographic Traveler* brings you the best of Cuba in text, pictures, and maps. Divided into three main sections, the guide begins with an overview of history, geography, and culture. Following are nine regional chapters with featured sites selected by the author for their particular interest and treated in depth.

The selected regions are arranged geographically. A map introduces each chapter, highlighting the featured sites. Walks and drives, plotted on their own maps, suggest routes for discovering an area. Features and sidebars give intriguing detail on history, culture, or contemporary life.

The final section, Travelwise, lists essential information for the traveler—pre-trip planning, getting around, and emergencies—along with with a selection of hotels, restaurants, shops, outdoor activities, entertainment, and special events. It also has a glossary of useful words and phrases.

To the best of our knowledge, all information is accurate as of the press date. However, it's always advisable to call ahead when possible.

Color coding

130

Each region is color coded for easy reference. Find the region you want on the map on the front flap, and look for the color flash at the top of the pages of the relevant chapter. Information in **Travelwise** is also color coded to each area.

Visitor information

Museo Nacional de Bellas Artes

🇦 61 E3
✉ Calle Rafael, bet. Zulueta & Monserrate
☎ 7/861-3858
🕐 Closed Mon.
💲 $

Practical information for most sites is given in the side column (see key to symbols on back flap). The map reference gives the page number of the map and grid reference. Other details are address, telephone number, days closed, entrance charge in a range from $ (under $5) to $$ (over $5). Other sites have information in italics and parentheses in the text.

TRAVELWISE

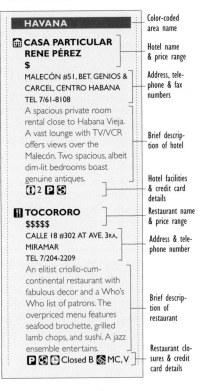

Color-coded area name

Hotel name & price range

Address, telephone & fax numbers

Brief description of hotel

Hotel facilities & credit card details

Restaurant name & price range

Address & telephone number

Brief description of restaurant

Restaurant closures & credit card details

Hotel & restaurant prices

An explanation of the price bands used in entries is given in the Hotels & Restaurants section (beginning on p. 238).

REGIONAL MAPS

Grid letter

Drive start point

Important featured site

Road label

La Habana (Havana)

Playa Baracoa

Road number

Adjacent chapter

Important featured town

Province name

- A locator map accompanies each regional map, showing that region's location in the country.
- Cities and points of interest described in the chapters are bolded and highlighted on each map.
- Adjacent regions are shown, each with a page reference.

WALKING TOURS

Red numbered bullets link sites on map to descriptions in the text.

Direction of route

Start point

Path

Walk route

Featured site on walk route

- An information box gives the starting and ending points, time and length of walk, and places not to be missed along the route.

DRIVING TOURS

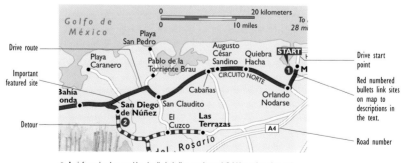

Drive route

Important featured site

Detour

Drive start point

Red numbered bullets link sites on map to descriptions in the text.

Road number

- An information box provides details including starting and finishing points, time and length of drive, and places not to be missed along the route, or tips on terrain.

NATIONAL GEOGRAPHIC

TRAVELER

Cuba

About the author & photographers

After studying geography at the University of London and Latin American studies at the University of Liverpool, Christopher P. Baker settled in California and established a career as a travel writer, photographer, and lecturer. He has written several guidebooks about Cuba and Havana, as well as ones to Jamaica, The Bahamas, Turks & Caicos, and California. He is author of the *National Geographic Traveler: Costa Rica* (2000), and National Geographic Adventure Press's *Mi Moto Fidel: Motorcycling through Castro's Cuba* (2000).

Pablo Corral Vega is the author of four photographic books: *Bare Earth; Silent Landscapes: The Andes of Ecuador; Ecuador: From Magic to Mirror,* and National Geographic's *Andes.* As director of the Discovering Ecuador project, he invited 38 photographers from 11 countries to spend one week photographing his homeland, resulting in a book published in 1994. He photographs for NATIONAL GEOGRAPHIC and other magazines and lives in Quito, Ecuador.

Cristobal Corral Vega has worked on various film documentaries in his native Ecuador, as well as contributed as photographer to many publications. His subjects have included bull fighting, religious art, residential design, and tourism. He is coauthor of the book, *Ecuador: De la Magia al Espanto,* published in 1996; and author of *Ecuador: Espacios de Luz,* published in 1998.

History & culture

The Cuban flag emulates the colors of the U.S. flag.

Cuba today

CUBA. AN ISLAND OF MAJESTIC ROYAL PALM TREES, DAY-GLO SUGARCANE fields, and soft textures. A land of revolution, haunting music, and bedeviling charms. Ethereal and romantic, Fidel Castro's captivating, chimerical isle is filled with mystery and contradictions, a place where communism takes on soft-textured tropical layers. Visitors thrill to Cuba's complexities and perplexing duality, to its lilting serenity, its delicious rums and rhythms, to the Cubans' vivacity and easy spontaneity.

So close and yet so far, Cuba is only 90 miles (145 km) from the neon-lit malls and fast food franchises of Florida—yet separated by a cultural and political gulf ten times that distance. Despite four frustrating decades of animosity between the U.S. and Cuban governments, Cuba—one of the most engaging and exhilarating destinations in the Western Hemisphere—has lost none of its romantic appeal. Tourism is booming, with travelers from Canada and Europe drawn by an open-arms welcome from the island's citizens and the exotic appeals of an unexpectedly haunting realm ripe with eccentricity and eroticism.

Visitors are awed by the time warp that is Cuba. Havana, erstwhile sultry seductress of the Caribbean, is today a stage set. Once glamorous, now patinated by age, it recalls the 1950s when the city was, in Somerset Maugham's piquant phrase, "a sunny place for

Havana sparkles by night. Rising above the waterfront Malecón is the Hotel Nacional, built in 1930.

century French rococo mansions, while art deco theaters from the 1920s blend into the cool, columned arcades of old palaces in a style called Mudejar. Fortunately, much of Cuba's colonial architecture, at least, is being restored.

Beyond the townships, you'll encounter an altogether different montage of timeless vignettes. Silver-sheathed royal palms rise over tobacco fields lovingly tended by *guajiros* (peasant farmers) in straw hats. Oxen plow the cinnamon-colored soil into furrows or lumber down country roads, pulling rickety carts piled high with sugarcane. Cuba is synonymous with sugar: Virtually everywhere you travel you are within sight of cane fields rippling in the breeze. Cuba's exotic, tropical beauty owes much to such calming landscapes. There are beaches, too, dazzlingly white, shelving into waters unbelievably blue, as in an ad for Havana Club rum. And mountains, perfect for birding and hiking. It is easy to understand why Cubans call their isle *"Mi cubita bella,* my beautiful little Cuba."

Cuba, however, is far removed from the picture-postcard cliché. What most enchants visitors is the potential for adventure. It's the way the Cubans are full of spontaneity and impromptu fun. The way they wring pleasure from poverty, draw you into their lives, and crank up the music, filling the air with salsa and sensuality. Tourists who restrict themselves to sightseeing without engaging the people will leave without having experienced—and shared—the real magic of Cuba.

You could easily fill your time in Havana—a gritty, seductive city full of museums, theaters, and nightclubs—with sweet rum and the world's finest cigars to be enjoyed fresh from factories that are open to view. But there's also traditional music and dance to be experienced in Santiago de Cuba. You can scuba dive off the Jardines de la Reina, fish to your heart's content in the lagoons of the Ciénaga de Zapata, go birding in the rain forests of the Cuchillas del Toa, or hike in the Sierra del Escambray. Such a highlights-of-Cuba itiner-

shady people." Cuba's old sauciness lingers on, beloved by Cubans and found in even the most remote urban backwater. Everywhere, classics from the heyday of Detroit—corpulent Chryslers, chrome-laden Cadillacs, and Studebakers with broad, grinning grilles—rumble down the road on underinflated tires, evoking nostalgia like Elvis Presley tunes of the same era. They are a metaphor, this four-wheeled flotsam, for the state of the island, notably the urban landscapes, many of which resemble classical ruins.

The fact that Cuba's cities ache with pathos and penury is part of the enigmatic allure. Cuba's remarkable colonial cities—Camagüey, Remedios, Santiago de Cuba, and Trinidad, to name a few—are repositories of architectural gems dating back centuries and boasting a spectacular amalgam of styles. Eighteenth-century Spanish cathedrals fuse into 19th-

ary barely scratches the surface, however. For these reasons and more, most visitors vow to return again soon.

CUBANS

Cubans have a uniquely profound culture steeped in Spanish and African traditions. The population of about 11.2 million is fiercely appreciative of its heritage. Strongly nationalistic, *los cubanos* combine a love of tradition with a progressive attitude. They are proud of their distinct identity, their *cubanía*, much of it forged during the years of socialist experiment under Fidel Castro.

Cuba's original inhabitants may have numbered as many as 300,000 indigenous peoples. Predominant in the areas where the Spanish first explored were the Taino, members of the Arawak Indian tribe from South America. Most of these aborigines succumbed to disease and the ruthlessness of 16th-century Spanish conquistadores. As the early Spanish colonists

Fashion-conscious Cubans wear imported clothes, brightening Havana's streets.

cleared the forests and planted sugarcane, African slaves were imported to Cuba; in time, as many as 600,000 arrived. They were joined by merchants, seafarers, and entrepreneurs who came from England and Europe in large numbers throughout the 18th and 19th centuries. These foreign groups were quickly assimilated into the mainstream Spanish-speaking culture. In the 1790s, a large infusion of French immigrants added Gallic ways to the culture. They were followed during the next century by Chinese indentured laborers, who coalesced in Central Havana. Thousands of North Americans settled during the 19th century, which also witnessed a vast emigration of Cubans to the United States. This was a decisive time in the formation of Cuban nationality as North American ways and values were increasingly adopted into the Cuban

lifestyle and used as standards for change as Spanish colonialism came to an end in 1898.

The early 1900s saw the arrival of Jamaicans in Santiago and Guantánamo provinces, where English can still be heard. North Americans continued to flood the island; throughout the first half of the 20th century, U.S. businesses controlled much of the Cuban economy and added to the vigor of Havana's lifestyle. Following the revolution in 1959, most foreign-born residents left Cuba—

along with tens of thousands of Cubans— and were gradually replaced by Soviets and other Eastern Europeans. Shunned by the host population, the Soviets kept to themselves; they departed Cuba in the 1990s, leaving few lasting reminders of their presence. Today Cuba is accumulating a resident population of foreign businessfolk—mostly Canadian and European.

In affinities, Cubans look north, not east to Spain. While Cuba's relationship with the

United States continues to be fraught with tension, Cubans hold no animosity toward Americans—United States travelers are feted as long-lost friends and can travel freely.

THE CUBAN CHARACTER

The Cubans' distinct identity owes much to four decades of socialism focused on reshaping the human character to form the "New Man"—a person who puts what's best for society before personal ambition. (In Cuba,

While youngsters cool off in the Río de Miel near Baracoa, a man washes his car. Cubans are fastidious about their 1950s *cacharros*.

the term "revolution" is used to refer to the building of a more equal society.) An intensely moral people, Cubans are highly considerate of others. They are gracious and generous to a fault, willing to share what little they may have. They are confident and unreserved, and display resounding gaiety in the face of adver-

sity. Cubans also take pride in personal clean-
liness and are unafraid of physical contact.
(One reason the Soviets were disliked is that
they didn't use deodorant.) They are great jok-
ers, known for a sharp and creative wit and
risqué innuendo; most *chistes* are aimed at
themselves and the absurdities of life in Cuba.
The population is highly literate and displays a
voracious intellectual appetite—the product
of the government's emphasis on education.
This is apparent when you observe well-

behaved Cuban schoolchildren in their prim
uniforms displaying impressive levels of
knowledge. Part of their education—and an
essential aspect of becoming a New Man—is
to also perform manual labor. Urban youths
are sent to work as seasonal laborers in the
fields and to develop a sound work ethic.

Cubans are intensely patriotic and proud
of the independence that the Cuban revolution has brought. However, most Cubans love
American culture. Youth dress in the latest

fashions, as much as their meager budgets allow. Cubans also share a northern work ethic. They are entrepreneurial and wizards of invention—a requirement in a society where nothing gets thrown away, and new or replacement parts are almost impossible to come by. *Resolver*—to resolve, to overcome obstacles with ingenuity—is a common concept. The economic crisis of recent years, however, has seriously challenged Cuba's value system. Youths are especially frustrated.

A former mansion turned tenement in Havana awaits restoration; as many as one-half of city dwellers live in decaying buildings.

About 50 percent of the population claims to be atheist, reflecting decades of state suppression of religion. In 1991, however, the Communist Party ceased denying membership to those who subscribed to a religion, and a year later the constitution was amended to characterize the nation as secular rather than atheist. Roman Catholicism, introduced by the Spanish, is resurgent, and Protestant evangelism has made inroads. Santería (spirit worship), introduced by slaves, and other Afro-Cuban religions that blend native African beliefs and Roman Catholicism are widely practiced in Cuba.

ERASING COLOR & CLASS

About 55 percent of Cuba's inhabitants are of Spanish-African ancestry. Throughout the colonial epoch, the white, Spanish-born population looked down on the blacks and the *criollos* (island born), regardless of color. Colonial Cuba was a hierarchical society, with whites at the top of the scale and blacks at the bottom, though relations were notably more relaxed than in the United States.

On the eve of the revolution, Cuba was a relatively developed yet divided society with a huge, predominantly white middle class spread throughout the island's cities. A large, predominantly black underclass lived in marginal conditions, often without basic amenities. The majority of the rural population—white and black alike—was mired in poverty.

Castro's revolution outlawed institutionalized racism and dramatically improved the lot of most blacks and those who lived in rural areas. Malnutrition and common diseases were eradicated. Although racism still exists and blacks make up a large proportion of the impoverished, Cuba is today marked by a relatively harmonious intermingling of ethnicities. The social leveling of the revolution also destroyed the middle classes, separating many families and reducing them to a level of poverty that all but the most privileged Cubans share today; almost every Cuban family has at least one family member who has left Cuba to seek a better life. This quest for a classless society has diminished class consciousness. Cubans call each other *companero* (companion) and greet each other, even as strangers, with a *beso* (kiss) and/or *abrazo* (hug). Doctors, lawyers, and other highly trained specialists are no longer regarded as a "separate class."

Nonetheless, Cuban society retains marked inequalities. Today's privileged class is formed of senior Communist Party officials and military figures, who enjoy benefits denied to most

Cubans; and of leading artists, musicians, and sports figures, who, uniquely in Cuba, are permitted to own modern cars. More recently, a new class of nouveau riche—*macetas*—with access to dollars has emerged.

LIVING CONDITIONS

Cuba's annual per capita income in 2001 was estimated at an equivalent of $1,700. Its standards of free universal education and primary health care are high: Both life expectancy and infant mortality are on a par with those of developed nations. Housing and many staples are subsidized, albeit in short supply. And the state provides exemplary care for the elderly and indigent. Thanks to foreign investment, many improvements have been made to the

telecommunications system in recent years, but access to computers and the Internet is severely proscribed by the government.

The revolution eradicated urban homelessness by erecting prefabricated apartment dwellings and by reallocating homes seized from families who fled Cuba. The government then neglected the cities, however. Most urbanites today live in overcrowded housing, much of which is crumbling; many inhabit *solares* (slum dwellings), often hidden from view behind more substantial houses. Rural dwellers typically live in traditional rustic *bohios* (thatched huts of wood or adobe); the majority now have electricity, though many homes still lack running water. Rural folk follow a simple life, tending their tobacco fields,

Cuba's inherent joie de vivre explodes during Carnival in Santiago de Cuba. The celebration dates back to the 18th century, when slaves were permitted a carousal.

coffee, and cows, or laboring for low pay in the sugarcane fields.

Material shortages are a fact of daily life. The average urbanite spends long hours struggling to get by. Following the revolution, restaurants, private businesses, and farms were seized by the state, while communist bureaucrats established a dysfunctional distribution system—the *acopio*. Many staples vanished long ago, and *puestos* (grocery stores) are now without food. Despite broad accomplishments in preventive medicine, the health-care system

At a neighborhood meeting of the **Committee for the Defense of the Revolution**, the national anthem blares on a boom box as citizens stand at attention.

suffers debilitating shortages while Cuba's prestigious biotech industry exports state-of-the-art medicines. City dwellers rely on the government *libreta* (ration book), which meets only a fraction of Cubans' needs. A thriving black market attempts to make up for shortfalls exacerbated by the four-decades-long U.S. embargo. Nothing is thrown away; thus the mummified yet still functional 1950s jalopies that litter the streets. Outside Havana, the most common means of transportation is the horse-drawn cart.

The state employs all workers, who are paid in near-worthless pesos: the average monthly wage is about 350 pesos, or just over $13. Although Cubans are industrious, workplace ennui is rampant: Cubans joke that "Fidel pretends to pay us, and we pretend to work." Cash sent from relatives in Miami brightens many Cubans' lives. Those without access to dollars scrape by. The scramble for dollars has eroded an ostensibly egalitarian society and given rise to *jineteros* (hustlers) and *jineteras* (prostitutes). Private enterprise remains illegal, with few exceptions. Licenses are granted for self-employment in several sectors, but many Cubans find the conditions untenable.

SIMPLE PLEASURES

Cubans can conjure tropical excitement out of thin air. On weekends, families pile into their '50s DeSotos and Chevies and head to the beach to play volleyball while couples flirt under the *palapas* (thatched shade umbrellas) and palms. Women pull their *sillones* (rockers) onto sidewalks to share gossip while men, shirtless in the heat, slap dominoes on tables strategically placed in puddles of shade. They smoke cigars, swig cheap *aguardiente* (white rum), and come together for impromptu *cumbanchas*—the local word for a street party, when radios are cranked up and couples dance groin-to-groin, overtly sexual rumbas. Flirting is a national pastime; the population is sexually liberal and has elevated casual sex to a defining element of their national culture.

Machismo—part of Cuba's Spanish heritage—remains. Unsolicited compliments, for example, are freely offered to female passersby. Cuba's progressive record in women's rights is impressive, yet females still adore coquetry. Cuban women are at ease with their bodies and determined to show them; even in rural communities, women of all ages and sizes sashay past in form-fitting spandex, carrying themselves with sensual self-assurance.

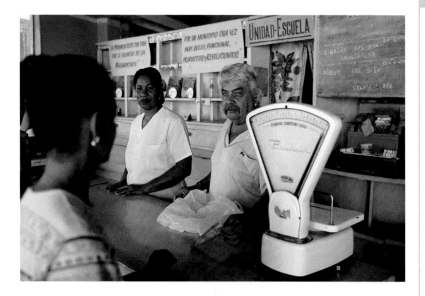

Bare shelves are not unusual in a state-run *puesto* (grocery), supplied by a dysfunctional distribution system that bucks the law of supply and demand.

GOVERNMENT & POLITICS

The 1976 Constitution defines Cuba as a socialist state run by Fidel Castro, who is named as president of the Republic, first secretary of the Communist Party, president of the Council of State, and president of the Council of Ministers. Power resides with the Communist Party, which greatly influences decisions made by each government body.

The Council of Ministers effectively runs the country under the direction of Castro, who chooses the members. The council drafts bills for submission to the National Assembly, which meets twice annually to ratify legislation and government appointments. Members are elected by national ballot; elections are held every five years. The Council of State functions as the executive committee of the National Assembly. The People's Supreme Court, whose president and vice president are chosen by Castro, is the highest judicial body. Castro's presidential office, the Council of State, Council of Ministers, and headquarters of the Communist Party are housed in the Presidential Palace, on the east side of the Plaza de la Revolución, in Havana.

The country is divided into 14 provinces: Pinar del Río, Havana, Matanzas, Villa Clara, Cienfuegos, Sancti Spíritus, Ciego de Ávila, Camagüey, Las Tunas, Holguín, Granma, Santiago de Cuba, and Guantánamo, plus the city of Havana. Isla de la Juventud (Isle of Youth) is a "special municipality." Each province is run by an elected Provincial Assembly, while municipal councils run the day-to-day affairs of 169 *municipios*.

The Communist Party of Cuba (PCC) is the sole political party. No other political entities are permitted. The PCC is led by a Politburo and Central Committee, whose members are elected by party members. The party occupies a central role in all state institutions, including mass organizations such as the Union of Communist Youth and Federation of Cuban Women. The government controls all communications and media and tightly restricts information. The military is under the command of Castro's younger brother, Raúl Castro, who is also vice president of the Republic, vice president of the Council of State and the Council of Ministers, and vice secretary of the Communist Party.

Castro uses the force of his personality to bolster mass support. At nationally televised rallies he invokes Cuban nationalism and anti-United States rhetoric to keep the revolution-

ary spirit alive. His charisma, and the existence of the U.S. embargo, which Castro blames for his country's problems, is central to his role as Cuba's head of state. In effect, Castro acts as an absolute authority, and nothing is permitted that meets his disapproval—especially opposition to the government.

The Ministry of the Interior (MININT) maintains a dossier on every Cuban citizen on which any transgressions are recorded. Anyone considered disloyal to the revolution risks losing his or her job or entitlements. Cubans who refuse to toe the line become outcasts in a society where everyone relies on the state to get by.

Secret police are ubiquitous, and Cubans live in constant dread of police informers. Fear of mentioning Castro's name is ingrained—Cubans draw a hand down their chin in an allusion to his beard.

CUBANS & THE REVOLUTION

Cubans are split between those who support Fidel Castro and those who crave personal control of their own lives. Loyalists point to

Cuba's impressive welfare programs and generous subsidies, to its remarkable achievements in education and health, to the way the revolution has eradicated the worst destitution; they compare the country with Haiti and other nations still beset by true poverty. Castro's base of support is in the countryside, where many of the promises of the revolution have been realized.

In the cities, support for the revolution has eroded along with many of the benefits once supported by Soviet largesse. In general, urbanites are weary of sacrifice and paternal-

Locals relax and chat in Plaza Mayor, Trinidad. Located in the heart of the old town, the square is surrounded by a cathedral and four museums housed in colonial mansions.

ism that shoehorns them into conformity and weighs down on daily life. They seek the reality of material progress and roll their eyes at Castro's "socialism or death!" His greatest adherents are the PCC members invested in a system that rewards them. ■

Food & drink

CUBANS HAVE AN OBSESSION WITH FOOD, AND NOT BECAUSE THEY'RE gourmands. They fantasize about what is no longer available; scarcity is the rule. Cuban fare is extremely simple, and it can be delicious. Havana claims a fistful of notable restaurants, but beyond the capital city, dining is usually meager and bland.

Comida criolla, the native cuisine, is country food—the fare of *el campo*—relying on lowly ingredients. Fried or roast chicken (*pollo frito* or *pollo asado*) and roast pork (*cerdo asado*) are the ubiquitous dishes—usually served with sides of white rice (*arroz*) and black beans; rice mixed with black beans (*moros y cristianos*); or rice mixed with red kidney beans (*congrí*)—and enlivened occasionally by *sofrito*, a paste of garlic (*ajo*), chopped onion, peppers, and lime sizzled with vegetable oil in a hot skillet.

Plantains (*plátanos*) or root vegetables such as cassava (*yuca*) or sweet potato (*boniato*) play supporting roles. The plantain—a relative of the banana—is served fried in strips when ripe (*maduro*), or as fried chips (*mariquitas* or *chicharritas*) or thick fried rounds called

tostones before it has ripened. Boiled and mashed, plantains make *fufú*. The accompanying salad rarely extends beyond lettuce, cucumber, and tomato; be prepared for string beans or shredded cabbage.

Seafood is scarce beyond Havana or coastal communities, though lobster (*langosta*) is widely available and usually a bargain. Many tourist venues, alas, charge top dollar for lobster and shrimp (*camarones*). The fish of choice is red snapper (*pargo*), and in the eastern provinces sea bass (*corvina*) is often served; less common is grouper (*cherna*), swordfish (*emperador, serrucho*), and marlin (*aguja*). Beef and steaks (*bistec*) can be found only at better state restaurants but rarely live up to U.S. standards. A popular menu item is

INGREDIENTES
* **UNA REVOLUCIÓN VERDADERA**
* **UN PUEBLO QUE LA DEFIENDE**
* **UN PARTIDO ÚNICO**
* **UN LÍDER HISTÓRICO**

Agricultural produce for sale at a "farmer's market" (left). One take on the perfect recipe for a *cuba libre* (above)

bistec uruguayano, pork steak stuffed with ham and cheese and deep fried. Occasionally you might find rabbit *(conejo),* or *ajiaco,* a classic stew of pork and root vegetables.

In most hotels, breakfasts are a simple buffet—*mesa sueca*—with cold cuts, cheese, boiled eggs, pancakes, fruits, and sponge cake the ubiquitous items. Cuban households might serve a plain tortilla and bread and butter *(pan con mantequilla).* Beyond home, urban Cubans rely on peso street stalls selling bland but filling pizzas, and snacks such as small turnovers *(empanadas)* filled with meat, washed down with *refresco*—chilled fruit drinks.

Fruits are also in short supply (most fruits are pulped to make juice), except at farmer's markets *(mercados agropecuarios),* which the state has permitted since 1993. Here you'll find oranges *(naranjas),* grapefruit *(toronjas),* mangoes *(mangos),* pineapple *(piña),* guava *(guayaba),* bananas *(plátanos),* and papaya (locally called *fruta bomba),* and favorites such as *mamey colorado, guanábana,* and *marañón.* Coconuts are less common since they are not

traditionally used in cooking, except around Baracoa, where they form the basis for Cuba's only regional cuisine.

Despite so much sugar, Cuba's dessert scene rarely extends beyond cookies and sponge cakes, deep-fried donut rings *(rosquitas),* puff pastries *(pasteles)* filled with cheese meringue or guava paste, and caramel custard *(flan).* Cubans, however, are ice-cream fanatics and favor the excellent Coppelia brand, best followed by espresso coffee, drunk thick and sugared *(café cubano). Café americano* is coffee diluted with water. A *cortado* is espresso served with milk, and a *café con leche* is served with more milk than coffee. Milk, however, is hard to find, except in delicious *batidos*—milkshakes often made with fruit.

Sugarcane is the source of Cuba's excellent rums. In the countryside, the working man's drinks are *aguardiente,* cheap clear white spirit, and *guarapo,* fresh-squeezed sugarcane juice, sold at roadside *guaraperías.* Cubans are also beer drinkers. The *clara* brew, issued on the ration *(libreta),* is best avoided, as is wine, which is stored well only in better restaurants. ∎

Cuban history

ON OCTOBER 28, 1492, CHRISTOPHER COLUMBUS TOUCHED LAND ON AN island he believed to be Japan. It was actually Cuba, a tropical paradise the explorer pronounced the "fairest on earth." Within a year, Spain asserted sovereignty over the island, beginning a long, bitter history made all the more poignant by the island's beauty. Fidel Castro's revolution, launched in 1956, traces its lineage back four centuries in a continuum of struggle by the Cuban people against the self-aggrandizement of colonial powers.

FIRST PEOPLES

Although archaeological excavations in Cuba have unearthed carved and polished stone dating back about 10,000 years, the first significant pre-Ceramic culture was that of nomadic hunters and gatherers who settled the archipelago about 8000 B.C. By about 2500 B.C., a second migratory group had settled the coasts, where they made their living by farming and fishing. Eventually both of these groups were displaced by one more advanced —the Taino—a tribe related to the Arawak of South America, who began to settle the Cuban archipelago between A.D. 700 and 800.

The peaceable Taino were skilled agriculturalists whose flourishing civilization was based on the cultivation of corn and yucca. They lived communally in thatched rectangular huts called *bohíos*; circular huts called *caneyes*; and huts called *barbacoas* that were built on stilts in lagoons or other marshy areas. The huts were typically arranged around an open space called a *batey,* with as many as 20 families forming a village under the leadership of a *cacique,* or chief. They painted their bodies and wore only the briefest of garments—loincloths for men and *naguas,* a type of cotton apron, for women—and considered flattened foreheads such a desirable mark of beauty that infants' heads were pressed between boards to restrict their development.

The Taino had no written language or metals and used neither the wheel nor beasts of burden. However, they were accomplished potters and were so adept at weaving wild cotton and *henequen* (hemp) into ropes and hammocks that, ultimately, Spanish conquistadores forced them to weave sailcloth for Spanish vessels. The Taino traded with neighboring islands, taking to the sea in large *canoas* (canoes) hewn from tree trunks.

Religion played a central role in their lives.

The tribe worshiped a pantheon of gods who were thought to control nature's whims and who displayed their wrath when hurricanes bore down on the isle. During religious ceremonies, which were attended by all in the village, the *behíque,* or priest, would initiate conversations with the gods. First, he purified himself through self-induced vomiting, then he inhaled a powder concocted from the dried leaves of different hallucinogenic plants through a hollow wooden object shaped like a Y. Once the *behíque* achieved the desired state, he conversed with the gods about events— past or future—that affected the village, especially in regard to sickness or crops.

An estimated 300,000 indigenous people inhabited Cuba when the first Europeans arrived, including descendants of some of the earliest inhabitants who were clinging to existence in the far west of the isle. What remains of their cultures is limited to pottery shards, petroglyphs, cult objects—called *cemíes*— carved in stone, and words such as "canoe," "hammock," "hurricane," and "tobacco."

FIRST EUROPEANS

On August 3, 1492, the Genoese explorer Christopher Columbus (1451–1506) set out from Spain on his first voyage to find a western passage to the East Indies. Sailing aboard the *Santa Maria* and accompanied by the caravels *Niña* and *Pinta* and a crew of 87, Columbus made first landfall in the Bahamas. There he took on indigenous guides, who told him of a large island called Cuba that lay to the southwest. After threading through coral-laced shallows, the expedition sighted the island on October 27. Columbus first landed in today's Bahía de Bariay, in the northeast province of Holguín. He scouted along the north coast for a month, arriving at a site that he called Puerto Santo, identified by a large, flat-topped mountain, today believed to be the Silla of Gibara. He then continued onto the Punta de Maisí and east to another island, which the indigenous peoples called Haiti and Columbus named Hispaniola, before returning to Spain. Columbus believed that he had found Japan by the western route, and he named the islands the West Indies, christening their inhabitants "Indians." Columbus returned three more times to the Americas, convinced that beyond Cuba, on the continent, lay the palaces of the Great Khan of Cathay, with their gold, precious stones, and the spices of which Marco Polo had written.

In 1508, Columbus's son, Diego, was named governor of the Indies and commissioned to lead an expedition to colonize Cuba. He set sail to Cuba in 1510, accompanied by Diego Velázquez (1465–1524), Hernán Cortés (1485–1547), and 300 men. In 1511 they established the first settlement, today's Baracoa, at the island's far eastern end. Six other crude *villas* followed by 1515: today's Bayamo, Camagüey, Sancti Spíritus, Santiago

In this engraving by F. Bartolozzi, a Taino chief greets Columbus on his first landfall in Cuba.

de Cuba, Trinidad, and Havana.

The Taino were viewed as heathen and quickly put to work by the conquistadores, who received land grants and were allotted a specific number of Indian laborers under the *encomienda* (a modified form of feudalism) system. The gentle Indians were no more suited, or inclined, to harsh labor than were the Spaniards, and the once-noble indigenous peoples began to decline. The Taino were briefly rallied to resistance in 1510 by Hatuey, a heroic chieftain who had fled neighboring Hispaniola after his own people were crushed. Hatuey's insurrection failed, and he was burned at the stake.

Suffering from malnutrition, disease, and spiritual sickness, the Indians found a friend in Bartolomé de las Casas (1474–1566), a Dominican friar who arrived with Velázquez. Las Casas' job included identifying sites for washing gold and also winning the commit-

ment and loyalty to the Crown of all the tribes and communities in the areas of displacement. Las Casas witnessed the massacre of Indians and soon devoted his energies to helping them. He succeeded: In 1542 the encomienda system, ostensibly established with the purpose of converting the heathen to Christianity, was abolished. But by then it was too late. European diseases such as smallpox, measles, and tuberculosis had combined with sword and musket to swiftly fell the Indians. In less than a century, Cuba's indigenous population was all but extinguished.

COLONIAL HEYDAY

Lust for gold filled the minds of the conquistadores who descended on the New World. The Spanish found traces of the precious metal in Cuba but soon exhausted the early mines. The island then became the supply base for expedi-

Santiago de Cuba was a bustling port in the 19th century.

tions bound for Mexico and other destinations. On one such foray, in 1519, Hernán Cortés and his army sailed to Mexico, where they confronted Aztec emperor Montezuma in his capital and defeated him. Cortés retreated, to return in 1521 to complete his conquest and to plunder the empire's wealth.

Indeed, Cuba's importance to Spain lay in its strategic location. The island commanded the sea routes to the Gulf of Mexico, and Havana's sheltered harbor fronted the fast-flowing Gulf Stream, which carried treasure-laden galleons to Spain. Havana was poised for a gilded future, evidenced in 1532, when Francisco Pizarro (1476–1541) conquered the Andean empire of the Incas. Gold, silver, and jewels poured into Havana as treasure fleets—*flotas*—assembled for the twice-yearly journey, under naval escort, to Spain.

The island's own wealth lay in its rich soil.

Native forests were felled and hardwoods shipped to Spain, and tobacco—along with sugar and other crops—was planted to feed the new smoking craze sweeping Europe. Cattle ranching also became widespread and Cuban leather grew highly prized throughout Europe. The Spanish monarchy, however, made little effort to develop the colony. It enforced a Crown monopoly; only the ports of Havana and Santiago de Cuba were entitled to trade (and only with the mother country), and exports were heavily taxed. Colonists were forbidden to manufacture; even the most mundane item had to be imported from Spain.

Unjust laws promote lawlessness, and many colonists resorted to smuggling. Havana prospered on two-way trade as English, Dutch, and French seamen took advantage of the restrictions to smuggle in goods and much-needed slaves to work the fields. By the mid-16th century, sugarcane plantations were developing rapidly, and with them the slave trade. English sea captains such as John Hawkins (1532–1595) and his kinsman, Sir Francis Drake (1540–1596), began their illustrious seafaring careers by bringing in slaves for Spanish planters and slipping away with gold, jewels, sugar, and hides under the noses of usually corrupt Spanish officials. When the Spanish armada sent to invade England was defeated in 1588, breaking the back of Spanish sea power, the flow of ships packed with African slaves crossed the ocean unchecked.

THE AGE OF PIRATES

The increased slave trade in the West Indies and the constant warring between Spain and England, France, and Holland during the 16th and 17th centuries brought new enemies to Cuba and its neighboring islands—pirates and *corsarios*, or corsairs. While most pirates acted independently in their harassment of Spanish vessels, corsarios were li-censed by Spain's rivals and acted with permission and protection as they plundered ships, cities, and plantations.

Havana was a choice target of such privateering. It first fell in 1547, to French pirate Jacques de Sores, who razed the town before sailing off with its treasures. In May 1586, Francis Drake arrived off the coast of Havana with 23 ships. The terror-filled citizens waited for the privateers to attack. What they didn't know was that the plague had broken out among the fleet. After four long days, Drake sailed away. The beleaguered city was ransacked numerous times thereafter, notably in 1662, when notorious English buccaneer Henry Morgan made off with even the church bells.

In 1697 the Treaty of Ryswick put an end to privateering, and England agreed to suppress piracy. But those were fickle times. To safeguard its treasures, Spain's King Philip II ordered the construction of a system of fortresses. Havana was protected by El Morro castle, dating from the late 16th to early 17th centuries and situated on a cliff at the entrance to the bay and harbor. The city prospered, every year growing more elegant and sophisticated,

with its gleaming architecture of wrought-iron balconies and carved mahogany doors. Then, in June 1762, a British army stormed El Morro, turned its guns on Havana, and captured the eastern part of the island, from the Bahía del Mariel to Matanzas. The English immediately opened Havana to unrestricted trade. The flag of St. George flew over Cuba for a mere 11 months before the territory was returned to Spain in exchange for Florida. But a new vitality had gripped the land. Cuba was about to enter its golden age.

SUGAR & SLAVERY

Once the doors to trade had been opened, Spain found it impossible to close them again. Free trade, including with newly burgeoning North American colonies, boosted the island's

rural economy, which was based on tobacco, cattle, and sugar. Unparalleled expansion in Cuba's sugar industry in turn created an unprecedented demand for slaves to clear forests and work the fields. British slave traders became a permanent fixture in Havana. By the end of the 19th century, the total number of slaves imported to the island since its colonization was more than 600,000. In addition, almost 100,000 immigrants from North America, Spain, and elsewhere in Europe came to Cuba to labor in the fields.

The successful slave revolt of 1791 in Santo Domingo (today's Haiti) destroyed that nation's sugar industry. Thousands of refugee planters resettled in Cuba, bringing their expertise with them. Sugar prices soared. Cuba—by 1827 the world's largest sugar pro-ducer—prospered as never before. Provincial cities such as Camagüey, Cienfuegos, and Trinidad flourished as Creole merchants and planters established cultural institutions and erected the magnificent stone palaces and mansions that still grace these cities today.

The introduction in the early 19th century of a new type of sugarcane that produced juice with a higher sugar content and more flavor, as well as the advent of steam power and railroads midway through the century, further strengthened the sugar-based economy. For those who toiled daily in the fields, however, life was brutal; with good reason, Spanish officials feared a rebellion. The majority of slaves

Cutting and loading the canes on the Plantation of Las Canas

were *criollos* (born in Cuba) and lived in cities as domestics or laborers. Although many bought their freedom over time and prospered on their own, others remained under the thumbs of their masters. After 300 years of slavery on the island, African blood, beliefs, and traditions mingled with those of the Spanish, and a distinct criollo culture emerged.

WARS OF INDEPENDENCE

Most criollos identified with their homeland, considering themselves Cuban instead of Spanish. Heavily taxed and harshly ruled by Spanish-born *peninsulares*, the island-born population had independence fever. By 1835, only Cuba, Puerto Rico, and the Philippines still belonged to Spain, which responded to the criollos' nationalist sentiments with brutality. Spain fought hard to hold on to the last, and most valued, of its possessions. When

sugar prices crashed in 1857, however, Cuba was ripe for revolt.

First war of independence: Ten Years War (1868–1878)

On October 10, 1868, a plantation owner in eastern Cuba named Carlos M. de Céspedes freed his slaves and, in an oration known as the *Grito de Yara* (Cry of Yara), declared war against Spain. Fellow planters joined him, and soon an army of poorly armed black and white insurgents had formed, calling themselves *mambísi*, after a freedom fighter named Juan Mambí who had battled for independence in Santo Domingo (Haiti). The mambísi were pitted against 100,000 Spanish troops who had rushed to the island. Cuba was ravaged as the patriots, led by Dominican-born Gen. Máximo Gómez and the popular mulatto Col. Antonio Maceo, fought a guerril-

The 1898 explosion of the U.S.S. *Maine* in Havana harbor was a pretext for war.

la war that divided the nation.

After a long, hard decade of fighting, the nationalist campaign fizzled. The war had claimed 250,000 lives and left a trail of destruction. Although Spain subsequently ended slavery in two stages (final abolition came in 1886), it clutched the island even more tightly in its iron fist.

Second war of independence (1895–1898)

The independence spirit was kept alive by poet and journalist José Martí, living in exile in the United States. In 1895, with Gómez, Martí returned to Cuba as leader of nationalist forces newly organized under Maceo. Though Martí was killed in the first skirmish of the new war, the mambísi swept across Cuba, defeating Spanish forces and torching the sugarcane fields and plantations. Desperate to hold onto their island jewel, Spanish forces seemingly stopped at nothing—including herding 200,000 people from Cuba's rural areas into concentration camps, where thousands died.

Spanish–American War (1898)

Stories of the cruel treatment meted out to the rebels stirred strong support in the U.S. for the mambísi movement, and the country eagerly followed news of the war. Americans already were heavily invested in Cuba's sugar industry, and the U.S. government, which had long coveted Cuba, was under pressure to intervene. Then, on February 15, 1898, a U.S. warship—the U.S.S. *Maine*—exploded in Havana harbor. Whether it was by accident or intent may never be known, but that act of aggression spurred the U.S. Congress to declare war on Spain on April 21, 1898.

In swift order the Spanish were routed—notably at a pivotal engagement on July 1 in Santiago de Cuba, where Theodore Roosevelt led a charge up San Juan Hill. Spain ceded control of Cuba to the United States in December 1898, under the terms of the Treaty of Paris. Thus began a new epoch in Cuba's long history of colonial rule.

A GOVERNMENT IN FLUX

On January 1, 1899, the U.S. military occupied Cuba, where it ruled until May 20, 1902. During that period, the United States wrote the Cuban constitution. It included the Platt Amendment, which granted America use of the Guantánamo naval base and the right to intervene in Cuban affairs to preserve the country's independence and stability. The United States sent troops to Cuba off and on over the next two decades to maintain or place friendly governments in power and to protect American business interests. The amendment was repealed in 1934, although the two countries reaffirmed the agreement to lease the Guantánamo naval base to the United States.

Years of war had devastated the Cuban economy, making the country ripe for American investors. The billions of dollars that flowed into Cuba reinvigorated the economy, notably in sugar, which enjoyed boom years from 1915 to 1920. The influx of money also funded grand civic constructions, plus hotels, casinos, and nightclubs. Although poverty riddled the countryside, the Cuba of the 1920s had evolved to become the world's wealthiest tropical country—and gracious, salacious Havana was the Jewel of the Caribbean. Tourists flocked there for the good and bad in equal measure, taking all the more pleasure in their carousing because of the enactment of Prohibition in the United States.

In 1924, Gen. Gerardo Machado (1871–1939) won the presidential election, initiating a period of unbridled corruption. Popular discontent was expressed on the streets and met with brutal repression. When the Great Depression hit, Cuba's one-crop economy crashed, and the country descended into violent chaos. In 1933 a general strike toppled Machado. Within six months, a 32-year-old army sergeant named Fulgencio Batista (1901–1973) seized power. Supportive of U.S. business interests and no less venal than his predecessors, Batista also proved himself a capable, enlightened reformer; notable social and political advances were made in the country. He won the 1940 presidential race but he was voted out of office in 1944 and retired to Florida, leaving Cuba in the hands of a series of corrupt and mostly inept politicians. The country was plagued by waves of street gangsterism and political assassinations.

In 1952, Batista returned to run for president once more. Fearful of losing his bid for office, however, he staged a bloodless *golpe de estado* (coup d'état) before the balloting could be held and reinstated himself as president. Hand-in-hand with Batista came the Mafia, who flocked to Havana following FBI crackdowns in the U.S. The city entered its frivolous heyday as Americans gravitated to the international playground to indulge in sun, sand, and sin.

One of Cuba's congressional hopefuls whose political ambitions had been thwarted by Batista's coup was a 25-year-old lawyer named Fidel Castro. Castro devoted himself to ousting Batista. On July 26, 1953, his revolutionary group—later to be called the 26th of

Fulgencio Batista enacted progressive social reform but ended up venal and corrupt.

July Movement—struck at the Moncada barracks in Santiago de Cuba. The armed assault was a failure, but the torture and assassination of 59 captured revolutionaries angered many Cubans and ignited popular support for the rebels. Castro was sentenced to 15 years' imprisonment but served only 22 months. Immediately upon his release, he launched an anti-Batista crusade. On July 7, 1955, he departed for Mexico to prepare a guerrilla force that would return to overthrow Batista, whose increasingly ruthless and corrupt regime was despised by the public.

THE FIGHT TO TOPPLE BATISTA

On November 25, 1956, Castro and 81 other revolutionaries set out from Tuxpán, Mexico, in a 38-foot-long, barely seaworthy, overloaded cruiser called the *Granma*. (The boat was named for the previous owner's grandmother.) Seven days later the rebels landed in Los Colorados, on the south coast of what is now Granma province. Batista's forces attacked the landing party, killing eight men in combat and assassinating 18 in the days that followed. Remarkably, survivors of the battle included the rebels' leaders: Fidel Castro, his younger brother Raúl, Camilo Cienfuegos (1923–1959), and a young Argentinian doctor named Ernesto "Che" Guevara (1928–1967). The beleaguered band took sanctuary in the Sierra Maestra.

Castro fought a war of attrition in the mountains while urban guerrillas attacked police stations and mounted a terror campaign in the cities. Batista's armed forces and police fought back with increasing brutality, which only further alienated Cuban citizens. By spring 1958, the rebel army controlled the mountain regions of Oriente. Expanding into the province of Las Villas, Castro opened new fronts under the command of Raúl Castro and Juan Almeida Bosque—and, later that summer, under Camilo Cienfuegos and Che Guevara, who had proved himself Castro's most capable and trusted commander.

After a series of victories, on December 30 Che's troops derailed an enemy troop train and captured the key city of Santa Clara. The following morning at 2 a.m., Batista fled Cuba for self-imposed exile. Castro led a triumphant parade to Havana, arriving on January 8, 1959, to a tumultuous welcome.

During his crusade to depose Batista, Castro claimed to have forsaken all allegiance to communism, and in July 1957 he issued the Sierra Maestra Manifesto, committing himself to "free and democratic elections." With Batista out of the picture, however, things changed quickly. With backing from the United States, a provisional government was established in Cuba, led by respected judge Manuel Urrutia Lleó (1901–1981). Castro simultaneously set up a secret parallel government that worked to subvert Urrutia and promote a far-reaching revolution. This was

Castro's disciplined and motivated guerrilla soldiers proved effective against Batista's army.

announced in May 1959, when Castro, who controlled the armed forces, enacted an agrarian reform law that confiscated large landholdings without compensation. Meanwhile Che presided over summary trials that sent thousands of Batista supporters and counter-revolutionaries to the firing squads. Fearing for their lives, professionals and property owners—including architects, doctors, and engineers—fled Cuba en masse (approximately two million Cubans have departed since the revolution). In July, Castro manipulated Urrutia's resignation and took power, to the popular acclaim of the peasantry and working classes. On May 1, 1960, he suspended the Constitution and announced that "the people" had declared elections unnecessary.

The previous year, the Soviet Union had officially recognized Castro's revolutionary government. Trade and defense agreements quickly followed. Between August and October 1959, Cuba sold 500,000 tons (453,600 tonnes) of sugar to the U.S.S.R., with another million tons (907,200 tonnes) to follow six months later. The Soviet Union also began to lend financial,

technical, and economic support to the island, with the goal of developing industrial, energy, mining, and farming operations. Experts came to the country to train Cubans in science, industry, and defense. When Soviet oil began arriving in Cuba in 1960, President Dwight D. Eisenhower (1890–1969) instructed U.S.-owned refineries not to process it. Castro reacted by nationalizing the refineries. By January 1961, Castro had nationalized all U.S. property in Cuba, and the United States broke off diplomatic ties. A trade ban was imposed in March 1961 that is still in effect today.

CATASTROPHE & CRISIS

While popular with less well-to-do Cubans, Castro's increasingly radical measures generated intense opposition—including among his former commanders, many of whom were later imprisoned or forced into exile. By 1960 counterrevolutionary bands had established a guerrilla front in the Sierra del Escambray; the Lucha Contra Bandidos—Fight Against Bandits—would take Castro six years to quell. Meanwhile, in Miami seething exiles, trained

Castro made his first speech in Santiago de Cuba in 1959 after toppling Batista's regime.

and equipped by the CIA, plotted their return. On April 15, 1961, they bombarded Cuban airfields as a prelude to landing ground forces. On April 17, an invasion force 1,400 strong arrived at Playa Girón, located on the Bahía de Cochinos—the Bay of Pigs. Their intent was to link up with the anti-Castroites and incite a counterrevolution. The exile force was swiftly defeated, however, and the debacle served only to strengthen Castro's hold over Cuba.

Despite his victory, Castro feared a U.S. invasion. It is unclear who initiated the visit, but in the summer of 1962 a Soviet delegation arrived in Cuba to propose the installation of medium-range missiles and nuclear arms. On October 14, U.S. intelligence detected those nuclear missiles. President John F. Kennedy (1917–1963) ordered them removed and placed U.S. forces on combat alert. The resulting standoff took the world to the brink of nuclear war. After 13 days, the Soviets backed down in exchange for a promise that the United States would not invade Cuba.

tarianism and the desire to contribute to the collective welfare. Che Guevara, as Minister of Finance and Industry, supervised radical economic reforms that culminated in 1968, when the government seized all private businesses. Socialist planning replaced "market anarchy." The result was chaos. As early as 1962, the economy was in shambles and rationing was introduced. Attempts to diversify the sugar-based economy failed miserably, prompting a disastrous effort, in 1970, to produce a bumper crop of sugar—10 million tons (9,072,000 tonnes). Most of Cuba's resources were dedicated to that goal, and the economy nearly ground to a halt. In the end, Castro sacrificed thoughts of a self-sufficient nation and supplied sugar to the Soviets in exchange for oil, rice, grains, and other staples.

While the Soviets had adopted a policy of coexistence with the U.S., Cuba's iconoclastic leader was intent on exporting his revolution and baiting his U.S. nemesis. In 1966, Castro launched his Fifth International, with the goal of creating "as many Vietnams as possible." International revolutionaries took military training in Cuba, and Cuban troops fanned out to aid leftist movements in Africa. In 1965, Che Guevara departed to lead revolutionary movements abroad; he was killed in Bolivia in 1967. Cuban doctors and technical specialists provided aid throughout the Third World, while at home campaigns were launched against intellectuals, homosexuals, Roman Catholics, and other "social deviants."

A GLIMMER OF HOPE

Castro's adventurism added frost to the icy relations between Havana and Washington. In 1977, however, in an effort at rapprochement with the island nation, President Jimmy Carter eased the trade embargo and lifted travel restrictions. The two nations even established Interests Sections as a prelude to restoring full diplomatic relations. But tensions flared again in 1980, in part because of Cuba's continuing aid to Marxist regimes in Africa and the Middle East. When 12 Cubans sought refuge in the Peruvian Embassy in Havana that year, Carter announced that he would welcome political refugees from Cuba. Castro promptly sent off disaffected citizens, prisoners, and other "antisocial elements." More than 120,000

THE REVOLUTION

Castro was now free to pursue his socialist revolution. Literacy brigades fanned out into the countryside to teach uneducated peasants to read and write. Money flowed into improving health care, and prices of rents, utilities, and transportation were dramatically lowered. The cities, however, were neglected as energies were focused on raising rural living standards. The state also eroded personal liberties and worked to destroy the middle class in an effort to create the "New Man"—an individual motivated not by personal ambition, but by egali-

refugees boarded boats for Florida. The incident sealed Cuban–U.S. hostility over the next years, with the U.S. dealing Cuba a blow in 1983 when American forces ousted the Cuban-backed regime in Grenada.

A brief dalliance with free-market experiments in the mid-1980s bolstered Cuba's faltering economy, but Castro ended the flirtation in 1986 and swung back toward communist orthodoxy. He rejected Mikhail Gorbachev's policy of perestroika (restructuring), which was meant to revive the Soviet Union's ailing economy by introducing some elements of capitalist competition. After perestroika failed, the Soviet bloc began to unravel in 1989, precipitating a crisis in Cuba as oil, foodstuffs, and other goods upon which the island relied ceased to arrive. Warlike austerity

measures were imposed in Cuba during the "Special Period," as it is called, and the economy slipped into a coma. In April 1992, President George H. W. Bush tightened the screws by signing the Cuban Democracy Act, which further restricted trade with Cuba—including supplies of food and medicines—and was designed to cause Castro's demise. Cuba's population faced terrible hardships, riots broke out, and a grim slogan from the 1960s reappeared: ¡Socialismo o Muerte!—Socialism or Death!

MODERN TIMES

The Cuban government urgently enacted reforms. A ban on possessing U.S. dollars was ended, self-employment for certain occupations was legalized, and foreign corporations were invited to partner with Cuban state com-

panies, with an emphasis on developing tourism. Meanwhile, thousands of Cubans fled the island. The exodus turned into a flood following deadly riots in Havana in August 1994. More than 30,000 *balseros* (boat people) washed up in Florida before Washington and Havana negotiated an accord to stem the tide.

A new crisis arose in February 1996, when Cuban MiGs shot down aircraft operated by a Cuban-American exile group over the Straits of Florida. As a result, President Bill Clinton signed into law a hard-line measure that threatened new sanctions.

Tourism from Europe, Canada, and Latin America (but still not the U.S.) had grown phenomenally, helping provide the revenue Cuba needs for economic recovery. Cuba received a further boost in January 1998, when

Fidel Castro greets former President Jimmy Carter in Havana on May 12, 2002 (above). At left, a Cuban woman watches one of Castro's televised speeches.

Pope John Paul II made a highly significant visit, initiating a loosening of restrictions on religion. The state, however, reined in self-employment as it reasserted control of the reenergized economy.

In September 2001, Castro fainted during a speech, raising speculation about his health. Two months later, Hurricane Michelle blasted across much of Matanzas and Villa Clara provinces. President George W. Bush offered humanitarian assistance. Castro chose instead to buy much-needed foods and medicines, taking advantage of the repeal by the U.S. Congress, in October 2000, of a prohibition on sales of those items to Cuba—the first such economic transaction between the two nations in 40 years. ■

Land & landscape

CUBA IS A TROPICAL EDEN, AN INTENSELY GREEN MONTAGE OF LYRICAL landscapes caressed by warm trade winds. Westernmost and largest of the West Indies islands, it lies just south of the Tropic of Cancer and is separated from the United States by the 90-mile-wide (145 km) Straits of Florida. It is washed along the north coast by the azure Atlantic, while the gentle Caribbean Sea, the color of green grapes, laps its southern shore. Its size can take visitors by surprise: Elongated and gently arcing, this 780-mile-long (1,255 km) island slants to the southeast, broadening gradually and ending at Punta Maisí. Cuba's nearest neighbor—Haiti—lies 48 miles (77 km) to the east, across the Windward Passage. To the west, the island tapers down to the tendril-thin Península de Guanahacabibes, ending at Cabo San Antonio. Within Cuba's 42,830 square miles (110,922 sq km) is a kaleidoscope of landscapes.

Cuba's vast plains are a gently undulating sea of chartreuse—sugarcane fields, dusted in summer with delicate white blossoms. Semi-desert merges into mountain rain forest, and white-hot beaches dissolve into seas that gleam an impossible peacock blue. Offshore, scores of coral cays dot the hazy horizon. Throughout the isle, the scenery unfolds dramatically—palm-tufted, and framed in the distance by mauve-colored *mogotes* (see pp. 102–103), rounded limestone hillocks that are Cuba's signature landforms. Between the mogotes are valleys filled with loamy soil the color of ripe tomatoes. Oxen till the fields, and tropical scents rise up from the fragrant earth.

Some 14 percent of the island's land mass is protected in 80 national and 195 local reserves. These include 14 national parks, 22 ecological reserves, 8 nature reserves, 11 wildlife reserves, 2 protected natural landscapes, and 11 flora reserves. Seven protected areas are designated as UNESCO biosphere reserves: the Península de Guanahacabibes and Sierra del Rosario, in Pinar del Río; Baconao and Cuchillas del Toa in Santiago de Cuba; Parque Nacional Alexander Von Humboldt in Guantánamo; Ciénaga de Zapata in Matanzas; and Buenavista and Parque Nacional Caguanes-Santa Maria in Ciégo de Ávila.

One-fifth of the population lives in Havana, a sprawling coastal city in the northwest part of Cuba. A majority of the rest live in provincial capitals and dusty agricultural towns scattered throughout the country.

The Valle de Viñales is among the most beautiful of Cuba's landscapes.

FAR WEST

Cuba's far west is made up of mountains and plains. West of Havana, the Cordillera de Guaniguanico fringes the narrow north coast, where offshore isles float in a warm, fecund sea. Divided into four ranges—Sierra del Rosario, Sierra de los Organos, Alturas de Pizarra del Norte, and the Alturas y Montañas de Pizarra del Sur—and dramatically sculpted with plump mogotes, these mountains are cut through with deep valleys. They culminate in the broad Valle de Viñales, whose rich red soils have proved perfect for growing tobacco. The pine-clad Sierra del Rosario offer good hiking and birding, especially at Soroa and Las Terrazas. Caves provide opportunities for exploration. East of Havana, rolling uplands—*alturas*—enfold the port city of Matanzas. Broad plains extend inland from the southern shore, flat as a pool table and just as green from the sugarcane that swathes much of the land. The rivers that flow south from the mountains eventually lose themselves amid swampy marshlands. These are drained by watery sloughs that transform the coastal low-lands into a patchwork of rice paddies and lagoons, and tan carpets of sedge. Profuse coral reefs and warm waters draw scuba divers

to Bahía de Corrientes, sheltered by the slender, scrub-covered Península de Guanahacabibes, a rugged refuge for wildlife.

WESTERN PLAINS

Swampland extends across much of the vast *llanuras* (flatlands) of southern Matanzas like a soggy carpet. The *ciénaga* (swamp) that smothers the shoe-shaped Zapata peninsula forms a 1,745-square-mile (4,520 sq km) wetland teeming with gamefish, crocodiles, and birds that can be viewed by boat or from blinds. Manatees inhabit more remote regions of the reserve. From the north, citrus groves push up against the swamps. The richest soils are tilled for potatoes, legumes, and sugarcane, extending into Villa Clara and Cienfuegos provinces across plains as flat as a carpenter's level. The region is traversed east to west by the Autopista Nacional (the nation's only freeway) and, to the north, by the Carretera Central, connecting time-weary towns like pointillistic dots on an emerald canvas. The Península de Hicacos, jutting from the north shore, is the setting for Cuba's major resort, Varadero. The southern shore boasts Playa Girón, a white-sand beach that was a landing site during the 1961 Bay of Pigs invasion. Tucked into a deep bay is Cienfuegos, an industrial port that wears its history on its sleeve.

CENTRAL UPLANDS

Dominating the midpoint of Cuba, a rolling massif rises gradually from the north coastal plain. The uplands stairstep southward in ridges enfolding exquisite valleys studded with mogotes; the fertile vales of Vuelta Abajo are a regional center of tobacco production. Farther south, the ragged Sierra del Escambray rise abruptly over a narrow coastal plain, attaining 3,762 feet (1,140 m) atop Pico San Juan. Upper slopes wear a lush green shawl of eucalyptus and pine. Birds such as the Cuban trogon *(tocororo)* and the *zunzún*, or Cuban emerald hummingbird, brighten the woodlands, which are easily explored at Topes de Collantes. From there trails lead to cascading waterfalls. The old city of Trinidad sits on the southeast flank of the mountains; Playa Ancón—the region's only white-sand beach—unfolds nearby and is being developed for tourism. Eastward lies the Valle de los

Ingenios, historically important as a center of sugar production. The waters of Presa Zaza teem with bass, providing another angle on adventure. The regional capitals of Santa Clara and Sancti Spíritus, straddling the Carretera Central, serve as gateways to the region.

EASTERN PLAINS

Spanning five provinces, the plains of east central Cuba put the island's scale in perspective. To the west, pancake-flat Ciego de Ávila province is farmed in sugarcane fields, which sprawl across the llanuras inland of the Atlantic and Caribbean shores. A narrow upland spine—the Periplano de Florida–Camagüey–Las Tunas—runs east–west through the center of Camagüey and Las Tunas provinces. Growing in scale as it swings north through Holguín, this ridge culminates in the Grupo Montañoso Maniabón, dramatically adorned with mogotes. These rolling

uplands are dominated by *ganaderias* (cattle ranches) and *vaqueros* (cowboys), who add an intriguing element to the terrain. North of the Periplano, the verdant landscapes wither to a lowland savanna carpeted by scrub and wild grassland munched by floppy-eared, humped cattle. Arching east, the Río Cauto cascades down from the Sierra Maestra, snakes across a great green wash of plain, and pours into the Golfo de Guacanayabo. Swampland extends along the sparsely populated southern shore. The north coast is incised with deep bays and dabbed with the white-sand beaches of Guardalavaca, Pesquero, and Santa Lucía—all of which are resorts in the making.

EASTERN SIERRA

Saw-toothed mountains define eastern Cuba. The Sierra Maestra—the dominant chain—extends along an east–west axis from Cabo

Ox-drawn plows cast a time-warp beauty over Cuba.

Cruz to the city of Santiago de Cuba. These are Cuba's highest peaks, rising to 6,475 feet (1,974 m) atop Pico Turquino—high enough that dwarf forest is ribboned with wispy cloud tendrils. Much of the forest is protected within Parque Nacional Pico Turquino. The mountains plummet to a narrow, ruler-straight coast that lies in a rain shadow; in places the coastline is so dry that cactuses push up within yards of the sea. Gray-sand beaches have attracted a bevy of resorts whose emergence in recent years attempts to bring a new cachet to the region. The culturally rich city of Santiago de Cuba and dowdy Guantánamo city are surrounded by mountains at the head of long, narrow bays. The cities simmer in intense heat, and the cool, pine-clad mountains that lie north and east are deluged by rain. Moisture-laden clouds race in from the east to dump their cargo, and bruised clouds swirl ominously about the windswept summits of the Sierra del Purial, Sierra del Cristal, and Cuchillas del Toa. Dense, humid forests teem with birds, today protected within a series of national parks being promoted for outdoor adventures.

OFFSHORE ISLES

Scores of low-lying cays, large and small, are separated from the mainland by warm, shallow seas. The majority span a 300-mile (480 km) arc stretching east–west in a long line at an average distance of 15 miles (24 km) off the north coast; they are known collectively as the Archipiélago de Sabana-Camagüey. One cay, Cayo Coco, is connected to the mainland by an isthmus measuring a hairbreadth; three more by *pedraplenes*—causeways—that shoot across the limpid lagoons where flamingoes wade. The seaward shores are edged by frost-white sands and coral reefs and turquoise ocean. The Cuban government is wise to the untainted allure of the cays—hotels are going up thick and fast.

The Archipiélago de los Canarreos (south of Havana province) and Jardines de la Reina (south of Ciego de Ávila and Camagüey provinces) are similar jewels in a sapphire sea. Cayo Largo, part of the Canarreos grouping, offers perhaps the finest beaches in all of Cuba and is fully stocked with tourist hotels. Its largest island, Isla de la Juventud, draws visitors to see crocodiles lumber around in the Lanier swamp; it is also a good destination for birding. Stunning beaches are swept by warm currents that bring ashore marine turtles, and scuba divers are awed by the wrecks and coral reefs off Cabo Francés.

FLORA & FAUNA

Over the course of four centuries, two-thirds of Cuba's forest cover has been felled to make room for sugarcane fields, yet remnants of almost every native ecosystem remain. More than half of the island's 6,700 plants species are endemics, for example, lending even the cities a quintessentially Cuban persona.

The undisputed symbol of Cuba (it graces the national coat of arms) is the ubiquitous royal palm, rising over the lyrical landscapes like silver-sheathed Corinthian columns. Cuba has some 90 species of palms, including the endangered antediluvian cork palm, found only in Pinar del Río. Among the most striking of other tree species are giant kapoks, with roots flanged like missiles; towering ceibas (silk cotton trees), revered in the Santería religion; and the *jagüey,* dropping its roots from its branches.

Flowering species speckle the forests of the cays in Impressionist colors: yellow *corteza amarilla,* scarlet *poró,* and bright orange *Spathodea,* locally called the Jesús Cristo tree because it blooms bloodred at Easter. Frangipani, hibiscus, and bougainvillea brighten colonial townscapes; bromeliads, orchids, and other epiphytes also thrive in the hot, humid climate. The national flower is the *mariposa blanca,* or white butterfly, whose pendulous white blossoms emit an exquisite scent.

Wide variety also exists in the wildlife that populates Cuba's varied landscapes. Mammals include deer, wild boar, and the *Solenodon cubanus* or *almiquí,* an endangered insectivore found only in the Sierra del Cristal. The *jutía*—a cat-size rodent living in uplands and offshore cays—is more common. It looks like a fat, tailless squirrel with thin legs and the tiptoeing gait of a deer. At night, bats command the sky. Cuba has 27 species, from the diminutive butterfly bat—160 together would weigh one pound—to the Jamaican fruit bat, with a wingspan of 20 inches (50 cm).

Shell games

The Cuchillas del Toa in the eastern Oriente region are known for *Polymita pictas*—a tiny species of land snail, unique to the region, known for its colorful shell. Each snail has its own color scheme. Some are bright yellow, others orange or white or black. The majority are whorled in delicate, multicolored stripes. The snail shells were initially colorless, according to local legend. One snail grew jealous of the local beauty and asked to borrow some green from the mountains, blue from the sky, yellow from the sands, and so on, and the other snails followed suit. Alas, locals collectors have decimated their numbers. ■

Royal palms rise over the Sierra del Cristal.

Of Cuba's 46 lizard species, the most colorful is the blue anole, in its debonair cloak of blue and green. When threatened, the male unfolds an orange dewlap below its throat to signal a territorial warning. Lizards are harmless. So, too, are the several species of nonpoisonous snakes, the iguanas in their headdresses of leathery spines, and dozens of amphibian species, including the world's smallest frog—the *Eleutherodactylus iberia,* which measures 3/4 of an inch (18–19 mm). Cuba also has six species of painted land snails (see sidebar left). About 200 species of Cuba's plant and animal species are listed as endangered or threatened, including hawksbill, green, and loggerhead turtles, which nest on the beaches of Isla de la Juventud and the southern cays.

Making a comeback is *Crocodylus rhombifer,* the indigenous Cuban crocodile that was hunted to near extinction. It is protected in the Zapata and Lanier swamps. This saurian giant is far more pugnacious than the American crocodile, and it is present across a broader range. Zapata's waters also shelter the endangered manatee and vast populations of avian fauna—from the purple gallinules and jacanas to scarlet and white ibis with long, curving beaks jabbing for tasty morsels. The sandhill crane is found only in the Lanier swamp, populated also by the emerald green Cuban parrot *(cotorra)* and by the roseate spoonbill, named for its spatulate bill. Flocks of greater flamingo wade the lagoons of Zapata and Cayería del Norte. They're lovely to watch outstretched, skimming the water as they fly.

The ivory-billed woodpecker was thought to be extinct until the bird was sighted in the Cuchillas del Toa in the mid-1980s, prompting the Cuban government to declare the region a protected area. The Cuban green woodpecker and red-billed woodpeckers are common, as are turkey vultures and cattle egrets, white as snow against the cane fields. Pelicans call the shorelines home, while frigate birds hang in the sky like kites tethered on invisible strings. Of the 354 species of birds recorded in Cuba, 21 are endemics, including the charming bee hummingbird, or *zunzuncito,* the world's smallest bird (it barely tips the scales at 1/14th of an ounce). The elegant Cuban trogon or *tocororo,* plumed in the colors of the Cuban flag, is beloved as the national bird. ■

Architecture

CUBA'S ENORMOUS SUGAR WEALTH SPAWNED A TROVE OF GLORIOUS BUILD-
ings in centuries past. The island's varied and distinctive architecture spans four centuries
and showcases a dizzying amalgam of styles—from 16th-century colonial asceticism and
17th- and 18th-century baroque to 19th-century neoclassic and neo-Gothic, plus a stunning array of 20th-century designs. The range is vast, be it the fine city mansions of
wealthy families or the simple wood-frame houses of coastal settlements. Tourism is
spurring efforts to preserve the past and also providing the much-needed resources to do
so—none too soon, because precious buildings collapse daily.

**The colonial-era interior patio (left) was adapted from the classic Moorish inner court.
Trinidad's Iglesia de la Santísima (right) epitomizes the colonial style.**

Throughout the centuries, Cuban architects
have shown remarkable creativity while adapt-
ing their vision to local conditions. The greatest concentration of buildings is in Havana,
which boasts one of the world's finest bodies
of 20th-century architecture in art nouveau,
eclectic, beaux arts, art deco, and modernist
styles. The regional cities and towns tempt
visitors, too, with their colonial structures.
The entire city of Trinidad is a designated
UNESCO World Heritage site, as is Old
Havana and the fortress in Santiago de Cuba.
Though many buildings are in ruins, the communist system has prevented the kinds of
private, for-profit projects that might have
demolished architectural treasures. Whole
cities are frozen in time, untouched by the
wrecking ball or contemporary sprawl.

EARLY COLONIAL STRUCTURES
(16TH & 17TH CENTURIES)

The first rustic settlements were built of wood
and thatched with palm fronds in indigenous
style. These simple *bohíos* are still a staple of
rural areas. As towns developed, adobe and
later limestone replaced wood. The Laws of

the Indies (1537) systemized Spanish plans for colonial settlement and called for plazas to be built every four blocks and presided over by a church. Early churches were simple and austere but for the exquisite carved wood altars adorned with elaborate gilt filigree. The period also saw the construction of forts, such as the Castillo de la Real Fuerza. Built between 1558 and 1577 and adjoining Havana's Plaza de Armas, its sharp-angled bastions are haloed at night in ghostly moonlight.

more ornate, with interiors in the Mudejar style (a blend of Islamic and contemporary European styles, especially Gothic). They had flamboyant baroque facades with portals crowned by scalloped motifs, and huge wooden doors studded with rosehead nails in Spanish style. The Catedral San Cristóbal (1748–1777) offers the finest example. Major cities also had convents. Most still stand today, their cloistered courtyards hidden behind rammed-earth walls, offering a quiet retreat.

The Gran Teatro, dating from the early 1900s, represents Havana at its neo-baroque best. It was built as a private club for descendants of Galician immigrants.

The grid-block pattern decreed by law lent orderliness to city development, with buildings adjoining one another along the narrow streets. The typical 17th-century house was of unadorned Spanish style, with two stories built around an inner courtyard. On the plazas, houses typically boasted a portico and loggia to provide shade and rain protection (see pp. 140–141 for more on the colonial style).

BAROQUE & VERNACULAR COMBINED (18TH CENTURY)

By the 18th century, churches had become

Many structures had *alfarjes* (carved wooden ceilings) that in Cuba often showed a nautical influence—not surprising, since many of them had been crafted by shipbuilders.

In Cuba the embellishments of European baroque style were usually reserved for the main front door. Wooden *rejas* (grilles protecting a window) provided decorative touches, while *vitrales*—stained-glass windows—flooded rooms with tinted light. Cuban cities evolved their own individual styles, such as the projecting turned-wood roof brackets and multicurved *arco mixtilíneo* (doorway lintel)

of Camagüey's houses; the gingerbread of Varadero's wooden beachfront dwellings; and the trompe-l'oeil interior wall paintings of Sancti Spíritus province. Provincial 18th-century houses were typically single story; in Havana, two-story homes prevailed. As Havana expanded, the wide avenues that led out of the city became lined with tall structures fronted by porticoed arcades.

The elaborate Teatro Tomás Terry, built in 1889 in Cienfuegos, is a fine example of neoclassic architecture.

NEOCLASSIC GRANDEUR (19TH CENTURY)

The *ingenio,* or plantation complex, a fixture in rural areas, featured a sugar refinery *(central),* a distillery, storehouses, a *barracón* (living quarters) for slaves, and, of course, the plantation owner's house. Cuba's plantation economy generated great wealth and spawned an early 19th-century boom in civic and private construction. Havana's *criollo* middle classes and aristocracy built *quintas*—neoclassic villas set in gardens in the suburbs—and grandiose mansions, such as the imposing Palacio Aldama (1840–1884), on Havana's Parque de la Fraternidad. Many were in Palladian style, then popular in Europe. The 19th century also witnessed a return to a more restrained, neoclassic style in church building.

Civic structures reflected the growing influence of European neoclassicism. Examples include El Templete, erected in 1828 in Havana's Plaza de Armas to celebrate the city's founding, and theaters such as the Teatro Sauto (1863) in Matanzas, and Teatro Terry (1889) in Cienfuegos. Corinthian columns

and lavishly decorated interiors ruled the day; ornate ironwork grilles and railings replaced wooden rejas.

MODERNIST INFLUENCES (20TH CENTURY)

The end of colonialism ushered in a period of radical change as architects and planners worked to elevate Cuba to the artistic avant-garde in an outpouring of European-inspired architectural styles. Soaring neo-Gothic spires rose above the Havana skyline. Art nouveau, which evolved in Europe from 1905 to 1920, came to Cuba as highly decorative houses in Belgian, French, or, principally, Catalonian styles. In Havana, the style was fostered by Catalans who settled the city. The Palacio Cueto (1906), on the southeast corner of Plaza Vieja, evokes this Gaudiesque influence.

Pride of heritage found expression in Spanish revival as aristocratic Spanish communities vied with one another to build social clubs that exhibited regional influences. Examples are Havana's Centro Asturiano (1927) and Centro Gallego (1915)—now the Gran Teatro. Spanish revival heavily influenced the eclectic style—what Cuban novelist Alejo Carpentier called "style without style."

In Havana, a fine example is the Palacio Presidencial (1920) by architects Paul Belau and Carlos Maruri. Now the Museo de la Revolución, the building's facade is imbued with classical allusions and Spanish revival overtones as seen in its ornate towers and ground-floor portals (see pp. 73–75). The nearby Residencia de Dionisio Velasco (1912), now the Spanish Embassy, and the Cuban Telephone Company (1927) by Leonardo Morales, at Dragones and Aguila, are other fine examples. Eclectic was particularly favored by provincial domestic architects. The streets of Pinar del Río city, for example, are lined with confections dripping with effusive stucco.

The 1920s brought about beaux arts, introduced by the École des Beaux-Arts in Paris. Pompeiian frescoes and Corinthian columns appeared, as did elaborate stained-glass appointments by Tiffany's. During this period, which dominated public buildings until the early 1940s, most Cuban cities erected grand civic edifices in neoclassic style.

Havana gained a monumental look, thanks in no small part to the colossal, symmetrical Capitolio (1912–29), the country's prime example of the beaux-arts style. The neo-classic structure, which emulated the capitol in Washington, D.C., had a counterpoint in beaux-art statues designed to convey Cuba's newfound confidence and pride. Notable, too, was the classically inspired University of Havana (1902–1940), with an 88-step entrance by French landscape designer Jean-Claude Nicolas Forestier.

By the late '20s, the art deco style—terra-cotta motifs, veneer panels, banded facades—became the rage. Most magnificent of Havana's art deco structures is the Edificio Bacardí (1930), by Esteban Rodríguez, Rafael Fernández Ruenes, and José Menéndez, the most completely art deco commercial building in Cuba. Its granite exterior is accented by multi-hued terra-cotta and its interior by the lavish decorative art that marked the style.

Cuba's art deco heyday coincided with that of the movie theater; an example is the pink-pastel exterior of the Cine-Teatro Fausto (1938). Art deco evolved into a sinuous, more

The Palacio de El Valle in Cienfuegos was completed in 1917 in ostentatious, neo-Moorish style. Moroccan craftsmen added fretted interiors, stained-glass windows, and balustraded rooms.

streamlined style with a fondness for curves and freestyle strokes. Buildings were meant to represent "velocity in motion," as in Havana's National Bus Terminal (1948–51) on Avenida Rancho Boyeros. The near complete absence of decoration and sensual nonchalance that marked the style is superbly expressed in movie houses such as Havana's Cine América (1941), where the vaulted auditorium seems to grow from the tiers of curvilinear box seats. The '30s and '40s also saw art deco high-rise apartment buildings erected in Havana and Santiago de Cuba. The rounded balconies of the Solimar apartment block (1944), located at Calle Soledad #205 between San Lázaro and Animas in Centro Habana, are fine examples of the style.

The post-World War II boom years ushered in modern rationalism. Austere monumental buildings of fundamentalist proportions went up, such as the Edificio Focsa (1956) apartment complex and the National Library, National Theater, and government buildings of Plaza de la Revolución. Emerging to pioneer the new style was a new generation of gifted young architects, including Mario Romañach, Silverio Bosch, and most significantly Max Borges Recio, who evoked tropical sensuality in his Club Náutico swimming club (1957) and Tropicana nightclub (1951–56). Each building was characterized by arcing shell vaults and large expanses of glass. These architects spearheaded a movement of great importance as Hispanic influence was being swept away by the U.S. model.

Modernity was adopted by the middle classes and spread throughout Havana as new residential districts emerged. In fact, the greatest experimentation took place in the construction of private houses. During the boom years of the early 20th century, Cuba's burgeoning and discerning middle classes sought quality housing in the latest architectural vogues. The evolution of a huge middle class in the decades between 1920 and 1959 saw lavish single-family residences in eclectic, neoclassic, and revivalist styles go up all over Havana. The most notable examples are in Nuevo Vedado and the upscale suburbs of Miramar and Country Club (today's Cubanacán). Thousands of such gems can be admired simply by walking the streets. On a par with anywhere else

El Futuro gas station in Havana seemed futuristic when built in the art deco heyday (above). Coppelia ice-cream shop (below), located in Havana's Vedado district, made a bold postrevolutionary statement when it was constructed in 1966. The concrete structure sits in lush gardens.

in the world, these stunning houses struggle to be acknowledged for their artistic worth as a collective asset of the nation's cultural heritage.

The same time period saw the construction of a new breed of high-rise casino-hotels influenced by the architecture of Miami Beach. The Hotel Riviera's (1957) prodigal use of curves and broad cantilevered eaves aerodynamically complemented the days of finned Cadillacs, while the opening of the landmark Havana Hilton Hotel (1958)—now the Habana Libre—with Hilton's neon-lit name emblazoned across it, confirmed that Havana was indeed enjoying its place in the sun.

POSTREVOLUTIONARY ARCHITECTURE (LATE 20TH CENTURY)

Many Cuban architects fled Cuba after 1959. The decades that followed witnessed a drastic upheaval in how architecture was perceived and practiced. Suffering under the rigid yoke of Soviet-influenced postmodernist dictates, the urban landscape was hammered and sick-led into disharmony with Cuba's past. Brutish apartment blocks of prefabricated concrete—a cheap and practical solution to the severe housing shortage—were built by untrained *microbrigadistas* (volunteer construction teams), fortunately outside Havana. A brief fling with new forms of artistic expression brought forth Havana's National Arts Schools complex (1961–65), conceived to be the jewel in the crown of revolutionary architecture. The romance ended, however, when the architects' vision proved too experimental for communist tastes.

As the revolution progressed, resources for construction dwindled. Havana's Coppelia ice-cream parlor (1966) and Las Ruinas restaurant (1972), both of pressed concrete, are among the few postrevolutionary edifices with aesthetic appeal. Santiago de Cuba's postmodernist Hotel Santiago (1986)—a massive assemblage of geometric forms in primary colors—led the way for a new era of stylish contemporary structures. These have been echoed in new resort projects now sprouting across the island nation. ■

Culture

CUBA'S VIBRANT CULTURAL SCENE STIRS THE SOUL AND IMAGINATION OF visitors. Operating in a virtual vacuum for the better part of 40 years, Cuban artists have explored boundaries of self-expression without influence from the rest of the world. So fertile and evolved are the arts that Cuba's creative performers set the world abuzz—and not simply with their infectious music. Cuba is an international trendsetter in cinema, literature, and the fine arts.

Cuban culture has its roots in the fusing of Spanish and African cultures. The national identity and spirit in the arts draw inspiration from a passionate and turbulent history—an expressive searching over centuries of a creative people confined in an authoritarian world. The literary scene, for example, has long found its inspiration in Cuba's continuum of struggle against oppression and tyranny. And Cuba's talented photographers, painters, and sculptors have produced a visceral and dynamic collection of work that provides a visual commentary on Cuban society's aspirations and social tensions.

The revolutionary government's shifting attitude toward the arts has both bolstered and stifled artistic expression. In 1961 the government began to shoehorn artists, writers, and intellectuals into ideological conformity, expressed in Fidel Castro's maxim, "Within the Revolution, everything. Against the Revolution, nothing!"

Today the scene is more liberal, though politically unpalatable works remain subject to official censure. Nonetheless, the Ministry of Culture has been committed to sponsorship of the arts in every field. Budding talent is identified at an early age, and the most gifted students are boarded at special art schools. The Escuela Nacional de Arte, or National School of Art, founded in Havana in 1960, oversees 41 schools across the nation, covering the spectrum of fine art, music, theater, ballet, and folkloric and modern dance. The most talented artists attend the Instituto Superior de Arte, Cuba's premier school, in Havana.

Havana has scores of art galleries and museums, and no township is without its museums, Casa de la Cultura, and/or Casa de la Trova, where under state sponsorship Cuba's rich cultural heritage is kept alive. The Galería Genesis exists to promote artists' work. In 1991 artists were granted copyright to their creations and, in a unique arrangement within Cuba, permitted to retain 85 percent of receipts on sales through a state agency.

FINE ARTS

Early Cuban painters adopted the Spanish style. It was not until the 1800s that a national Cuban style arose. Led by José Nicolás de la Escalera (1734–1804) and Vincente Escobar (1762–1834), the movement was characterized by an idealized vision of black culture. The opening in Havana in 1818 of the Escuela de Pintura y Escultura de San Alejandro—the School of Painting and Sculpture—under the direction of French artist Jean Baptiste Vermay (1786–1833) lent new vigor to the arts community. It was responsible for infusing neoclassicism from the French and Italian schools into romantic landscapes, a direction pursued in the second half of the 19th century by such artists as Esteban Chartrand (1824–1884).

By the turn of the 20th century, Cuba came under the sway of Europe's avant-garde movement. Cuban painters adapted international styles to local themes, notably the emblematic figure of the *guajiro* (peasant farmer) favored by painter Carlos Enrique (1900–1957). Meanwhile, Victor Manuel García (1897–1965) helped inspire a cadre of Cuban artists who experimented in the style of Postimpressionists such as Gauguin.

The most acclaimed Cuban painter—Wifredo Lam (1902–1982)—was born to a Chinese father and an Afro-Cuban mother. He studied at Vermay's *academía*, then left for Spain in 1936. Lam moved between Havana,

"Interior of Juan Bautista Sagarra's House," by Manuel Vicens, in the Museo Bacardí, shows 19th-century upper-class life.

Marseilles, and Paris. He was influenced by the surrealists—notably Picasso, who took the young Cuban under his wing. Lam immersed himself in African culture and adopted the theme of Afro-Cuban mysticism in his exploration of the magical-surrealist style. His works fetch up to a million dollars each on the world market. Many of his best paintings hang in Havana's Fine Arts Museum.

The influence of Picasso is also felt in the work of Amelia Peláez (1896–1968), known for her abstract ceramic murals. A re-creation of a 525-piece mural by Peláez adorns the facade of Havana's Hotel Habana Libre. Inside the hotel, a mosaic by acclaimed contemporary ceramacist and sculptor Alfredo Sosabravo (1930–) graces the lobby.

What experts call a true renaissance of Cuban art occurred in the 1980s. The island's artists portrayed ideas in a way they never had. They began to participate in formal exhibits and compete artistically and commercially on

an international level. The work of such artists as Los Carpinteros (the collaborative name of Cuban artists Alexandre Arrechea, Marco Castillo, and Dagoberto Rodríguez), Pedro Alvarez, Esterio Segura, and others today forms part of the collections of major museums and art institutions around the world.

Cuba's contemporary art community has evolved a profoundly experimental and easily recognizable genre, not least in a vast and sophisticated body of political poster art and street billboards. The influence of Afro-Cuban religious culture remains dominant in the wildly imaginative, idiosyncratic works of such artists as Pedro Pablo Oliva (1949–), Nelson Domínguez (1947–), and Manuel Mendive (1944–). Themes of eroticism are another constant element of art from this sensual isle. Visitors are often shocked at the highly graphic sexual content on public view, as in the evocatively symbolic works of Chago Armada and Aldo Soler. The past decade has

Central stage in this Camagüey painting are Che Guevera, Elián Gonzáles, and José Martí.

also seen a profusion of works catering to the tourist market: Street scenes showing antique Yankee *cacharros* (cars) are a popular theme. Other artists parody the style of Salvador Dalí, whose tortured surrealism serves as metaphor for their own vision of contemporary Cuba.

Work in sculpture and ceramic arts has been no less expressive. Roberto Fernández Martínez finds inspiration in African myth for his totemic oversize sculptures. The exquisitely crafted figures of Rita Longa (1912–2000), Cuba's most famous contemporary sculptor, stand at the entrances to the Riviera Hotel and the Terminal de Omnibus; her ballet dancer has become the emblem of the Tropicana nightclub.

A recent outpouring of contemporary jewelry designs displays a quintessential Cuban passion for creativity—for example, in the use of antique silver cutlery entwining black coral. Nothing is thrown away in Cuba, where recycling is itself an art. Artist Gilberto Kindelán collects glass and metallic tidbits from fallen

buildings and crafts them into exquisite art nouveau lamps. And the recent tourism boom has sparked a revolution in crafts such as leatherwork, earthenware pottery, and wood carvings—predominantly of nubile women.

LITERATURE

Injustice and social turmoil are the grist for great literature, and Cuba, with a long history of both, has produced dozens of authors and poets whose works are profound. The *criollo* patriot and national hero José Martí (1853–1895) is revered for his poetry and prose, which passionately decry injustice and espouse the cause of independence. Martí was among a long line of Cuban exiles who produced their best works abroad. Cirilo Villaverde (1812–1894), for example, wrote *Cecilia Valdés* while in exile. Alejo Carpentier (1904–

1980) wrote many of his surrealistic novels in Venezuela during the Batista era. And Virgilio Piñera, author of *Cold Tales*, and Guillermo Cabrera Infanta, known for his comedic *Three Trapped Tigers*, set in the seedy Havana of Batista days, are two of the many authors estranged from their country since the 1960s.

One who stayed on the island that inspired him was mulatto poet Nicolás Guillén (1902–1989), who lent lyrical and passionate beauty to his *poesía negra* (black poetry) by drawing on the anguish of slavery. After the revolution, Guillén, a committed socialist, helped found the PCC-controlled UNEAC—Cuban National Union of Writers and Artists—and became Cuba's poet laureate. Alejo Carpentier returned to Cuba in 1959 and remained loyal to the revolution—a prerequisite for being published in contemporary Cuba.

Most of the best writers of the 1960s and '70s fled, however or were forced to leave. Avant-garde writer José Lezama Lima (1912–1976), author of *Paradiso,* was elevated to literary director of the National Cultural Council before running afoul of Fidel Castro. Similarly, Reinaldo Arenas (1943–1990) and Carlos Franquí (1921–), both Castroite guerrillas and brilliant essayists, were later forced into exile.

In the 1980s the works of many forbidden authors were resurrected, and the 1990s saw a new body of literature produced, including works by women. Historically, women have not been well represented in Cuban literature, with the exception of La Avellaneda in the 19th century, famed for her sensitive poems, and Dulce María Loynaz (1902–1997), former director of the Cuban Academy of Language. She was acclaimed as Cuba's finest recent poet.

Unfortunately, material shortages and ideological restrictions have conspired to keep undiscovered an entire generation of Cuban authors. Although Cuba is a country of avid readers, due in large part to the revolution's emphasis on literacy, bookstores and libraries are few and meagerly stocked, and books are recycled until they crumble to dust.

FILM & THEATER

Cubans are devout moviegoers. Since 1959, Cuba has produced high-caliber movies through the state-controlled film institute, Instituto Cubano de Arte e Industria del Cine.

The institute has granted great latitude to intellectuals such as Tomás Gutiérrez Alea (1928–1996), a brilliant producer of populist satires on communist life. His *Fresa y chocolate (Strawberry and Chocolate,* 1994), which portrays the repression of homosexuals, was nominated for an Academy Award. A respected international film festival takes place annually in Havana.

Theater came to Cuba from Spain during the colonial period. In the 19th century, Teatro Bufo, a vernacular tradition, evolved as Cuba's version of a national theatrical experience. It combined music, dances, and *guarachas* (country ballads), and introduced three popular characters representing Cuban identity: the Spaniard *(el Gallego),* the Mulata (a beautiful

mestiza), and the Black Guy *(el Negrito).* The three characters would sing and interact with the audience, using sarcastic language and often introducing political issues.

In the 1950s, Vicente Revuelta, considered the father of Cuban theater, founded Teatro Estudio. Revuelta's space was a haven for many important actors and directors, including Roberto Blanco, Bertha Martínez, and Abelardo Estorino, the most important living Cuban playwright.

A new generation of actors, directors, and critics entered the theater in the 1980s. Today there are about 60 professional theater groups and numerous community theater groups across the country. Two important theater festivals take place biennially in September.

Conjunto Folklórico members rehearse at the Palenque de los Congos Reales, near Plazuela Segarte, in Trinidad.

MUSIC & DANCE

From traditional folk music to rumba and rap, music is Cuba's lifeblood. Since the revolution, the government has promoted folkloric over commercial music and in 1961 founded Conjunto Folklórico Nacional to revive appreciation for traditional music and dance. And Cubans have held fast to their roots: The seductive rhythms and soulful beats pulsing through the streets owe much to the fusion of Spanish and African sounds.

Spaniards introduced rural folk music to the isle. Cuba quickly developed a distinctive

Groups such as Grupo Salsa Matriz infuse Cuba with sensual rhythms.

criollo folk music—*guajiras*, or *trovas*—using a tradition of poetry in song. Singing of their sorrows and joys, entertainers improvised to the musical accompaniment of a guitar, lute, gourd instruments, and *tres* (a Cuban guitar with three sets of double strings). Guajiras remain popular today and can be heard performed at Casas de la Trova nationwide. "Guantanamera"—the love song written in 1928 by José Fernández (1908–1979)—is the most famous. The *nueva trova* has evolved, as performed by Silvio Rodríguez, with cutting lyrics that focus on contemporary life.

This fusion of sweet folk music with African rhythms and instruments is the basis for modern Cuban popular music, beginning with the *danzón*, which evolved from the French contredanse in the late 19th century and proved popular through the 1920s. Danzón formed the basis for *son*, which was popularized in the 1920s by radio and by groups such as the Trío Matamoros. Son derives from the mountains of Guantánamo province, where it was performed with guitar, *claves, maracas, bongos*, and the *marímbula*—a sound box of Bantu origin played by plucking metal tongues. The music typically uses *décima* verses—octosyllable ten-line stanzas. *Son changüí*—a fast, country version of son as performed by Orquestra Revé—remains quite popular in Guantánamo.

Beginning in the 1930s, U.S. jazz bands that toured the isle influenced Cuban music. The formation of brassy big band sets—

orquestras típicas—opened the way for the evolution, in the '60s and '70s, of a Latin-jazz, dance-oriented sound called salsa. Played by such acclaimed dance bands as Los Van Van, salsa is a high-spirited, fast-paced, and uniquely Cuban fusion of jazz and traditional rhythms. A variation, and the latest Cuban trend, is new-wave salsa, or timba. This potent blend of keyboards and percussive Afro-Cuban groove is performed by groups such as Bamboleo and ¡Cubanismo!

Today, rock and roll bands enjoy government sponsorship. And the success of the 1996 movie *Buena Vista Social Club*, which brought together and made international stars of four elderly, half-forgotten master players—Ibrahim Ferrer, Ruben González, Eliades Ochoa, and Compay Segundo—has rekindled interest in son. Jazz, too, is enjoying a renaissance.

Cuba has also produced accomplished classical musicians. Composer-pianist Ernesto Lecuona (1896–1963) performed to acclaim throughout Europe and wrote many classical pieces, operas, and songs inspired by Afro-Cuban rhythms. Leo Brouwer is a classical composer and guitarist of world renown, and Frank Fernández, an internationally recognized classical pianist, frequently performs with Cuba's Orquestra Simfónica Nacional. The world-famous Ballet Nacional de Cuba, founded in 1940 by Alicia Alonso, performs through a year-long season. The Camagüey Ballet and Ballet Folklórico de Oriente also raise the curtain to ovations abroad. ∎

Ethereal and exciting, Cuba's history-steeped capital city is remarkable for its colonial fortresses and cathedrals and stunning array of 20th-century architectural styles. Other enthralling attractions include cigar factories, a museum dedicated to the revolution, and bars haunted by Hemingway's ghost.

Havana

Gran Teatro de la Habana

Havana

HAVANA IS A GRITTY, STEAMY, SHELL-SHOCKED, IRRESISTIBLE CITY FINGER-
ing out around a flask-shaped bay like an aged Spanish fan. Much of this vast, sprawling
metropolis of 2.2 million people has suffered from decades of neglect, its decaying buildings and potholed streets bespeaking difficult times. Yet this monumental city is also as
grandiose and romantic as any Europe or the New World can offer. Its charming historic
core is a fairy-tale jewel with a grid of intimate streets lined by baroque churches, palaces,
castles, and mansions—eloquent evocations of the once mighty power of Spain.

Havana is one of the world's great historical
cities, resembling—and this is perhaps its
greatest charm—an abandoned stage set still
waiting for the curtain to rise. Founded on its
current site in 1519, San Cristóbal de la
Habana rapidly evolved to become Spain's key
to the New World, brimful of architectural
gems. The Pearl of the Antilles remained a
prosperous city into the mid-20th century,
gradually acquiring handsome parks, leafy
boulevards, belle epoque mansions, streamlined
art deco blocks, modernist villas, grandiose
monuments, and other lavish structures that
boasted of Havana's wealth and the showy exu-
berance and sophistication of Cuban culture.
Havana's relatively lax morals drew Yankees,
tempted by the lures of casinos, *mojitos* (a rum
cocktail), and more sinful indulgence: live sex
shows, cocaine parlors, and other esoteric
frontiers of the libertine Latin mystique.

After the revolution, monuments to those
on the wrong side of history came down, while
others to politically correct heroes went up
alongside museums that wave a flag for the
socialist cause. Street names were also changed,
so that many streets have both an old and new
name, the former being preferred by locals.

The postrevolutionary era has been hard
on Havana. Neglected for four long, hard
decades, the once-proud city sank into decline.
Monstrous Soviet-style apartment blocks
replaced the shantytowns of prerevolutionary
Cuba with their own form of blight. Though
the neglect and dishevelment invoke a profound melancholy, the city has avoided the kind
of population onslaught—and shantytowns—
that have deluged Mexico City and other capitals. Greater Havana, comprising 15 *municipios*,
or municipalities, retains an amalgam of colonial-era villages, engulfed by the greater
metropolis but still rich in historical allure.

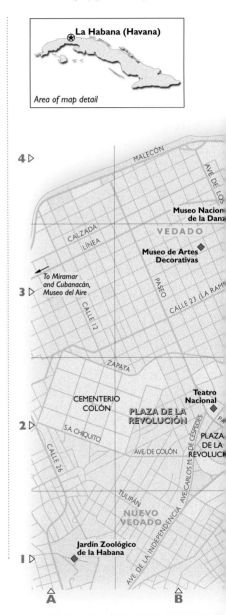

La Habana (Havana)

Area of map detail

The city's colonial core—Habana Vieja (Old Havana)—was declared a UNESCO World Heritage site in 1982. Bit by bit, the government is restoring its venerable structures, a rich blend of architecture dating back 400 years.

Other pockets of Havana are on the upswing as tourism in the post-Soviet era writes a new chapter. Ritzy hotels have sprouted. A trade center in Miramar is expanding, while commercial billboards and fast-food outlets are going up. Gleaming Mercedes taxis now streak past sock-hop-era jalopies and overloaded Hungarian buses belching fumes.

Though the strip clubs and brothels are gone, chased away by Castro & Co.'s puritanical strictures, Havana is still sensual, still steeped in an irrepressible, sunwashed tawdriness. It is best appreciated nose-to-nose,

through close contact with its vivacious, hospitable people who enjoy life to the fullest, as much as their budgets allow.

The most interesting sites concentrate around the four main plazas of Old Havana. The old city deserves a three-day minimum, and Vedado, Miramar, and outlying districts a day each. Though spread out, Havana is a walker's city, nonthreatening and beckoning you to touch the past through the soles of your feet.

Keep in mind that descriptive exhibits at museums are mostly in Spanish. English-speaking guides are available at most sites, where permission to photograph usually costs extra. Venues, hours, and telephone numbers change often. A heavy police presence helps keep crime at bay, although petty thievery still abounds and *jineteros* and *jineteras*—touts and prostitutes—attempt to pry dollars from tourists. ∎

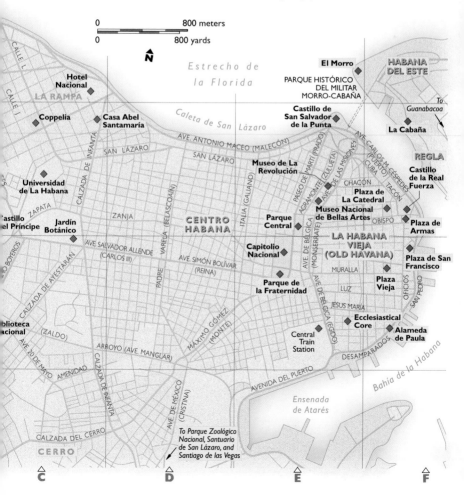

Like the dramatis personae of a Greek play, Havana wears many faces. A performance in Plaza de Armas pays tribute to the government's accomplishments in the arts.

Habana Vieja

Replete with cultural and historic attractions, Old Havana is a 350-acre trove of intriguing attractions guaranteed to enthrall for days. Its four main squares are graced by an architectural A-list of palaces, castles, and mansions, many turned into restaurants, boutique hotels, galleries, and eclectic museums. Much of Old Havana—crammed to bursting point with 74,000 people—is a lived-in museum: decrepit, yes, and now lacking its fortified walls . . . but fascinating, too, for the earthy, timeworn appeal of life lived in the darkening shadows of Cuba's past.

In 1977, Old Havana was declared a national monument, and the following year a major restoration project was declared. The need was urgent: Most of Old Havana's 3,157 structures had deteriorated to a point of dilapidation. Three decades on, having been named a UNESCO World Heritage site in 1982, the remarkable effort has lent new vigor to the world's most authentic colonial collection.

The flavor of bygone days is heady along narrow streets, lined with beautiful mansions adorned with graceful *portales* setting off their exquisite facades. The symptoms of the 20th century are soon forgotten as you stroll the plazas and cobblestoned streets bathed in incandescent light, past buildings whose bright pastels—lemon yellow, guava green, tangerine, like tropical fruits—compete with the dazzling blue hue of the sky.

A logical place to start is Plaza de Armas. ■

Plaza de Armas

FIRST LAID OUT IN 1519 AS A PARADE GROUND, HAVANA'S oldest plaza became the center of city life and the seat of government throughout 383 years of Spanish tenure. A small park lies at its heart, framed by tall palms that cast cooling shadows over a statue of the 19th-century revolutionary leader Carlos Manuel de Céspedes.

Important 18th-century buildings of coral limestone edge the plaza. Most notable is the **Palacio de los Capitanes Generales,** on the west side, from where the governors *(capitanes generales)* enforced Spanish rule. Fronted by a wide loggia, the three-story structure wraps around a central courtyard. Marble stairs lead up to sumptuous rooms housing the **Museo de la Ciudad** (Museum of the City). Its many treasures reflect the history of Havana and Cuba and include the **Hall of Mirrors** (Sala de los Espejos), where the transfer of power from Spain to the United States took place on Jan. 1, 1899.

Clockwise around the plaza, the 1772 **Palacio del Segundo Cabo** (Palace of the Second Lieutenant, *tel 7/862-8091),* in Moorish-inspired Cuban baroque style, was originally built as a post office. Later it housed the vice governor, became the Senate building, and today hosts the **Cuban Book Institute** (Instituto Cubano del Libro); it's open by guided tour.

The plaza opens northeast to a pocket-size castle, **Castillo de la Real Fuerza.** The second oldest fortress in the Americas, it was completed in 1577. Gleaming suits of armor in the foyer beckon you to the **Museo de la Cerámica** *(tel 7/861-6130),* which displays pottery through the ages. The weather vane atop the northwest watchtower is a copy of **La Giraldilla de la Habana,** cast in honor of Inéz de Bobadilla, who served as Cuba's only female governor while her husband, Gov. Hernando de Soto, fruitlessly searched for the Fountain of Youth (the original statue is in the Museo de la Ciudad).

El Templete, a tiny Greco-Roman-style temple dating from 1828, sits adjacent, marking the site where the first Mass was held in the then tiny hamlet, in 1519. Outside, votive offerings placed by Santería believers adorn the base of a sacred ceiba tree. The mansion to the south is the former Casa del Conde de Santovenia, today the **Hotel Santa Isabel.** Its mellowed antiquity recalls the day in 1867 when the palace became the city's first hotel.

Be sure to pop into the **Taberna del Galeón** *(tel 7/33-8476),* tucked off the square on Calle Baratillo. It serves rum samplers within its chilled confines. On the south side of the plaza, the **Museo Nacional de Historia Natural** displays Cuban flora and fauna. ■

Plaza de Armas
- Map p. 67 & 61 F3

Museo de la Ciudad
- Palacio de los Capitanes Generales, Calle Tacón #1, bet. Obispo & O'Reilly
- 7/861-5779
- $

Castillo de la Real Fuerza
- Calle O'Reilly #2
- 7/861-6130
- $

Museo Nacional de Historia Natural
- Calle Obispo #61, bet. Oficios & Baratillo
- 7/863-9391
- Closed Mon.
- $

The Palacio de los Capitanes Generales

Plaza de La Catedral

THE MOST INTIMATE (AND THE YOUNGEST) OF OLD HAVANA'S main squares, this compact plaza was originally a swamp. The area was drained and laid out in the late 17th century. From lowly beginnings arose aristocratic mansions and the baroque splendor of the Havana cathedral. Today, troubadours roam the square while *mulattas* in traditional costume add color to the sense of a *temps perdú.*

Plaza de La Catedral

🅰 Map p. 67 & 61 F3

Museo de Arte Colonial

✉ #61 Plaza de la Catedral

☎ 7/862-6440

💲 $

Centro de Arte Contemporáneo Wifredo Lam

✉ Calle San Ignacio #22, at Empedrado

☎ 7/861-2096

🕐 Closed Sun.

💲 $

Fundación Alejo Carpentier

✉ Calle Empedrado #215, bet. Cuba & San Ignacio

☎ 7/861-5506

🕐 Closed Sat.–Sun.

Dominating the plaza is **Catedral San Cristóbal** *(tel 7/861-7771),* built between 1748 and 1777 and locally known as Catedral de la Habana. Dedicated to Christopher Columbus, the baroque cathedral once contained a casket thought to contain the bones of the explorer; they were returned to Spain in 1899. Its rippling facade is framed by campaniles whose bells, according to legend, were cast with a dash of gold.

The 1720 Casa del Conde de Casa Bayona, on the plaza's south side, exemplifies the elegant symmetry of period architecture, with an inner patio surrounded by Tuscan pilasters. It holds the **Museo de Arte Colonial,** overflowing with antiquities.

On the square's east side stand the **Palacio del Marqués de Arcos** and **Casa del Conde de Casa Lombillo,** both dating from 1740. The latter later became the

city's first post office; you can still insert letters into the mouth of a grotesque face inset in the wall. On the west side, the **Casa de los Marqueses de Aguas Claras** (1751–1775) now serves as a restaurant and bar.

The **Centro de Arte Contemporáneo Wifredo Lam,** at the square's northwest corner, honors famed Cuban artist Wifredo Lam (1902–1982) by showing artists exhibiting at Havana's Art Biennale. Steps away, at Calle Empedrado #207, is **La Bodeguita del Medio,** the tiny *bodega* where Errol Flynn and, occasionally, Ernest Hemingway quaffed their *mojitos.* Immediately west, the 1809 Casa de la Condesa de la Reunión was the setting for much of 20th-century novelist Alejo Carpentier's *The Enlightenment.* Today it houses the **Fundación Alejo Carpentier,** dedicated to the author's memory. ∎

Plaza de San Francisco

THIS OPEN PLAZA—AT CALLE OFICIOS AND THE FOOT OF Calle Amargura—has changed little since the days when Spanish galleons creaked at anchor, holds bulging with treasure laden for Spain. The harbor is now hidden by the Aduana, or customs building, erected in 1914 and recently converted, in part, into the spiffy new Terminal Sierra Maestra, where cruise ships dock. Horse-drawn carriages still clatter upon the relaid cobbles, and the surrounding streets, lined with the former homes of wealthy merchants, gleam afresh like confections in stone.

Commanding the plaza's north side is the five-story **Lonja del Comercio de La Habana** (Goods Exchange; tel 7/866-9587 or 7/866-9588), built in 1909 in a neoclassically inspired eclectic style with a dome topped by a bronze figure of Mercury. Recently gutted and refitted in contemporary vogue, it still functions as a mercantile venue for foreign corporations. The grand houses along the plaza's west flank today serve as restaurants, galleries, and boutiques for the tourist trade.

The **Fuente de los Leones** (Fountain of the Lions), erected in 1836, graces the square on its south side, drawing pigeons and children to its splashing waters. The *fuente* stands in delicate counterpoint to the baroque **Iglesia y Convento de San Francisco de Asis**, dating from 1719–1738, which looms behind. It was here that Processions of the Cross once set out each Lenten Friday on a pilgrimage to Plaza del Cristo. The church, built between 1580 and 1591 and modified in the 18th century, is topped by a 120-foot-high (36 m) bell tower. The gold-gilt cedar altar, alas, was removed following the English invasion of 1762; after a Protestant service was held here, the Catholics considered the church defiled and thereafter no services were held. Today it hosts classical concerts.

A portion of the crypt is visible beneath glass (people were buried here according to rank; nobles near the altar, baptized black slaves near the door). Note the trompe l'oeil that extends the perspective of the nave. The nave opens to the cloisters of the convent, consecrated in 1739 and now exhibiting religious treasures in the **Museo de Arte Religioso.** The life-size bronze outside the convent is that of the **Caballero de París,** a stylish tramp famous throughout Havana in the 1950s. ∎

Glossary of architectural details

Alfarje: Carved wooden ceiling featuring angled beams set in star patterns.

Azulejo: Glazed Spanish tile.

Cenefa: Band of decorative plasterwork on interior walls.

Mamparsa: Intricately decorated inner door.

Mediopunto: Wooden or stained-glass arch window designed to filter strong sunlight.

Portale: Massive doorway with elaborate baroque moldings.

Postigo: Smaller door contained within a larger *portale.*

Reja: Elongated grille protecting a window. ∎

Plaza de San Francisco

⬛ Map p. 67 & 61 F2

Iglesia y Convento de San Francisco de Asis

✉ Calle Oficios bet. Amargura & Teniente Rey

☎ 7/862-3467

💲 $

Dinner beneath the stars

A folkloric *espectáculo* (show) is held monthly beneath the romantic glow of lanterns in both Plaza de La Catedral and Plaza de San Francisco. See p. 261.

Walk: The heart of Habana Vieja

This circuit follows cobbled streets that echo with the footsteps of history and trace a path through the heart of quintessential Havana—a restored seven-by-two-block core forming a rhomboid, with the city's main squares at each quadrant. The walk passes the finest of Old Havana's architectural gems that are sprinkled throughout a harmonious network of narrow streets newly emerged from restoration. Some streets are pedestrians-only. The walk is best done between 8 a.m. and noon to avoid the midafternoon heat.

Start at the southwest corner of **Plaza de Armas** ❶ (see p. 63), where Calle Obispo is lined by early colonial houses with exquisite touches: wood balconies, *mediopuntos,* and mahogany carriage doors. One of the many buildings now housing part of the **Oficina del Historiador de la Ciudad** *(Calle Obispo #119)* is located in Havana's oldest house, dating from 1598. After quaffing a glass of mineral water at **Casa del Agua "La Tinaja"** *(Calle Obispo #109),* turn south onto Calle Oficios.

On your right is a fine Moorish inspiration, the **Casa de los Árabes** ❷ *(Calle Oficios #16, tel 7/861-5868, closed Mon.),* celebrating Arab culture in Cuba, with carved saddles, rugs, and other Oriental exhibits. The Casa del Obispo, next door, is a former bishop's palace and today houses the **Museo Numismático** *(Calle Oficios #8, tel 7/861-5811, closed Mon.),* drawing coin-lovers for its collection dating

back 500 years. Opposite, the **Depósito del Automóvil** *(Calle Oficios #13)* displays vintage autos. Continue south to Calle Obrapía. Here, the **Hostal Valencia** *(tel 7/867-1037),* a classic Spanish-style posada, is worth a stop for its atmospheric restaurant.

Continuing south on Oficios, you enter **Plaza de San Francisco** ❸ (see p. 65). The block facing the Iglesia y Convento de San Francisco de Asís contains some of the prettiest colonial houses in Old Havana, including the **Galería Carmen Montilla Tinoco** *(Calle Oficios #162, tel 7/33-8768, closed Sun.).* Behind its soft-pink-and-green facade, the cutaway rear wall opens to a sculpture garden highlighted by a 3-D mural by Alfredo Sosabravo. Follow Oficios two blocks to Calle Muralla and the **Antigua Cámara de Representantes** *(Calle Oficios #211, tel 7/863-4352),* with a neoclassic lobby lit through stunning stained-glass

Havana's lively art scene is displayed at Calle Tacón's artisans' market.

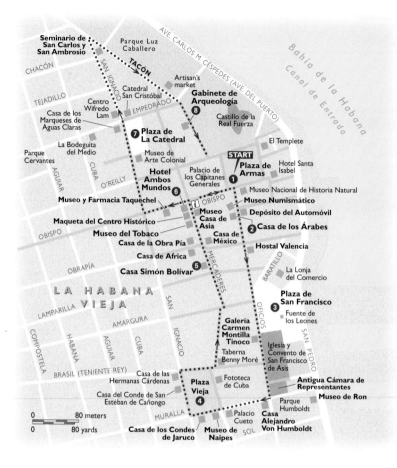

windows. Built in 1929, it has housed the Ministry of Education and the Municipal Assembly. It now exhibits things related to all its history, as well as the **Museo de Campana de Alfabetización** (Museum of the Literacy Campaign; *closed Mon., $*).

Catercorner is the **Casa Alejandro Von Humboldt** (*Calle Oficios #254 bet. Sol & Muralla, tel 7/863-9850, closed Mon.*), where displays honor the German explorer who in the early 1800s catalogued the island's flora and fauna. The park opposite features his bust and is backed by the Casa del Conde de la Mortera, now housing the **Museo de Ron** (Museum of Rum; *Calle San Pedro #262 at Sol, tel 7/861-8051, $*), where guided tours explain the stages of rum production. Exhibits include a 1:22.5 scale model of a 1930s town.

🅜 See area map pages 60–61
▶ Plaza de Armas
🔁 1.5 miles (2.4 km)
🕐 2 hours
▶ Plaza de Armas

NOT TO BE MISSED

- Museo de Ron
- Casa de Africa
- Maqueta de Centro Histórico
- Museo y Farmacia Taquechel

Retrace Muralla west to **Plaza Vieja** ④ (see p. 69). Exit north along Calle Mercaderes. Cross Calle Lamparilla and stop in at **Casa Simón Bolívar** ⑤ (*Calle Mercaderes #156, tel 7/861-3988, closed Mon.*), dedicated to

Troubadours serenade diners at La Bodeguita del Medio, off Plaza de La Catedral.

Venezuelan culture. Note the statue to Bolívar (1783–1830), the great South American liberator, in the *plazuela* (little plaza) opposite. At Obrapía, the **Casa de México** (*Calle Mercaderes #116, tel 7/861-8166, closed Mon.*) celebrates Mexican culture with fine exhibits that include Aztec jewelry.

Fifty yards west, on Obrapía, is the lemon-and-cream **Casa de la Obra Pía** (*Calle Obrapía #158, tel 7/861-3097, closed Mon.*), the 16th-century home of a charitable nobleman whose pious acts lent the street its name. Entering through a portal brought from Cádiz in 1686, you stand within a courtyard framed by arched galleries that open to rooms displaying contemporary art and exhibits dedicated to author Alejo Carpentier. **Casa de Africa,** opposite, houses artifacts honoring African culture. (Currently undergoing restoration, it has moved part of its collection to the Casa Alejandro Von Humboldt; see p. 67).

Return to Mercaderes and turn left. This block features the **Museo del Tabaco** (*Calle Mercaderes #120, tel 7/861-5795, closed Mon.*), above the Casa del Tabaco on your left; upstairs are displays of tobacco miscellany. Fifty yards farther, visit the **Maqueta del Centro Histórico** (*Calle Mercaderes #114*), featuring a 1:500 scale model of Old Havana in minutest detail. Also worth perusal is the **Museo Casa de Asia** (*Calle Mercaderes #111, tel 7/863-9740, closed Mon.*), opposite; upstairs you'll find mother-of-pearl furniture, weaponry, kimonos, and other delights from the Orient.

Nearby, at the corner of Calle Obispo, you may be irresistibly drawn to the piano-bar lobby of the **Hotel Ambos Mundos** ❻ (*tel 7/860-9529*). Take the lattice-gate elevator to the fifth floor, where Room 511 (*closed Sun.*) is preserved as it was when Hemingway lodged here in the 1930s and wrote *For Whom the Bell Tolls.* Exit and follow Obispo west 50 yards (45 m) to the **Museo y Farmacia Taquechel** (*Calle Obispo #155, tel 7/862-9286*), an apothecary founded in 1898 and filled with illustrated ceramic jars of potions and herbs.

Turn right on Calle San Ignacio and step north two blocks to **Plaza de La Catedral** ❼ (see p. 64). Exit north along San Ignacio to Calle Tacón. Forming Old Havana's boundary, this street runs inside what remains of Havana's fortified wall. Turning right on Tacón, note **La Maestranza de Artilleria,** which contains a section of the wall and vestiges of one of the most important colonial artillery manufacturers. The wall fronts the **Seminario de San Carlos y San Ambrosio,** a Jesuit seminary established in 1774. It is closed to visitors, but striking for its baroque facade.

Check out the **artisan's market** that extends to the tiny plazuela at Tacón and Empedrado. To return to Plaza de Armas, turn right and follow Tacón one block. En route, stop by the **Gabinete de Arqueología** ❽ (*Calle Tacón #12, tel 7/861-4469, closed Mon.*), in a mansion showing pre-Columbian exhibits, plus 18th-century wall murals depicting life of the times. ∎

Plaza Vieja

PLAZA VIEJA—OLD SQUARE—WAS ORIGINALLY THE VENUE
for Havana's slave market and fiestas. A few years ago, the capacious
square was in a sorry state, not least for the architectural decay that
followed after a parking garage was built here in the 1930s. Today,
relaid with cobbles, it shines after a renovation nearing completion.

Plaza Vieja
Map p. 67 & 61 F2

Museo de Naipes
Calle Muralla #101
7/860-1534
$

At its heart is a fountain—a copy of
the original—in the shape of four
dolphins cavorting in a shell-like
bowl. It is framed to all sides by
gracious colonial homes fronted at
their bases by broad loggias. The
Casa de los Condes de Jaruco
*(Calle Muralla #107, tel 7/862-3577,
closed Sun.)*, on the south side, is
perhaps the most important such
structure, with wrought-iron balconies and stained-glass *mediopuntos.* Commissioned in 1732, this
former residence of the Count of
Jaruco houses the Cuban Cultural
Foundation, featuring commercial
art galleries. Just east, the **Museo
de Naipes** displays a collection of
playing cards.

Notable on the plaza's west
side are the **Casa del Conde
de San Estéban de Cañongo**
and, next door, on the northwest
corner, the neoclassic **Casa de las**
Hermanas Cárdenas, with
superb baroque woodwork. The
latter houses the **Centro de
Desarrollo de Artes Visuales**
*(Calle San Ignacio #352 at Teniente
Rey, tel 7/862-3533, closed
Sun.–Mon.);* beyond its towering
carriage doors, a workshop trains
artists in making cloth dolls and
other crafts. A fine sculpture by
Alfredo Sosabravo (1930–) graces
the inner patio, and the upper story
features a contemporary art gallery.

The **Casa de Juan Rico de
Mata,** built in 1752 on the plaza's
east side, today hosts photo exhibitions in the **Fototeca de Cuba**
*(Calle Mercaderes #307, tel 7/862-
2530).* Soaring above the plaza to
the southeast is the art nouveau
Palacio Cuerto; it is slated to
reopen as the Palacio Vienna Hotel.
The **Taberna Beny Moré** graces
the northeast corner. ■

City overview
For an overview of the
city, visit the Cámara
Oscura *($),* a simple
device that projects a
360-degree view of
Havana.

**Sunlight gilds
Plaza Vieja,
highlighting the
restoration now
sweeping Old
Havana.**

Antigua Iglesia de San Francisco de Paula, on Desamparados

Ecclesiastical Core

**Antigua Iglesia
de San Francisco
de Paula, on
Desamparados**

**Ecclesiastical
Core**
🗺 61 E2

**Iglesia y
Convento de
Santa Clara**
✉ Calle Cuba bet. Sol
& Luz
🕐 Closed Sat.–Sun.
💲 $

**Casa Natal de
José Martí**
✉ Calle Leonor Pérez
#314
☎ 7/861-3778
🕐 Closed Mon.
💲 $

Note
Most churches in Havana close noon–3 p.m.

OFTEN OVERLOOKED BY VISITORS, THE SOUTHERN HALF of Old Havana—bounded south and east by Avenida San Pedro (Desamparados) and, to the west, by Avenida de Bélgica (Egido)— abounds in beautiful churches and convents dating from the 1700s.

The area is now primarily a residential quarter of sagging walls and makeshift scaffolding. Community-oriented restoration is underway, notably around Calle San Isidro.

One block east of Egido, between Calles Lamparilla and Brasil, is quaint **Plaza del Cristo,** anchored by the **Iglesia del Santo Cristo del Buen Viaje.** This Franciscan hermitage dates from 1640 (reconstructed 1932). A short stroll away, on Calle Compostela between Luz and Acosta, the **Iglesia y Convento de Nuestra Señora de Belén** was begun in 1712 and later served as a hospice and government ministry.

Cuba's first convent, **Iglesia y Convento de Santa Clara,** was begun in 1638. Its Salon Plenario offers concerts beneath a Moorish-style ceiling. Originally a hermitage for freed slaves and later a sanctuary from the law, the 1638 **Iglesia Parroquial del Espíritu Santo** (*Calles Cuba & Acosta*) is Havana's oldest church. The 1867 **Iglesia y Convento de Nuestra Señora de la Merced** (*Calle Cuba at Merced*) draws devotees of Santería for the Feast Day of the Virgen de la Merced every September 24.

Egido follows the course of the old city walls, razed in 1863. Only fragments remain, notably the **Puerta de la Tenaza,** at Egido and Desamparados, the sole city gate still standing. The lemon-and-cream house across the street from the nearby railway station is the **Casa Natal de José Martí,** filled with the personal effects of Cuba's national hero, born here on Jan. 28, 1853. ■

Parque Central & nearby

BUSTLING AND PIVOTALLY PLACED PARQUE CENTRAL commands the threshold to Old Havana, accessed via Calle Obispo. A social node for Cubans and a tourist rendezvous, the park is surrounded by important buildings in baroque, art deco, and art nouveau styles, including several hotels, major museums, theaters, cigar factories, and important terminuses for pesos-only taxis and buses.

Parque Central & nearby

🅰 61 E3

Visitor information

✉ Calle Obispo #521, bet. Villegas & San Ignacio

☎ 7/863-6884

Gran Teatro de la Habana

✉ Paseo de Martí #458 at San Rafael

☎ 7/861-3078

🕓 Performances held Fri., Sat., & Sun.

💲 $$

PARQUE CENTRAL

Royal palms rise elegantly over this two-block-long park, hemmed by Paseo de Martí and Calle Agramonte, and by Calles Neptuno and San Martín. At its heart rises a statue of José Martí erected in 1905 of Carrara marble. Baseball fans gather at the *esquina caliente* (hot corner) to argue the fine points of pelota.

Four historic hotels stand over the park. Wedged into the northeast corner is the **Hotel Plaza** *(Calle Agramonte #267, tel 7/860-8583)*, in eclectic style, with a triangular lobby supported by Corinthian columns aglow in light filtering down subaqueously through a stained-glass skylight. The **Hotel Parque Central** *(Calle Neptuno bet. Agramonte & Prado, tel 7/860-6627)* dominates the park's north

side; though refitted in contemporary guise, elements of its elegant facade remain. On the west side, the venerable **Hotel Inglaterra** *(Paseo de Martí #416, tel 7/860-8595)* boasts a wedding-cake facade and an extravagant lobby flush with archways and patterned *azulejos*. Winston Churchill is among the notables who slept here in the late 19th century. The rooftop bar offers fine views over the square. The **Hotel Telegrafo,** on the northwest corner, recently opened.

Havana's most exorbitant neo-baroque structure, the adjacent **Gran Teatro de la Habana** resembles a confection in stone. To each corner, four towers are tipped by angels. Initiated in 1907 as the Centro Gallego (a Galacian social club), it evolved into an illustrious

Leafy Parque Central, with its centerpiece statue honoring José Martí, is a gathering place for Cubans. Here a band waits to perform at a military wedding.

theater that drew luminaries of the operatic world. The National Ballet and Opera still perform here; rehearsals are open to view.

The grand structure dominating the park's east side is the international division of the **Museo Nacional de Bellas Artes** (Fine Arts Museum). It occupies the Centro Asturiano, built in 1927 with a Renaissance facade and a staircase suffused in light from a stained-glass window depicting Columbus' discovery of the New World.

Museo Nacional de Bellas Artes

- 🅜 61 E3
- ✉ Calle Rafael, bet. Zulueta & Monserrate
- ☎ 7/861-3858
- 🕐 Closed Mon.
- 💲 $

Along the Prado, a popular promenade for more than two centuries

Museo de Tesoro Reclamado

- ✉ Ave. Carlos M. de Céspedes, at Prado
- 🕐 Closed Mon.–Tues.
- 💲 $

Exhibits span the globe and include many works by European masters.

PRADO (PASEO DE MARTÍ)

Spilling north from the park's northwest corner, this tree-lined boulevard slopes down to the mouth of the harbor channel. When laid out between 1772 and 1852, the Alameda de Isabel II (renamed the Prado in 1904) ran outside the old city walls, with an elevated promenade dividing two one-way causeways. It was adopted by the city's nobility, who built their mansions, dance halls, and fencing schools in palatial style. French landscape designer Jean-Claude Nicolas Forestier gave it its current look in 1929, with bronze lions, marble benches, and wrought-iron lampposts.

Among the baroque gems is the **Palacio de los Matrimonios** (Palace of Civil Marriages; *Prado #306, tel 7/862-5781)*, in the old Casino Español. Built in 1914 in Spanish Renaissance style, its opulent interior, albeit badly deteriorated—a mini-Versailles dripping with frescoed stucco—casts an appropriate spell over lovers who come to get hitched.

The Prado also boasts fine examples of Moorish style, notably at the 1908 **Hotel Sevilla** *(Calle Trocadero #55, tel 7/860-8560)*. Glistening with *azulejos*, it was inspired by Granada's Alhambra. The upper-story restaurant-bar, sumptuously neoclassic, is a good spot to settle over a Mary Pickford cocktail (rum, pineapple, grenadine), invented here. The art deco style is represented by the **Cine-Teatro Fausto,** at the corner of Calle Colón.

Parque de los Mártires, at the base of the Prado, honors Cubans who have died for the spirit of independence. Among them was José Martí, who between 1869 and 1870 broke rocks here at the former Prado prison. The park features the **Monumento a los Estudiantes de Medicina,** a small temple honoring eight medical students executed here in 1871, falsely accused of desecrating the tomb of a Spanish loyalist.

Across Avenida Carlos M. de Céspedes, **Castillo de San Salvador de la Punta,** built between 1589 and 1600, commands the stub of land facing **El Morro castle** (see p. 78). In colonial days, a chain was stretched between the two castles each evening to seal the harbor mouth. Today it houses the **Museo de Tesoro Reclamado,** full of salvaged treasure.

ALONG AGRAMONTE & MONSERRATE

Calle Agramonte (locally called

Zulueta), a block east of the Prado, slopes northeast from Parque Central toward the harbor channel. Monserrate runs parallel to Agramonte to the east. Between the two, at their base, lies **Plaza 13 de Mayo,** merging northward into **Parque de los Mártires.** Here a monument honors Gen. Máximo Gómez, the Dominican-born commander of the liberation army during Cuba's wars of independence. He sits astride his bronze charger atop a granite plinth of Corinthian columns. The art nouveau building at the base of Agramonte is the former **Palacio Velasco,** built in 1912 and today housing the Spanish Embassy.

The 1902 Casa de Pérez de la Riva, at the base of Monserrate, functions as the **Museo de la Música** *(Calle Capdevila #1, tel 7/861-9846, closed Sun., $).* It traces the history of Cuba's vivacious music back through colonial times, with a large collection of instruments and original scores from around the world.

MUSEO DE LA REVOLUCIÓN

Monserrate follows the course of the old city wall. A remnant watchtower—**Baluarte del Ángel**—still stands to the south side of Plaza 13 de Mayo. Facing it is a SAU-100 Soviet tank supposedly commanded by Fidel Castro at the Bay of Pigs. Together they guard the **Museo de la Revolución,** housed in the former Presidential Palace, initiated in 1920 with interior decor by the firm of Louis Comfort Tiffany. In 1957 the palace was the site of an unsuccessful attempt to overthrow General Batista; look for the bullet holes in the foyer.

Sumptuous salons today glorify the revolution that finally toppled Batista, part of a chronological presentation of Cuba's political devel-

opment, from slave uprisings to joint space missions with the ex-Soviet Union. All descriptions are in Spanish (except for the exhibit detailing the failed Bay of Pigs invasion), but you need no words to comprehend the stories behind the gory photos, submachine guns, and bloodstained shirts worn by guerrillas. Keep an eye out for one of Che's famous berets, as well as the diorama of Che and Camilo Cienfuegos emerging from the forest of the Sierra Maestra.

Occupying the grounds to the rear, a glass encasement—**Memorial *Granma*—**enshrines

A baroque balcony along the Prado

Museo de la Revolución
- 61 E3
- Calle Refugio #1, bet. Agramonte & Monserrate
- 7/862-4091
- $

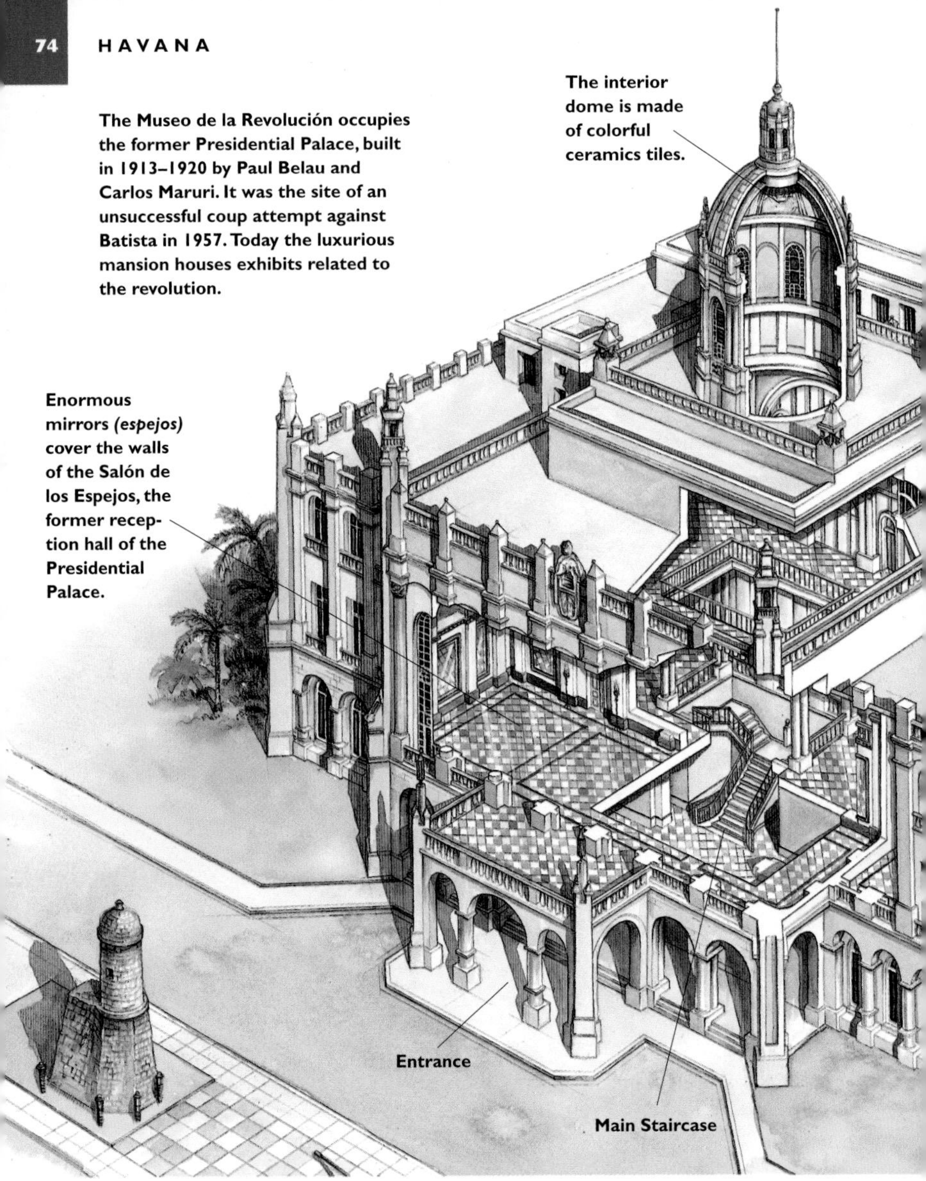

The Museo de la Revolución occupies the former Presidential Palace, built in 1913–1920 by Paul Belau and Carlos Maruri. It was the site of an unsuccessful coup attempt against Batista in 1957. Today the luxurious mansion houses exhibits related to the revolution.

The interior dome is made of colorful ceramics tiles.

Enormous mirrors (espejos) cover the walls of the Salón de los Espejos, the former reception hall of the Presidential Palace.

Entrance

Main Staircase

Fábrica de Tabaco La Corona

- Calle Agramonte #106
- 7/862-0001
- Closed Sun.
- $

the vessel that brought Fidel Castro, Che Guevara, and 80 other rebels from Mexico to launch the revolution. They landed on December 2, 1956, on the southern coast of Oriente province, marking the commencement of the Liberation War in the Sierra Maestra mountains. Also outside the museum are other vehicles involved in the revolution, including planes and tanks,

plus a piece of a U.S. spy plane shot down in the 1970s.

The **Fábrica de Tabaco La Corona,** on the museum's west side, provides the inside story on cigars, rolled here since 1888. José Martí was baptized on February 12, 1853, in the **Iglesia del Santo Angel Custodio,** to the east. The gleaming white Gothic church boasts fine stained glass and

MUSEO DE LA REVOLUCIÓN

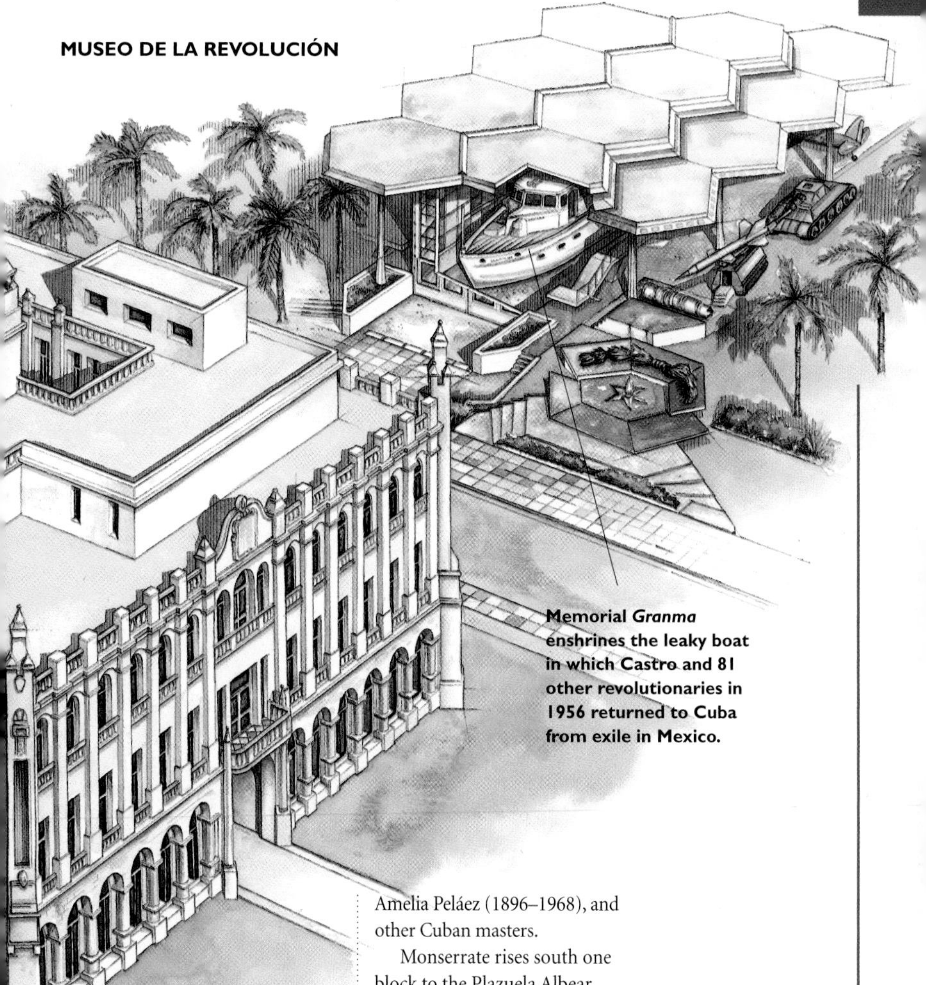

Memorial *Granma* enshrines the leaky boat in which Castro and 81 other revolutionaries in 1956 returned to Cuba from exile in Mexico.

Amelia Peláez (1896–1968), and other Cuban masters.

Monserrate rises south one block to the Plazuela Albear, overshadowed by the **Edificio Bacardí,** erstwhile headquarters for the Bacardí rum company. This soaring art deco masterpiece, erected in 1929 of coral limestone and pink granite, boasts terra-cotta tilework and a pyramidal roof topped by the famous Bacardí bat. A block south is a bar and restaurant called **El Floridita** *(tel 7/867-1300).* Spruced up in its original 1930s art deco style, the establishment is haunted by Hemingway's ghost; he sipped his sugarless double daiquiri here. A chain prevents idolaters from sitting on Papa's hallowed barstool. ∎

features prominently in *Cecilia Valdés,* Cirilo Villaverde's 19th-century novel.

MORE PLACES NEAR PARQUE CENTRAL

The **Museo Nacional de Bellas Artes** (Fine Arts Museum; Cuban section), in a recently remodeled 1955 modernist structure, displays works by Wifredo Lam (1902–1982),

Museo Nacional de Bellas Artes

✉ Calle Trocadero, bet. Agramonte & Monserrate

☎ 7/863-9042

💲 $

A *torcedor* demonstrates the deft hand skills essential for rolling the world's finest cigars.

Habana gold

A fat cigar is a defining image of Cuba, as quintessential as rum and salsa dancing. World-famous brands such as Cohiba, Montecristo, and Romeo y Julieta, made in Havana's eight cigar factories, are acclaimed as the finest in the world.

The individual character of a cigar depends on its blend of the filler, binder, and wrapper leaves, or *liga*. Every cigar variety and brand has a recipe, and each factory has a tobacco master who ensures the liga is appropriate to the specific Havana being rolled.

When dried and fermented leaves arrive in the tobacco factory *(fábrica)*, they are moistened to restore their elasticity, then flattened and stripped of their midribs. The rough leaves are sorted by size, classified according to color, texture, and quality (there are between 11 and 15 grades, and more than 75 colors in each category), then sent to the workshop *(galera)* to be rolled into cigars. First, the *torcedor* rolls two or three *seco* leaves (for strength) in his or her palm. This is then wrapped in *ligero* leaves (for aroma) and *volado* leaves (for even burning) to form the filler. The filler is enfolded by binder leaves, called *capotes,* and rolled until the familiar torpedo shape emerges. After being pressed in a tubular mold, this cylindrical "bunch" is wrapped in a pliable *capa* leaf, then rolled with the flat of a *chaveta*, a rounded, all-purpose knife that is the torcedor's only tool. Finally, a quarter-sized piece of wrapper is folded and sealed at one end.

Manuel dexterity is all important to ensure that the cigar is neither too tight nor too loose; otherwise, it won't draw. Torcedors usually follow in family tradition and, after a formal apprenticeship, graduate from petite Coronas to larger and specialist sizes. An experienced roller can roll more than 100 cigars a day. Torcedors are permitted to smoke as many cigars as they wish on the job. For entertainment, a *lector* reads the daily news aloud, followed by excerpts from literature.

A guillotine cuts the cigars to size. They are then fumigated, rechecked for quality, and sorted by color according to six categories ranging from greenish-brown *(pariso verdoso)* to darkest brown *(oscuro)*. The cigars are then stored in a cool room before being laid out in pine or cedar boxes—darkest on the left, lightest on the right—sealed with a green-and-white label, signifying *puro habanos.* Each cigar wears a paper band imprinted with the brand's logo, and the boxes are adorned with richly emblazoned labels.

While export-brand cigars are hand-rolled in Havana, regional, small-scale factories produce lesser-quality cigars for the domestic market. ∎

Parque de la Fraternidad

OPENING TO THE SOUTHWEST OF PARQUE CENTRAL, THIS swath of greenery, split by merging roads, was laid out in its present form for the sixth Pan-American Conference, hosted by Havana in 1928; formerly the city's railway station (and before that, the military parade ground) stood here. The park is anchored by a grand ceiba tree—the Árbol de la Fraternidad Americana (Tree of American Brotherhood)—and by busts to continental heroes, not least Abraham Lincoln. The marble fountain at the base of the Prado, the Fuente de la India de la Bella Habana, sculpted in 1837, depicts an Indian queen brandishing a shield bearing Cuba's coat of arms.

Parque de la Fraternidad
- 61 E2

Capitolio
- 61 E2
- Prado bet. San Martín & Dragones
- 7/860-3411
- $

Fábrica de Tabaco Partagás
- Calle Industria #520, at Dragones
- 7/862-0086
- Closed Sat.–Sun.
- $$ (includes tour)

The domed edifice to the north is the **Capitolio,** soaring 205 feet. Inspired by Washington's Capitol, this neoclassic structure was erected between 1912 and 1929 to house Cuba's own two-chamber Congress. The stone staircase, flanked by bronze figures representing Labor and Virtue, ascends to a monumental portal with bronze doors adorned with bas-relief panels depicting scenes in Cuban history. The 394-foot-long (120 m) **Hall of the Lost Steps,** breathtakingly aglimmer with gold leaf and marble, features a 59-foot-tall (17 m) statue of La República, holding a lance and shield which bears the arms of Cuba. At her feet, inset in the floor, is a 23-carat diamond (supposedly a fake; the original is said to reside with Castro) marking the zero milestone for Cuba's roads. Galleries lead to semicircular pavilions that housed the **Senate** and **Chamber of Representatives.** The **Cuban Academy of Sciences's** library is on the ground floor.

Visitors receive an aromatic welcome at **Fábrica de Tabaco Partagás,** behind the Capitolio, as prelude to a riveting tour of this cigar factory, in operation since 1845. A surflike baroque roofline caps the exquisite frontage. Tucked in the park's southwest corner, the neoclassic **Palacio de Aldama,** built between 1840 and 1844 with a facade of Ionic columns, is highlighted by frescoes depicting scenes from Pompeii—an unlikely venue for the Institute of the History of the Communist Movement and Socialist Revolution *(tel 7/862-2076).* ■

The Capitolio

El Morro castle &
La Cabaña fortress

COMMANDING THE ROCKY PENINSULA THAT GUARDS Havana harbor, El Morro castle and La Cabaña fortress together formed the largest Spanish military complex in the Americas. Today, enshrined in the Parque Histórico Militar Morro–Cabaña, the structures echo to the bootsteps of soldiers in period costumes, while museums and a nightly cannon firing add to a past that seems cinematic.

**El Morro castle
(Castillo de los
Tres Reyes del
Morro)**

🅰 61 E4 & inside
back cover

✉ Parque Histórico
Militar Morro–
Cabaña, Carretera de
la Habana, Habana
del Este

☎ 7/863-7941

💲 $

**La Cabaña
fortress
(Fortaleza de
San Carlos de la
Cabaña)**

🅰 61 F3 & inside
back cover

✉ Parque Histór-
ico Militar Morro–
Cabaña, Carretera de
la Habana, Habana
del Este

☎ 7/862-0617 or
7/862-0619

💲 $

The park, approached via the tunnel that dips beneath the harbor channel, sprawls a mile across La Cabaña, the long windswept ridge that displays a blunt cliff face—a natural palisade—toward Old Havana. Northward, the ridge slopes down to the sea. El Castillo de los Tres Reyes del Morro went up between 1589 and 1630 to guard the harbor entrance. Stout and strong, it withstood the English siege in 1762 for 40 days until breached by a massive explosion. When the English departed 11 months later, the Spanish lost no time in securing their precious city with a mightier complex to guard the land route. Ten years in construction, the Fortaleza de San Carlos de la Cabaña cost 14 million duros (as the currency of the time was called)—enough that Spanish King Charles III jokingly asked for a telescope, saying that such a monstrous structure must surely be visible from Madrid.

A military compound, off-limits to visitors, occupies much of the park.

EL MORRO CASTLE

Named for the knobby promontory on which it was built, this compact castle squats at the headland, over-looking the ocean. Conceived by military engineer Juan Bautista Antonelli (1550–1616), it is shaped in an irregular polygon in Milanese military tradition and surrounded by moats hewn from bare rock. The castle worked in conjunction with the **Castillo de San Salvador de la Punta** (see p. 72), across the bay, to catch enemy ships in a crossfire.

Enter El Morro via a drawbridge that funnels you along the Tunel Aspillerado (Loopholed Tunnel), to the **Plaza de Armas,** the military parade ground. The plaza was filled in 1763—after the fortress was restored following the English assault—with a two-story structure built as a garrison for a thousand men. A ramp leads to a series of batteries: **Baluarte de Austria,** with cannon in their embrasures pointing down at the moat; **Baluarte de Tejeda,** facing east; and **Batería de Velasco,** named for the Spanish general and governor who initiated the castle's construction.

The **Surtida de los Tina-jones** displays the great earthen-ware vases (see p. 161) that once held rapeseed to fire the lantern of the 35-foot-tall (10 m) **light-house,** erected in 1844. The light-house still functions, albeit today flashing an electric lantern. You can enter ($) and ascend to the balcony for a stupendous view.

To the south, a ramp leads down from the castle to the **Baluarte de los Doce Apóstoles** (Battery of the Twelve Apostles), named for the dozen cannon dating from the Spanish-American War. The erst-while powderhouse is now a little bar—El Polvorín.

LA CABAÑA FORTRESS

Symbol of Spanish rule for more than three centuries, this awesome bastion, built between 1764 and 1774 in the shape of an isosceles triangle, sprawls over 25 acres (10 ha). Initiated in 1763 following the English invasion of Cuba, it was designed and built by French engineers. Its stone ramparts, 40 feet (12 m) thick in places, have stood fast against all comers for centuries. A genius of strategic invention, the fortress comprises successive lines of defense, each convoluted and higher than the last, with a complicated system of moats, so that the hapless invader who overcomes any line finds himself trapped in the next.

You enter La Cabaña via the monumental baroque portal. Beyond, a drawbridge spans a dry moat carved from solid rock and extending eastward to **El Foso de los Laureles** (Moat of the Laurels), used as an execution ground over the centuries. The castillo served as a prison for nationalist rebels in the 19th century and, later, for Batista henchmen and suspected anti-Castroites fol-lowing "*el triunfo de la revolución,*" when Che Guevara set up head-quarters here and oversaw their dis-patch by firing squad.

The sally port opens to the **Plaza de Armas.** At the west end stand the **Museo Comandancia del Che,** with mementoes recalling the days when Che presided; and the **Capilla de San Carlos,** a simple chapel with an exquisite altar. To the east, a looping cobbled street is lined with former barracks whose vaulted ceilings, built to withstand enemy cannonballs, now lend the rooms an air of ecclesiastical calm. Some have been converted into two Spanish bodegas. Others house the **Museo de Fortificaciones y Armas,** stocked with eclectic armaments, including Roman ballisters.

La Cabaña changes by night, when torches are lit and tourists gather to watch Cuban soldiers cos-tumed in 18th-century military garb march along the ramparts and touch a spark to a cannon, marking the end of the day. In colonial times, the *kaboom* announced the closing of the city gates and draw-ing of a chain across the harbor. ■

El Morro guarded Havana with walls ten feet thick until overwhelmed by the English in 1762.

Centro Habana & Cerro

Centro Habana & Cerro

🗺 61 C1, D1, D2, D3

Museo Lezama Lima

✉ Trocadero #162, bet. Consulado & Industria

☎ 7/863-4161

🕐 Closed for restoration

💲 $

Cine América

✉ Avenida de Italia #253 at Neptuno

☎ 7/862-5416

PREDOMINANTLY RESIDENTIAL, CENTRO HABANA (CENtral Havana) is laid out in a rough grid receding inland from the Malecón, the gracefully sinuous shoreline boulevard that links Old Havana to Vedado. The district of Cerro (Hill) sprawls to the south. Here the street life is lively, offering an entrée to fascinating microcosms of city life.

Lying due west of Old Havana, Central Havana—usually referred to as Centro—evolved during the late 19th century as a residential district. Its block-after-block of buildings are similar to those of Old Havana, though taller and lacking interior patios. Corroded by sea air, many have been lost to decay. The dilapidated buildings along the Malecón (see sidebar p. 84) are being restored. The first building to metamorphose

was the Club Unión casino, now housing the **Centro Cultural de España** *(tel 7/862-3165)*, which celebrates Spanish culture. Three blocks inland, the former home of author José Lezama Lima (1910–1976) is now the **Museo Lezama Lima** *(closed for restoration)*.

Westward, the Malecón sweeps past the **Monumento a Antonio Maceo,** dedicated to the the brilliant black general, second

Renaissance style. The broad arch spanning the road outside is the **Pórtico Chino,** the Dragon Gate announcing the official entry to **Barrio Chino.** Centro's Chinatown was once the largest (in population) in Latin America. The infamous Shanghai Theater was here, offering cabarets "of extreme obscenity," according to English writer Graham Greene (1904–1991). After the revolution, the Chinese fled Cuba en masse. The restaurants along Calle Cuchillo serve a remnant Cuban-Chinese population of about 300 Chinese-born naturals and several thousand descendants; **Restaurante Pacífico** was once favored by Castro, who later cleaned out the whorehouse and opium den.

Avenida Salvador Allende (Carlos Tercero) forms an axis for Centro and, east of Padre Varela (Belascoaín), slopes east to **Parque de la Fraternidad** as **Avenida Simón Bolívar.** Sites of interest include the **Gran Templo Nacional Masónico;** the **Freemason's Temple;** and the Gothic **Iglesia del Sagrado Corazón** (1914–1922), remarkable for its gargoyles. Step down Padre Varela to the **Fábrica Romeo y Julieta,** where the famous cigar brand has been manufactured since 1875. Padre Valera continues south to **Cuatro Caminos,** Havana's bustling 19th-century market hall.

Centro rises southward to **Cerro,** a 19th-century residential district where the well-to-do built summer houses in Italianate style, concentrated along the Calzada de Cerro. Today the serpentine road aches with pathos and penury, its colonnaded mansions crumbling to dust. One venerable home houses the **Fábrica de Ron Bocoy,** a small rum factory. James Michener used the house as a venue for his 1989 novel, *Caribbean.* ∎

in command under Gen. Máximo Gómez during the wars of independence. A short stroll inland up Calle San Lázaro leads to **Callejón de Hamel,** an alley ablaze with evocative murals—the inspiration of local artist Salvador González.

Slicing Centro north–south is **Avenida de Italia** (Galiano), which, with Neptuno and San Rafael running perpendicular, form Havana's once elegant, now impoverished shopping streets. The **Cine América** is one of the world's great art deco theaters. Intersecting Galiano farther south, **Zanja**— named for a colonial aqueduct that ran through here—forms Centro's axis. Towering over the junction is the 1927 **Cuban Telephone Company** building *(Calle Aguila #565),* in flamboyant Spanish

Centro Habana's dense street life colors Calle Neptuno.

Restaurante Pacífico
✉ Calle San Nicolás, bet. Zanja & Dragones
☎ 7/863-3243

Gran Templo Nacional Masónico
✉ Avenida Salvador Allende, bet. Padre Varela & Lucena
☎ 7/870-5642

Iglesia del Sagrado Corazón
✉ Avenida Simón Bolívar, bet. Padre Varela & Gervasio
☎ 7/862-4979

Fábrica Romeo y Julieta
✉ Calle Padre Varela #528, bet. Desague & Peñalver
☎ 8/870-5915

Cuatro Caminos
✉ Calle Máximo Gómez, bet. Arroyo & Matadero

Fábrica de Ron Bocoy
✉ Calle Máximo Gómez, bet. Patria & Auditor
☎ 7/870-5642
💲 Free guided tours

Vedado

A Chevy Bel-Air and Hotel Havana Libre recall Havana's 1950s heyday.

MEMORIES OF 1950s MOBSTER EXCESS LINGER ON THE streets of Vedado, studded by high-rise hotels and commercial offices at its core. Its broad, tree-shaded *calles* (streets), lined with mansions of the erstwhile well-to-do, make for pleasant strolling. To the south, Plaza, or Nuevo Vedado, hosts the government ministries. Museums and other attractions abound.

Beginning in 1859, an elegant new district was laid out upon the reserve (*vedado*), the wide expanse west of Centro that in colonial days served as a buffer zone in the event of an attack on the city. Divided by broad boulevards into a quilt of graceful blocks, this leafy district blossomed in the early 20th century, when wealthy Cubans and other North Americans built small apartment buildings and villas in neo-classic beaux-arts style. **Calle 17**—novelist Alejo Carpentier's "row of magnificent mansions"—boasts several stunning exemplars of beaux-arts villas. Among them is the 1927 Casa de José Gómez Mena, a fittingly sumptuous venue for the **Museo de Artes Decorativas,** brimming with chinoiserie and gleaming antiques. Seven blocks west at **Parque Lennon** (*Calles 15/17 & Calles 6/8)*, a bronze statue of ex-Beatle John Lennon (1940–1980) by Cuban artist José Villa draws admirers.

LA RAMPA & VICINITY
The area around La Rampa, the inclined boulevard linking Calle L with the Malecón, is Havana's business and hotel district, full of cinemas, jazz clubs, and modern high-rises harking back to the 1950s. At its base is the neo-Renaissance-style **Hotel Nacional** (*Calles O & 21, tel 7/33-3564)*, inaugurated in 1930 and sitting atop a bluff occupied by a battery of colonial-era cannon. Reached via a palm-lined drive, this graceful

grande dame—its lobby agleam with *azulejos*—remains a favorite of an international clientele.

Minimalism in high-rise 1950s design is epitomized by the **Hotel Capri** (*Calle 21 & Calle K, tel 33-3747)*, where actor George Raft (1895–1980) famously refused entry to a revolutionary mob who had come to trash the casino; and by the 21-story **Habana Libre** (*La Rampa & Calle L, tel 7/33-4011)*, which began life in April 1958 as the Havana Hilton. In January 1959, Castro set up headquarters on the top floor and bearded revolutionaries lounged around in its glamorous domed lobby, marking the end of the high-rolling heyday. A reproduction of a remarkable mural by Amelia

Peláez graces the facade.

Catercorner, the beloved **Coppelia** ice-cream parlor, serving 30,000 people daily, is not to be missed (see p. 244).

A classically inspired staircase, **Las Escalinatas** leads from Calle L to the Acropolis-like **Universidad de La Habana.** Founded in Old Havana in 1728, it moved to its current location in 1902. During the Republican era, the staircase was the setting for violent rallies. The university library boasts exquisite art deco; the **Great Hall** features a splendid mural by Armando García Menocal (1863–1941). The Felipe Poey Science Building houses the **Museo Antropológico Montané,** with a superb collection of pre-Columbian art; and the **Museo de Ciencias Naturales,** dedicated to the natural world. Both were recently restored.

Nearby, the Renaissance home of Orestes Ferrara (1910–1912) is now the **Museo Napoleónico,** displaying a collection devoted to the French Emperor amassed prior to the revolution by Cuban millionaire Julio Lobo. Decor includes period furniture.

ALONG THE MALECÓN

From the base of La Rampa, the Malecón (see sidebar p. 84) sweeps westward past the **Monumento a las Víctimas del Maine,** erected in 1925 in homage to the 288 sailors killed when the U.S.S. *Maine* exploded in Havana harbor in 1898, sparking the Spanish-American War. Nearby is the **Tribuna Antimperialista,** inaugurated in 2000 as a setting for anti-American demonstrations. Here, erected in response to the Elián González situation, a bronze statue of José Martí holding the boy in his arms points an accusatory finger at the U.S. Interests Section (the former U.S. Embassy), one block west at the junction with Calle L.

The **Monumento a Calixto García,** at the base of palm-shaded Avenida de los Presidentes (Calle G), was erected in 1959 to honor the hero general of the wars of independence. Mobster Meyer Lansky owned the **Hotel Riviera,** farther west at the base of Paseo. Opened in 1958 and still displaying its original kitschy decor, it remains a monument of sorts to him. The seafront boulevard ends at **La Chorrera fortress,** built in 1645 at the mouth of the Río Almendares.

CEMENTERIO COLÓN

Havana's vast and remarkable necropolis, at Zapata and Calle 12, was laid out between 1871 and 1886. It spans some 125 acres (50 ha) of fabulous statuary and mau-

Many of Vedado's beaux-arts mansions are crumbling to dust (top); others have been restored for embassies or government use (above).

Cementerio Colón
◪ 60 A2 & B2

Plaza de la Revolución
- ✉ 60 B2

Memorial José Martí
- ✉ Plaza de la Revolución
- ☎ 7/59-2351
- 🕐 Closed Sun.
- 💲 $

Museo Postal Cubano
- ✉ Avenida Independencia at 19 de Mayo
- ☎ 7/851-5551
- 🕐 Closed Sat.–Sun.
- 💲 $

Casa–Museo de Máximo Gómez
- ✉ Avenida Salvador Allende, bet. Infanta & Luaces
- ☎ 7/79-8850
- 🕐 Closed indefinitely for renovation
- 💲 $

The Malecón

Havana's serpentine seafront drive, the Malecón was laid out in 1901 by the U.S. governor, Gen. Leonard Woods (1860–1927); it twines 5 miles (7 km) west from the base of the Prado to the Río Almendares. The seawall is the great meeting point for habaneros, notably lovers, and for children who come to swim in the square baths (baños de mar) hewn from the shoreline rocks. In inclement weather, waves cascade over the seawall; the once glorious colonial structures facing the ocean have proven incapable of withstanding the corrosive assault. Many are being restored. ∎

soleums representing a flamboyant array of styles. Cuba's finest lie here: from novelist Alejo Carpentier and world chess champion José Raúl Capablanca (1888–1942) to Gen. Máximo Gómez and revolutionary heroines Haydee Santamaría and Celia Sánchez. Many funerary monuments are dedicated to professions, such as actors and firemen. The collective pantheons also include those of martyrs, such as the students who died in the 1958 attack on the Presidential Palace.

Supplicants attribute miraculous healings to **La Milagrosa,** the tomb of Amelia Goyre de Hoz, who died in childbirth in 1901. The flower-covered grave is a favorite of childless women who come to ask good fortune by knocking three times on the tomb.

PLAZA DE LA REVOLUCIÓN & VICINITY

Originally called Plaza Cívica when laid out in the 1950s atop the **Loma de los Catalanes** (Hill of the Catalans), this vast open swath is surrounded by government min-

istries in monumental style, plus the **Biblioteca Nacional** (National Library; tel 7/55-5442) to the east; and **Teatro Nacional** (tel 7/879-3558), with a glazed convex facade, to the west.

Looming over the barren, 11-acre (4 ha) square is the 59-foot-tall (17 m) **Monumento a José Martí,** hewn of granite and marble and showing the Cuban hero of independence in a contemplative pose. The statue, by Juan José Sicre, is dwarfed by a granite obelisk towering 295 feet (90 m). At its base—shaped as a five-pointed star—is the modern **Memorial José Martí,** a small museum with engravings, photos, documents, and films that honor the "intellectual author" of the revolution. An elevator ($) whisks visitors to the top of the tower, where an observation platform offers a 360-degree view of Havana from the city's highest point.

The labyrinthine government palace to the rear is the enormous **Palacio de la Revolución,** erected as the Palace of Justice in 1953–57 with a monumental gravitas inspired by the fascistic 1942 Universal Exhibition in Rome and the Trocadero in Paris. Off-limits to visitors, here Castro & Co. hatch their policies of state.

The facade of the stark stone **Ministerio del Interior,** on the plaza's north side, bears a ceramic mural by Amelia Peláez overshadowed by a five-story-tall face of Che Guevara—the universally recognized image photographed by Alberto "Korda" Gutiérrez (1928–2001). Cast in bronze, inscripted with the words *"Hasta la victoria siempre,* Toward victory, always," it is perhaps the most photographed site in Havana.

On the plaza's northeast corner stands the Ministerio de Informática y Comunicaciones, its **Museo Postal Cubano** displaying postage stamps from around the world. Time your visit for the rallies held January 1, May 1, and July 26, when Cubans carrying banners troop by to demonstrate their loyalty to the revolution.

Avenida Boyeros runs north from the plaza to the **Castillo del Príncipe,** hidden from view (and off-limits) atop a hill at the base of Avenida de los Presidentes. The **Monumento a José Miguel Gómez** commands the crest of the broad *avenida,* lined with dramatic *jagüey* trees. To the east, Avenida Salvador Allende (Carlos III) fronts the **Quinta de los Molinos,** commissioned in 1837 as the summer palace of the *capitanes generales.* The villa was gifted to Gen. Máximo Gómez in 1899 and today houses the dour **Casa–Museo de Máximo Gómez** *(closed for renovation).* ■

The Malecón is a 24-hour social center for habaneros.

One of Miramar's tree-shaded mansions

Miramar & Cubanacán

Miramar & Cubanacán

🅰 60 A3 & inside back cover

Visitor information

✉ Infotur, Avenida 5ta & Calle 112, Miramar

☎ 7/204-7036

Museo del Ministerio del Interior

✉ Avenida 5ta & Calle 16, Miramar

☎ 7/203-4432

🕐 Closed Sun.–Mon.

💲 $

Maqueta de la Habana

✉ 113 Calle 28 #113, bet. Avenida 1ra & 3ra, Miramar

☎ 7/202-7303

🕐 Closed Sun.–Mon.

💲 $

Acuario Nacional

✉ Avenida 1ra & Calle 60, Miramar

☎ 7/203-6401

🕐 Closed Mon.

💲 $

WEST OF THE RÍO ALMENDARES LIES THE SPRAWLING *municipio* of Playa, a region of supreme architectural charm divided into districts *(barrios)* that include the tony seafront precinct of Miramar—full of grandiose, green-lawned mansions—and, to the west, Cubanacán, where once exclusive houses of the long-departed wealthy line leafy hills. The areas are perfect for touring by car.

MIRAMAR

The '30s, '40s, and '50s live on in the eclectic architecture of Miramar, from classical interpretations of colonial architecture to uninhibited free-form compositions. Anchoring Miramar is **Quinta Avenida** (Avenida 5ta), the main east–west boulevard and the westerly extension of the Malecón, beyond a tunnel beneath the Río Almendares. Stunning beaux-arts, art deco, and modernist villas edge this palm-shaded thoroughfare, known as "Embassy Row." Many mansions have metamorphosed in recent years as commercial outlets—ground zero in Havana's quasicapitalist remake epitomized by the sprouting of the Miramar Trade Center and a conclave of upper-end hotels.

A highlight is the **Museo del Ministerio del Interior,** dedicated to showcasing attacks on the current government; among the James Bond-style exhibits are poison capsules used by the CIA in an attempt to assassinate Castro.

Ecclesiastical sites of interest include the **Iglesia de Santa Rita** *(Avenida 5ta at Calle 26, tel 7/209-2298),* with parabolic arches. Its 1943 statue of Saint Rita was controversial in its day because of sculptor Rita Longa's unique style. Also here is the Romanesque **Iglesia San Antonio de Padua** *(Calle 60 #316 at Avenida 5ta, tel 7/203-5045),* featuring a majestic, albeit now unplayable, organ. Built in 1949, the church is overshadowed by the former Soviet embassy—a towering unsightly cubist fantasy erected in the 1980s and which today houses the Russian Embassy.

The **Maqueta de la Habana** (City Model) displays a fascinating 1:1,000-scale reproduction of Havana made of recycled cigar boxes. Every building is there, color-coded by age: red for colonial, yellow for the Republic, and ivory for postrevolutionary.

Avenida Primera parallels the shoreline and leads west to the **Acuario Nacional,** the National

Aquarium, opened in 1960. You can view an assortment of turtles, sea lions, fishes, and other sealife. Dolphin shows are featured.

West of Miramar, the shorefront of **Flores** is lined with erstwhile private clubs and *balnearios* (beach resorts) established in the early 20th century to serve the upper classes and, since the revolution, a more democratic clientele.

CUBANACÁN

Cubanacán—nicknamed Cuba's Beverly Hills—was developed beginning in the 1920s, when the city's wealthy built posh country estates along sinuous, sloping streets. Many homes were abandoned—"donated to the revolution" is the government's phraseology—when Castro took power and their occupants fled to Miami. The reclusive neighborhood is still exclusive: Many homes are embassies or protocol houses granted for the use of visiting foreign dignitaries and Cuban officials.

In 1960 the former Havana Country Club was converted into a site for the **Instituto Superior de Arte** (National Arts School), conceived by Castro to be an exemplar of the possibilities of revolutionary architecture. This extraordinary complex was partially built between 1961 and 1965 before being deemed too experimental; the commission was canceled. Amazingly, in 2001 the original architects, Cuban Ricardo Porro and Italians Vittorio Garatti and Roberto Gottardi, were commissioned to revamp and complete the project.

Nearby is the **Palacio de las Convenciones** (*Calle 146, bet. 11 & 13, tel 7/202-6011*), Cuba's premier convention site, built in 1979 to host the Conference of Non-Aligned Countries. It abuts, to the south, the resplendent turn-of-the-20th-century mansion of the Marques de Pinar del Río. Abounding with 1930s art deco glass and chrome, this stupendous villa functions as **Fábrica el Laguito,** where the finest of Cuban cigars—the Cohibas—are rolled.

Southward, Cubanacán extends into the region of **Siboney,** a center for biogenetic research. ∎

Fábrica el Laguito

✉ Calle 146 #2302, Cubanacán

☎ 7/208-2218 & 7/208-2486

🕐 By appt. only

Tropicana

Havana's most spectacular nightclub, the Tropicana is one symbol of prerevolutionary Cuba that was not allowed to die. The twice nightly show is world-famous for its flamboyant cabaret routines highlighted by showgirls' stupendous costumes that hide very little. The Tropicana opened on New Year's Eve in 1939 in an open-air theater in the Buena Vista district south of Miramar. Max Borges Recio designed the current theater, dating from 1951–1956; he adapted modernism to the tropical climate in his "mambo-style" club. Surrounded by luxuriant gardens, the central stage is open to the sky—meaning, if it rains, the show is canceled. Though expensive (between $50 and $70), shows are often fully booked; reserve ahead. ∎

Backstage at the Tropicana

Cabaret Tropicana

✉ Calle 72 #4504, Marianao

☎ 7/267-1717

🕐 Closed Mon.

$ $$

Keeping the faith

About three-quarters of Cubans admit to some kind of Afro-Cuban religious belief. Followers of Santería—by far the most popular of these religions—come from all walks of life. Even Fidel Castro is thought to believe in Santería. Nonetheless, the Castro government discouraged Santería during three decades. Since the 1980s, the state has been more lenient, and the religion has flourished. Today many Cubans practice both Santería and Roman Catholicism. Other popular religions with roots that twine back to Africa include Palo Monte and Abakuá.

A Santería priestess performs a ceremony to honor deceased ancestors (above and right).

During centuries of colonial rule, West African slaves brought to Cuba clung to their ancestral religions. The Spanish permitted slaves to practice their religion in the belief that it would help avoid slave rebellions. Practice was restricted, however, to ethnic social clubs, or *cabildos,* and each cabildo was required by law to be patronized by a Roman Catholic saint. As a result, the various African cults unified as *la regla de ocha* (the way of the saint). The resulting religion—Santería—hid behind a facade of Catholicism, with various saints representing the *orishas,* the spiritual emissaries of Olofi (God) in the traditional Yoruba religion of what are now Nigeria and Benin.

There are more than 200 orishas recognized in Africa; 56 are worshiped in Cuba.

Among them, Changó, god of passion and lightning, is represented by the colors red and white; he embodies manhood and virility, and his Catholic equivalent is Santa Bárbara. His femme fatale equivalent is Ochún, goddess of sweet water, fertility, and love; she is represented by La Virgen de la Caridad, whose color is yellow. Yemayá, symbolizing motherhood and the sea, wears blue and white; her equivalent is the Virgen de Regla. Obbatalá, who symbolizes creation and peace, is associated with the Virgen de la Merced and dresses all in white. Santería balances the moral proscriptions of Roman Catholicism; orishas are hedonistic, licentious, and fallible.

Orishas are thought to play a role in each individual's destiny and can be called upon to perform miracles and solve everyday problems. Every *santero* or *santera,* or practitioner of Santería, has a spirit altar where offerings such as rum, cigars, fruits, and flowers are made to one's personal orishas, who "live" in clay or porcelain pots kept in one's home. Each pot, arranged in hierarchical order, contains consecrated stones thought to embody the spirit of the orisha.

Santeros and santeras—often identified by their necklaces of colorful beads—use divination to communicate with their orishas. Simple questions can be answered using a fresh coconut divided into four sections. More complex oracles are interpreted by an *oriaté,* who elucidates prophecies through divination with cowrie shells; or one's high priest, who offers counsel and guidance.

Any follower of Santería may choose to become a santero or santera by undertaking an elaborate initiation (involving animal sacrifice) that will set his or her feet on *la regla de ocha* under the guidance of a godparent. During this time, the initiate, or *iyawó,* may be possessed by a specific orisha, who will act as personal guardian for the rest of his or her life.

At ritual ceremonies, three *batá* drums are used to invoke the orishas, who may "mount" a santero or santera, who goes into trance. Such ceremonies are private. Tourists can experience faux ceremonies at theaters, museums, and tourist complexes, but to experience

the real thing, you will need to evolve a close friendship with a santero.

Palo Monte, similar to Santería, but deriving from the Congolese Bantu religion, believes in the redemptive power of the dead, which, as in voodoo, may be used to affect the destiny of another person. Abakuá, from Nigeria, is a monotheist, hermetic cult practiced by all-male secret societies dedicated to social justice and welfare (initiation, however, traditionally involved murder). Members *(ñañigos)* worship representations of the spirits, called *iremes* or *diabolitos,* who dance dressed head-to-toe in hooded burlap outfits. Initiates *(ekobios)* hear sacred voices in sacred drums. ∎

Regla & Guanabacoa

**Regla &
Guanabacoa**
🅜 61 F3 & inside
back cover
**Visitor
information**
✉ Rumbos Regla, Calle
Albuquerque &
Martí
☎ 7/97-0297

**Museo Municipal
de Regla**
✉ Calle Martí
#158, bet. Facciolo
& La Piedra
☎ 7/97-6989
🕓 Closed Mon.
💲 $

**At Iglesia de
Nuestra Señora
de Regla**

THESE CONTIGUOUS *BARRIOS,* RISING ON THE EAST SIDE
of Havana harbor, are centers of Santería (see pp. 88–89), and community life is infused with the spirit of ancient African rhythms.
Shrines dedicated to the Afro-Cuban pantheon abound, as do centuries-
old Roman Catholic convents and churches.

The harbor town of **Regla** evolved
as a smuggling port for slaves. It is
reached by a rustic passenger ferry
(lanchita) from the Muelle de Luz
on Old Havana's Avenida del
Puerto. The ferry deposits you
beside the **Iglesia de Nuestra
Señora de Regla** *(Calle Santuario
#11, tel 7/97-6228, closed Mon.),* an
endearing hermitage dating from
1687 that draws adherents of
Catholicism and Santería alike. A
gilt altar gleams within the simple
church, which bustles with devotees
mumbling bequests to the statues of
saints, and to the black Virgen de
Regla (the Roman Catholic equiva-

lent of Yemayá, goddess of the sea).
Nearby, the **Museo Municipal
de Regla** provides a grounding in
Regla's Santería associations. A short
stroll leads to **Colina de Lenin**
(Lenin Hill), where a ten-foot-tall
(3 m) visage of the Russian revolutionary (1870–1924) inset in rock
surveys Regla.

Guanabacoa, just east of
Regla, was founded in 1607 and
became an important bastion in
protecting the approach to Havana.
In the 18th century, it gained popu-
larity among the nobility for its
mineral springs and as an ecclesiastical center. The **Iglesia Parroquial
Mayor** *(Calle Division #331, tel 7/97-
7368),* on the main square, has a fine
baroque altar. Adjoining, the **Museo
Histórico de Guanabacoa** *(closed
for renovation)* is devoted to the
town's evolution.

Among the abundant religious
sites awaiting restoration is the
**Iglesia y Convento Santo
Domingo** *(Calle Santo Domingo
#407 at Lebredo, tel 7/97-7376).*
Erected in 1728, it boasts a spectac-
ular *alfarje* ceiling in Mudejar style.

As in Regla, the practice of
African-derived cults is a long-held
tradition, earning Guanabacoa the
nickname the *"pueblo embrujado"*
(bewitched village). The streets
reverberate to the beat of the *batá*
drum. Guanabacoa has birthed
some of the nation's finest percus-
sionists and other musicians, and
its **Casa de la Trova** *(Calle Martí
#111, bet. San Antonio & Versalles,
tel 7/97-7687)* is a fine spot to savor
traditional Afro-Cuban music. ∎

Habana del Este

EXTENDING EAST OF THE CITY, MILES OF CONTEMPORARY
suburbs comprise Habana del Este. Making amends are a quaint fishing hamlet with powerful Hemingway associations and the scintillating beaches of Playas del Este, to which habaneros flock in droves
on sun-splashed weekends.

Habana del Este is accessed via the
tunnel that burrows beneath the
harbor channel and widens into the
Via Monumental. Rising over the
highway are various sports stadiums built for the 1991 Pan-
American Games. Although touted
as a tourist base, there is little appeal
to **Villa Panamericana,** the residential town originally built
to house the athletes and press.

Two miles (3.2 km) east of Villa
Panamericana begin the sprawling
twin dormitory cities of **Alamar**
and **Celimar.** Together they add
up to a monstrous postrevolutionary blight proclaimed by Castro as a
socialist triumph. The high-rise
community, covering more than 6
square miles (15.5 sq km), was
hastily erected by untrained volun-
teers *(microbrigadas)*. They have
since degenerated into a not-so-
lofty (but safe) slum.

COJÍMAR
More engaging is the village of
Cojímar—squatting in a cove
between Villa Panamericana and
Alamar—with its red-roofed cottages. A diminutive fortress—**El
Torreón**—guards the entrance to
the cove where the English came
ashore in 1762 to capture the isle
for King George. Fronting it is the
**Monumento a Ernest
Hemingway,** a classical rotunda
surrounding a limestone pedestal
bearing a bust of Papa, molded
from various brass items donated
by local fishermen.

Hemingway frequented **La
Terraza de Cojímar** *(Calle Real*

#161 at Candelaria, tel 7/93-9232),
a bar-cum-restaurant overlooking
the cove where he berthed his boat,
El Pilar. The author's memory
lingers at the mahogany bar and on
the walls, adorned with black-and-
white photos of him with his prize
trophy fish. La Terraza, which
Hemingway immortalized in *The
Old Man and the Sea* and *Islands in
the Stream,* is a good place to enjoy
paella and to sip a Coctel Fuentes,
named in honor of Hemingway's
former skipper, Gregorio Fuentes
(1897–2002); Fuentes, whom Castro
named a national hero in 1993, lived
at Calle Pezuela #209 *(tel 7/65-2285).*

Playa Bacuranao

Habana del Este
 61 F4 & inside
back cover
**Visitor
information**
Infotur Santa María,
Avenida de las
Terrazas & Calles
10 & 11
7/96-1111

TARARÁ

The Via Blanca, the main east–west highway, spans the Río Tarará. On the river's right bank begins a tendril of white sand that unspools eastward for several miles. Here, tucked in a cove at the river mouth, is the **Marina Puertosol Tarará** *(tel 7/97-1462)*, offering scuba diving and water sports. The coral offshore makes for good snorkeling and diving. Passports required.

A residential community extends eastward. A newly renovated resort here *(Cubanacán Hotels, tel 7/97-1616)* focuses on health tourism, but it is more famous as the setting for the **José Martí Pioneer City,** dedicated to treating the child victims of the 1988 Chernobyl nuclear catastrophe. It was here, in 1959, that Che Guevara came to recuperate from the debilitations wrought by three years of fighting; and that Castro, using his visits as a pretext, established a secret government to undermine the democratic government of President Urrutia created in the immediate aftermath of Batista's ouster.

PLAYAS DEL ESTE

Popular with Cubans for its sand like pulverized sugar, this 4-mile-long (6 km) beach (divided by name into four sections) draws habaneros to flirt beneath the palms and swim in the warm turquoise sea. **Playa El Mégano** and **Playa Santa María** to the west are backed by hotels and villas that before the Special Period (see p. 38), were popular holiday venues for Cuban families. Today they are reserved for foreign tourists. Other than the gorgeous beach, the hotels and restaurants are dour, and the entertainment desultory. Thatched *ranchitas* (small thatched huts) serve grilled seafoods, and water sports are offered.

A lagoon—**Laguna Itabo—** and mangrove swamp, good for viewing birdlife, extend behind Playa Boca Ciega; biologist Alberto Quilez offers tours *($$)*, and water bikes and kayaks are for hire at Mi Cayito *(tel 7/97-1339)*, a small island with a restaurant. Farther east, **Playa Guanabo** fronts the old village of Guanabo, which offers cottages of colonial charm. ■

Havana's outskirts

NEGLECTED TO LARGE DEGREE BY TOURISTS, HAVANA'S outer reaches offer genuine delights, not least colonial-era outposts that still move to a 19th-century pace. Hemingway's former home is a de rigeur attraction, and the district of Arroyo Naranjo-Boyeros offers the bucolic charms of a vast recreational park and the national botanical garden.

FINCA VIGÍA

For pilgrims, the highlight of the Hemingway Trail is this 20-acre estate, dominated by a colonial house perched atop a hill in San Francisco de Paula, 8 miles (12 km) southeast of Havana. Appropriately, it is called Finca Vigía—Lookout Farm. The author lived here in between his travels for nearly 20 years, making it his most permanent home. Remodeled and now the **Museo Ernest Hemingway,** it remains much as Hemingway left it when he departed Cuba in 1960.

The simple, Spanish-style house is strewn with trophies, firearms, more than 9,000 books and magazines, and artwork by Picasso. The heads of antelope, impala, and buffalo that Hemingway killed on safari look down from the walls. A four-story tower, adjacent, was intended as Hemingway's study. He thought it too isolated and continued to write in the main house, often standing on a kudu rug with Boise, his favorite cat, at his feet (he had 50–70 cats). Guides follow your every move, and no photos are allowed.

Hemingway's well-varnished sportfishing cruiser—*Pilar*—is docked in a pavilion overlooking the swimming pool where Ava Gardner swam nude.

PARQUE LENIN

This vast park in Arroyo Naranjo Boyeros, 14 miles south of central Havana, is popular with Cuban families, drawn on weekends to the

A writer's life

Ernest Hemingway lived in Cuba for the better part of 20 years, drawn initially by his "great, deep blue river" teeming with billfish. He arrived in April 1932 and made the Hotel Ambos Mundos his first pied-á-terre. Handily, it was a stone's throw from what would become his favorite bar, El Floridita. Later, the irascible author would drive into town from Finca Vigía to carouse with politicians, movie stars, bullfighters, and ordinary folk who found their way into his novels, including *The Old Man and the Sea*. In 1960, Hemingway was forced to decide between divided loyalties. He donated his Nobel Prize for Literature to his adoptive island. In November 1960 he left for Spain, then Key West, never to return to Cuba. ■

Havana's outskirts

▲ inside back cover

Finca Vigía & the Museo Ernest Hemingway

✉ Calle Vigía, Km 2.5+, San Francisco de Paula

☎ 7/91-0809

🕐 Closed Tues.

💲 $

ExpoCuba

- ✉ Carretera del Rocío, Km 3.5
- ☎ 7/57-8284
- 🕐 Closed Mon.–Tues., & Sept.–Dec.
- 💲 $

Jardín Botánico

- ✉ Carretera del Rocío, Km 3.5
- ☎ 7/54-9159
- 🕐 Closed Mon.–Tues.
- 💲 $

carousels, a narrow-gauge steam-train ride, rodeos, horseback riding, and boating. Concentrated at the south end are a series of monuments, museums, and galleries, including **Galería de Arte Amelia Peláez,** on Calle Cortina, displaying works by this famous Cuban ceramist. Nearby, the **Monumento a Celia Sánchez** honors the revolutionary heroine (see sidebar p. 195) who conceived the park; she ran the secret network that supplied Castro's guerrillas with arms and became Castro's closest confidante. Honoring the park's namesake is the 30-foot-tall (9 m) **Monumento Lenin,** carved of marble by Soviet sculptor L. E. Kerbel (1917–).

The facilities are simple and meager. An exception is **Las Ruinas** restaurant, a prefab construction built in 1972 around the remains of an 18th-century sugar mill. Shady bamboo copses and greenswards are good for picnics.

EXPOCUBA

Carretera El Globo leads south from Parque Lenin to this complex—a self-congratulatory cross between a trade fair and museum—that pays homage to Cuba's accomplishments in industry, sports, science, and culture. Its 25 pavilions span the nation's individual provinces, with live music, crafts displays, and other exhibits that profile Cuba's diversity. ExpoCuba boasts a large display of vintage rolling stock, plus a maritime pavilion with various seacraft. It is served by railway from the Tulipán Railway Station *(Calle Tulipán, tel 7/81-4431),* in Nuevo Vedado.

JARDÍN BOTÁNICO

Laid out between 1968 and 1984, and extending over 1,480 acres, Cuba's national botanical garden appeals for its sheer grandness. More than 20 miles of road thread the park, partitioned by tropical regions and divided into zones that reflect Cuba's own varied ecosystems. A highlight is the exquisitely landscaped Japanese garden centered on a lake full of koi. The **Rincón Eckman Glasshouse,** named for Erik Leonard Eckman (1883–1931), who pioneered the study of botany in Cuba, features separate glasshouses exhibiting mountain plants; cactuses; and epiphytes, bromeliads, and ferns. The entrance is opposite ExpoCuba. ■

The cactus garden at the Jardín Botánico

The revolution is one subject that has inspired Cuba's artists.

More places to visit around Havana

ALAMEDA DE PAULA

Rising alongside Avenida del Puerto, this 200-yard-long (183 m) elevated pedestrian causeway makes for pleasant strolling. Marble benches and wrought-iron lamps add a romantic note. **Columna O'Donnell,** a carved column spouting from a fountain and erected in 1847, honors the Spanish navy; it was named for a *capitane generale.* At its southern end, the rotund and recently restored **Iglesia de San Francisco de Paula** occupies a traffic circle, at the junction with San Ignacio and Leonor Pérez. Before the revolution, the area was a red-light district. Hints of the past linger at **Dos Hermanos** *(Avenida del Puerto #304 at Sol),* a bar where Hemingway sipped *mojitos,* his famed rum cocktail. 61 F2

CASA ABEL SANTAMARÍA

Appealing to the revolution-curious, this apartment-unit-turned-museum, once occupied by martyred revolutionary hero Abel Santamaría, is revered as the early headquarters for Castro's M-26-7 movement. Fidel's work-desk and other original furnishings are in place. Abel and Haydee Santamaría, brother and sister, are honored in a photo gallery (he was brutally tortured and killed for the cause; in 1980 she committed suicide). 61 C3 ✉ Calle 25 #164, bet. Infanta & O ☎ 7/870-0417 🕐 Closed Sun.

JÁRDIN ZOOLÓGICO DE LA HABANA

Though the exhibits circle the tropics—from crocodiles and jaguars to gorillas and hippopotamuses—Havana's inner-city zoo, in Nuevo Vedado, is depressingly austere and suffers from a severe lack of funds. Loud-speakers add to the torment by blasting out deafening music. 60 A1 ✉ Avenida 26 & Zoológico ☎ 7/881-8915 🕐 Closed Mon. 💲 $

MUSEO DEL AIRE

For serious aviation buffs, **Havana's Air Museum,** in the La Coronela district, offers 27 biplanes, MiG jet fighters, helicopters, and missiles, mostly of Soviet provenance. A museum tells the Cuban version of the Bay of Pigs invasion, features a model plane collection, and has a section dedicated to space aviation. 60 A3 & IBC ✉ Avenida 212, bet. Calles 29 & 31 ☎ 7/271-0632 🕐 Closed Mon. 💲 $

MUSEO NACIONAL DE LA DANZA

Cuba's fine dance tradition is celebrated at this recently opened museum, housed in a restored mansion. The exhibits span musical scores, photographs, and wardrobes that include the personal collection of Alicia Alonso (1921–), the founder and *prima ballerina absoluta* of Cuba's National Ballet. Even Nijinsky's marriage certificate is here. 60 B4 & IBC ✉ Calle Linea #365 at Avenida de los Presidentes ☎ 7/831-2198 🕐 Closed Sun.–Mon. 💲 $

PARQUE ZOOLÓGICO NACIONAL

Although dismaying for the grim conditions in which most of the 784 animals (representing 91 species) are kept, Cuba's national zoo, covering 865 acres (350 ha) in Boyeros, about 11 miles (18 km) southwest of central Havana, makes amends with two attractions of note. A bus tour *(every 30 minutes, 0.40 centavos)* takes visitors through the **Pradera Africana,** an African wildlife park where elephants, rhinos, and zebra roam free; and the **Foso de los Leones,** a giant pit filled with lions. It has an **Area de Reproducción** where visitors can witness endangered species procreating. A **Zoo Infantíl** features opportunities to pet animals and offers rides to children. 🄰 61 D1 & IBC ✉ Avenida Soto, off Calzada de Bejucal ☎ 7/44-7613 🕐 Closed Mon.–Tues. 💲 $

SANCTUARIO DE SAN LÁZARO

Cuba's foremost pilgrimage site, the **Church of San Lazarus,** on the western outskirts of Rincón, draws supplicants year-round. They come to seek cures from San Lázaro, patron saint of sickness and disease (his African equivalent is Babalú Ayé, god of healing in Santería). Holy powers are ascribed to the waters that flow from a fountain behind the church. A leprosarium and AIDS sanatorium are nearby. Time your visit for December 17, when thousands of believers flock. 🄰 61 D1 & inside back cover ✉ Carretera de San Antonio de los Baños ☎ 0683/2396

SANTIAGO DE LAS VEGAS

Steeped in bucolic charm, Santiago de las Vegas, in the *municipio* of Boyeros, 14 miles (22 km) south of central Havana, harks back to a quieter era. Its red-tile-roofed houses are in country style. **Plaza Mayor** boasts a handsome church, plus a marble statue of Juan Delgado González, leader of local Mambí forces during the wars of independence. Gen. Antonio Maceo (1845–1896), the mulatto hero general of the wars of independence, is buried at **El Cacahual,** a mile south of town. His massive granite mausoleum commands a hilltop that offers views over the site of the skirmish at San Pedro, where Maceo was killed on December 7, 1896. 🄰 61 D1 ■

Sanctuario de San Lázaro draws supplicants from far and wide.

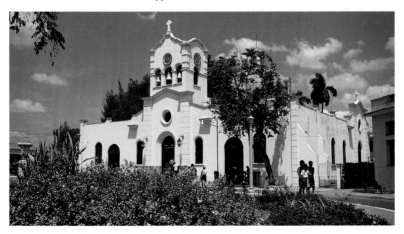

Blessed with stunning limestone formations and spectacular caverns, this lovely region is a bonanza for hiking, while pristine coral reefs guarantee splendid diving, and ox-carts plough broad valleys where the world's finest tobacco grows.

Far West

A delicate *Ralonia* at
Orquideario Soroa

The Iglesia Sagrado Corazón adds to Viñales's charm.

Far West

ALMOST EVERY TOURIST WHO VENTURES FORTH FROM HAVANA THINKS TO head to the Valle de Viñales, the crown jewel of Cuba's scenic attractions and the defining image of the far west. It's a choice made with good reason. Here, broad valleys are quilted with tobacco farms, and oxen till loamy, lipstick-red fields framed by dramatically sheer-sided *mogotes* (see pp. 102–103) that look like they just fell from their own picture postcards. Viñales is but one of many such valleys tucked within the Cordillera de Guaniguanico—the mountain spine that runs east–west through Pinar del Río province. Paved, albeit potholed, little-trafficked roads twist into the mountains, unveiling pastoral scenes that carry you back through the centuries.

On its eastern margin, the far west region encompasses a portion of Havana province. Relatively flat and fertile and intensely farmed, it mostly lacks sites of touristic interest. Exceptions are found in such timeworn colonial towns as Artemisa and San Antonio de los Baños; and in *presas* (reservoirs) stocked with largemouth bass.

Pinar del Río ("pine forest by the river") province, farther west, is predominantly mountainous. Prior to the Spanish arrival, the area was a retreat for the various Indian tribes driven west by succeeding invasions that culminated with conquest by Spain. The region's development came relatively late in the day when settlers (predominantly from the Canary Islands) planted tobacco in the early 18th century. The following century, French settlers planted coffee plantations in the Sierra del

Rosario; the coffee industry later fell into ruin, but the first glimmers of revival now show.

Heavily forested, the sierra also formed a base for counterrevolutionary bands in the early years following Castro's takeover. Peaceful today, the mountains lure hikers and birders, notably to the ecotourism sites of Soroa and Las Terrazas; and spelunkers tempted to cool off in the many underground caverns—one cave system in the Valle Santo Tomás comprises more than 15 miles of underground passages.

The scenery builds westward, culminating in the splendor of the Valle de Viñales and neighboring vales, where the intrepid hiker might find patches of endemic cork palm, tracing a lineage back more than 200 million years. The eponymous provincial capital is a draw for its colonial structures.

To the south sprawls a vast alluvial plain, smothered in a rippling ocean of sugarcane. The marshy shore is popular with hunters who come to down waterfowl. Tantalizing

beaches are few, although the Cabo Corrientes offers scintillating sand and superb diving, as does the necklace of coral cays—the Archipiélago de los Colorados—off the north shore. As yet none of the upscale resort hotels planned here has opened. Westward, the land peters down to an arid peninsula protected as the Parque Nacional Península de Guanahacabibes, selected as a UNESCO biosphere reserve.

Three routes access the far west region. The Circuito Norte twines along the north coast, delivering marvelous mountain and ocean vistas. The Carretera Central, once the main highway linking Havana with the city of Pinar del Río, runs along the southern flank of the mountains, connecting a string of unremarkable colonial towns. These days, most travelers opt for the *autopista*—a fast highway that cuts an arrow shot through the countryside, but is devoid of markings and sights—and there is no shortage of Cubans desperately beseeching rides. Drive carefully! ■

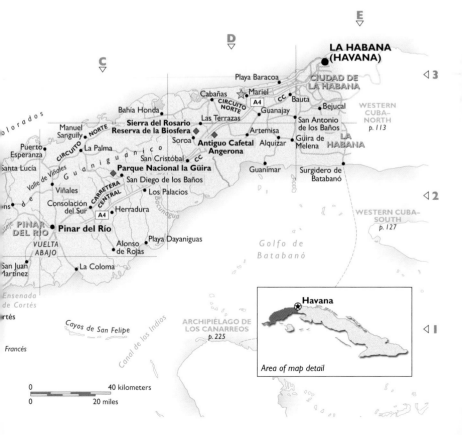

Sierra del Rosario
Reserva de la Biosfera

PINE FORESTS CLAD THE HILLS OF THE SIERRA DEL ROSARIO, rising to 1,640 feet (500 m) and beneficiary of two decades of reforestation of teak, mahogany, cedar, and pine. Named a UNESCO biosphere reserve in 1984, this 61,775-acre (25,000 ha) park is alluring to hikers and to botanists drawn, not least, to a fine orchid garden.

This reserve protects an area that over the centuries had been heavily logged and cleared for coffee estates. The Castro government initiated a pine replanting program in 1967. Rich in biodiversity, the forests are habitat to at least 98 species of birds that include parrots, trogons, and the national bird—the *tocororo*.

Deer and *jutías* are common, as are harmless snakes and amphibians, including *Sminthilis limbatus*, the world's second smallest frog.

LAS TERRAZAS

Touted as Cuba's prime ecotourism site, this *complejo turístico* (tourist complex; *$*) is centered on an eponymous peasant village built around Lago San Juan in 1971 as part of the reforestation initiative. Several residents work as artists; worth a visit is the **studio of Lester Campo** (*Edificio 4*). You can swim in the nearby **Baños de San Juan,** a series of pools and cascades.

The restored **Cafetal Buena Vista** coffee plantation, dating from 1801, is now an atmospheric restaurant. A peasant family welcomes visitors to the simple **Hacienda Unión,** where rustic meals are served. The **Centro Ecológico** is a research center with modest exhibits; you can hire guides for hikes here and at **La Moka** (*tel 82/78600*), a fine hotel amid woods overlooking the village and lake.

SOROA

This ecoretreat has been a draw since colonial days, when mineral baths were opened. The Baños Romanos are today dour, but the **El Salto cascades** have lost none of their beauty. Prime draw is **Orquideario Soroa** (*tel 85/2558*), an orchid garden created by a Spaniard in the mid-1940s. Built into a craggy hillside, it blazes with 700 species. ∎

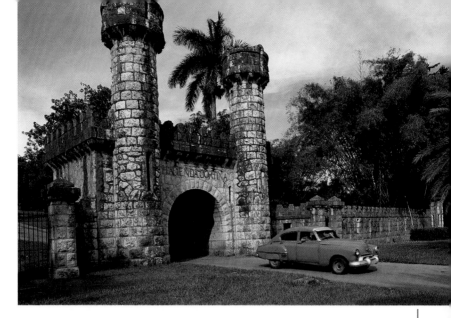

Parque Nacional la Güira

The dramatic entrance to Parque Nacional la Güira dates back less than a century.

SPANNING 54,000 ACRES (21,850 HA) OF THE SIERRA DE LOS Organos, this park enshrines scenic valleys filled with cave-studded *mogotes* (see pp. 102–103)—one cave, of awesome dimensions, played a role during the 1962 Cuban missile crisis. Ruins, a botanical garden, and splendid hiking round out the appeals.

The park is most commonly approached from its south side, off the Carretera Central, via a mock fortress that opens to **Hacienda Cortina.** Now mostly in ruins, this once imposing medieval-style mansion of Cuban millionaire attorney Manuel Cortina, with its lavish gardens, was seized by the government following the revolution. Part of the house is now a museum containing original tapestries and what little remains of the furnishings.

The access road winds up through sylvan glades—predominantly of pine—to **Cabañas de los Pinos,** a now abandoned tree-house hotel complex conceived by revolutionary heroine Celia Sánchez (see p. 195) following the revolution.

A side road drops down to sinuous valleys, farmed in the traditional manner into a quiltwork of tobacco and corn fields. It makes for a superlative drive. Signs point the way to **Cuevas de los Portales,** 10 miles (16 km) north of Hacienda Cortina. Of dramatic scale and impressive beauty, the cave forms the hollow of a sheer-sided mogote cut through by the Río Caiguanabo. The cathedral-like vault soars 90 feet (27 m) and forms a habitat for bats. Ornate dripstone formations resemble giant organs.

The cave's scale and reclusivity lured Che Guevara, who set up headquarters here during the Cuban missile crisis, when he commanded the Western Army. His bedrooms, tucked inside a small recess inside the cave, and makeshift "office" are maintained. Guides are on hand. A *campismo* (basic camping facility with cabins) was closed at press time, but slated for renovation. ■

Parque Nacional la Güira
⚑ 99 C2

Towering topography

Much of Cuba comprises what geologists call classic karst topography: irregular limestone terrain studded with conical mountains, divided by flat valleys and precipitous ravines, and underlain with labyrinthine caves. The most striking component of this geology, the signature feature of Cuba, is the conical mountains called *mogotes* (haystacks). They speckle the landscape, adding to Cuba's surreal beauty.

The product of uplift and erosion over millennia, mogotes owe their genesis to an erstwhile limestone seabed formed during the Jurassic period, beginning some 160 million years ago, when the compressed remains of myriad shells and other aquatic life accumulated on the ocean bottom. Gradually the great plateau was thrust from the sea.

Limestone is extremely porous and succumbs to the dissolving action of rainwater and underground streams as water drains through structural joints. Rainwater also interacts with limestone to form a mild carbolic acid. In Cuba, heavy tropical rains and high temperatures speed the acidic assault on the permeable rock. Eventually, chemical action erodes the limestone into a network of

Cuba's renowned beauty is never better displayed than at sunset in the Valle de Viñales (above), while sheer *mogotes* add drama to the valley's timeless landscapes (below).

huge underground passages and caves. In due course, the roofs of the largest caverns collapse, forming the mogotes' accompanying great valleys, some measuring as much as half a mile (0.8 km) across.

Many mogotes are freestanding and conical in shape, like upended bullets soaring as high as a thousand feet. Others, as seen from above, wind for miles in sinuous chains. All are rounded and sheer-sided and rise above the flat, fertile valleys whose vertical walls give a sense of being walled in. Many mogotes are undercut at their bases, as if by the action of waves. In fact, it's a result of erosion by groundwater whose acidity content is increased by decomposed vegetation.

The mogotes are further broken down by plants whose roots expand incipient cracks in the rock. Vegetation roots in hollows where soils accumulate, forming natural bowls and hanging planters, like densely packed arboretums. Since rainwater drains rapidly, the surface soil is dry. Hence, the dome-shaped hilltops themselves are sparsely vegetated. But the mogotes' sheer sides are overgrown with luxuriant greenery: thick brush, epiphytes, lianas, and mountain species that have adapted to tough conditions, such as caiman oaks, sierra palms, and the rare cork palm, which grows only in the karst terrain of Valle de Viñales. North-facing slopes typically are lusher, with a heavier preponderance of epiphytes, ferns, and mosses. More than 20 species of flora are endemic to the mogotes of Viñales.

So specialized is the environment that specific mogotes often harbor species of fauna absent even on neighboring hummocks. This is especially true of certain species of mollusks: Each elevation holds several unique species of land snails. One snail genus, *Chondropomete,* whose long eyestalks blaze a fluorescent orange, has evolved a unique defense against predators: It glues itself beneath rocky outcrops and hangs by a home-made elongated suspender.

Similar terrain exists elsewhere, notably in neighboring Puerto Rico and Jamaica, as well as the Guangxi region of southern China and the karst region of Croatia's Dalmatian Coast. ■

Viñales

Viñales
99 C2

THE VALLE DE VIÑALES CLAIMS STUPENDOUS SCENERY—unequivocally Cuba's finest. Cut into the Sierra de los Organos and ringed by *mogotes*, the valley is quilted with red, fertile soils and green *vegas* (fields), where the world's finest tobacco is grown. Cast in a quintessential Cuban time warp, the valley's one main town, Viñales, resounds to the creak of ox-drawn carts and the *clip-clop* of hooves. Fine hotels offer the most absorbing of views.

A fruit stop at day's end in Viñales. See more photos of the valley on pp. 40–41 & 102–103.

Peasant farmers—*guajiros*—tend the tobacco fields, dressed in straw hats and white linens or well-worn army fatigues. They have no machinery to help with their work; only white oxen to draw wooden ploughs and comb the rich soils into rows. Many of the guajiros own the land they till (although they must sell their entire crop to the government at a fixed rate). Feel free to enter the vegas and tent-shaped thatched curing sheds to ask for a lesson in Tobacco 101.

Adding to the valley's pastoral idyll, chickens, horses, pigs, and cattle scurry about the fields, even in the road, while snowy white egrets jab for insects. Palm fronds and the orange blossoms of

Spathodea burst over the scene.

The valley is splendid for hiking. Take a qualified guide if you plan on scaling a mogote. The mogotes are also riddled with caverns to explore.

Valley views are at their best at dawn and dusk, when the mogotes glow molten and the *bohios* (thatched huts) below are lit by the warm glow of lanterns. The best vantages are enjoyed from the **Hotel Los Jazmines** and **Hotel La Ermita** (see p. 245), perched atop the valley's southern wall.

VIÑALES VILLAGE

A spell seems to have been cast over Viñales, a sleepy cowboy village first founded in 1607. It is centered on a small colonial plaza that boasts a fine 19th-century church and the **Casa de la Cultura.**

The few places of note are arrayed along the main street—**Calle Salvador Cisneros,** lined with pine trees and statues and venerable colonial houses. One—the former home of independence heroine Adela Azcuy (1861–1914)—is now a **Museo Municipal,** with a modest showing. The **Jardín de las Hermanas Carmen y Caridad,** at the east end of Cisneros, is a luxuriant garden maintained by the Miranda sisters. Be sure to dine at **Casa de Don Tomás** *(Calle Salvador Cisneros #140, tel 8/93-6300),* serving country fare in a mellowed 1822 wooden mansion; or at **Casa del Veguero** *(tel 8/93-6080),* just south of town, where you can visit a *casa de tabaco* (tobacco barn).

MONUMENTO NACIONAL DE VIÑALES

So exquisite is the Viñales region that it is ennobled as a national monument, which incorporates a series of narrow, interconnected valleys that open up to and include the much larger Valle de Viñales. West from Viñales village, the road to the village of Pons passes through the **Valle de Santo Tomás,** whose walls are riddled with miles of connected chambers—the **Cuevas de Santo Tomás.** South of Pons, you are treated to the **Valle de San Carlos**—a tight-hemmed Viñales in miniature.

One mile west of Viñales, a side road leads into the **Valle de los Guasas,** a vast amphitheater where the road dead-ends beneath the sheer-faced **Mogote Dos Hermanas.** The beauty of this mogote is marred by the **Mural de la Prehistoria,** a 300-foot-long (180 m) mural in naïve style commissioned by Castro in 1961 to pro-file the evolution of socialist man. The rustic restaurant *(tel 8/93-6260)* at its base serves wholesome meals accompanied by traditional music. A trail leads up the mogote to **Los Acuáticos,** the home of locals who welcome visitors interested in the curative powers of their healing waters; guides can lead you. The nearby **Campismo Dos Hermanas** *(tel 8/93223)* has a small **Museo de la Prehistoria** *(closed Mon.).*

North of Viñales, the mogotes close in to form the pinched **Valle de San Vicente;** a drive through

Exploring Cueva del Indio by boat

the valley is a roller-coaster ride whose drama is enhanced by rocky formations suspended on the side walls like plicated curtains. The **Cueva de Viñales,** 2 miles (3 km) north of Viñales, is a curiosity for its dripstone formations that act as a backdrop to the nightly cabaret-disco. Guided tours are offered by day.

More interesting are the nearby **Cueva del Indio,** underground caverns that in places attain heights of 300 feet. They can be explored partway by foot and the rest by motorized boat. Endemic species of blind crustaceans and fish inhabit the pea-green waters, while bats flit overhead. ∎

Museo Municipal

✉ Calle Salvador Cisnero #115, Viñales

☎ 8/93359

🕐 Closed indefinitely for restoration

💲 $

Tobacco rows

It is appropriate that the world's finest tobacco is Cuban. *Nicotiana tabacum* has been cultivated in Cuba since pre-Columbian times. It was hallowed by the indigenous Taino, who smoked it through tubes made of hollowed wood called *cohibas.* Today, the image of a mustachioed tobacco farmer *(veguero)* attentively coddling his tobacco plants is a quintessential image that personifies Cuba.

A cousin of the potato, tobacco is a member of the nightshade family. Two varieties are grown in Cuba. The *corojo,* which provides the cigar's large, thin wrapper leaves, is grown under fine sheets of mosquito netting *(tapados)* to protect against harsh sunlight and ensure leaves that are smooth and pliable. The *criollo,* used for filler leaves, is grown in direct sunlight, which brings out the fullest of flavors derived from oils that are a protective response to the sun.

Tobacco requires near-constant sunlight and minimal rain during its growing season. October to January are the prime months, after the rains have ceased. Seeds are planted in a mix of sand and ashes under beds of straw that are removed upon germination. After about 45 days, seedlings are transplanted to the fields and laid out in rows.

The maturing plants are handled with great tenderness—vegueros are even known to talk to their leaves to stimulate growth. When the plant attains a height of five feet (1.5 m), the central bud is nipped off before flowering to encourage leaf growth.

The leaves grow in pairs, with six or more pairs on each plant. They are harvested January through March in six phases according to the leaves' respective positions. The lowest leaves are snicked off first, two-by-two, with a small sickle. The leaves above them are gathered in one-week intervals as they mature, until the *corona,* the top leaf of the plant, is taken.

The harvested leaves are sewn together and strung up on long poles, or *cujes,* arranged in rows in thatched barns *(casas de tabaco* or *secaderos);* the barns are aligned east to west

Viñales's ideal climate and rich soils are perfect for growing tobacco (right). Leaves hang like kippers in a *secadero* (above right).

for exposure to even sunlight. Here they are left to dry for about 60 days, during which time the leaves lose about 85 percent of their water and turn a reddish-gold color, the green chlorophyll having turned to brown carotene.

Once cured, the leaves are taken down and bundled into wooden cases to be sent to a sorting house, where they are left to ferment for up to three months. This reduces the resin and nicotine content. The leaves are then graded and sent to the factories to be moistened and fermented again for 60 days to remove ammonia and other impurities. After drying, the leaves are packed in bales wrapped in palm bark, which helps keep the leaves at a constant humidity. After aging for up to four years, they are ready to be rolled into the world's finest cigars (see p. 76). ■

Pinar del Río
◩ 99 C2
Visitor information
✉ Cubatur, Calle Martí #115
☎ 82/78405
🕒 Closed Sun.

Fábrica de Tabacos Francisco Donatién
✉ Calle Antonio Maceo #157 at Ajete
☎ 82/3424
🕒 Closed Sun.
💲 $

Fábrica de Bebidas Guayabita
✉ Calle Isabel Rubio #189, bet. Cerefino Fernández & Frank País
☎ 82/2966
🕒 Closed Sun.
💲 $

Museo de Ciencias Naturales
✉ Calle Martí #202 at Ave. Comandante Pinares
☎ 82/3087
💲 $

Pinar del Río's Restaurante Rumayor features a jazzy Afro-Cuban folkloric show and cabaret (see p. 245).

Pinar del Río

THE SLEEPY, DOWN-AT-HEELS PROVINCIAL CAPITAL OFFERS limited appeal for tourists other than as an overnight stop. It is known, however, for its neoclassic structures graced by art nouveau facades, and a miscellany of modest attractions—including a tobacco factory and esoteric museum—are worth a visit before moving on.

Pinar del Río, 90 miles west of Havana, was founded in 1669 and named for the pine forests that once grew here. It grew wealthy in the following century as Cuba's main center for cigar production. When the factories moved to Havana in the late 19th century, its fortunes declined.

Today, this town of 148,000 retains a laid-back rusticity, despite such modern amenities as a university and stadium. Its dusty streets boast flamboyant colonial facades, notably along the main street, **Calle Martí.** Most buildings cry out for restoration. Fortunately, city fathers answered the call to save the **Teatro José Jacinto Milanés,** built in 1898 in Italianate Renaissance style at the juncture of Calles Martí and Colón. And the renovated **Hotel Globo** (*Calle Martí at Calle Isabel, tel 82/4268*) gleams with impressive tilework.

The most interesting site is the **Fábrica de Tabacos Francisco Donatién,** a diminutive cigar factory where you can watch rollers conjuring cigars for domestic consumption. To better appreciate your visit, take a guided tour (*$*).

Guayabita, a nationally acclaimed brandy made of the guayaba fruit, has been distilled at the **Fábrica de Bebidas Guayabita/Casa Garay** since 1892; tastings and guided tours are offered.

Peer into the **Palacio Gausch,** built by a local doctor between 1909 and 1914, with a gauche baroque frontage incorporating Gothic gargoyles, Athenian columns, and other elements inspired by his travels. Inside, the **Museo de Ciencias Naturales** offers a no-less-eclectic parade of exhibits that includes seashells and a motley assortment of dinosaurs cast in cement.

The modest **Museo Provincial de Historia** (*Calle Martí #58, tel 82/4300, $*) presents the history of town and province. Exhibits include weapons and period furnishings. ■

Parque Nacional Península de Guanahacabibes

Parque Nacional
Península de
Guanahacabibes

🅰 98 A1

**Visitor
information**

✉ Contact Centro
    Ecológico, La Bajada

☎ 82/93359

💲 $$

EXTENDING LIKE A WITCH'S FINGER INTO THE GULF OF Mexico, the 60-mile-long (96.5 km) Península de Guanahacabibes is virtually uninhabited. Smothered in cactuses and scrubby woodland, and edged by a corona of sugar-white beaches, the slender promontory is a pristine refuge best known for its superlative diving in the translucent waters of Bahía de Corrientes.

Prior to the Spanish conquest of Cuba, this remote region had become a point of refuge for the indigenous Siboney (also known as the Guanahatabeys), driven west by the Taino. Several archaeological sites attest to the tenure of these early residents. Today, the small community of **Villa San Juan** raises bees, while impoverished charcoal-burners eke a living cutting mangroves on the swampy north coast. Otherwise, the region is mostly left to wild pigs, deer, *jutías* (large rodents), iguanas, and copious birdlife, including parakeets, Cuban trogons, and endangered great lizard cuckoos.

The flat, semiarid peninsula is enshrined as a 250,806-acre (101,500 ha) national park and UNESCO biosphere reserve. It is divided into two sections: the El Veral and Cabo Corrientes reserves. Facilities for tourists are nonexistent, although three hiking trails are currently open. Obligatory guides can be hired at the **Centro Ecológico,** an ecological research station located where the paved access road first meets the shore, at the tiny community of La Bajada.

The road splits here. To the left, you'll swing around the east end of Bahía de Corrientes to **Villa María la Gorda** *(tel 82/78131)*, a dive resort fronted by a modest beach. The bay extends south to Cabo Corrientes and offers premier diving, with spectacular coral formations and the possibility of seeing

dolphins and whale sharks. There are even sunken galleons to explore. The bay was once a haven for pirates, and the most prominent physical feature hereabouts is named, according to local lore, for the endowments of the woman (María la Gorda, or Fat Mary) who serviced them.

West from La Bajada, a dirt road extends 34 miles (54 km) along the length of the peninsula's southern shore and deposits you at a lighthouse at **Cabo de San Antonio** (Cuba's westernmost point). The views down over the cactus-studded raised limestone platform are inspiring. The lighthouse is backed by a military outpost; ask before taking photographs. In springtime, tens of thousands of land crabs swarm across the road on their mating and egg-laying endeavors. ∎

Bathtub-warm waters are a snorkeler's delight at María la Gorda.

Travel notes
A permit (obtained at Villa María la Gorda, tel 82/78131) is required to travel to Punta Cajón. There's a military checkpoint on the access road, about 2 miles (3 km) before the shore; you'll need to show your passport.

The ecoresort of Las Terrazas nestles in the Sierra del Rosario Reserva de la Biosfera.

Driving the north coast

Although most travelers heading west from Havana opt for the fast *autopista,* which sweeps through the southern lowlands of Pinar del Río, Circuito Norte, which hugs the north shore, is far more appealing. This roller-coaster ride offers seductive vistas of peacock-colored waters and dramatic *mogotes,* and the bucolic calm of sleepy coastal towns interspersed among rolling canefields.

The 90-mile (145 km) drive along Route 1-1 (the Circuito Norte) begins at **Mariel ❶,** a run-down port city 28 miles west of Havana. It's known as the departure point for the "boatlift" of 1980, when 120,000 Cubans (many of them criminals released from jail) fled their homeland for Florida.

West of Mariel, the sense of urban enclosure gives way to more calming sensations as the road narrows down to do a twisty two-lane tango along a ridgetop between lime-green sugarcane fields and the rich blue Atlantic. *Centrales* (sugar factories) rise over the fields. Traffic is limited, with a preponderance of tractors and creaking wooden carts pulled by white oxen dropping long stalks of cane as they go. Potholes are numerous, as are the usual obstacles—bicycles, cattle, and, during the *zafra* (sugar harvest), steam trains shunting to and from centrales.

You'll pass through forlorn fishing villages,

with signs pointing to various *campismos*—Cuban holiday camps. They're dismaying and not worth the detour. Gradually the Sierra del Rosario rises to the south. Numerous side roads lead into the cool, pine-clad mountains. At

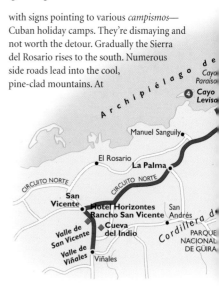

San Diego de Núñez, ❷ you might opt to detour inland and follow the twisting road up to **Soroa** and **Las Terrazas,** two ecological tourist communities in the **Sierra del Rosario Reserva de la Biosfera** (see p. 100). However, to make the most of these sites, you will add several hours to your journey.

Back on the Circuito Norte, you pass through the unremarkable town of **Bahía Honda.** Seven miles (11 km) farther west, turn south for a brief detour for a close-up view of **Pan de Guajaibón** ❸, a dramatic, mauve-colored sugarloaf soaring 2,294 feet (699 m). The detour—which snakes 9 miles (14 km) up through coffee country, with glossy-leafed bushes aligned in neat rows— peters out at the ramshackle hamlet of **Rancho Canelo.** From here, you can hike to the base of the mountain.

West of Las Pozas, the coastal views open up, with the cays of the **Archipiélago de los Colorados** floating in the turquoise shallows of Enseñanza de la Mulata. The road drops to the coastal plain, offering only occasional tantalizing glimpses of the sea. At **Playa la Mulata,** 8 miles (13 km) beyond Las Pozas, stop to admire the plaque, which tells you that Ernest Hemingway used Cayo Paraíso, offshore, as a base for antisubmarine operations from his yacht—*El Pilar*—during World War II. About 5.5 miles (8.8 km) farther west, a turn-off leads 2 miles (3 km) north to the ferry berth for **Cayo Levisa** ❹ *(tel 8/33-4042),* a prime dive site with sparkling beaches (ferries run twice daily).

The road pitches in great sweeping curves as it leads you southwest to the unassuming town of **La Palma.** At **San Vicente,** 20 miles (32 km) farther, turn south for Viñales; there's a gas station just south of the junction. It's time to break out your camera as the road climbs gradually between sheer *mogotes,* with the views growing more sublime by the mile. You'll pass the **Hotel Horizontes Rancho San Vicente** *(tel 8/93-6201),* a partially restored spa hotel, and **Cueva del Indio** (see p. 105). Beyond, the valley opens up dramatically into the **Valle de San Vicente** (see p. 105), an amphitheater that you exit via a narrow defiles that deposits you in the **Valle de Viñales** and the charming eponymous village (see pp. 104–105). ∎

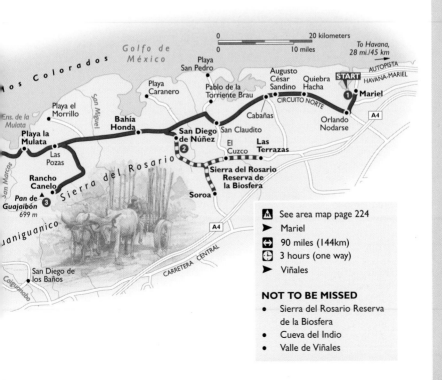

To Havana, 28 mi./45 km

START Mariel ❶

◭	See area map page 224
►	Mariel
↔	90 miles (144km)
⏱	3 hours (one way)
►	Viñales

NOT TO BE MISSED
- Sierra del Rosario Reserva de la Biosfera
- Cueva del Indio
- Valle de Viñales

The ruins of Antiguo Cafetal Angerona, once one of Cuba's largest coffee and sugar estates

More places to visit in the far west

ANTIGUO CAFETAL ANGERONA

This coffee *finca*, 10 miles (18 km) west of Artemisa, in Havana province, was built in 1813 for Cornelius Sausse and grew to become one of the largest coffee and sugar estates in Cuba, with 450 slaves. The ruins are approached by a long drive that ends by the former great house. You can explore the subterranean cisterns, and the watchtowers that shadow the *barracón*, where slaves were kept when not toiling the fields. The finca, which became a sugar estate following Sausse's death, was used by James Michener as a setting in his 1989 novel, *Caribbean*. 🅰 99 D2

SAN ANTONIO DE LOS BAÑOS

Despite its forlorn appearance, this small town, 19 miles south of Havana, clings to its colonial charm, concentrated around the main plaza. Its main draw is the **Bienal Internacional del Humor,** a comedy festival held every two years. The festival has spawned the **Museo del Humor** *(Calle 60 at Calle 45, tel 650/2817),* displaying cartoons from around the world—with a strongly anti-imperialist bias. 🅰 99 D3

SAN DIEGO DE LOS BAÑOS

This small, sleepy place, half a mile (0.8 km) north of the Carretera Central, about 38 miles east of the town of Pinar del Río, has been an important spa town since the late 19th century. The mineral springs, which hover around 100°F (38°C), feed subterranean whirlpool baths at the **Balneario San Diego** *(tel 8/37812),* where treatments are offered. The **Hotel Santiago** is a jaded architectural curiosity (it accepts Cuban guests only), as is the Greek Orthodox-style church on the main plaza. Tourists are billeted at the handsome **Hotel El Mirador** (see p. 245; *Calle 23, tel 82/78338),* a restored 1950s mansion now run by Servimed and specializing in medical treatments. 🅰 99 C2

VUELTA ABAJO

While lacking the grandeur of the Valle de Viñales, the flat but fertile soils of Vuelta Abajo produce unequivocally the finest tobacco in Cuba—outclassing even that of Viñales. At the region's heart is the colonial town of **San Juan y Martinez,** 15 miles (24 km) west of Pinar del Río. The most famous of the plantations is **Hoyo de Monterrey,** which even has its own cigar label. At **San Luís,** Alejandro Robaina also farms one of the most famous *hoyos* (plantation) in Cuba, carrying on a family tradition of tobacco production that extends back to 1845. His home doubles as the **Museo de Alejandro Robaina,** full of miscellany related to tobacco and cigar production. The plantation is 6 miles (10 km) west of Pinar del Río; turn south off the highway for 5 miles (8 km). 🅰 99 C2 ■

Slender peninsulas fringed by beaches, beautiful tobacco country, villages that explode in firework revelry, and mausoleum and monuments to Che highlight this coastal plain.

Western Cuba–North

Festive mask at the Museo de las Parrandas, Remedios

Western Cuba—North

EAST OF THE CUBAN CAPITAL, THE ISLAND FATTENS OUT, WITH THE LIMESTONE uplands of Havana province shouldering against the broad plains, or *llanuras,* of Matanzas province. Green and flat as a billiard table, these plains possess Cuba's richest soils, ideal for growing sugarcane. Narrowing eastward, they edge along the coast in the cusp of low hills that comprise the soft, rolling landscape of Villa Clara province.

Scenic only at the hilly extremes, the region offers scant delights along the shore. Mangroves creep into the calm waters of the Archipiélago Sabana-Camagüey, a series of coral cays that forms an unbroken necklace between 5 and 15 miles offshore. The cays extend east of the Península de Hicacos, a thin sling cast from the mainland of Matanzas province. Sugar-coated, the peninsula hosts Varadero—Cuba's Cancún—drawing package tourists to its famous 7-mile (11.5 km) beach lined with more than 30 hotels. Despite a bagful of offerings—water sports, scuba diving, and golf, to name a few—Varadero disappoints, not least because Cuban citizens are turned away, sapping resorts of the vivacity and passion that are the hallmarks of the Cuban spirit. A new resort playground is emerging farther east, at Cayo Santa María and neighboring cays.

East of Varadero, a broad plain extends inland from the coast. Since the 19th century, this area has been Cuba's most fertile sugar-growing region, a landscape of Day-Glo green canefields with tornadoes of black smoke eddying up from *centrales* (sugarcane processing plants) that, during the *zafra,* or sugar harvest, taint the idyll with the cloying smell of molasses. "White gold"—sugar—paid for towns such as Matanzas and Cárdenas, where museums and edifices of note can still be found.

The cities are linked to Havana by the Carretera Central, built between 1926 and 1931 as the country's main highway and today connecting dusty farming towns whose former prominence has since been usurped by the Autopista Nacional, farther south.

The Vía Blanca, or Circuito Norte, accesses the north coast. Rising eastward into the Alturas del Nordeste, it offers a splendid entrée to the beauty of upland Villa Clara south of the rich coastal plain. Royal palms stud the valleys where *vegueros* (tobacco grow-

ers) tend their plants and till the fields with oxen. Most travelers journey through Villa Clara to pay homage to Che Guevara in the provincial capital of Santa Clara. The heavily industrialized city is remarkable for its towering statue and soulful mausoleum to Santa Clara's adopted revolutionary hero, and as the site for the decisive battle that toppled the Batista regime. Santa Clara draws the three main highways to itself and spins the Circuito Norte shooting back toward the coast via Vuelta Arriba—an important tobacco-producing region—to Remedios, a colonial charmer that moves to the lassitude of yesteryear. Steeped in colonial antiquity, Remedios is especially enticing

for its year-end *parrandas*—battles of fireworks that erupt during Christmas week. There are caverns to explore in the hills and vales surrounding Matanzas, where a once popular spa destination—San Miguel de los Baños—awaits restoration. ■

The gentry once flocked to Balneario San Miguel in San Miguel de los Baños to soak in its mineral baths.

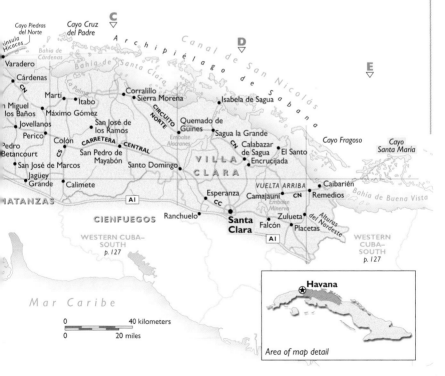

Havana to Matanzas

A COASTAL ZONE OF PRIM COVES AND GOLDEN BEACHES extends between the cities of Havana and Matanzas. Uninspiring stretches of raised coral, some marred by oil derricks and overpowered by the stench of sulphurous fumes, meld into more graceful vistas that reveal the beauty of inland valleys studded by *mogotes* (see pp. 102–103). A venerable sugar processing plant and equally aged rum factory make intriguing stops on any journey between the two cities.

The Puente Bacunayagua sweeps travelers high above a river canyon, with stunning views all around.

Havana to Matanzas

🅼 144 A2 & B2

Vintage rails

Providing a splendid entrée to the beauty of rural Cuba, the Hershey train runs leisurely between Casablanca (on the north shore of Havana harbor) and Matanzas. As it wends through the Valle Yumurí, it stops at remote way stations where *guajiros* (peasant farmers) in traditional country dress clamber aboard or alight. A highlight is a stop at the old Hershey estate, where you can explore the now-tumbledown village. Antique Spanish cars provide the current service, originally inaugurated in 1916 and resumed in 1998. The train operates five times daily *(schedules change frequently, tel 7/862-4888)*. ∎

Eastward, beyond Playas del Este, the Vía Blanca (Rte. 2-1.3) hugs the shoreline, offering little of note for the first 10 miles (16 km). Beyond Boca de Jaruco, the mouth of the Río Jaruco, oil derricks appear. Looming beyond is an oil-fed electrical-generating plant at the edge of **Santa Cruz del Norte.** Here the taint of molasses emanates from **Fábrica Cubaron** *(closed to the public),* which produces Havana Club rums.

Swoop south 3 miles (5 km) to **Camilo Cienfuegos,** a community serving an eponymous *central* (sugarcane processing plant). Before the revolution, the Pennsylvania-based Hershey chocolate company owned 69 square miles (18,000 ha) of land here to farm sugarcane; it was centered on the purpose-built village—christened "Hershey"—complete with movie theater, baseball field, and hotel. Though ramshackle, the town is worth a quick browse.

At **Puente Bacunayagua,** 66 miles (106 km) east of Havana, travelers trundling along the highway are treated to a spectacular vista. Here, a 1,030-foot-long (314 m) bridge hangs over a canyon at the mouth of the Río Bacunayagua, 361 feet (110 m) below. To the south sprawls the **Valle Yumurí,** its rolling green landscape dotted with palms. No stopping is allowed on the bridge. A *mirador* (viewing platform) overlooking the highway offers a chance to capture the picture-postcard setting on camera. ∎

Matanzas

Matanzas' Parque Central

Matanzas
▲ 114 B2
Visitor information
✉ Infotur, Plaza de la Libertad, Calles 83 & 290

Museo Provincial Palacio de Junco
✉ Calle 83 (Milanés) & Calle 212, bet. Magdalena & Ayón
☎ 45/24-3464
⊕ Closed Mon.
$ $

LONG-KNOWN AS THE "ATHENS OF CUBA," THE PORT CITY of Matanzas offers its share of neoclassic structures of note. It is hardly a picturesque city, however, despite its dramatic location on a sweeping bay—Cuba's largest—enfolded by hills. Matanzas is known for its traditional music, strongly influenced by African rhythms.

Matanzas (population 126,000) was founded in 1693 between the mouths of the Yumurí and San Juan Rivers. Before that, it was best known for Dutch pirate Piet Heyn's attack on the Spanish treasure fleet in 1628; two dozen gold-laden galleons were sent to the bottom of the bay.

The city was named for either a massacre *(matanza)* of Spaniards by Indians in 1510, or that of pigs killed to supply fleets of ships. It became a main center for the disembarkation of slaves and an outlet for the produce of the rich inland valleys. The city grew wealthy during the mid-19th-century heyday of sugar and evolved a café society that found its expression in civic construction and in music and dance—the *danzón,* a derivative of the French quadrille, was invented here in 1879, and the city is considered the "queen of rumba."

Today, tankers and freighters anchor in the bay, surrounded by sugar-loading and oil-refining facilities and industrial factories. For a

splendid view, head up Calle 306 to **Ermita de Monserrate,** a ruined hilltop hermitage; and **Parque René Fraga,** at Bonificio Byrne and Calle 312.

THE HISTORIC CORE

Reparto Matanzas, the early colonial core, is laid out in a grid west of **Plaza de la Vigía,** the original town plaza. Its pride is the **Teatro Sauto,** built in neoclassic style in 1863. With its tiered balconies, bronze columns, and classical statuary, it ranks among the world's finest theaters for opera. To learn something of local history, call in at the **Museo Provincial Palacio de Junco,** in the former Palacio Junco, a neoclassic structure with arcades built in 1838 by a wealthy planter.

The plaza merges into **Parque de los Bomberos** (Fireman's Square), where antique fire engines dating back more than a century are on display in the quaint neoclassic firehouse, now the **Museo de los Bomberos.** Opposite, one

A variety of old-time remedies line the shelves of the Museo Farmacéutico.

Museo Farmacéutico

✉ Calle 83 (Milanés) #4951, bet. Santa Teresa & Ayuntamiento

☎ 45/24-3179

$ $

of Cuba's most treasured publishing houses, **Ediciones Vígía** still produces fine hand-printed works.

Plaza de la Libertad, four blocks west, has a bronze statue of José Martí. To each side are buildings of note: to the north, the **Biblioteca** (library) and adjoining **Casa de la Cultura,** in the former Lyceum Club and Casino Club, respectively; and to the south, the **Hotel Louvre** and the **Museo Farmacéutico.** The latter—the Pharmaceutical Museum—occupies an 1882 pharmacy that has been preserved as it was in yesteryear. Carved wooden shelves are lined with ornate porcelain jars and crystal flasks containing all manner of cures. Note the green, red, and white stained-glass windows; they were red, white, and blue until Spanish authorities demanded that they be changed to Spain's colors.

The partially restored **Catedral de San Carlos** (Calle 282, bet. Calles 83 & 85) was built in 1878 and boasts a beautiful frescoed ceiling.

REPARTO VERSALLES

Settled by French refugees from Haiti in the early 19th century, this district lies north of the Río Yumurí. To get there, cross the arched **Puente Concordia,** built of stone in 1878 with decorative columns. Worth perusal are the neoclassic **Iglesia de San Pedro Apóstol** (Calles 57 & 270), and the **Cuartel Golcuría,** a military barracks-turned-school that was attacked by Castroite rebels on April 29, 1956.

Serious history buffs might consider visiting **Castillo de San Severino,** rising over the port at the east end of Reparto Versalles. The castle, which served as a prison during the wars of independence, is accessed via the Centro Politécnico on Calles 57 and 230. It is not set up for tourists yet, but the *custodio* is usually happy to give a tour for a small tip.

The terminus of the Hershey train is here (see p. 116; Calle 262 at 67, tel 45/24-4805). ■

Varadero

CUBA'S LODESTONE OF TOURISM, VARADERO, LOCATED 88 miles (141 km) east of Havana, lures vacationers with a diamond-dust beach edging the length of an 11-mile-long (17 km) peninsula. Half of the nation's hotels are here—from budget options to inter-national-chain resorts. If sun, sand, and sea are your thing, this could be for you. But Varadero caters mainly to Canadian and European package-tourists and, being off-limits to Cubans, is soulless for it.

Jutting out into Bahía de Cárdenas, the pencil-thin **Punta Hicacos** is being developed as a Cuban Cancún. The beaches on the north shore shelve into turquoise waters whose coral reefs tempt divers with a world more exquisite than a casket of gems—notably in **Parque Nacional Marino Cayo Piedras del Norte,** with its sunken plane, frigate, and missile launcher.

Varadero village evolved in the 1880s as a summer resort for mainland residents; the red-roofed wooden houses can still be seen along Avenida 1ra. In the 1920s, U.S. chemical industrialist Irénée du Pont developed much of the peninsula with private villas. By the 1950s, grand hotels and casinos sprang up, luring Hollywood figures.

Du Pont's Spanish-style man-sion, now a restaurant called **Las Américas** *(tel 45/66-7750),* com-mands a headland at the east end of the main beach. The home, which features the original library and ball-room (now a bar), is open to view. Du Pont's 9-hole golf course has metamorphosed into the 18-hole Varadero Golf Club *(tel 5/66-7788).* Nearby, dolphins perform at the **Delfinario** *(tel 45/66-8888).*

Parque Retiro-Josone *(Avenida 1ra, bet. Calles 55 & 59)* offers a bucolic retreat with a lake surrounding a mansion seized by the government in 1959. The **Museo Municipal de Varadero** *(Avenida 1ra at Calle 57, tel 45/61-3189, $)* displays exhibits on local

flora and fauna; the **Salón de Deportes,** upstairs, honors Cuba's excellence in sports, including the rowing regattas for which Varadero was once famous. To see cigars being rolled, pop into **Casa Vegueros** *(Avenida 1ra & Calle 27).*

Parque Ecológico Varadero, a 730-acre swath of scrub at the island's east end, is being developed for ecotourism. Marked trails lead to numerous caves, including **Cueva Ambrosio,** containing Indian drawings. ■

Varadero
▲ 115 B2
Visitor information
✉ Avenida 1ra at Calle 23
☎ 5/66-7743

Note
Mosquitoes can be a problem; sulphurous fumes from nearby petrochemical installations frequently foul the air.

Above the tourist paradise of Varadero

Santa Clara

Santa Clara

⬣ 115 D1

Visitor information

✉ Rumbos, Calle Independencia #167

☎ 422/21-8118

Museo Histórico Nacional

✉ Escuela Abel Santamaría, Calle Esquerra at Central

☎ 42/20-3041

🕐 Closed Sun.

💲 $

El Bulevar, Santa Clara

THIS IMPORTANT INDUSTRIAL AND UNIVERSITY CITY, provincial capital of Villa Clara province and gateway to the eastern provinces, lies at the heartland of Cuba. The city (pop. 210,000) has strong associations with Che Guevara (see pp. 122–123), who here led the final, successful battle of the revolutionary war to topple Batista.

Santa Clara, 170 miles east of Havana, was founded in 1689 when residents of nearby Remedios relocated to escape the Insurrection (see p. 124). The city was fought over fiercely during the wars of independence and later proved critical in the ouster of General Batista when it was attacked in 1958 by Che Guevara's rebel army. After three days of battle, Santa Clara was captured and Batista fled Cuba the next day. Che's remains were interred here in October 1997 to popular excitement.

Worth seeking out are **Iglesia Buen Viaje,** at Calles Pedro Estévez and Pardo; and **Iglesia del Carmen,** on Plaza del Carmen. The latter, dating from 1748, still shows the bullet holes fired from the police station across the street during Che's attack.

PARQUE VIDAL

This park—named for independence hero Col. Leoncio Vidal—lies at the city core. Shaded by poinciana and *guásima* trees, the colonial plaza is ringed by a two-tier walkway divided by a rail that in colonial days separated whites from blacks.

Neoclassic buildings surround the square, including (on the east side) the **Palacio del Gobierno Provincial,** the former town hall now housing the library. On the northwest corner stands **Teatro de la Caridad** (tel 42/20-5548), built in 1885 on behalf of the poor of Santa Clara and funded by local noblewoman-philanthropist Marta Abreu de Estéves (1845–1904); her bronze bust looks over the plaza. An exquisite fresco by Spanish-Philippine artist Camilo Salaya graces the theater's dome.

Next door, a beautiful 18th-century mansion contains the **Museo de Artes Decorativas,** displaying a sumptuous collection of paintings and antiques spanning three centuries. The nondescript structure on the southwest side is the **Hotel Santa Clara Libre,** notable solely for its historic importance as site of a battle to oust Batista's troops.

The **Museo Histórico Nacional,** in Reparto Osvaldo Herrera, is a curiosity in passing. Its eclectic exhibits range from natural history and colonial furniture to Villa Clara's role in the independence and revolutionary wars. It is housed in the city's former military barracks—now a school, Escuela Abel Santamaría—where Che accepted the surrender of the city. It's hard to find; ask for directions.

HOMAGE TO CHE

Calle Independencia slopes downhill to the Río Cubanicay and the remains of the **Tren Blindado,** an armored train sent to reinforce Batista's forces. On December 29, 1958, a rebel band led by Che derailed the train loaded with munitions and 408 men. After a short battle, the troops surrendered. The monument comprises four carriages arrayed as they came to rest in a tangle; one is now a museum. The story of the battle is given on an adjacent obelisk.

Now head out to **Plaza de la Revolución.** The vast concrete plaza is dominated by artist José Delarra's bronze statue of Che, bearing a rifle, with his other arm in a sling. It was erected in 1987 for the 20th anniversary of the revolutionary's death. The splendid **Mausoleo del Che** is tucked into the rear. Photographs, mementoes, and other miscellany trace Che's life, from childhood in Argentina to his death in Bolivia in 1967. His green fatigue jacket is here, as is his black beret with five-pointed star. No photos are allowed. Adjacent is a simple, somber mausoleum where Che's remains are inset in the wall, along with those of 17 other guerrillas killed in the ill-fated Bolivia campaign. An eternal flame—lit by Castro on October 17, 1997—adds to the stirring effect. ■

Museo de Artes Decorativas

- ✉ Parque Vidal #3 at Luis Estévez
- ☎ 42/20-5368
- 🕑 Closed Tues.
- 💲 $

Mausoleo del Che

- ✉ Plaza de la Revolución at Avenida de los Desfiles
- ☎ 42/20-5878
- 🕑 Closed Sun.

What is it about Che?

Ernesto "Che" Guevara is Cuba's most revered revolutionary hero. His steely visage—the famous image of the "Heroic Guerrilla" wearing his signature beret with five-pointed star—is seen across Cuba on everything from billboards to key chains. A chief architect of the Cuban revolution, this Argentinean is still invoked as the model for the New Man, someone unselfishly committed to socialist ideals. As an icon for an entire generation, Che remains today an inspiration for idealists both within and beyond the island.

Ernesto Guevara (1928–1967) was born in Rosario, Argentina, to an intellectual middle-class family. He trained as a doctor then, seeking to sow some wild oats, set out to explore South America on his Norton motorcycle. The poverty and injustice he saw awakened his socialist passions. In 1954 he witnessed the CIA's overthrow of Guatemala's socialist Arbenz government. Embittered, he fled to Mexico City, where he met Fidel Castro and signed on with Castro's guerrilla army-in-training—the 26th of July Movement. In time, he became Castro's closest friend and was known simply as Che, the Argentinean equivalent of the American "buddy" (he was also called *el chancho*—the pig—because he rarely bathed).

Che was one of only 17 rebels who survived the *Granma* landing in December 1956. A daring and reckless fighter, Che proved himself a brilliant field commander; he was beloved by his troops, many of whom committed to him for the rest of their lives—*los hombres del che*. In the decisive battle at Santa Clara in December 1958, Che won a stunning victory that sealed the fate of the Batista dictatorship. After *el triunfo*, Che led the tribunals that sent thousands of counterrevolutionaries to be executed at the wall. He was given Cuban citizenship and shaped the revolution hand-in-hand with Castro. Che negotiated key treaties with the Soviet Union, supervised agrarian reform, and oversaw the transformation of the economy as Head of the National Bank (from 1959) and Minister of Finance and Industry (from 1961).

The committed Marxist denied himself any

The larger-than-life hero looms over the Plaza de la Revolucíon in Santa Clara (above), while a mosaic in Matanzas (right) honors the "Heroic Guerilla."

privileges and demanded sacrifice and austerity of others. He sought to crush individualism and to replace the desire for material gain with moral incentives inspired by altruism and the collective welfare. A brilliant intellectual, Che also wrote poetry, played chess, and authored several books.

An anti-imperialist, the restless romantic clung to his fervid dream of inspiring international revolution. In 1965, he renounced his Cuban citizenship and departed Cuba in secret to train leftist rebels in the Congo. The following year he appeared in Bolivia with a Cuban force, intent on sparking continent-wide insurrection. It was a disaster. Bolivian peasants betrayed him, and in 1967 Che was executed by the Bolivian army and buried in a secret grave.

Castro subsequently built a cult of Che. A "We will be like Che" campaign, invoked in the '60s, still attempts to keep revolutionary fervor alive. His motto—*Hasta la victoria siempre* (Ever onward to victory)—is splashed across Cuba. In 1997 his mortal remains were unearthed in Bolivia and taken to Cuba. ■

Iglesia del Buen Viaje is one of two fine churches gracing Remedios's Plaza Martí.

Remedios
🅜 115 E1

Museo de la Música Alejandro García Caturla
✉ Parque Martí #5
🕐 Closed Mon.
💲 $

Museo de las Parrandas
✉ Máximo Gómez #71
🕐 Closed Mon.
💲 $

Museo de Historia Local
✉ Calle Antonio Maceo #56, bet. Avenida General Carilla & Fe del Valle
🕐 Closed Mon.

Remedios

SECOND ONLY TO TRINIDAD IN PROVINCIAL COLONIAL charm, Remedios—one of Cuba's oldest settlements—clings to its well-preserved past. Spruced up after being named a national monument, its streets vibrate with color and never more than at year's end, when the otherwise somnolent town explodes in firework fever.

The town was founded in 1514 close to the Atlantic and, due to predation by pirates, relocated in 1544 to its present position, 26 miles northeast of Santa Clara. Remedios grew to become the region's most important town until the late 17th century, when catastrophe befell. In 1682 a priest was asked to exorcize the devil. He declared that the village was possessed by evil legions of demons. The Inquisition descended and numerous inhabitants were burned at the stake and their houses put to the torch. Many villagers abandoned Remedios to found a new township—today's Santa Clara (see pp. 120–121).

The town, untouched by modernity, is replete with venerable churches, houses, and other buildings spanning the last 300 years. Many are fronted by *rejas* (grilles protecting the windows) and graced by tall Spanish doors. Remedios receives very few tourists, and simply wandering the streets is its own reward.

Your starting point is **Plaza Martí,** an intimate square graced by tall palms shading a bandstand and wrought-iron benches. The ocher **Parroquial Mayor de San Juan Bautista** rears over the plaza. Dating from 1682, the church's interior features a baroque gilt altar and a vaulted mahogany ceiling, noteworthy for its stylized floral decoration. To the north, the **Museo de la Música Alejandro García Caturla** honors musical prodigy Alejandro García Caturla (1906–1940), a foremost composer, liberal social activist, and iconoclast. Born to a wealthy family, he was elected as an incorruptible municipal judge and assassinated in 1940, reputedly for refusing bribes from a local policeman due to come before Caturla on charges of beating a woman to death. Caturla's musical scores and instruments are among the exhibits.

On the plaza's southwest corner stands the **Hotel Mascotte** *(tel 42/39-5144),* newly restored to serve tourists. A plaque on the exterior wall of this small grande-dame hotel recalls that on February 1, 1899, Gen. Máximo Gómez and Robert P. Porter, acting on behalf of President William McKinley, negotiated the honorable discharge of the Mambí army following the Spanish-American War.

Worth a look, too, is the tiny **Iglesia del Buen Viaje** *(Calle Alejandro del Río #66),* occupying a small *plazuela* facing east onto Plaza Martí. Fronting it is a marble statue of Cuba's symbolic Indian maiden.

Be sure to visit the **Museo de las Parrandas,** one block east, to learn about the fascinating *parrandas* unique to the region and for which the town is famous (see sidebar right). Exhibits include flags, parade costumes, floats, and samples of fireworks used for the

Christmas festivities, when the two sides of town and neighboring villages do battle.

To learn more about Remedios' intriguing history, stop by the **Museo de Historia Local,** housed in a beautiful mansion. Guides are available to lead tours. ■

Taking a break: students at Remedios' Escuela Mártires de Barbados

Noisy nights

At year's end, the sky over Remedios and neighboring villages literally explodes in bright lights, when communities divide into rival sections to do battle for status in an orgy of pyrotechnic insanity. The Mardi Gras-style festival, called *Parrandas Remedianas,* dates from the early 19th century. Lasting through the night, the parranda begins when neon-lit murals towering 90 feet over the plaza are lit, and the entire town crowds onto the plaza. Rum flows freely, fueling wild displays of bravado as a barrage of homemade fireworks is unleashed. Each side also presents a parade float, which emerge around 3 a.m. Points are added up, but it is the bombast of fireworks rather than any artistic creativity that takes precedent in deciding the winner. ■

More places to visit in Western Cuba–North

CÁRDENAS

Founded in 1828, this sprawling port town is located 8 miles southeast of Varadero. The Cuban flag was first flown here, in 1850, when Venezuelan adventurer Narciso López launched an ill-fated invasion to spawn Cuban independence. Worth a visit are the **Catedral de la Concepción Inmaculada,** on Plaza Colón; and the **Museo Oscar María de Rojas** (*Calle Calzada #4, tel 45/52-2417, closed Mon.*), with eclectic displays portraying the city's past. The **Plaza Molokoff,** a domed market hall at Calle 12 and Avenida 3, is noteworthy. Cárdenas is most famous as being the home of Elián González, the child who became the object of a custody battle after being rescued at sea off Florida in November 1999.  115 B2

CAYO SANTA MARÍA

Currently being developed for tourism, this cay is the last of a 35-mile-long parade of cays sprinkled across the Bahía de Buena Vista, off northeast Villa Clara. Some 28 hotels are slated for the enclave of cays, served by a new 10,000-foot airstrip. Gorgeous beaches gird the isles' seaward side. The **Barco San Pasqual—**a tanker-turned-hotel off Cayo Francés—caters to scuba divers. The cays are linked to the mainland by a *pedraplen* (raised causeway); a toll applies. No Cubans are allowed. 115 E2

CUEVAS DE BELLAMAR

This mammoth cave system, at Finca la Alcancia, 3 miles southeast of Matanzas, has more than 2 miles of viewable chambers full of dripstone formations and marine fossils dating back 25 million years. Hour-long guided tours are offered. 114 B2 Closed Mon.

PLAYA JIBACOA

Playa Jibacoa, 38 miles east of Havana, is being developed for international tourism; the plan includes two golf courses and several luxury hotels. Coral formations offer fine snorkeling and diving offshore. The shore is dotted with *campismos*—back-to-basics "villa-hotels" for Cubans, to whom the beaches may soon be off-limits. The most famous—**El Abra** (*open to tourists*)—is touted as an "eco-camp," but lives up to this only in name. 114 A2

SAN MIGUEL DE LOS BAÑOS

This once thriving spa town nestles in the hills 25 miles southeast of Matanzas. It evolved in the mid-1800s, when the gentry sought the cure in local mineral baths. The town, still lived in, is in sad destitution but is fascinating for a taste of the beauty that once was. The **Balneario San Miguel,** the bathhouse erected in vaguely Muslim style, is slated to be restored, along with the rest of the town. 115 B2 ■

Horse-drawn buggies in front of the Catedral de la Concepción Inmaculada in Cárdenas

The glint of sugar-white beaches and the gleam of cobbled plazas draw visitors to a region whose diverse attractions include a vast wetland good for birding and fishing, and beautiful Trinidad, a time-warp colonial town that's a UNESCO World Heritage site.

Western Cuba–South

Young pioneers at the Ismadillo camp, between Trinidad and Cienfuegos

WESTERN CUBA–NORTH
p. 113

0   40 kilometers
0   20 miles

ARCHIPIÉLAGO DE LOS CANARREOS
p. 225

Mar Caribe

Western Cuba–South

SPANNING THE PROVINCES OF MATANZAS, CIENFUEGOS, AND SANCTI Spíritus, this region is remarkable for the variety and scope of its beauty, leaving an indelible impression on those who venture here. It is not hard to understand why this area has become one of Cuba's most popular destinations. The Autopista Nacional—the nation's sole freeway—cuts a swath through the western lowlands and skirts more easterly mountains, linking Havana with the city of Sancti Spíritus and enabling swift access to all sites via paved roads that feed south from the arterial highway.

The west comprises a vast plain farmed in sugarcane and citrus. It is also home to the pristine wetlands of the Ciénaga de Zapata, unparalleled in the Caribbean as a refuge for rare bird and other animal species. Spoonbills and neon-pink flamingoes forage in the shallows while crocodiles bask on the mudflats. Anglers are hooked on the lure of Zapata, but the area has a place in history as well. Here is the swampy Bay of Pigs, the spot where in April 1961 CIA-trained Cuban exiles sworn to overthrow Castro attempted to invade their former homeland. Today, tourists relax and sun themselves along the string of white-sand beaches that edge the famous shore. Playa Ancón, near Trinidad, is the finest beach on the coast. There and at Playas Larga and

Girón, dive facilities will outfit you to take the plunge in admiration of groves of black coral and spectacular sponges.

Pockets of Old World charm can be savored in the once prosperous cities of Sancti Spíritus and Cienfuegos. The latter is a charming port city with a well-regarded botanical garden and a small castle (the only one in the region).

Trinidad, a 19th-century living museum, enchants visitors who metaphorically step back in time. Its status as a UNESCO World Heritage site is testament to its unique importance. Adding to the calming sense of a *temps perdú*, some tourists choose the popular option of staying with a local family.

Cienfuegos and Trinidad unfold against

Area of map detail

a backdrop of kelly green—the Guamuhaya mountains, colloquially called the Sierra del Escambray. Perched amid these cool heights is a spa hotel; from here hiking trails radiate through lush forests of pine and eucalyptus, cut through by tumbling rivers. To the east, the fertile Valle de los Ingenios was the setting during past centuries for dozens of sugar plantations and today is also a UNESCO World Heritage site. The landscapes grow larger as the coast highway—Circuito Sur—swings up through the Alturas de Banao, where the wild, whiskey-brown crags resemble those of the Scottish Highlands. Horseback riding is offered at working *fincas.*

Completing the picture of nature in all its glory, in the southeastern quarter of the region, the wetlands of Sancti Spíritus province are full of limpid lagoons. Migratory waterfowl flock to these vital reserves, including those surrounding the man-made lake Presa Zaza.

Overall, tourist facilities in the region are scarce. But this may change soon, as recent years have seen the beginnings of construction on major beaches, which were badly damaged when Hurricane Michelle whipped ashore in November 2001, causing devastation throughout southern Matanzas. ■

Horse-drawn carriages in Sancti Spíritus

Parque Nacional Ciénaga de Zapata

Parque Nacional Ciénaga de Zapata

🗺 128 A2 & B2

Visitor information

✉ Oficina del Parque Nacional, Playa Larga

☎ 459/7249

Centro Ecológico

✉ Route 3-1-18, Km 21

💲 $

Only a mother could love these babies at La Boca de Guamá crocodile farm.

CROCODILES. FLAMINGOES. ANTEDILUVIAN GARFISH. THE vast Ciénaga de Zapata swamp—the Caribbean's largest wetland ecosystem—harbors a veritable Noah's ark of wildlife within its 1,745-square-mile (4,468 sq km) swath of mangroves, sawgrass, *marabú* brush, and lagoons.

Mirroring the Everglades of Florida, Zapata unrolls across a vast triangular peninsula that comprises a virtually unexplored wilderness, where sloughs and lagoons speckle a spread of tall sawgrass punctuated with clumps of hardwoods and palms. The tan carpet yields to mangrove jungle along the fringe. The wetlands surround the 13-mile-long (21 km) Bahía de Cochinos (Bay of Pigs) inlet, incised into a limestone plain that is fractured and honeycombed with *cenotes*, or water-filled sinkholes.

The park protects more than 900 species of flora, 171 bird species, 31 reptile species, and 12 mammal species. Many, such as the rare Zapata rail, are found only here. The Ciénaga de Zapata also protects a rare population of Cuban parrots. Sandhill cranes, ibis, and flamingoes are among the stilt-legged waders. Crocodiles slosh

about in the shallows. Ancient *manjuarí* (garfish) and equally endangered manatees live in the brackish lagoons, notably around the mouth of the Río Jatiguanico. Migratory waterfowl are particularly abundant October through April—a good time to visit. **Laguna de las Salinas** is recommended for fishing; contact Rumbos *(tel 459/3224)*. Tarpon, bonefish, and snook ply the waters.

Route 3-1-18 links the Bay of Pigs with the Autopista Nacional (the turn-off is at Jagüey Grande) and leads past the **Centro Ecológico,** where a museum details Zapata's ecosystems. The road meets the shore at **Playa Larga,** a small fishing village and landing site during the 1961 Bay of Pigs invasion (see sidebar p. 133). Guides are required and can be hired at the Playa Larga ranger station; you'll need your own car.

LA BOCA DE GUAMÁ

This tourist complex *(tel 459/ 2456)*, 11 miles (18 km) south of the autopista, features a host of tourist attractions, including a ceramics workshop. The highlight is the *criadero de cocodrilos* (crocodile farm), where endemic Cuban crocodiles are bred. Step up on a raised platform for a better view of the breeding lagoons. You can sample crocodile meat at the adjacent **La Boca Restaurant.** With luck, you might spot these fearsome reptiles during a boat ride to the large lake called **Laguna del Tesoro.** At its heart is **Villa Guamá** *(tel 459/5551);* 13 islands connected by boardwalks form a hotel complex of modest appeal. ■

Mangroves

Mangroves are halophytes—plants that thrive in salty conditions. Four species are found in Cuba, and the areas they inhabit teem with wildlife.

The dense, glutinous mud that mangroves live in contains almost no oxygen. Most mangroves form aerial roots, drawing in oxygen through spongy bark. One species sends out underground roots that sprout long lines of offshoots; these poke through the surface of the ground like upturned nails.

Mangroves propagate swiftly. The mangrove blooms briefly in spring, then produces a fruit from which sprouts a fleshy seedling shaped like a plumb bob. This pendulous seed, which can grow to a foot (30 cm) in length, germinates on the branch then drops like a dart. The seeds stick upright in the mud and send out roots.

A seedling can grow 2 feet (60 cm) or more its first year. By the third year it has become a mature bush, sprouting seeds that establish themselves around the parent's roots. The web of roots helps protect land against erosion by waves and builds land by filtering out silt brought to the sea by rivers. As the land builds up in their lee, the mangroves eventually strand themselves and die on land they've created.

Mangroves are vital aquatic nurseries for creatures such as oysters, sponges, crustaceans, fish, even stingrays and baby sharks. So important are these habitats that the destruction of mangroves has an inordinately harmful effect on the marine ecosystem. The nutrient-rich muds also foster the growth of microorganisms that are a food source for larger species, such as shrimps and snails.

The redolent mangroves are favored by scores of bird species, not least white ibis, flamingoes, roseate spoonbills, and the great blue heron (one of ten heron species inhabiting the halophyte wetlands of Cuba). Cormorants, pelicans, and frigate birds favor the mangroves for nesting. The Cuban parrot and bee hummingbird are also present, as is the common black hawk. *Jutías,* lizards, crocodiles, and snakes abound too. ■

Nature's land builders: mangrove roots at Laguna del Tesoro

Playa Girón

Playa Girón

🅰 128 B1

Museo Girón

✉ Playa Girón

💲 $

PLAYA GIRÓN HAS LOVELY BEACHES AND GREAT DIVING; *cenotes* (limestone sinkholes) and coves filled with warm waters offer prime snorkeling. But the area is best known for a single event: The 1961 Bay of Pigs invasion, which aimed to topple the young Castro regime, took place at Girón Beach.

Beyond Playa Larga, Route 3-1-18 unfurls toward the mouth of the Bahía de Cochinos, then swoops east along the rugged limestone shore. As you drive, note the 161 obelisks placed alongside the road—they honor the Cuban nationals killed during the invasion of 1961.

Beaches are few and far between; here the shore is lined with mangroves. Before the revolution, impoverished *cenagueros* (swamp people) eked out a meager living by burning and selling mangroves as charcoal. In 1960, Castro ordered a highway built into the swamp, and a hospital and teachers arrived, but the isolated communities remain impoverished. The area was badly affected in November 2001, by Hurricane Michelle, which flattened hundreds of flimsy thatched houses and caused widespread flooding when an 18-foot (5 m) storm surge rolled in. Fortunately, the entire region had been evacuated.

To cool off, stop at **Los Cenotes,** 5 miles (8 km) east of Playa Larga, for a dip in the 60-foot-deep (18 m) cenote; or at **Cueva de los Peces,** where a

Playa Girón today. Four decades ago, it was the Bay of Pigs battlefield.

Cubans demonstrate an antiaircraft gun used during the Bay of Pigs invasion.

Bay of Pigs invasion

In 1959, the CIA conceived a plan to land Cuban exiles in Cuba to topple Castro's regime. President John F. Kennedy vetoed an initial plan for a landing at Playa Ancón as too ambitious. Thus, on April 17, 1961, about 1,400 heavily armed exiles were put ashore at the Bay of Pigs. The landing craft grounded on coral that CIA analysts had dismissed as seaweed, and most heavy armor was lost. The supply ships were sunk by Cuban aircraft (which survived a preemptive strike meant to destroy them) as Castro directed the defense. Although U.S. jets flew reconnaissance, President Kennedy refused to order air strikes (however, six U.S. pilots did fly combat; four were killed). After 72 hours of ferocious fighting, the U.S. task force withdrew, abandoning most of the exiles—who were later traded back to the U.S. in exchange for 53 million dollars in food and medicines. ∎

flooded cave is popular with scuba divers. **Caleta Buena,** an exquisite coral cove 5 miles (8 km) east of Playa Girón, offers snorkeling in waters teeming with fish.

The beach at Playa Girón is one of the finest along the island's south coast; the **Playa Girón Scuba Diving Center** *(tel 59/7294)* offers dives. The area is popular with international vacationers, who probably regret their decision to come here—a concrete barrier stretches across the bay, cutting off tide and view; tourist facilities are few and mediocre; and a chain-link fence keeps Cubans away. The sole site of interest is **Museo Girón,** which displays a Sea-Fury fighter, Soviet T-34 and SAU-100 tanks, and other armaments from the 1961 battle; maps trace the course of events. Political commentary mocks the Cuban exiles and portrays the hardships of the cenagueros on the eve of the invasion.

In spring, the crushed carapaces of migrating crabs litter the road; those who repair tire punctures do a good business. ∎

Cienfuegos

Cienfuegos
🅰 128 C1
**Visitor
information**
✉ Avenida 54, Calles
29 & 31, Cubanacán
☎ 432/55-1680
🕐 Closed Sun.

**Museo Histórico
Provincial**
✉ Avenida 54 #2702
at Calle 27
☎ 432/51-9722
🕐 Closed Mon.
$ $

**Parque Martí's
bandstand**

IMBUED WITH FRENCH INFLUENCES, CIENFUEGOS IS ONE of Cuba's loveliest and liveliest cities, well worth a visit. Officials have put a shine to the colonial core, and sites of architectural interest dot the city. Stifling hot due to its sheltered position within a vast bay it is Cuba's third largest port city (population 139,000).

Though the city's name appropriately means "100 fires," it was actually named for Don José Cienfuegos, the Spanish captain-general who in 1817 approved a plan to settle French emigrés from Bordeaux and Louisiana in the area. Located 151 miles (244 km) southeast of Havana, the city prospered as a port for sugar and cattle. Today the sprawling city boasts Cuba's largest oil refinery and bulk sugar terminal, and the dome of a never-completed nuclear reactor rises eerily over the bay.

A broad boulevard—**Paseo del Prado** (Calle 37)—runs north–south through the city center. Its promenade, lined with busts of distinguished persons, bustles at night and on weekends. Avenida 5 de Septiembre, which leads east to Trinidad, passes by the **Necrópolis Tomás Acea** ($). This grand building is notable for its entrance gate, which boasts 64 columns—it was modeled on the Parthenon—and for its grand neoclassic tombs. At Calle 25 and Avenida 46, catch the ferry that serves **Perché,** a scenic fishing village inside the entrance to

the **Teatro Tomás Terry** *(tel 432/51-3361)*, opened in 1890 and worth a peek inside for the exquisite bas-relief of Dionysius in the proscenium and the 950-seat, Italian-style auditorium constructed of carved cedar. In its heyday, Enrico Caruso and Sarah Bernhardt performed here. Steps away is the **Colegio San Lorenzo,** with a gracious neoclassic facade. On the south side, the **Casa de la Cultura** *(tel 432/51-6584)*, located in the baroque **Palacio Ferrer** *(Calle 25 #5403)*, is in sad disrepair; ascend the *mirador,* however, for a view of the town. Lining the west side of the square are the **Galería Maroya,** displaying art; the **Museo Provincial,** brimful of period furnishings and tracing regional history from pre-Columbian days through the revolutionary war; and the red-domed **Ayuntamiento de Cienfuegos,** the seat of local government *(closed to the public).* Slake your thirst at the **Palatino,** a colonial-era bar with a patio.

The **Museo Histórico Naval** at the old naval base has a motley collection of vessels and related items. On September 5, 1957, officers here staged an ill-fated revolt against Batista.

PUNTA GORDA

South of the colonial core, the Prado becomes the Malecón, extending along the Punta Gorda peninsula, a once-exclusive area that recalls 1950s American suburbia; Detroit classics occupy driveways of the art deco bungalows. It is a pleasant 1.5-mile-long (2.4 km) stroll or carriage ride. At its base is the town's architectural jewel—the **Palacio de Valle** *(tel 432/55-1226)*. It was built between 1913 and 1917 by Acisclo del Valle y Blanco, who imported Moroccan craftsmen to design in Mudejar and Gothic style. It is now a restaurant. ∎

Museo Histórico Naval
- ✉ Avenida 60 & Calle 21
- ☎ 432/6617
- 💲 $

Museo Provincial
- ✉ Avenida 54 at 27
- 🕐 Closed Mon.

Cienfuegos Bay. The community nestles in the shadow of the **Fortaleza de Nuestra Señora de los Angeles de Jagua,** built between 1738 and 1745 to protect against pirates.

PUEBLO NUEVO

Pueblo Nuevo, the colonial core, extends west of the Prado. Avenida 54 links the Prado with **Parque Martí,** the palm-shaded main plaza laid out in 1839 with a bandstand, triumphal arch, and a statue of José Martí guarded by marble lions. The square is surrounded by stately structures of the belle epoque era. To the east is the **Catedral de la Purísima Concepción,** dating from 1869. It is resplendent with a Corinthian altar, vaulted ceiling, and French stained-glass windows of the Twelve Apostles.

A counterclockwise tour passes

Sierra del Escambray

Sierra del Escambray
🗺 128 C1 & 129 D1

THE SAW-TOOTHED ESCAMBRAY, CUBA'S SECOND HIGHEST mountain chain, rises precipitously from the coast east of Cienfuegos. Pine studded and a luscious green, these sierra—reaching 3,762 feet (1,147 m) atop Pico San Juan—offer breathtaking views of the landscape below.

The town of Yaguanabo Alto nestles at the foot of the mountains (above). *Mariposa blanca*—white butterfly—is Cuba's national flower (bottom).

The thickly forested Guamuhaya mountains, locally called the Sierra del Escambray, sheltered Che Guevara's Second Front in the late 1950s. Following Castro's victory, counterrevolutionaries were also based here (they weren't overcome until 1966). It is cool and moist at these heights (visitors should bring a jacket), and air plants weigh heavily on the moss-laden boughs of Caribbean pine and eucalyptus. The many bird species include *cotorras* (parrots).

Tumbling rivers have gnawed deep ravines into the precipitous southern flanks, where the vales are farmed in coffee. For scenic value, follow the **Valle de Mataguá,** studded with *mogotes* and featuring great dripstone formations that cling to the mountainside. The **Valle de Yaguanabo** is no less scenic, offering waterfalls and **Cueva Martín Infierno,** with exquisite gypsum flowers (*flores de yeso*) and a stalag-

mite soaring 220 feet (67 m).

Northward, the sierra ease into Villa Clara province. The long grades—the views are among the most sublime in Cuba—coil down through narrow valleys carpeted in rows of coffee bushes, descending through a landscape of sepia-toned *bohíos* (thatched huts) and lime-green tobacco fields to the tidy agricultural town of **Manicaragua.** Inset in the slopes southwest of Manicaragua is **Embalse de Hanabanilla,** a lake favored by anglers. Fishing and scenic boat trips are offered at **Hotel Hanabanilla** *(tel 42/20-2399).*

TOPES DE COLLANTES

This ecotour and spa complex nestles in the mountains, 13 miles (21 km) northwest of Trinidad. In its midst stands the towering, blunt-faced **Kurhotel** *(tel 42/54-0180),* approached via a monumental stone staircase. The spa-hotel was erected in 1936 by Fulgencio Batista as a sanatorium for victims of tuberculosis; after the revolution the disease was eradicated in Cuba.

The park is laced with hiking trails—steep and demanding—that lead to the **Salto Vega Grande** and **Salto de Caburní** waterfalls. Treks are offered *(contact Gaviota, tel 419/54-0117),* including to **Hacienda Codena,** a center for birders and hikers, with an orchid garden and trails leading to waterfalls and caves. Beware the steep road from Trinidad to Topes de Collantes—the hairpin turns hide deep troughs filled with gravel. ∎

Trinidad

TUCKED BETWEEN THE SIERRA DEL ESCAMBRAY AND THE Caribbean Sea, Trinidad is Cuba's colonial treasure. Its recently restored historic core is unequaled for its trove of pastel houses from the isle's golden age. Designated a UNESCO World Heritage site in 1988, Trinidad and the Valle de los Ingenios are living monuments to a way of life going back nearly 500 years.

Trinidad (population 30,000) nestles against a breeze-swept hillside, with views toward both mountain and sea. Founded by Diego Velázquez in 1514, it was Cuba's third settlement. A short-lived gold mine cast a warm glow on the town and its port of Casilda, point of departure for conquistador Hernán Cortés, who set out for Mexico in 1518 to conquer the Aztec empire for Spain. Fleets bearing the spoils of Mexico soon filled Trinidad's vaults. But Havana eclipsed the southern city, which became an outpost for smugglers, pirates, and slave traders. The abundance of slaves stimulated the local sugar industry, and Trinidad entered its golden age as profits from the 18th-century sugar boom bankrolled the construction of fine houses, churches, and convents. Eventually, however, the town was overshadowed by developments elsewhere in the country, and it began a slow demise.

In the 1950s, Trinidad was decreed a national monument. New development was prohibited and a restoration project was begun. Today the city is remarkably unsullied by tourism, and life moves at a yesteryear pace. About 6,000 Trinitarios still inhabit the colonial core, where the *clip-clop* of horses' hooves echoes down cobbled streets. It is a joy to wander the maze of traffic-free lanes—designed higgledy-piggledy, to thwart pirates—especially at dawn and dusk when sunlight gilds the timeworn, red-tile-roofed houses. (Note the caged songbirds hung on

Trinidad

⚑ 128 C1

Visitor information

✉ Rumbos, Calle Simon Bolívar #422

☎ 419/6464 or 419/6404

Built in 1740, Iglesia Nuestra Señora de la Candelaria de la Popa is the oldest Trinidad church still standing.

Museo Romántico

✉ Calle Fernando Hernández Echerrí #52 at Calle Simón Bolívar

☎ 419/4363

🕐 Closed Mon.

💲 $

Museo de Arqueológia y Ciencias Naturales

✉ Calle Simón Bolívar #457

☎ 419/3420

🕐 Currently closed for repairs

💲 $

Museo de Arquitectura Colonial

✉ Plaza Mayor, Calle Cispalda #83, bet. Cristo & Plaza Real del Jigüe

☎ 419/3208

🕐 Closed Fri.

💲 $

Museo de la Lucha Contra Bandidos

✉ Calle Echerrí #59 at Piro Guinalt

☎ 419/4121

🕐 Closed Mon.

💲 $

Colonial-era bedroom furnishings displayed at the Museo Romántico

exterior walls in centuries-old tradition.) Rent a room in a colonial mansion to really savor the town most fully (look for signs).

PLAZA MAYOR

The old town's compact main square is dominated by a simple cathedral and five exquisite colonial mansions painted in pastel yellow, pink, green, and blue. At its heart is a park with a statue of Terpsichore, the muse of dancing and song, and bronze greyhounds in the shade of royal palms, framed by wrought-iron fences draped with hibiscus.

The **Iglesia de la Santísima Trinidad** (Holy Trinity Church), today known as the Parroquial Mayor, was built in 1892. Inside, it wears a simple Victorian-Gothic motif but note the marble altar and statuary, including the 18th-century Cristo de la Vera Cruz (Christ of the True Cross). Just west, the **Palacio Brunet,** built in 1808, is Trinidad's most beautiful mansion. Now restored, it houses the opulent **Museo Romántico,** brimful of period furnishings and bespeaking 18th-century wealth. Highlights include lovely tilework, beautiful arched stained-glass windows, and a carved cedar ceiling.

To the southwest is **Casa**

Padrón, fronted by iron railings. The mansion houses the **Museo de Arqueológia y Ciencias Naturales,** which displays not-so-enticing exhibits ranging from pre-Columbian culture to local flora and fauna. German explorer Alexander von Humboldt stayed here during his sojourn to Cuba in 1801. Facing it on the east is the pale blue Casa de los Sánchez–Iznaga, former home of a wealthy sugar baron and today the **Museo de Arquitectura Colonial.** Here maps, scale models, and other exhibits demonstrate the architectural techniques that gave Trinidad its unique charm.

COLONIAL TREASURES

The streets fanning out from Plaza Mayor are replete with colonial treasures. The El Futuro district, west of the plaza, is highlighted by the **Antiguo Convento de San Francisco de Asís,** dating from 1813. Climb the original bell tower for a view. Today the convent houses the **Museo de la Lucha Contra Bandidos** (Museum of the Fight Against Bandits), where exhibits portray the fight to eradicate counterrevolutionaries based in the Sierra del Escambray from 1959 to 1966. Nearby, **Casa**

Carlos Merlin *(Ciro Redondo #261)* is one of several houses of smugglers and pirates who were among the citizenry during the 17th and 18th centuries.

The **Palacio Cantero** *(Calle Simón Bolívar #423)* was acquired by Justo Cantero, a powerful plantation owner. Still filled with stylish period furnishings, it is today the **Museo Histórico Municipal.** Tracing the town's history, it displays such miscellany as slave stocks and a fountain that supposedly spouted gin for gents and eau de cologne for ladies. You can ascend to the rooftop watchtower for fine views of the city.

Other mansions that speak of the glittering 18th-century lifestyle include **Casa de González Gil** *(Calles Maceo & Bolívar),* **Casa de Manuel Meyer Cantero** *(Calle Izquierdo #111; visits by request),* and **Casa del Dominicano** *(Calle Bolívar #518).* At the latter, **Teresa Paulette Cajigas** welcomes visitors to come peruse her vast collection of Christ figures. Nearby, the **Palacio Iznaga** *(Calles Bolívar & Muñoz)* awaits its reopening as a hotel.

FARTHER AFIELD

A stroll east from Playa Mayor brings you to **Plaza Santa Ana** *(Calles Camilo Cienfuegos & José Mendoza),* overlooked by the ruins of **Iglesia Santa Ana.** On the east side stands the fortress-like **Carcel Real** (Royal Prison), newly restored as a cultural center containing a ceramics workshop and artisans' workshops beneath the shaded arcade of its inner courtyard. Five blocks east and one south is **El Alfarero Cerámica** *(Calle Andrés Berro Macias #51, at Pepito Tey & Rubén Batista),* where members of a family cooperative shape clay into fine pottery.

If you crave more revolutionary lore, check out the **Casa de los Mártires de Trinidad,** *(Calle Zerquero #254),* honoring locals who died fighting to oust Batista and, later, counterrevolutionaries. Nearby, the **Fábrica de Tabacos** *(Calles Maceo #403 at Colón, tel 419/3282),* a small cigar factory, permits free visits. **Parque Céspedes,** two blocks south along Colón and one east on José Martí, is the town's official main square; it is ringed by government buildings such as the town hall—**Ayuntamiento**—and by **Iglesia de Paula;** peek in at the statuary.

Overlooking the town is the **Iglesia Nuestra Señora de la Candelaria de la Popa,** built in 1740 and in dire need of restoration. To its rear, the **Cueva de Ayala,** full of dripstone formations, serves as a disco. ∎

The 19th-century Iglesia de la Santísima Trinidad, on Plaza Mayor, epitomizes the Cuban colonial style of architecture.

Museo Histórico Municipal

✉ Calle Simón Bolívar #423, bet. Francisco Gómez Toro & Gustavo Izquierdo

☎ 419/4460

🕐 Closed Fri.

💲 $

Colonial legacies

Cuba's colonizers brought with them a Spanish aesthetic that they adapted to the tropical clime. Glorious buildings from centuries past display the evolution of an architectural heritage influenced by Mudejar style.

Cuba's first colonial settlements were of single-story adobe dwellings with palm fiber roofs. By the 17th century, houses had become more complex. Typically built of local limestone, with two stories and tiled wooden roofs, they followed the Moorish convention of having an inner courtyard that permitted air to circulate through the house—a design that lasted four centuries.

The ground floor was devoted to commerce and the upper stories to private apartments. Relatively austere, their facades were softened by turned wooden balconies and by ornamental *portales,* doors with elaborate baroque moldings that through the years grew large enough to admit a horse and carriage. Typically, these massive doors contained smaller doors—*postigos*—set at face level. The patio was accessed by an inner archway of intricate multifoil design. The hall *(zaguán)* between portal and patio was usually open to the public; inner arcades provided access to *dependencias*—commercial rooms that opened to the street. The rooms around the patio's perimeter were given to offices and storage, while those at the rear of the house surrounded a *traspatio* and were devoted to stables and domestic activities. Houses facing the plazas and main boulevards featured facades embellished by porticos—galleried walkways with arches supported by columns, providing shelter from sun and rain.

A staircase led to the private quarters—a chapel, kitchen, dining room, and bedrooms. Rooms were divided by *mamparsas,* intricately decorated inner doors something like saloon swing doors, to provide privacy while retaining a sense of communal living. By the 18th century, the typical town house had added a low-ceilinged mezzanine level *(entresuelo),* either below or above the second story and given over to offices and slave quarters.

The greatest evolution of form was in ornamentation, notably in windows, which were initially protected by wooden panels and later by the addition of ornate grilles—*rejas* or *barrotes*—of lathe-turned wood. By the 19th century, when neoclassic forms were adopted in town house design, elaborate metal grilles had replaced wood. Colored glass began to appear on the engraved panels, which featured slatted shutters *(persianas)*. These decorative windows evolved into fanciful geometric patterns, with larger windows topped by *mediopuntos*—arches that support the windows. The stained glass filtered the sun and cast diffused colors into household interiors. Additional artistic touches were lent by *cenefas*—bands of decorative plasterwork—on interior walls

The beamed roofs were often built by shipbuilders and frequently enhanced by *alfarjes*—wooden ceilings featuring angled beams set in exquisite star patterns in Mudejar fashion. ■

This typical 18th-century home (top) has *postigos* (smaller doors set within larger ones), *rejas* (ornate window grilles), and a balcony with turned wooden railings. *Mediopuntos* top windows at the Hotel Tejadillo, Havana (left), while an *alfarje* shows Moorish inspiration (above).

COLONIAL TRINIDAD STROLL

Colonial houses edge Trinidad's cobbled streets.

Colonial Trinidad stroll

Exploring the heart of colonial Trinidad, this walk follows narrow cobbled streets that wind from the main plaza into the ancient barrio of Tres Cruces, where the earthy street life is as intriguing as that of any individual site. The quarter features the city's prime concentration of exquisitely restored colonial mansions-turned-museums. There are some short but steep grades, with the ground uneven underfoot, but the ambling is peaceful and traffic-free. Wear comfortable shoes, and set out in early morning or late afternoon to avoid the midday heat.

Begin your walk at the Antiguo Convento de San Francisco de Asís. It now houses the **Museo de la Lucha Contra Bandidos** ❶ (see p. 138). Exiting the museum, walk south 80 yards (73 m) to the palm-shaded **Plaza Mayor** and the newly restored Palacio Brunet, now the **Museo Romántico** (see p. 138), on your left.

Proceed south 50 yards (46 m) and enter the **Iglesia de la Santísima Trinidad** ❷ to admire the vaulted ceiling, carved statuary, and sacred icons. Catercorner to the cathedral, facing you on your left as you exit, is the Casa de los Sánchez–Iznaga, now housing the **Museo de Arquitectura Colonial** ❸ (see p. 138). Descend the south face of the square 50 yards (46 m) to Calle Rubén

Martínez Villena and pause to admire the facade of the grand mansion before you. The home of local art critic Carlos Sotolongo, it is full of period furnishings *(visits by request).* Next door, the **Casa de Aldeman Ortíz,** at the corner of Calle Simón Bolívar, beckons you upstairs to look at artwork in the **Galería de Arte del Fondo Cubano de Bienes Culturales** *(Calle Simón Bolívar #418, tel 419/3590).*

Exiting, continue along Rubén Martínez Villena to the plaza's west corner, and Casa Padrón, housing the **Museo de Arqueológia y Ciencias Naturales** (see p. 138). Proceed along Villena, noting the **Templo de Yemayá** *(Calle Villena #59)* on your left; it features Santería altars and hosts occasional religious ceremonies. A few steps farther is **Plaza Real del Jigüe** ❹, an enchanting plaza where the **Restaurante El Jigüe** *(tel 419/6476)*, with a facade of ceramic tiles, offers refreshments. Mass is still held beneath the calabash tree at its heart, planted in 1929; the tradition dates back to 1513, when the first Mass was held here. Note the original stone-and-lime masonry exposed in a portion of the **Ayuntamiento y Cárcel**—the old town hall and jail—on the southeast corner.

After three more blocks you'll emerge on **Plaza de las Tres Cruces** ❺, an undeveloped area of bare earth in the heart of Trinidad's oldest neighborhood; the three wood crosses denote the terminus of the city's annual Easter procession. Turn right and right again on Calle Juan Manuel Márquez. Turn left on Calle Bolívar and climb the steep, narrow path 200 yards (183 m) to **Iglesia Nuestra Señora de la Candelaria** ❻ (sometimes called Ermita la Popa), the city's oldest church. It is closed for restoration, but the view is superb.

Retrace your steps downhill then turn left on Calle José Mendoza. After three blocks, turn right onto Calle Juan Manuel Márquez, which descends 70 yards (64 m) past a trio of houses with photogenic elevated galleries.

Turn left at Calle Jesús Menéndez into intimate, triangular **Plazuela de Segarte** ❼, surrounded by venerable houses fronted by *rejas* and tall carriage doors. At the junction with Calle Fernando Hernández Echerrí is the **Casa de la Trova** *(Leonor Pérez, tel 419/6445)*, where traditional music performances are hosted. You will see Plaza Mayor 100 yards (91 m) east. En route, on your right, pause to admire the **Casa de los Conspiradores**, with an impressive ocher facade and wooden balcony. Reentering Plaza Mayor, ascend the wide staircase to the **Casa de la Música** ❽ *(tel 419/3414)*, exhibiting musical instruments through the ages. ∎

🅼 See area map pages 128–129
▶ Plaza Mayor
↔ 1.5 miles (2 km)
🕑 2 hours
▶ Plaza Mayor

NOT TO BE MISSED
- Museo Romántico
- Plaza Real del Jigüe
- Casa de la Música

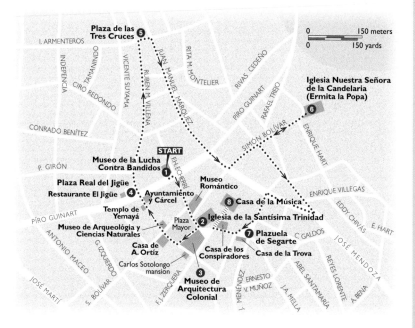

Península de Ancón

CURLING AROUND THE SHELTERED WATERS OF THE Ensenada de Casilda like a shepherd's crook, the pencil-thin Península de Ancón is fringed by fine beaches whose white sands shelve into warm, tranquil green-blue waters. The longest and most beautiful beach—a stone's throw from Trinidad—is being developed.

LA BOCA

This charming fishing village, beside the mouth of the Río Guaurabo, 5 miles (8 km) west of Trinidad, is favored by Trinitarios on weekends for its proximity to town and for its pocket-size beaches tucked into tree-shaded coves. Exposed coral heads provide pedestals for enjoying vistas of the **Sierra del Escambray** while cooling your heels in jade waters. Bougainvillea bowers spill over simple, timeworn red-tile-roofed cottages—many of them offering rooms for private rental. A string of beaches backed by sea grapes unspools south along the peninsula and await development. Facilities are limited—bring a packed lunch.

The **Casa Museo Alberto Delgado,** 2 miles (3 km) east of La Boca, honors a Castro sympathizer killed during the counterrevolutionary war. Nearby, **Finca María Dolores** (tel 419/3581), on the north bank of the Río Guaurabo, is an old-time working farm. Here, you can witness cockfights (the roosters' spurs are clipped to appease tourists' sensitivities) and traditional farm activities.

PLAYA ANCÓN

This 2-mile-long (3 km) sliver of beach vies for honors as the most beautiful shoreline along the south coast of Cuba. The turquoise Caribbean proves perfect for snorkeling and for scuba diving amid coral reefs—notably **Cayo Blanco de Casilda,** with the largest black coral grove in Cuba. The **Hotel Ancón** (tel 419/6120) and new, adjacent **Hotel Brisas Trinidad del Mar** (tel 419/6500) offer scuba diving and water sports, including sailboats, as does the **Puertosol Marina Trinidad** (tel 419/6205), which also has a "seafari" to Cayo Blanco. On-going development is changing the face of the placid beach, with several large-scale hotels slated to open.

The barren swath of marsh backing the peninsula draws birds in abundance. A shuttle runs regularly between Trinidad and the beach, 10 miles (16 km) away. ■

Trinitarios cool off at La Boca.

Valle de San Luís

NICKNAMED VALLE DE LOS INGENIOS FOR THE SUGAR MILLS *(ingenios)* that once dotted this broad sprawling valley, the Valle de San Luís draws its appeal from its scenic beauty and historic value as an open-air museum recalling the heyday of sugar. Some of the estate houses and mills still stand; others are being restored to their former grandeur, broadening the appeal of the bucolic landscape.

Valle de San Luís
🅰 129 DI

Hacienda Iznaga
✉ Iznaga
☎ 419/7241

The Carretera de Sancti Spíritus, linking Trinidad with the city of Sancti Spíritus, cleaves a path through the Valle de San Luís, which was named a UNESCO World Heritage site for its ingenios legacy. Fields of sugarcane, green as limes, carpet the valley, framed to the north by a crescent of mountains and to the south by the Caribbean Sea. During the 18th century, this was Cuba's most productive sugar-growing region, with 40 mills to attest to its wealth and importance. By the mid-19th century, the aging mills—many of which were destroyed in the wars of independence—proved unable to compete with the more advanced central plantation system that had been introduced elsewhere in Cuba.

Hacienda Iznaga is the most complete estate in existence, with a 148-foot-tall (45 m) tower that serves as the valley's emblem. The main house, completed in 1845, sits atop a breeze-swept hillock 8 miles (13 km) east of Trinidad. It features period costumes and other exhibits, and a restaurant serves up food and vistas across the valley. The slave quarters and warehouses still stand. You can ascend the 136 stairs of the tower (Torre de Manaca Iznaga) for the sweeping view. Local artisans sell lace items at its base.

Hacienda los Molinos, farther east, operates as a cattle *finca.* Guided horseback trips head into the nearby **Alturas de Sancti Spíritus,** and there are rooms for overnight stays. Nearby, the **Casa**

Guachinango welcomes visitors for horseback rides and *criollo* fare at this restored 18th-century hacienda. The Italianate **Hacienda Jesús de Nazareno de Buenavista,** and **Casa del Ingenio Guaimaro,** boasting fine murals, are being restored; follow signs from the highway. The latter will feature a **Museo de Caño de Azúcar** (sugarcane museum).

A steam train *(Rumbos, tel 419/6464)* runs scenic rides from the Trinidad terminal into the valley. ■

The seven-story tower at Hacienda Iznaga

Sancti Spíritus

Sancti Spíritus
⚑ 129 D1

DESPITE ITS SIZE AND REGIONAL IMPORT AS PROVINCIAL capital at the midpoint of Cuba, Sancti Spíritus is limited in its tourist appeal and can be fully explored in a day. Quaint colonial streets are worth browsing, bolstered by a historic church of note.

This city of 105,000 straddles the Carretera Central, 245 miles (394 km) east of Havana. Founded in 1522 on the east bank of the Río Yayabo, Sancti Spíritus prospered on sugar and the slave trade. It has an expansive colonial core that has been partly restored.

At the city's heart is the bustling **Plaza Serafín Sánchez,** named for a local patriot killed in 1896. The **Biblioteca** (library) and **Centro Provincial de Patrimonio Cultural** (Provincial

Dominoes is a national pastime in Cuba.

Center of Cultural Heritage), on the west side, and the **Teatro Principal** and **Hotel Plaza,** to south and east, respectively, have neoclassic facades of modest appeal. Note the statue of local hero Judás Martínez Moles (1861–1915) in the *plazuela* tucked off the northeast corner.

Calle Independencia flows from Plaza Sanchez's southeast corner one block to the **Mercado Agropecuario,** where agricultural produce is sold. Immediately

to the plaza via Calle Céspedes, stop at the **Museo Casa de Serafín Sánchez,** where the local hero of the wars of independence was born.

THE COLONIAL CORE

Most sites of interest are concentrated southwest of Plaza Sánchez. Stroll 200 yards (183 m) along Calle Máximo Gómez to **Plaza Honorato del Castillo,** a triangular plazuela anchored by a statue of local doctor Rudesindo Antonio García Rojo. To the north and east are ancient arcades where bootblacks gather and a giant brass bell is displayed. The **Casa de la Trova,** on the west side, hosts performances of traditional music and dance. Dominating the plaza, to the south, is the splendidly preserved **Parroquial Mayor de Sancti Spíritus,** dating from 1680. The triple-tiered, 98-foot-tall (30 m) bell tower, topped by a cupola, was added in 1764. The church is simple within, with an *alfarje* ceiling of intricately crossed beams.

Following Avenida Menéndez as it curls south, you drop to the Río Yayabo, spanned by a triple-arched stone bridge completed in 1825. En route you'll pass the three-story Palacio del Vallé–Iznaga, the town's finest mansion and home to the **Museo de Arte Colonial.** Its 13 rooms are crammed with period furnishings and decorative pieces portraying the lavish lifestyle of an earlier time, when the mansion was owned by one of Cuba's wealthiest families. More modest abodes line Calle el Llano, an exquisitely restored cobbled street due east of Menéndez. Llano and the surrounding streets vibrate with color: Venerable low-roofed houses fronted by hanging lanterns and *rejas* of lathe-spun wood and wrought-iron are painted in every shade of soft pastel. At dusk, slanting rays splash the scene in fiery orange and violet. ■

south is the **Fondo Cubano de Bienes Culturales,** worth a peek for the artwork of painter Oscar Fernández Morera (1890–1946) displayed in its **Galería Oscar Morera** (*Calle Independencia #55, tel 41/27106, closed Mon.*). Follow Independencia north three blocks from the plaza to **Parque Maceo,** an intimate plaza anchored by a simple church—**Iglesia de Nuestra Señora de la Caridad.** On the park's southeast corner is the **Fundación de la Naturaleza y el Hombre,** a small museum celebrating the fantastic journey of writer Antonio Nuñez (1923–1998) and a team of Cubans in 1996, who paddled 10,889 miles (17,520 km) in dugout canoes from the source of the Amazon to the Bahamas. Returning

Fundación de la Naturaleza y el Hombre
- ✉ Calle Cruz Pérez #1, at Céspedes & Independencia
- ☎ 41/28342
- 🕓 Closed Sun.
- 💲 $

Museo Casa de Serafín Sánchez
- ✉ Calle Céspedes #112, at Sobral & San Cristóbal
- ☎ 41/27791
- 🕓 Closed Mon.
- 💲 $

Museo de Arte Colonial
- ✉ Calle Plácido #74, at Boquete de Guairo & Ave. Jesús Menéndez
- ☎ 41/25455
- 🕓 Closed Mon.
- 💲 $

Trinidad to Cumanayagua loop

Superbly scenic yet virtually devoid of traffic, this circular drive offers elevated vistas over the Caribbean Sea and the rolling quiltwork of Villa Clara. In a dizzyingly ascent into the lushly forested Sierra del Escambray, you'll experience some of Cuba's most pristine mountain scenery before snaking down through a quintessentially Cuban landscape of tobacco and citrus farms. There are some steep grades, with dangerous hairpin turns, that are slick in wet weather.

Begin in **Trinidad ❶** (see pp. 137–143), exiting west along Calle Pino Guinart and the Circuito Sur. Three miles (5 km) west of town, you'll see a sign for Topes de Collantes to the right; follow the road north as it dips and weaves through the Río Cañas valley. Gradually you ascend into the Sierra del Escambray; the road curves steeply—be cautious, because pine needles litter the surface and the curves are studded with large potholes. After 8 miles (13 km), you arrive at **Topes de Collantes ❷**, an area developed as a spa resort; stop to explore the Kurhotel *(tel 42/40219)* or hike one of the trails before continuing north; follow the road that curls around the hotel.

Two miles (3 km) north of Topes de Collantes, bear right at the Y-junction. The next few miles offer breathtaking views through gaps in the pine and eucalyptus forest. Dark, foreboding mountains rise to the west; eastward, you gaze down through the Valle de Caburní. About 8 miles (13 km) later, the road begins to corkscrew down the northern flank of the mountains to the village of **Jibacoa.** The slopes are patterned in rows of green corduroy—coffee bushes—coiling along the narrow valley sides. The descent eases, and the views northward open up, revealing *bohíos* (thatched huts), royal palms, and blood-red fields tilled by oxen.

Ten miles (16 km) beyond Jibacoa, you arrive at **Manicaragua ❸**, a modest agricultural town. Turn left in the town center onto

Transporting sugarcane near Jibacoa

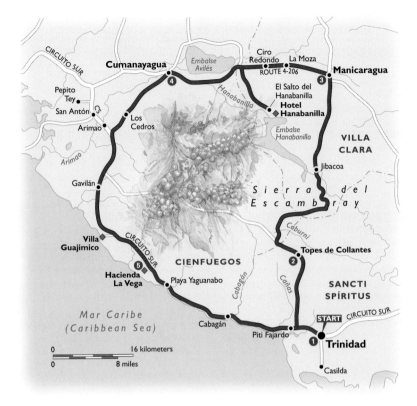

Route 4-206. Three miles (5 km) beyond the community of Ciro Redondo, turn left for **Embalse Hanabanilla** (5 miles/8 km), where you can dine at the **Hotel Hanabanilla** *(tel 42/20-2399)* and enjoy views of the pea-green lake.

Retrace your route to the main highway and continue west to **Cumanayagua** ❹. At the west end of town, go south. In season, a perfume wafts over the orange groves that extend for miles around. Beyond Los Cedros, you'll see the Circuito Sur. Turn left. The Escambray soon soar off to your left. The massif forms a rain shadow, and with it comes an abrupt change in the landscape: Citrus fades to golden grasslands grazed by humped cattle. The plain undulates with rounded hillocks.

After about 15 miles (24 km) beyond Los Cedros, the road touches the coast at the mouth of the Río La Jutía. Access the beckoning white-sand beach by a side road that leads west 1 mile (1.6 km) to **Villa Guajimico**

> 🗺 See area map pages 128–129
> ► Trinidad
> ↔ 96 miles (153 km)
> ⏱ 5 hours
> ► Trinidad

NOT TO BE MISSED
- Topes de Collantes
- Embalse Hanabanilla
- Hacienda La Vega

(tel 432/45-1206). Seven miles (11 km) farther south, you'll pass **Hacienda La Vega** ❺, a cattle *finca* where horseback rides are offered. The Escambray crowd down to the shore as you continue eastward, crossing rivers and deep ravines. White beaches sparkle on the river-mouth shoals. Beyond the Río Cabagán, you enter Sancti Spíritus province, 9 miles (14 km) beyond which you power up the hill that returns you to Trinidad. ∎

More places to visit in Western Cuba—South

AREA PROTEGIDA JOBO ROSADO
New in 2001, this nature reserve is located near the town of Yaguajay on the north shore of Sancti Spíritus. It protects 186 species of fauna, including endemic iguana subspecies and one of Cuba's largest colonies of endemic cranes *(Graus canadensis nesiotes)*. Visit some of at least 35 caverns to marvel at the subterranean galleries and pre-Columbian petroglyphs, including 17 large murals. **Gaviota** *(tel 7/204-5245)* offers tours that include a steam train ride from Central Simón Bolívar.  129 E2

CENTRAL AUSTRALIA
This sugarcane processing factory, on Route 3-1-18 a mile south of the autopista, was the site of Castro's headquarters during the Bay of Pigs invasion. The adjacent **Museo de la Comandancia** *(closed Mon.)* displays a hodgepodge of aircraft remnants. Built in 1904, the factory itself is off-limits; no photos are permitted. 128 B2

FINCA FIESTA CAMPESINA
Billed as a "peasant's farm," this tourist way station—at the junction of Jagüey Grande and Playa Girón, at Km 142 on the autopista—displays a *trapiche* (sugarcane press) where fresh-squeezed juice is served. Other features include a restaurant, a cock-

fight pit, and a small zoo with crocodiles, snakes, agoutis, deer, and birds. 128 B2 ☎ 59/3224

JARDÍN BOTÁNICO DE CIENFUEGOS
This 232-acre garden near Guaos, 10 miles (16 km) east of Cienfuegos, boasts more than 2,000 species of tropical plants, with hundreds that are rare. Rubber trees, bamboo, and cactuses are represented, as are more than 300 palm species. Edward Atkins, a New Englander and local sugar plantation owner, created the garden in 1899 to propagate more productive sugarcane strains. Harvard University later administered the garden; it became one of the largest, most beautiful collections in the tropical world. Today the Cuban Academy of Sciences maintains the garden, which is recovering from hurricane damage. It is approached via an avenue of palms that extends across the highway to **Pepito Tey,** a village with a *central* (sugar mill) of that name. 128 C1 ☎ 432/45115

PRESA ZAZA
Cuba's largest man-made lake supplies Sancti Spíritus province with fresh water and anglers with trout and largemouth bass. The lake is surrounded by wetlands alive with thousands of waterfowl. The **Hotel Zaza** *(tel 41/27015)* is a base for hunting and fishing. 129 E1 ∎

Royal palms stand sentry over Sancti Spíritus province.

Home to Cuba's most spectacular beaches, this idyllic region beckons divers to clear blue waters and coral reefs teeming with life. Resorts line offshore cays, while provincial cities offer pockets of colonial charm.

Central Cuba

Cayo Coco

Central Cuba.

THE HEARTLAND OF CUBA—COMPRISING CIEGO DE ÁVILA AND CAMAGÜEY provinces—is relatively sparsely populated and offers few sites of historical interest. Yet the region is one of Cuba's most visited, for here visitors come to sun themselves on glorious beaches or dive the coral reefs of the Cayerías del Norte off the region's north shore. The Carretera Central speeds through the heart of the region, and arterial highways permit forays afield. More scenic is the Circuito Norte, which parallels the north coast.

Ciego de Ávila province, the narrow waist of Cuba, is pancake-flat and lushly green. Citrus and sugarcane farms dot the landscape, and pineapple is grown around the eponymous capital city. Freshwater lakes offer prime fishing for bass. The heat builds gradually as you travel eastward, until the verdant landscape withers to a featureless plain shaded by broad trees spreading their gnarled branches long and low to the ground.

Neighboring Camagüey province is the

color of honey, a rolling upland plain where hot winds whistle through tall, rain-starved grasslands and *vaqueros* (cowboys) survey the land from their saddles. This was a forested region when Columbus came ashore. During the 17th and 18th centuries, the region evolved as the center of cattle-breeding. Camagüey province is still dominated by state-owned *ganaderías* (ranches).

The south coast is sparsely populated. Much is swampy, providing a habitat for

Under the rainbow in the central Cuban town of Manicaragua, where tobacco is king

large bird populations and crocodiles that slosh along the mangrove-lined shore. A few paved roads slice through the bright green carpet of sugarcane and sedge and lead to humble fishing villages, such as Júcaro and Santa Cruz del Sur. These serve as jumping-off points for forays to the Jardines de la Reina (Queen's Gardens)—a vast archipelago of coral cays and turquoise ocean shallows. Tourist facilities are meager, but scuba diving and sportfishing are offered. New eco-focused hotels are in the works.

Currently, development is concentrated on Cayo Coco and Cayo Guillermo, favored by Canadians, Europeans, and South Americans. Coco and Guillermo are part of the Jardines del Rey (King's Gardens), a larger system of cays and isles off the north coast. The hotel star ratings are overly generous, but the diving here and off Playa Santa Lucía (in northeast Camagüey) is fabulous; more than 50 coral species thrive in one of the world's longest reefs. Flamingoes inhabit the inshore lagoons, looking like feathered roses atop spindly pink stalks, quite at odds with their blue surroundings. Note that the cays do not have public transportation, and Cubans are forbidden to mingle with tourists.

As for the cities, Ciego de Ávila is rather forlorn. Save your urban exploration for Camagüey, where many buildings and plazas have been impressively restored. ■

Ciego de Ávila

Ciego de Ávila

🗺 153 B2

Visitor information

✉ Agencia de Viajes Islazul, Calle Joaquín Agüero #85

☎ 33/25314

THE PROVINCIAL CITY OF CIEGO DE ÁVILA DRAWS FEW visitors despite its strategic location midway between Sancti Spíritus and Camagüey. Cuba's main highway—Carretera Central (in town it is called Calle Chicho Valdés)—cuts through the heart of the city (population 85,000), where horse-drawn wagons predominate.

Officially founded in 1840, today Ciego de Ávila is known as the "pineapple town" for the acres of sweet, juicy *piñas* grown locally and processed at nearby Empresa Piña. The city is laid out in a grid centered on **Parque Martí,** graced by shade trees and Victorian-style lampposts. A small bust of national hero José Martí stands in the center of the plaza. The few buildings of note include, on the south side, the **Poder Popular**—the old town hall—dating from 1911. One block south, on Calle Joaquín Agüera where it crosses Calle Honorato de Castillo, is the baroque **Teatro Principal** *(tel 33/22086).* The theater's interior is elaborately decorated in baroque and neoclassic styles, highlighted by statuary and a grand marble staircase.

Other points of interest include the **Fortín de la Trocha,** at the west end of Calle Máximo Gómez. A remnant of Cuba's own Maginot Line, this is the only fortress still standing (see sidebar left). One block west, the Instituto de Segunda Enseñanza houses the **Museo Provincial** *(tel 33/28431),* with a motley collection of mounted fauna, pre-Columbian artifacts, and exhibits honoring local war heroes. ∎

Defense!

During the first war of independence (1868–1878), a defensive line of 43 forts extending 42 miles (67 km), from Morón in the north to Júcaro in the south, blocked the westward advance of the rebel army. The line, conceived by Spanish Gen. Blas Villate de la Hera and called La Trocha, was penetrated in 1875 but fortified during the second war of independence (1895–1898). Rebel forces under Gen. Antonio Maceo broke through the line again in 1895 and ravaged western Cuba. ∎

Along Calle Martí in Morón, a crossroads near Ciego de Ávila

Morón & nearby

GATEWAY TO THE JARDINES DEL REY, MORÓN IS A CROSS-roads town linking Ciego de Ávila to the Circuito Norte—the north coast highway. A place to stock up on supplies rather than a sightseeing destination in its own right, the City of the Rooster nonetheless boasts some intriguing architecture and adjoining wetlands to lure anglers and birders.

Morón (population 50,000) was originally settled in 1643 by Andalusians, who named it after their hometown in Spain. Its nickname derives from early days, when a corrupt judge who had earned the unflattering sobriquet "the cock of Morón" was banished from town. In the 1950s, Fulgencio Batista presided over the unveiling of an emblematic rooster at the southern entrance to Morón. It was toppled following the revolution, but a **bronze rooster** replaced it in 1981; it stands beside the clock tower outside the Hotel Morón on Avenida Tarafa, the town's main boulevard.

Tarafa runs north past a 1923 Teutonic-style railway station with wrought-iron awnings, and becomes Calle Martí. Lined with columned porticos, Martí leads into the old quarter, centered on **Parque Agramonte,** at the north end of town. This tiny square, currently being restored, is surrounded by a simple church—**Iglesia de Lourdes** (tel 335/3634)—and quaint, red-tile-roofed houses painted in soft pastels. Among them is the **Casa Parroquial,** the traditional home of the priest. A visit to the **Museo Caonabo** is worthwhile for its collection of pre-Columbian artifacts.

A vast wetland system of sedges and mangroves spreads over the coastal plains north of town. At its heart is **Laguna de la Leche** (Lagoon of the Milk), a jade jewel lent its opaque complexion by deposits of gypsum. Gawky flamin-

goes tip-toe around, and quails, ducks, and other waterfowl flock in to the saltwater lake in such numbers that the rush of their wings makes a muffled roar. Their presence draws hunters to **Aguachales de Falla,** a game reserve on the lake's northwest shore. Anglers flock to **Centro Pescadores la Redonda** (tel 335/2236), a fishing lodge on the shores of Laguna la Redonda, which bubbles with over-size largemouth bass, tilapia, and carp. The Morón-Cayo Coco highway runs between the two lakes and passes **Comunidad Celia Sánchez,** a rural community built atop a hillock with houses in faux-timbered, high-gabled Dutch style—hence its colloquial name, **Pueblo Holandés.** If lingering by night, check out the local cabaret in **La Cueva** (tel 335/2239), a cave on Laguna de la Leche's south shore. ■

Morón & nearby

⚑ 153 B3

Museo Caonabo

✉ Calle Martí #374 at Sergio Antuña

☎ 335/4501

🕐 Closed Mon.

💲 $

Morón's large metal rooster is programmed to crow at dawn and dusk.

Jardines del Rey

Jardines del Rey
🅰 153 B3, C3
**Visitor
information**
✉ Rumbos S.A.,
Nuevitas
☎ 32/44754

SPANNING THE WIDTH OF CIEGO DE ÁVILA AND CAMAGÜEY provinces, this wilderness of sandy coral islands crouches 5 to 15 miles (8 to 24 km) offshore in a great line that parallels the coast for 248 miles (400 km). These island jewels beckon with whiter-than-white sands washed by waters of startling turquoise hues.

**Royal palms
sway on their
namesake beach,
Playa Palma Real,
Cayo Coco.**

The Jardines del Rey (King's Gardens) are one of the least disturbed areas of Cuba. Few among the 400 or so low-lying isles and cays are inhabited or even accessible, and only two—Cayo Coco and Cayo Guillermo—have been developed for tourism so far. The cays—also known as the Cayéria del Norte—are smothered in scrub and mangrove marshes that harbor *jabalí* (wild pigs), iguanas, and more than 150 species of birds. Reefs run virtually unbroken the entire length of the cays' north shores, offering superb snorkeling and diving. Be sure to pack insect repellent for the mosquitoes.

CAYO COCO

On Cayo Coco, 56 miles (90 km) northeast of Ciego de Ávila, at least half a dozen resort hotels now operate under foreign management, and Cuba plans to build 13,000 hotel rooms. Twelve miles (19 km) of

pedraplen (raised causeway).

Much of the cay is within **Parque Nacional El Bagá** *(tel 33/30-1061),* which has trails; a crocodile farm, butterfly garden, and cultural center are planned. Within its fold is **Cueva del Jabalí** *(tel 33/30-1206),* a dank cave-turned-bar with glittery cabarets at night. Plan guided horseback rides at **Sitio la Güira** *(tel 33/30-1208).* Sportfishing and diving are offered at **Marina Aguas Tranquilas** *(tel 33/30-1221),* on Playa Colorada, and at major hotels, where you can rent bicycles, scooters, and cars. Day tours from Havana *(Cubatur, tel 7/33-4135)* and other major towns are offered.

CAYO GUILLERMO

Two miles (3 km) west of Cayo Coco is Cayo Guillermo. Its chief draw is **Playa El Paso,** a 3-mile-long (5 km) beach. Farther west are **Playa El Medio,** backed by huge dunes, and **Playa Pilar,** named for Hemingway's sportfishing vessel. Water sports are available, and **Marina Cayo Guillermo** *(tel 33/30-1738)* offers "seafari" excursions and boat rentals.

CAYO SABINAL

The easternmost cay, Cayo Sabinal is reached by a road of hard-packed coral with police checkpoint (passports required). Sabinal is booked to receive 12,000 hotel rooms; go now, while it remains undeveloped.

The finest beach is **Playa Los Pinos;** you'll likely have the place to yourself. Food is served at a beach bar. Smaller **Playa Brava** and **Playa Bonita** extend west and east, respectively; the latter has a rustic bar. **Faro Colón,** an 1850 lighthouse, and the remains of a fortress—**Fuerte San Hilario**—guard the island's eastern tip. You'll need a 4WD vehicle to negotiate the soft sand that smothers the track. ∎

frosted sands line the 20-mile-long (32 km) Atlantic shore of the isle, divided westward into Playa Colorada, Playa Larga, and Playa Prohibida. To escape the crowds, venture to **Playa Los Flamencos** or take to the sea in a catamaran or windsurfer. On the smaller **Cayo Paredón Grande,** northeast of Cayo Coco, visit the **Faro Diego Velázquez,** an 1859 lighthouse at the cay's northern tip.

You can reach Cayo Coco from San Rafael via a 17-mile-long (27 km) causeway across Bahía de Perros (Bay of Dogs). At a security checkpoint *(toll),* show your passport.

The bay hosts the Caribbean's largest flock of flamingoes. At sunrise and dusk they fly over the tombolo; watch them at the **Parador La Silla** restaurant, midway along the

Reef world

Among the most biologically productive ecosystems on Earth, coral reefs encircle Cuba's shores—luring scuba divers and snorkelers from afar.

Coral reefs are built by tiny organisms called polyps—the corals. Each polyp, some no larger than a pinhead, secretes calcium carbonate from its base to form an external skeleton—a protective chamber in which it lives. But it's strength in numbers that produce a reef. New polyps can bud off the old, securing their own skeletons in the interstice and atop older polyps; some species beget offspring that smother their parents and use those skeletons as foundations on which to cement their own. Over the span of thousands of generations, millions of polyps work together to create an intricately structured limestone reef.

Reefs are divided into life zones defined by depth, water temperature, and light. Distinct corals inhabit each zone. They come in a profusion of forms: massive brain corals; translucent saucer corals; gracefully curled wire corals; elkhorn coral (named for its resemblance to an elk's antlers), which can span 10 feet; and pillar coral, which sends its perfectly cylindrical columns shooting sunward as high as 15 feet.

Each reef is a subaqueous metropolis that is also home to a multitude of other creatures: sea urchins, moray eels, lobsters, octopuses, anemones, tubular sponges, and, of course, fishes large and small. Huge grouper and cubera snappers hang suspended as if by invisible strings. Manta rays, and hawksbill and loggerhead turtles cruise leisurely by. Sharks lurk beneath ledges and inhabit tunnels. Schools of permit and crevalle jacks stream past, glittering like foil. And an endless parade of brightly colored fish add to the beauty: blue tangs, queen angelfish, yellow-and-purple fairy basslet, iridescent blue chromis, and black-and-white-striped sergeant-majors. ■

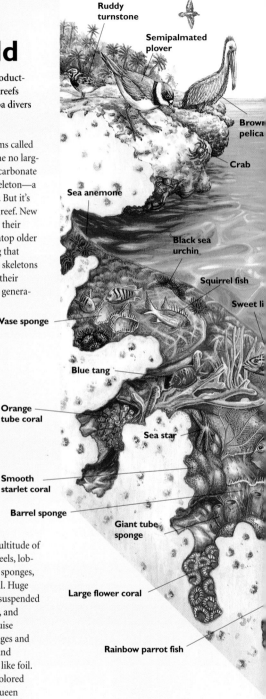

Ruddy turnstone
Semipalmated plover
Brown pelica
Crab
Sea anemone
Black sea urchin
Squirrel fish
Sweet li
Vase sponge
Blue tang
Orange tube coral
Sea star
Smooth starlet coral
Barrel sponge
Giant tube sponge
Large flower coral
Rainbow parrot fish

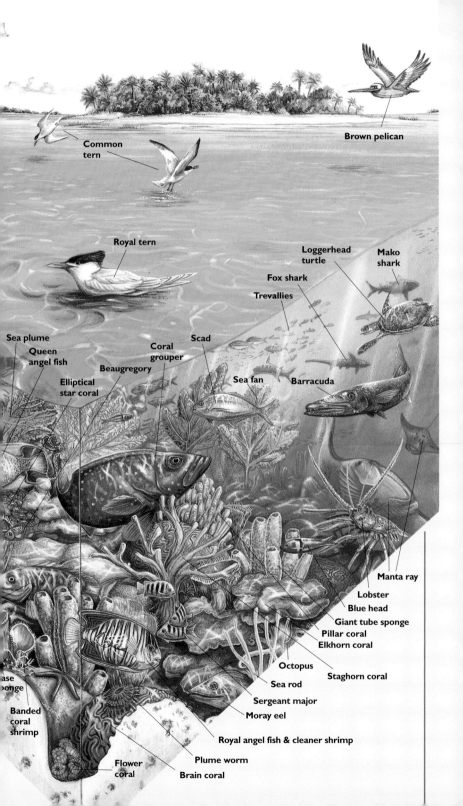

Brown pelican

Common tern

Royal tern

Loggerhead turtle

Mako shark

Fox shark

Trevallies

Sea plume

Queen angel fish

Coral grouper

Scad

Beaugregory

Elliptical star coral

Sea fan

Barracuda

Manta ray

Lobster

Blue head

Giant tube sponge

Pillar coral

Elkhorn coral

Staghorn coral

Octopus

Sea rod

Sergeant major

Moray eel

Royal angel fish & cleaner shrimp

Banded coral shrimp

...ase ...ponge

Plume worm

Brain coral

Flower coral

Camagüey evolved its own architectural style, simpler than that of Havana and typified by broad eaves supported by unadorned wooden beams.

Camagüey

Camagüey
153 B2
Visitor information
Islazul, Calle Ignacio Agramonte #448
32/29-2550

ONE OF THE ISLAND'S ORIGINAL SEVEN SETTLEMENTS, Camagüey is a labyrinth of narrow, winding lanes and cul-de-sacs; its defensive layout, once meant to thwart pirates, now serves to confound tourists. Persistence pays off, however, revealing the city's charms—its restored buildings, colonial plazas, and ubiquitous *tinajones,* the earthenware rain collectors that are a symbol of the city.

Founded in 1515 under the name Puerto Príncipe, Camagüey moved to its present site on the north bank of the Río Jatibonico in 1528. The town prospered from its position at the heart of cattle country—attracting pirates on numerous occasions—and by the 19th century it was the second largest city in Cuba (it has since been superceded by Santiago de Cuba).

COLONIAL PLAZAS
The heart of the city is compact **Parque Agramonte,** named

for Maj. Gen. Ignacio Agramonte (1841–1873), who led the city's rebel forces against Spain during the first war of independence. He is honored in bronze, riding his charger. On the south side of the park is the austere **Catedral Metropolitana de Nuestra Señora de Candelaria** *(tel 32/29-4965),* dating from 1864. First erected in 1530, the first structure was felled by an earthquake.

Plaza de los Trabajadores (Workers' Plaza) is an irregular polygon centered on an aged ceiba tree. It is dominated by **Cathedral Nuestra Señora de la Merced** *(tel 32/29-2740),* built in 1748. This stately church boasts a neo-Gothic gilt altar, baroque balconies, and a frescoed ceiling. Be sure to stop by the cloisters to the left, where supplicants pray beside the Santo Sepulcro, a silver coffin that prior to the revolution was borne through the town in procession. Skeletons are still on view in the catacombs below.

On the square's west side stands **Casa Natal Ignacio Agramonte,** birthplace of the aristocratic war hero. The 18th-century mansion, heavy with hardwood balustrades, was seized by the government during the war; it later served as the Spanish consulate. Impressively restored, it displays sumptuous period furnishings.

Photogenic **Plaza San Juan de Díos,** the most intimate square, is now a national monument surrounded by 18th-century houses gaily painted in bright pastels. The cream-and-green **Convento y Hospital de San Juan de Díos** dates from 1728 and features handsome arcaded cloisters added in 1840; the adjoining church boasts a splendid mahogany ceiling and commanding bell tower. The Centro Provincial de Patrimonio, which oversees the city's restoration, is housed here; a portion is being refitted as a hotel. The **Museo de San Juan de Díos** offers meager exhibits about the town's history.

FARTHER AFIELD
Six blocks west of Parque Agramonte, on Calle Martí, **Convento de Nuestra Señora del Carmen** is slated for a much-needed restoration. Built in 1825, this once noble convent overlooks a cobbled plaza lined with traditional 18th-century houses. The **Teatro Prin-**

cipal *(Calle Padre Valencia, tel 32/29-3048),* which once drew Enrico Caruso and other operatic luminaries, is also the worse for wear. It is open intermittently; pop in to admire the marble staircase, gilt chandeliers, and magnificent stained-glass windows *(vitrales).* The acclaimed Ballet de Camagüey still performs here.

Narrow but bustling Calle República leads north to **Museo Provincial Ignacio Agramonte,** housed in the former cavalry garrison. Its eclectic exhibits span natural history, decorative arts, archaeology, and culture.

The neoclassic **Instituto de Segunda Enseñanza** (Institute of Secondary Education) stands on the Río Jatibonico's south bank, at Avenida de la Libertad. Adjacent is **Casino Campestre,** a large park with statuary and a bandstand. ∎

Casa Natal Ignacio Agramonte
- ✉ Calle Ignacio Agramonte #459, bet. Independencia & Cisneros
- ☎ 32/29-7116
- ⏱ Closed Tues.
- 💲 $

Museo de San Juan de Díos
- ✉ Plaza San Juan de Díos
- ⏱ Closed Sun.
- 💲 $

Museo Provincial Ignacio Agramonte
- ✉ Avenida de los Mártires #2
- ☎ 32/28-2425
- ⏱ Closed Mon.
- 💲 $

Rain catchers

The earthenware jugs called *tinajones,* modeled on Spanish wine jars, were used during colonial times to collect water during a drought. Up to 5

feet tall and 10 feet in diameter, the jugs were usually sunk into the ground to keep the water cool. Legend suggests that visitors who accept a drink offered by a girl from a *tinajón* will fall in love and never leave town. ∎

Tinajones displayed in the Museo Provincial Ignacio Agramonte

A sunset glow mellows the rich hues of buildings edging Plaza San Juan de Díos.

Walk: Colonial Camagüey

This walk leads you back in time, down side streets linking hidden churches, small museums, and the city's three major plazas. You'll see much of the city's most intriguing colonial architecture. Some of the scenes are tumbledown, but pockets of renovation lift the spirit. Take time to stop and talk to locals who, with luck, might invite you into their homes, through ancient timber doorways to cool patios to the rear. Set out in late afternoon to miss the midday heat and view the plazas as they glow in the soft golden sunlight. *Jineteros* (hustlers) are especially numerous and persistent—steel yourself to be pestered.

Your starting point is the **Gran Hotel ①** *(tel 32/29-2093)*, midway down Calle Maceo, the city's sole pedestrians-only thoroughfare. The recently restored hotel deserves a look for its gleaming 19th-century decor. Walk north 50 yards (46 m) to the junction with Calle República, the city's central thoroughfare. You stand facing **Iglesia Nuestra Señora de la Soledad ②,** built in 1776. Its worn redbrick facade belies the exquisite interior, which showcases baroque frescoes and an imposing vaulted ceiling. Its lofty tower is a city guidepost.

Turn right and follow República to Calle Martí; turn left and walk two blocks to tiny **Plaza de la Juventud.** On its south side, on Calle Luaces, is **Iglesia del Sagrado Corazón de Jesús ③,** a neo-Gothic church built in 1920. Slip through the huge mahogany

doorway to admire the trompe l'oeil interior gleaming with gold and marble. Unfortunately, its once beautiful stained-glass windows were destroyed following the revolution.

Follow Luaces west to República, turn left, and walk 400 yards (366 m) to **Puente Jatibonico ④,** a metal bridge over the Río Jatibonico that dates from 1773. Turn right and follow the river, along Calle Matadero, where produce and livestock are sold in the open-air *mercado agropecuario.*

After two blocks turn right; this opens to cobblestoned **Plaza San Juan de Díos ⑤** (see p. 161), edged with brightly hued houses with red-tile roofs. Be sure to explore the **Convento y Hospital de San Juan de Díos,** which served as a hospital until 1902 and in various capacities since. One of the 18th-century houses on the plaza's north side has been converted into the pink-and-yellow **Campaña de Toledo** restaurant *(tel 32/29-5888)*, specializing in *criollo* meals and boasting intriguing ceramic murals. Inside the courtyard awaits a ceramics workshop—your chance to purchase your own *tinajón*.

After refreshments at the restaurant, exit the plaza to the northwest and turn right onto Calle Raúl Lamar for 50 yards (46 m), then left onto Calle Cisneros. Follow this north to **Parque Agramonte** 6 (see p. 160), where you might want to sit awhile and admire the *tinajones*, Victorian lampstands, and the venerable facades drenched in sunlight. A statue of General Agramonte presides. The palm trees at each corner of the square were planted by locals in secret tribute to four Cuban independence fighters executed by the Spanish in 1851. Be sure to call in at the **Casa de la Trova** *(Calle Cisneros #171, tel 32/29-1357)*, where on weekends folkloric music performances take place on the cool patio to the rear.

Continue north one block to Calle Hermano Agüero (10 de Octubre); turn left. On your right, 30 yards (27 m) ahead, is **Casa Natal Nicolás Guillén** 7 *(Calle Hermano*

Agüero #58, tel 32/29-3706), the birthplace, in 1902, of acclaimed poet, nationalist, revolutionary, and cofounder of the National Union of Cuban Writers and Artists. Guillén, who championed the cause of Afro-Cubans, was Cuba's poet laureate until his death in 1989. The small, pleasant home contains his library and personal possessions.

Return to Cisneros and go north two blocks to **Plaza de los Trabajadores** 8 (see pp. 160–161), anchored by the **Catedral Nuestra Señora de la Merced,** where your walk ends. ■

- ⊠ See area map page 153
- ▶ Gran Hotel
- ⬌ 1.5 miles (2 km)
- 🕒 3 hours
- ▶ Plaza de los Trabajadores

NOT TO BE MISSED
- Iglesia Nuestra Señora de la Soledad
- Plaza San Juan de Díos
- Casa de la Trova

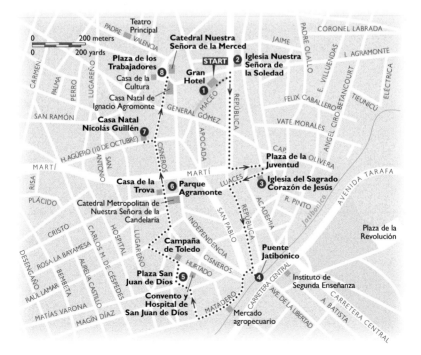

Santa Lucía

CUBA'S FOURTH LARGEST RESORT HAS MUCH TO OFFER IF your idea of a great getaway includes 12 miles (19 km) of sun-washed sand and great diving amid magnificent offshore coral reefs. There aren't a lot of amenities, nearby attractions, or even much local color to soak up. But there is the sun, the sand, and the sea.

Santa Lucía boasts the island's third longest beach and pristine turquoise shallows that are splendid for swimming and snorkeling. (Rubber waders are a good idea, as sea grasses smother much of the seabed.) Divers are not disappointed here either. Imagine huge gardens of black coral, massive sponges, nurse sharks, and an infinite number of zebra-striped, polka-dotted, rainbow-hued fish. Numerous shipwrecks litter the mouth of the Bahía de Nuevitas, including the steamship *Mortera*, which sank to a depth of 20 feet (6 m) in 1898. Diving and sportfishing are offered at **Shark's Friend Dive Center** *(tel 32/36-5182).*

The region is semiarid and flat as a pancake. For nature lovers, two mangrove-edged lagoons— **Laguna Daniel** to the south and

Laguna El Real to the north— harbor diverse birdlife, including flamingoes. The area is slated to be tapped for ecotourism.

Currently Santa Lucía, 75 miles (121 km) northeast of Camagüey, offers half-a-dozen mediocre hotels and some ancillary services along 3 miles (5 km) of beachfront. Cubans vacation in *campismos* and bungalows, but police keep them from mingling with tourists.

A highway runs along the shore; rented cars, bicycles, and mopeds share it with horse-and-trap taxis. The only place close by is **La Boca,** a colorful, ramshackle fishing hamlet 2 miles (3 km) north. The hamlet enfolds **Playa Los Cocos,** a beauty of a beach; the snorkeling and diving are sublime, and Cubans are permitted, enabling tourists a chance to mingle with locals. ∎

Jardines de la Reina

AN UNEXPLORED FRONTIER AWAITING DISCOVERY, THE chain of almost 700 islets and cays lying off the southern coast of central Cuba is slated for major development. This string of coral jewels in a sapphire sea is a mecca for divers, boaters, and self-reliant types who are undeterred, or even drawn, by a lack of facilities.

Jardines de la Reina
🗺 153 A1, B1

Three subgroups extending across 200 miles (322 km) of shallow sea compose the archipelago called the Jardines de la Reina (Queen's Gardens). The largest islands—the so-called **"Labyrinth of the Twelve Leagues"**—gather in a long line about 50 miles (80 km) offshore of Ciego de Ávila province and taper east into the neighboring province of Camagüey. This chain of stepping-stone isles shields the Golfo de Ana María, an underwater sea that is about as deep as the islands are high; it is bounded along the south by a nearly unbroken coral reef. Beyond it, barely a mile (1.6 km) from shore, the plateau drops off to a very dark 6,000 feet (1,829 m).

Eastward, scores of smaller cays scattered higgledy-piggledy across the western extent of the Golfo de Guacanayabo make up the second group. A third group, the **Cayos Ana María,** clusters close to the shores of Ciego de Ávila province. All are flat, sandy, and covered with swampy mangrove pools.

Tourism has yet to catch on here. The only road access is via a *pedraplen* (raised causeway) that delivers you to **Cayo Cocoa,** in the Cayos Ana María. The cay is devoid of all facilities; bring water and other supplies. You can fly (or sail) to **Cayo Caguamas;** it has a marina from which boat excursions set out to explore neighboring cays. Soon visitors will be able to overnight here, as they can on **Cayo Algodón Grande** and **Cayo Bartolo,** which host a small hotel

and fishing lodge, respectively. The vast flats are a supreme bonefish

Tourists take a boat ride out to explore the cays.

habitat, and catching them requires little skill. Fidel Castro once frequented the area, flying down to his personal isle—Cayo Piedra—to fish, dive, and entertain friends and lovers beyond prying eyes.

Four live-aboard dive boats also cater to scuba divers drawn by the diversity of sea life, including marine turtles and sharks. Many prime dive sites have yet to be explored. The convoluted passages through the archipelago became a graveyard for Spanish galleons—the seabed is a trove of doubloons and precious trinkets, while speculation contends that more treasure lies buried in the sand, courtesy of pirates such as Sir Francis Drake, who reputedly died here of dysentery in 1596.

Organize trips through **Puertosol marinas** *(tel 7/204-5923)* at Júcaro, 13 miles (21 km) south of Ciego de Ávila, and Santa Cruz, 47 miles (76 km) south of Camagüey; these marinas are also departure points for the cays. ■

Visitor information
✉ Grupo de Desarrollo del Circuito Náutico Jardines de la Reina Delegación de Turismo de Camagüey
☎ 32/27-2162

More places to visit in Central Cuba

KING RANCH

Prior to the revolution, this cattle *finca,* about 5 miles (14 km) west of Camalote and 1 mile (1.6 km) south of the coast highway, was one of the largest such operations in Cuba. Once part of the Texas-based King Ranch empire, it still operates as a cattle-breeding station and welcomes visitors to witness displays of horsemanship at a rodeo. You can rent horses for rides through the cactus scrub and pockets of forests. Rumbos *(tel 32/3612)* and Cubanacan *(tel 32/5241)* offer excursions from Santa Lucía.  153 C2

MINAS & AROUND

If you're heading to Santa Lucía, this small village, 23 miles (37 km) northeast of Camagüey, is worth a stop. Surrounded by arable farmland, its draw is the **Fábrica de Instrumentos Musicales** *(tel 32/96232, closed Sun., $),* a modest factory where

workers craft guitars, violins, cellos, and other musical instruments of varying quality. The *fábrica* was created prior to the revolution by Alvaro Suárez Ravinal, whose son still works here. Today, the factory is often idle due to a shortage of hardwoods and parts. Worth a look, too, is **Ingenio del Sol,** the remains of a historic sugar mill, about 10 miles (16 km) from Minas, near the village of San Miguel.

Minas is located in the **Sierra De Camajan,** with cliffs measuring up to 650 feet (200 m) in striking limestone gorges. The most famous ravine is **Pasaje de Paredones,** a popular excursion among Cubans.

If you wish to stare down the gullet of a hungry crocodile, visit the **criadero de cocodrilos** (crocodile breeding center) outside the village of Senado, about 5 miles (8 km) northwest of Minas. The farm is one of seven criaderos in Cuba. This one breeds American crocodiles for their skins (the endemic Cuban crocodile—*Crocodylus rhombifer*—is not raised here). You can see about 350 animals, from newborns to 15-year-old crocs. Lagoons are enclosed, permitting safe close-up viewing. There's a simple thatched restaurant-bar.  153 C2

MORÓN'S COUNTRYSIDE

The Sierra Jatibonico rise dramatically west of Morón, and any drive through the undulating terrain surrounding the towns of **Florencia** and **Chambas**—served by train from Morón—is a pleasure. Sugarcane, tobacco, and cattle are raised amid quintessentially Cuban landscapes. Rumbos offers horseback trips from **Campismo Boquerón** *(c/o Islazul, tel 33/25314),* near Florencia, that lead to a farmstead where a rodeo show and pig roast are hosted. During tobacco-picking season, the trips also include a visit to curing sheds. At Campismo Boauerón you can also swim in the Río Jatibonico and explore nearby *mogotes* (see pp. 102–103).  153 A3, B3 ■

Craftsmen at work in the Fábrica de Instrumentos Musicales in the village of Minas

Extreme in contrasts, this region offers colonial cities and sugar-white beaches, rides on a century-old steam train, and hiking to Fidel Castro's guerrilla headquarters.

Western Oriente

At the Museo Celia Sánchez

Western Oriente

THE SWEEPING, PALM-STUDDED PLAINS OF THE WESTERN ORIENTE REGION encompass Las Tunas, Holguín, and Granma provinces. With a backdrop of mountains that reach 6,475 feet (1,974 m) at Pico Turquino, Cuba's highest peak, the flatlands range in terrain from swamp to semidesert. The region is often overlooked by visitors, despite its many draws, which include fine beaches, ecosystems rich with bird species, and key historical sites.

The province of Las Tunas, named after the prickly pear cactus, lies to the east of Havana. It is cattle country in the south, flat and dry, easing to verdant green farther north. The eponymous capital city comes alive each June for a folklore festival, and the area plays host to a large cattle fair. Just to the east, Holguín province boasts a sprawling city of the same name, with quaint colonial streets at its core. The area's economy is dominated by sugar: During the *zafra,* or sugar harvest, the air is

filled with the cloying odor of molasses emanating from the sugar mills. To the northeast the Sierra del Cristal frame the green plains. These mountains are being developed for ecotourism, with trails and lodges atop the misty heights where Fidel Castro played as a boy. Laced throughout the mountains are cobalt, manganese, and nickel, which generate almost one quarter of the island's export earnings.

Mangrove forest lines much of the north coast, but it is the ribbons of talcum-fine

The beauty of Holguín province as seen from Mirador de Mayabe

beaches that attract the most attention, especially at Guardalavaca and Playa Pesquero, with its all-inclusive resorts offering water sports and a host of local excursions. These include a trip by steam train through the dramatic Grupo Montañoso Manabión mountains, known for Cuba's

foremost pre-Columbian site. Christopher Columbus stepped ashore there in 1492, near what is now the coastal town of Gibara.

Granma, extending south of Las Tunas and west of Holguín like a great arrowhead jutting into the Caribbean, comprises fertile plains watered by the Río Cauto, Cuba's largest river. The vast delta that opens to the Golfo de Guacanayabo is a swampy no-man's-land where crocodiles are king; a breeding farm is open to view. Granma is steeped in history: Independence was born at the city of Bayamo and at Carlos Céspedes's estate at La Demajagua. You can also visit the site where national hero José Martí was martyred, and where Castro came ashore to launch the decisive stage of the revolution. Parque Nacional del Desembarcardo del Granma is a cactus-studded environment laced with trails. So, too, is the Sierra Maestra, a sheer mountain chain where trails ascend to Castro's guerrilla headquarters and Pico Turquino. ■

D
▽

Cayo Saetía

caro

E
▽

Cayo Mambí

Moa

erra del Cristal

Sagua de Tánamo

o de ristal
31 m

Mayarí Arriba

Havana

Area of map detail

Las Tunas

Las Tunas
⚑ 168 B2

Museo Provincial
✉ Calle Francisco
Varona at Lucas
Ortíz Angel de la
Guardia
☎ 31/48201
🕐 Closed Mon.
💲 $

THIS UNASSUMING AND INTIMATE CITY STRADDLING THE Carretera Central is the gateway to the Oriente region. Though not a stand-alone draw, you can easily spend a half-day in the provincial capital while passing through. Sites include handsome colonial buildings, a museum to a homegrown revolutionary hero, and contemporary ceramic murals.

La Victoria de las Tunas—a name adopted in 1869 following a Spanish victory here during the Ten Years War—was a territory of Bayamo, but became a city in its own right in 1852. It is small in scale, with a compact town center that lost many original structures in an 1897 fire. The somnolent town of 120,000 has traditionally served as a regional center for the surrounding cattle industry; Cuba's largest annual horse and cattle fair is held here. It is also known as the City of Sculptures for the unique terra-cotta art forms found on the exteriors of many buildings.

THE HISTORIC CORE
At its heart, at the top of Avenida Vicente García, is **Parque**

The small-time capital of Las Tunas boasts a tidy, quiet town center.

Vicente García, the town's intimate main square honoring Maj. Gen. Vicente García González. A rebel leader who commanded nationalist forces during both wars of independence, it was he who ordered the city of his birth set ablaze in 1897. Admire his marble bust from marble benches set in the shade of begonias that ring the square. The park opens to smaller **Plaza Martiana de las Tunas,** home to a large, contemporary sundial sculpture that points to an embossed bust of José Martí.

On the northeast side of Parque Vicente García stands the **Museo Provincial,** housed in the old *ayuntamiento,* or town hall—an attractive white-and-blue structure with a handsome clock tower. The museum's displays include historical artifacts and photos, including a section on slavery and another profiling the life of Juan Cristóbal Nápoles, the town's famous 19th-century poet. Slip upstairs for a brief look at the timeworn natural history collection. The **Centro Histórico** *(tel 31/48201),* one block west, offers its own lean exhibits. Seek out the terra-cotta wall plaque showing the old city in bas-relief.

Avenida Vicente García, the bustling main street, slants west and is lined with aged buildings fronted by columned *portales.* Pop into the **Casa de la Cultura** *(Vicente García #8, tel 31/45401),* where poetry readings and music recitals are offered. Despite the conflagration that swept the city in 1897, the **Memorial Vicente García González,** where García was born, survived the blaze and—duly restored—now serves as a museum recalling those dramatic events. Exhibits include the homegrown hero's ceremonial swords.

ABOUT TOWN

At the foot of Vicente García, step across narrow Río Hormiguero. Facing you, on the north side of Calle Luca Ortíz, is a venerable wooden home that is now the **Memorial Mártires de Barbados,** dedicated to the 57 Cubans and 16 others who died in 1976 when their Cubana airliner was blown up in midair by Cuban-exile terrorists. The museum is housed in the former *casa* of Carlos Leyva González, Cuba's champion *florete* (fencer), who died along with the entire Cuban fencing team. Leyva's medals and fencing gear are among the displays. Note the metal sculpture in the form of a clenched fist, to the side of the house.

Reparto Aurora, northeast of the historic core, is the setting

for the austere **Plaza de la Revolución,** dominated on its north side by a monument of Maj. Gen. Vicente García González. The general is entombed here, in the **Mausoleo del Mayor General Vicente García González.** ■

El Cucalambé

If possible time your visit for June, when the town hosts the Jornada Cucalambeana (Cucalambé Folkloric Festival), drawing Cubans to hear *trovadores*—troubadours—celebrate the tradition of rhyming song. The festival is named for local poet Juan Cristóbal Nápoles Fajardo (1829–1862), nicknamed El Cucalambé. Nápoles was Cuba's preeminent composer of *décimas*—rhyming, eight-syllable verses that form the lyrics for songs. In 1856, Nápoles published a booklet of verses that celebrated the creole Cuban *guajiro* (peasant). His poems were enthusiastically received and contributed to the nationalist spirit of the times. The festival is held at Motel El Cornito, 4 miles west of town; cabarets are hosted here throughout the year. ■

A bronze bust of national hero José Martí keeps watch over Plaza Martiana de las Tunas.

Memorial Vicente García González
✉ Avenida Vicente García #5
☎ 31/45164
🕐 Closed Sun.
💲 $

Memorial Mártires de Barbados
✉ Calle Luca Ortíz #344
☎ 31/47213
💲 $

Baseball fever

Cubans are a peaceable people, though you'd never know it on a sunny afternoon in Havana's Parque Central. Here baseball fanatics gather at *la esquina caliente* (hot corner) to debate the fine points of the national sport. Arguments break out. Even the odd fight isn't unknown, so passionate are the Cubans for pelota, or *beisbol*. Cubans have been loco for baseball ever since the game was introduced by the United States in the 1860s.

In 1872, the Habana Baseball Club was founded as Cuba's first professional team. The first league was formed six years later. North American clubs headed south as early as 1881 to take on Cuban teams, and in the decades that followed, major league heros chased the sun to play "winter ball." Babe Ruth, Willy Mays, and Tommy Lasorda all played baseball for Cuban clubs. The exchange of talent went both ways. "The rush of Cubans to the big

leagues may cause an appeal for an amendment to the immigration laws," joked sports columnist W. O. McGeehan in 1919 after Cuban pitcher Oscar Teuro led the St. Louis Cardinals to a victory over the New York Giants. Even the revolution came to a halt during the 1957 World Series, when guerrilla commanders stopped operations to catch the final game. (Fidel Castro once tried out, unsuccessfully, for the Washington Senators.)

Cubans play the game with fierce determination. Boys grow up swinging a bat, which in Cuba means any stick they can get their hands on. No one has money for real bats, which in any event are as rare as gold in the stores. And no one has spikes or helmets. Bottle tops serve as stand-ins for baseballs. An entire school or neighborhood team might share a worn Cuban-made Batos glove. But what they lack in equipment, they make up in talent.

Sixteen provincial championship teams plus Havana's two teams play a 39-game season, which runs December to June. The top seven teams go on to play a 54-game National Series. Regional fans are assured of seeing their favorite team play live—the last game of each three-game series is played in a rural township. Cuba has nine major baseball stadiums. The largest, Havana's simple 55,000-seat Estadio Latinoamericano, is the yin to Dodger Stadium's yang, with none of its flashing scoreboards. And while the fans are partisan, they're also good socialists and applaud whenever the opposition scores a run.

In this land of egalitarianism, even professional baseball players earn only about 400 pesos (U.S. $18) a month. Not surprisingly, the U.S. professional leagues have been snapping up the best Cuban players like stolen bases. Cuban national team pitchers, in particular, have caught home-run fever. Rene Arocha fled Cuba in 1991 for the St. Louis Cardinals. Osvaldo Fernández left in 1995 and was signed by the San Francisco Giants. Rolando Arrojo defected during the 1996 Atlanta Olympic Games

(Cuba won the gold medal, thanks to slugger Orestes Kindelán and third baseman Omar Linares). Livan Hernández left Cuba in 1996 to join the Florida Marlins; the following year he won the World Series MVP award. And, in January 1998, Hernández's brother Orlando ("El Duque") slipped out of Cuba by raft to play for the New York Yankees … perhaps the ultimate victory of Yankee imperialism. ∎

Members of the Cuban Olympic baseball team celebrate after defeating Japan in the 1996 Olympics (left). An eye on the ball and a future (right). Practicing the perfect pitch (below)

Holguín

LYING WITHIN THE FOLD OF SURROUNDING HILLS THAT offer their own sites of interest, Holguín is a modern city with modest tourist facilities. But it is home to some of Cuba's most charming plazas and, for that reason alone, it is worth a visit.

In 1525 the Spanish granted the land around Cubanacán, the major Taino Indian settlement, to conquistador Capitán García Holguín, who founded a cattle estate that would eventually become Cuba's fourth largest city (264,000). During the 19th century, the city grew in prominence and was fought over in the wars of independence. But industrialization—Cuba's major brewery and a sugarcane harvester factory are here—and urban expansion in dour communist style have defaced the contemporary city. The city's saving grace is that its concentrated colonial core is attractive and the city has a vital culture, with mechanical organ groups a prominent feature.

Loma de la Cruz (Hill of the Cross) shoulders up to the north side of the city, providing a panoramic view over the great sweep of Holguín province. You can ascend by car or attempt a leg-trembling climb up the 458-step staircase that begins at the head of Calle Maceo (rest at the thatched restaurant west of the summit). The hill is named for the wooden cross erected here on May 3, 1790; a religious procession—the *Romería de la Cruz* (Pilgrimage of the Cross)—ascends the steps on the anniversary of that day.

CITY OF PARKS

The logical starting point for exploring is **Plaza Calixto García,** the town's expansive main square, which is laid out in ornamental pink and green marble. At its heart is a statue of the revered Gen. Calixto Iñiguez García sitting on horseback. García was born one block east, in **Casa Natal de Calixto García.** Today it is a museum displaying meager personal effects and exhibits tracing his role in the fight for independence. For more about regional history, check out the **Museo Provincial de Historia,** housed in the former Casino Español (a social club for Iberians),

graced by delicate wrought-iron balconies. Erected in 1860–1862, the building later became a barracks and is mockingly called "La Periquera"— parakeet's cage—after Spanish troops dressed in yellow, green, and blue uniforms were barricaded behind the grilled windows during the fighting of October 1868. It has a fine collection of pre-Columbian artifacts, including a polished peridot axe (the *hacha de Holguín*) carved in the shape of a human. José Martí's ceremonial sword is there as well, encased in glass.

Be sure to take in the **Casa de la Trova** next door, where *música campesina* (country music) performances are hosted on the patio, and the **Centro Provincial de Artes Plásticas** art gallery, on the park's southwest corner. Note, too, the art deco facade of the **Teatro Comandante Eddy Suñol** (named for a revolutionary hero), on the plaza's south side.

The **Museo de Historia Natural Carlos de la Torre,** 50 yards (46 m) south of Plaza Calixto García on Calle Maceo, displays a ragtag collection of mounted Cuban fauna, including a manatee, plus polymites—the dazzling colored snails endemic to Oriente (see sidebar p. 44). The museum is housed in a columned confection that melds Moorish elements into neoclassic style; note the *azulejo* tilework.

Maceo opens onto the intimate **Plaza Julio Grave de Peralta,**

Centro Provincial de Artes Plásticas art gallery
✉ Calle Martí #119
☎ 24/42-7490

The building that houses the Museo Provincial de Historia, on Parque Calixto García in Holguín, dates from 1862.

Holguín's hero

Born in Holguín on August 4, 1839, Calixto Iñiguez García rose to become commander-in-chief of the rebel army during the Ten Years War. On December 19, 1872, the general led the rebel assault that seized his home town from Spanish forces. He was captured in 1873 and taken to Spain. When the second war of independence broke out in 1895, García escaped to New York and returned to Cuba. In 1898 he again attempted to capture Holguín, but abandoned the siege to lead rebel forces in the battle for Santiago de Cuba following U.S. intervention. He died later that year and was reinterred in Holguín in 1980. ■

Museo del Estadio Calixto García

✉ Avenida XX Aniversario

☎ 24/46-2014

🕐 Closed Sat.–Sun.

💲 $

anchored by a marble statue of Gen. Grave de Peralta (1834–1872), who led the rebel assault in 1868 that captured Holguín from the Spanish. The venerable church on the east side is the recently restored **Catedral de San Isidro,** built in 1720 in dedication to the town's patron saint. Peek in to admire the wooden ceiling; the rough-brick church is otherwise austere. Note the mural in the northwest corner of the square, showing Fidel Castro leading a pantheon of revolutionaries from throughout the Americas.

Holguín's most pleasing square is cobbled **Plaza San José,** two blocks north of Plaza Calixto García. It is surrounded by old colonial houses and the charming **Iglesia de San José,** which dates from 1820 and features a domed neoclassic clock tower. Romantic tunes waft over the square each Sunday evening, when a mechanical organ is played.

BEYOND THE CORE

The city claims the nation's sole mechanical organ factory—**Fábrica de Órganos** (*Carretera de Gibara #301*)—where artisans craft organs, guitars, and other musical instruments in traditional fashion. Baseball fans might head to the stadium in the modern Reparto Plaza de la Revolución, east of downtown. The stadium features a **Museo del Estadio Calixto García,** with exhibits of sports memorabilia, including photos of Che Guevara and Castro playing baseball. Holguín's **Plaza de la Revolución,** to the rear of the stadium, hosts political rallies and is worth a quick browse in passing. Calixto García slumbers in a mausoleum opposite the huge provincial headquarters of the Communist Party. Adjacent is a bronze monument to the heroes of Cuban independence; note the Cuban flag draped in the form of Holguín province.

A broad boulevard—Avenida de los Libertadores (Carretera a Mayarí)—leads east from downtown and is named in celebration of various Cuban and continental "liberators." It is lined with monuments to Benito Suárez, Simón Bolívar, Máximo Gómez, Antonio Maceo, and Che Guevara—the latter, at Avenida de los Internationalistas—in impressive bas-relief.

MIRADOR DE MAYABE

Many visitors stop to buy a beer for Panchito the burro, in a stall beside the bar at Mirador de Mayabe (*tel 24/42-2160 or 24/47-3485*), 5 miles southeast of Holguín. This reconstruction of a farmstead has fruit trees, various farm animals on view in pens, plus a *valla* (cockpit) for cockfights. Horseback rides and accommodations are offered. A sundeck offers views across Valle de Mayabe. ■

Gibara & nearby

THE SLEEPY, WEATHER-BEATEN COASTAL TOWN OF GIBARA is a trove of salt-preserved architectural treasures. It is also famous as the site of Columbus's landing in Cuba. The presumed spot of the explorer's first footfall, in sparkling, flask-shaped Bahía de Bariay, is enshrined within a national park that also encompasses beaches, mangroves, and mountains.

Gibara & nearby
🗺 168 C3

Gibara, 21 miles (34 km) north of Holguín, dates from 1822. Once a wealthy port trading sugar. The town's fortunes declined when railroads arrived to steal the trade. The ruins of the **Fuerte el Cuartelón** fortress (a 30-minute hike from the town plaza) overlook still-elegant colonial buildings that earned Gibara the nickname Perla del Oriente (Pearl of the Orient). Waves break over the coral foreshore along which sweeps Gibara's seafront promenade.

Parque Calixto García—the main plaza, lined with *robles africanos* (African oaks)—boasts a small statue of Cuba's Indian maiden representing the freedom gained when the Spanish were dispelled in 1898. To one side of the plaza is the Byzantine-style **Iglesia de San Fulgencio.** Appealing, too, is the **Museo de Arte Decorativo,** exhibiting sumptuous period furnishings and paintings upstairs in a restored colonial mansion. Note the beautiful *mediopuntos.*

PARQUE NACIONAL CRISTÓBAL COLÓN

This national park was created to preserve the shoreline surrounding the site of Columbus's landing. A monument symbolizing the meeting of Old and New World inhabitants was erected in 1992, on the west side of Bahía de Bariay. It is accessed from the community of Frey Benito via a potholed yet scenic road. You can hike the **Sendero del Peñón** from the monument. A smaller monument

stands on the eastern shore at Playa Blanca; a plaque declares it the "site of the first landing of Christopher Columbus in Cuba." Take the road that leads northeast from the town of Rafael Freyre. ∎

Museo de Arte Decorativo
✉ Calle Independencia #19
☎ 24/34407
🕐 Closed Mon.
💲 $

Columbus in Cuba

Columbus's first New World landfall was in the Bahamas, whose inhabitants told him that gold could be found in Cubanacán (middle Cuba), which he translated as "Kublai Khan." On November 27, 1492, after a month exploring Cuba's north coast, Columbus's three caravels dropped anchor in a protected bay—he christened it Puerto Santo—framed by a flattopped mountain that "looked like an island." Despite claims otherwise, archaeologists believe the explorer described the Bahía de Bariay and the Silla de Gibara. ∎

A statue of Cuba's Indian maiden stands in the Parque Calixto García, outside the Iglesia de San Fulgencio.

Holguín to Banes drive

Dipping down to the shore and into the lush vales of the Grupo Montañoso Maniabón mountains (see p. 181), Route 6-241 carves a superbly scenic path through a landscape punctuated with an irregular pattern of limestone hummocks and ridges running to all points of the compass. Although the road is mostly in good condition, the usual hazards—potholes, bicycles, and ox-drawn carts—require constant caution.

Departing **Holguín** ❶ can be confusing. Exit Plaza Calixto García along Calle Martí and veer right along Avenida de los Libertadores; immediately beyond the baseball stadium (on your left), turn left onto Avenida XX Aniversario, which leads to Route 6-241 and Guardalavaca. The road dips and rises through wide-open rangeland grazed by Brahman cattle, with steep-faced *mogotes* (see pp. 102–103) studding the landscape ahead. Bright red crotons flame alongside the road, and you'll pass *bohíos* (thatched huts) fenced

by tightly packed cactuses shaped like candelabras, neatly and lovingly trimmed. For 10 miles (16 km) or more, the mark of the hedge clipper is on every bush.

About 21 miles (34 km) northeast of Holguín, just beyond the turn-off for Rafael Freyre (marked as Santa Lucía on some maps), you'll pass over a railway line. Pull over and admire the views of the mogotes to the east. Less than half a mile away (0.8 km), to the west, the railroad enters **Central Rafael Freyre** ❷, a sugarcane factory served by various antique steam trains (including an 1882 Baldwin 0-6-0) that during the *zafra* (sugar harvest) pass daily under the bridge. If you have a minimum of two hours to spare, you can rent a locomotive *(tel 24/20119 or 24/20300 ext 275; ask for Rodolfo Betancourt)* for trips through the sugarcane fields and into the Grupo Montañoso Maniabón. Photographers might want to drive ahead of the train to capture it as it comes puffing around the scenic Bariay bend. You'll be assigned an engineer to communicate with the train; be warned—you'll careen pell-mell down rough country lanes!

Ten miles (16 km) beyond Rafael Freyre you'll pass Bahía de Naranjo and, a short distance farther, the turn-off for **Playa Esmeralda** ❸. Three miles (5 km) on, turn left off the *carretera* and pause in the resort of **Guardalavaca** (see pp. 180–181). After an hour or two sunning on creamy white **Playa Mayor** and swimming in the warm turquoise waters, return to the highway and continue east. The road immediately heads south and cuts inland over the northernmost mogotes of the Grupo Montañoso Maniabón mountains. At the village of **Yaguajay,** turn right at the sign for **Museo Aborigen Chorro de Maita**

Statue of José Martí in Banes (left); a demonstration at the Museo Aborigen Chorro de Maita near Yaguajay (top right)

(see p. 181), Cuba's largest pre-Columbian archaeological site; it's 2 miles (3 km) uphill. After visiting the museum and a re-creation of an Indian village, head back to Route 6-241.

Beyond Yagaujay, the road drops down to the village of Cañadón, in the **Valle de Samá.** Tousled royal palms stand sentry over lime-green tobacco fields in the lee of sensuously rounded hills. You'll pass though the community of **El Salado,** where the freestanding knolls tower over the highway. The road snakes in and out of lush vales and deposits you, 18 miles (29 km) beyond Guardalavaca, on a

broad plain that sweeps east to the Bahía de Banes. Sugarcane stretches out before you, rippling in the breeze like folds of green silk.

Follow the road as it curves northeast to **Banes ❹,** with an atmospheric, well-preserved colonial core (note the town has no hotels). Fulgencio Batista was born here in 1901, and Fidel Castro was married in 1948 in the **Iglesia de Nuestra Señora de la Caridad.** The **Museo Indocubano** (see p. 198) is also worth a visit. ■

See area map pages 168–169
► Holguín
↔ 60 miles (96 km)
🕓 4.5 hours (one way)
► Banes

NOT TO BE MISSED
- Playa Mayor, Guardalavaca
- Museo Aborigen Chorro de Maita, near Yagaujay
- Iglesia de Nuestra Señora de la Caridad, Banes

Guardalavaca & nearby

Guardalavaca & nearby
🅰 168 C3
Visitor information
✉ Cubatur
☎ 24/30171

AS A RESORT DESTINATION, POCKET-SIZE GUARDALAVACA has been overtaken in recent years by Cayo Coco. But what it lacks in size it makes up in beaches and water. Adjacent *playas* are being developed with showy all-inclusive hotels, ecotour projects are evolving, and the area is rich with worthy excursions.

Guardalavaca (the name means "watch the cow") was created in the 1970s, when the area became popular with Soviet officials. Since their departure it has struggled to appeal to a more discerning clientele. The basic amenities are present—car rental, liquor store, souvenirs—but not much else. However, you can

Bringing in the cane at Central Australia

mingle with local Cubans, who, for now, are still granted access. The beaches—**Playa Guardalavaca** to the west and **Playa Las Brisas** to the east—are beautiful, and water-sports outlets rent equipment, including sailboards. Divers justifiably rave about the riotous glories of the undersea world: Giant groupers and sponges, for example, and even swordfish, are commonly seen slicing along a wall called **The Jump.** The reef begins just 200 yards (183 m) from shore.

PARQUE NATURAL BAHÍA DE NARANJO

This horseshoe bay, about 5 miles (8 km) west of Guardalavaca, is surrounded by mangroves and woodland, parts of which have been developed for ecotourism. **Reserva Ecológica Las Guanas,** on the eastern headland at the mouth of the bay, has trails that lead from an interpretive center; one deposits you at **Cueva Siboney,** a cave displaying Indian petroglyphs. You can rent horses at **Rancho Naranjo,** an equestrian center, and view exhibits of local flora and fauna at **Rancho Mongo,** a re-creation of a country *finca.*

The beaches that edge the shore on either side of the bay—**Playa Esmeralda** to the east, and **Playa Pesquero** to the west—are in the throes of development that will eventually gild the shoreline with a string of upscale, all-inclusive resorts. At least five hotels under foreign management have already opened. The bays offer fine snorkel-

Steam trains

During the sugar harvest, January through June, the countryside resounds around the clock with the whistles, hissing, and clanking of steam trains as sugarcane is unloaded at *centrales.* Cuba has some 285 steam trains still in operation—the largest collection of working U.S. steam trains in the world. Many date back more than a century; the oldest is an 1878 Baldwin 0-4-2T, at the Central Villena. Engineers spend the off-season tending to repairs to extract yet another year's labor from these centenarian relics. ■

Playa Guardalavaca, with its beautiful beaches and coral reef, is slated for future development.

ing and diving, but beware of the strong currents at Pesquero.

A small island—**Cayo Naranjo**—sits in the bay. Its draw is **Acuario Cayo Naranjo** *(tel 24/30132 or 24/30434)*, an aquarium where sea lions and dolphins perform daily at noon for tourists. You can swim with the dolphins for an extra charge. Excursions run from nearby hotels.

GRUPO MONTAÑOSO MANIABÓN

These dramatic mountain formations rise south of Guardalavaca and are made up of *mogotes* (see pp. 102–103) arranged in a bizarre topography that is among the most beautiful in Cuba. The valleys, with their rust-red soils, are cultivated in sugarcane and tobacco. The hills are replete with wildlife.

Tucked into these heights is **Museo Aborigen Chorro de Maita,** site of a Taino cemetery and the largest aboriginal burial site in the West Indies. A pit in the center of the hilltop museum displays some of the more than 100 skeletons unearthed here since 1930 (note the malformed skulls, intentionally flattened at birth). Ceramics, jewelry, and other artifacts can be seen (many of the finest remains are displayed at the **Museo Indocubano,** in Banes; see p. 198). For a sense of the Taino lifestyle, cross the road to **Aldea Taína** *(fee)*, an idealized recreation of an Indian village. ■

Museo Aborigen Chorro de Maita
- ✉ Route 6-241, Yaguajay
- ☎ 24/30422
- ⏱ Closed Mon.
- 💲 $

Sweet harvest

Cuba is a gently undulating sea of chartreuse. Rippling fields of *azúcar*—sugar—cover four million acres (1.6 million ha), or about 50 percent of the island's arable land. The local saying, *"sin azúcar, no hay país,* without sugar, there's no country,"* reflects the degree to which Cuba's economy depends on the crop. Although in the last decade tourism surpassed sugar as the primary source of foreign exchange, it is this single crop that has tethered Cuba to a string of colonial powers and to a history marked by alternating periods of prosperity and depression.

Sugarcane was brought to Spain by the Moors. It was introduced to Cuba in 1512 by Diego Velázquez, at a time when "white gold" was one of Europe's most valued commodities. Cuba's humid tropical climate and deep, fertile soils proved perfectly suited to growing *Saccharum officinarus*—a tall, reedlike grass whose hard, multijointed stalk is filled with spongy pulp containing sweet, juicy sucrose.

The plant requires plentiful rainfall during the growing season and a dry season to bring in the crop. It is propagated from cuttings, which are laid lengthwise about 12 inches (30 cm) apart in furrows, then covered with soil. The cuttings sprout multiple stems that grow in clumps. The thick stalks grow to more than 9 feet (3 m) high and mature about 12 to 18 months after planting, strewing the lime-green cane fields with wispy white blossoms.

In preparation for the *zafra*—the harvest—which takes place in the January through June dry season, the fields are set afire to burn off the long, scimitar-sharp, sword-shaped leaves. Today, most cane is cut by mechanical harvesters. Smoke-smudged *macheteros* dressed in straw hats and coarse linens have not been replaced entirely, though, and still wield their sharp blunt-nosed machetes to fell the charred stalks on hillsides and in valleys. A skilled machetero can cut more than four tons of cane a day, while the Cuban-designed combine-harvesters can cut twice that amount in one hour (a ton/0.9 tonne of sugarcane produces about 220 pounds/100 kg of sugar). The stalk is cut off close to the ground, where the sucrose concentrates, while the leafy top is lopped off and the leaves stripped from the stalk. The plant is left to regrow; after three crops, the field is usually plowed over and replanted.

The stems are taken to Cuba's 156 dilapi-

Macheteros cut the grass beside cane fields in preparation for the *zafra*, or sugar harvest.

dated sugar processing factories *(centrales)* that during the harvest operate around the clock. Here, the stems are shredded and crushed between huge rollers that squeeze out the juice *(guarapo)*. The liquid is boiled in a clarifier, where impurities settle out. A filtering step is next, then the clear sucrose is evaporated in a vacuum pan to remove excess water. This produces a viscous yet crystalline syrup. A centrifuge spins out the molasses syrup and leaves raw brown sugar crystals, which are sent to bulk shipping terminals for refining abroad. Nothing

is wasted. The mud—*vinasse*—from the clarifier is used as a fertilizer. The molasses goes to make rum. And the fibrous, pulpy cane waste *(bagasse)* is used as cattle feed, for cardboard and wallboard, and to fuel centrale boilers.

Cuba's early, labor-intensive sugar industry was reliant upon simple mills *(trapiches)* driven by oxen, mules, or slaves. It remained comparatively backward for almost two centuries; during the time monopolistic laws compelled Cuba to trade only with the homeland. The industry was also held back by a

shortage of slaves. Spain had been slow to take advantage of the slave trade dominated by the British, who in 1762 seized Cuba, opened the island to international trade, and introduced technological advances such as water-powered sugar mills *(ingenios)*, which the British had pioneered on their Caribbean island possessions. The brief British occupation gave Cuba's sugar industry a remarkable boost, assisted in 1791 when a slave revolt virtually destroyed the sugar industry on neighboring Santo Domingo (Haiti), then the world's largest producer.

Sugar had its heyday in Cuba in the 19th century, when the first railroads were laid and steam power and mechanization were introduced to the mills. Sugar became the foremost crop (it accounted for about 70 percent of Cuba's revenue), and Cuba became the world's largest producer. The wars of independence, however, ravaged the sugar industry, which passed largely into the hands of U.S. corporations after Cuba gained independence in 1898. Though the industry was modernized and the U.S. government made guarantees to buy Cuba's sugar, the nation became bound economically to the United States.

In 1960, Fidel Castro nationalized the sugar industry. Soon thereafter sugar was supplied to the Eastern bloc in exchange for rice, grain, and other staples, locking the island nation into a dependent relationship with the Soviets. The zafra became a yardstick for the success of the revolutionary economy. In 1970, Castro announced that the country would produce ten million tons of sugar that year. The entire economy was reorganized toward that aim, and those in the cities were sent to work in the fields. The effort failed, while the rest of the economy ground to a virtual halt. The resulting attempt to wean the economy off its dependence on sugar crops also failed; Cuba remained the world's largest sugar producer, averaging about eight million tons annually. Since the collapse of the Soviet Union, sugar production has slumped; the zafra has averaged less than four million tons annually since 1990. In 2002 the government began scaling back its sugar lands and closing down inefficient centrales. ■

The Sierra Maestra form a dramatic backdrop for cane fields and stands of royal palms.

Sierra del Cristal

VERDANT AND VIRGINAL, THE SIERRA DEL CRISTAL RISE east of Holguín, inland of the narrow coastal plain. Pine-clad and home to myriad species of flora and fauna, including many rare birds, these refreshing, unsullied heights beckon hikers and nature lovers undaunted by the lack of facilities.

A farmer plows a field the old-fashioned way near the town of Mayarí Arriba.

Few roads penetrate these mountains, which rise eastward and attain 4,346 feet (1,231 m) atop Pico de Cristal, where clouds swirl through the mist-sodden montane forest. Many endemic species thrive amid the lush landscapes including, at drier lower elevations, orchids that have uniquely adapted by growing neither leaf nor flower.

Pinares de Mayarí, located 10 miles (16 km) south of the town of Mayarí, draws visitors for birding and forest hikes at the **Parque Nacional La Mensura,** high in the Altiplanices de Nipe. (The road from Mayarí is rough—rent a four-wheel-drive vehicle for the trip.) Nearby, Gaviota (tel 24/53308) runs an alpine-themed ecoresort called **Villa Pinares de Mayarí.** Once serving communist guests but now catering to the tourist market, it overlooks a reservoir—**Presa Cupey;** there are trails and horses for guided rides to the **Salto de Guayabo,** a 280-foot (85 m) waterfall, where you have a fabulous view north to the Bahía de Nipe. Nearby is **La Planca,** a horticultural garden alive with colors and scents difficult to dampen in even the rainiest weather. Three miles (5 km) east of Mayarí, signs point the way to Farallones and **Saboruco,** a cavern complex containing fanciful dripstone formations plus modest pre-Columbian petroglyphs on the walls.

Farther east along the coast highway, turn south and ascend to **Parque Nacional Pico Cristal.** Cresting the mountains, you arrive at **Mayarí Arriba,** a bucolic town at the center of a coffee-producing area. The town, just 34 miles (55 km) northeast of Santiago de Cuba, is remote: Raúl Castro, Fidel's brother, established his military headquarters here. The **Museo Comandancia del II Frente** (Avenida de los Mártires, tel 22/25249) tells the tale. ∎

Sierra del Cristal
169 D2

Bayamo & nearby

Bayamo & nearby
🗺 168 B1

Casa Natal de Carlos Manuel de Céspedes
✉ Calle Maceo #57
☎ 23/42-3864
🕐 Closed Mon.
💲 $

Museo Colonial
✉ Calle Maceo #55
💲 $

BAYAMO, DATING FROM 1513, IS ONE OF THE ORIGINAL SEVEN settlements founded by Diego Velázquez. Its central plaza has been restored and sites of great importance in Cuba's history now gleam, although the town is otherwise somewhat shabby. Nearby, several sites associated with the long struggle for independence provide intriguing forays afield.

The early settlement of Bayamo was built atop a bluff overlooking the Río Bayamo (today lily-clogged), in the lee of the Sierra Maestra. Despite its inland position, the town thrived as a center for smuggling, drawing the attention of pirates. The most notable raid

Carlos Céspedes & the Grito de Yara

Carlos Manuel de Céspedes (1819–1874) is called the Father of the Nation. The wealthy estate owner, poet, and lawyer published the first journal of the independence movement—*Cubano Libro (Free Cuba)*. On October 10, 1868, the 50-year-old plantation owner freed his slaves at La Demajagua, near Manzanillo, and, in an oration known as the *Grito de Yara* (Cry of Yara), called for open revolt against Spanish colonial rule. Céspedes was named head of a rebel army and of the first Assembly of the Republic. When the Spanish captured his son Oscar, Céspedes refused to surrender himself in exchange for the life of his son, who was shot. Following the failure of the Ten Years War (1868–1878), Céspedes retired to San Lorenzo, in the Sierra Maestra, where he was ambushed and killed by Spanish troops. ∎

occurred in 1604 when a French pirate held the local bishop hostage. The citizenry came to his aid, but the bishop was killed, along with his captor. The town later prospered from the sugar trade.

By the mid-18th century, the center of economic activity had shifted to western Cuba, and Bayamo became a hotbed of independence sentiment—and the setting for some consequential events. On October 10, 1868, a local *criollo* landowner, Carlos Manuel de Céspedes, initiated revolt against Spain (see sidebar left). Ten days later, rebel forces led by Céspedes seized Bayamo, where a revolutionary junta was formed. In January 1869, with Spanish troops at the door, the rebels torched the city; it was finally recaptured by Gen. Calixto García in April 1898. Today the city's central core is a national monument.

The Carretera Central skirts the city center and few tourists call in on Bayamo, which lies midway between Holguín and Santiago de Cuba. Those who do stop visit the expansive main square—**Parque Carlos Manuel de Céspedes**—which is named for the nationalist revolutionary, who was born here. Note the granite column in the center of the park, topped by a larger-than-life bronze effigy of a dignified yet solemn Céspedes in frock coat, with bas-reliefs depicting scenes from his life. A bust, inscribed with the national anthem, "La Bayamesa" (see sidebar p. 188), honors composer Perucho

Figueredo (1819–1870).

On the plaza's north side is Céspedes's birthplace, a two-story house that, remarkably, survived the conflagration. **Casa Natal de Carlos Manuel de Céspedes** is now a museum tracing Bayamo's history and Céspedes's rise from law student to rebel president. Original furnishings grace the upstairs bedrooms, and Céspedes's law books and ceremonial sword are among the exhibits.

Next door, the **Museo Colonial** also features period furnishings, plus the original score of Cuba's national anthem, initially composed as a stirring martial song. On the square's east side, Céspedes proclaimed Cuban independence in front of the *ayuntamiento* (town hall), which was also the site of the first meeting of the Assembly of the Republic.

The park opens to the northwest onto the cobbled **Plaza del Himno Nacional,** surrounded by cream-colored colonial houses. The revolutionary anthem was first sung by a choir of women in the **Catedral de Santísima Salvador** *(tel 23/42-2514)* on November 8, 1868. The beautifully restored church, rebuilt after the

1869 fire, features an exquisite mural above the altar depicting the town's dramatic events. Slip into the **Capilla de la Dolorosa;** this side chapel, with a Mudejar-style ceiling, dates from 1740. The first flag of the republic, sewn by Céspedes's wife, is displayed here; note also the baroque gilt altar to the Virgen de Dolores, ornately adorned with faux fruit. The colonial building with red-tile roof facing the church entrance is the **Casa de la Nacionalidad Cubana**—the office of the city historian.

South along Calle de Céspedes, you'll pass several old buildings. Tomás Estrada Palma, first presi-

Horse-drawn buggies are the typical means of transportation in Bayamo (top). Above, Catedral de Santísima Salvador sits on the Plaza del Himno Nacional, Bayamo.

Dos Ríos

168 C2

dent of independent Cuba, was born at **Casa de Estrada Palma** *(Calle de Céspedes #158, tel 23/42-3670);* today, as the **Casa de la UNEAC,** it houses an art gallery. The **Retablo de los Héroes,** at Calles Martí and Amado Éstevez, is a bas-relief bronze sculpture of Francisco Aquilera (1821–1877), a local hero of the Ten Years War, and honors other local revolutionary and nationalist heroes in marble.

"La Bayamesa"

"The Bayamo Song" was first performed in 1868 during the Battle of Bayamo—in which its author, Perucho Figueredo, played a leading role. Two years later, he was captured by the Spanish and executed by firing squad. The anthem was officially adopted in 1940.

To battle, run, people of Bayamo

Let your country proudly observe you

Fear not a glorious death

For to die for your country is to live.

To live in chains is to live in insult and drowning shame.

Listen to the bugle calling you

To arms, braves ones, run!

DOS RÍOS

The site where independence leader and national hero José Martí met his death in 1895 (see pp. 190–191) is set in the midst of a semiarid alluvial plain, on the north bank of the Río

Contramaestra, 14 miles (23 km) northeast of Jiguaní and 32 miles (52 km) northeast of Bayamo. Few visitors make it to this most hallowed of sites. A path lined by a wall with a bronze bas-relief of Martí leads through a garden of white roses—an allusion to his poem, "Cultivo una rosa blanca … " (Cultivate a white rose). The wall contains an inscription of another Martí phrase: "When my fall comes, all the sorrow of life will seem like sun and honey."

Here, the **Monumento Martí**—a 30-foot-tall (9 m) simple concrete obelisk—is shaded by

palms. A bronze plaque notes: "He died at this place on 19 May 1895." Devotees to Martí arrive each May for anniversary celebrations in a vast, faceless plaza.

Approach Dos Ríos from the south; the road north of the site is alarmingly potholed. The journey itself is of note: Brahman cattle and goats forage the plains, which are frequently scoured by searing winds.

LOMA DE YAREY
Rising over a vast, barren pan of parched earth, this hill offers stupendous views and is well worth the detour from the Carretera Central (*turn N, 4 miles/6 km E of Jiguaní*). The road snakes steeply uphill, offering all-round vistas over the sprawling plains. To the south, in the far distance, the Sierra Maestra rise in great pleated ridges. There's a rustic hotel and restaurant—**Villa del Yarey** (*tel 23/42-7258*)—with thatched stone cabins and a swimming pool in the midst of a rock garden surrounded by gnarled *majagua* trees. Birders will appreciate the diverse avian fauna, which include Cuban solitaire, Cuban vireo, and red-tailed hawks. ∎

The musical group *La Familia* rehearses in Bayamo.

Revolutionary poet

The "spiritual father of the revolution," José Martí is the most revered person in Cuban history—a national hero and an inspiration to both Fidel Castro and to his opponents. The international airport is named after him, as are major plazas, theaters, and avenues throughout the island. His bust appears outside every school and important state building and in the town square of even the tiniest village. No study of Cuba is complete without understanding the legacy of this man of prodigious talents.

José Julían Martí y Pérez was born in Havana to Spanish immigrant parents on January 28, 1853 (his father, a policeman, came from Valencia; his mother was born in the Canary Islands). As a youth, he became involved in the movement against Spanish colonial rule and at 16 published an underground separatist newspaper. He was convicted of sedition and sentenced to six years, including six months hard labor at Havana's Prado stone quarry. Martí's sentence was commuted to exile on today's Isla de la Juventud (see pp. 226–229). Shortly thereafter, he was exiled to Spain, where he mixed in revolutionary circles, studied at Madrid and Zaragoza universities, and graduated with law and philosophy degrees.

Denied permission to return to Cuba, Martí began his luminous academic and literary career as a reporter in Mexico and, briefly, as a teacher in Guatemala. His revolutionary fire upset both the Mexican and Guatemalan governments, and he was forced to move on. When Spain issued a general amnesty in 1878, Martí returned to Cuba, where he renewed his revolutionary activities and was subsequently deported again to Spain. He traveled in France and Venezuela, and in 1880 settled in New York (a center for Cuban exiles) with his wife and son. He lived in exile for 15 years, working as a correspondent for U.S. and South American newspapers and, eventually, as the consul for Argentina, Paraguay, and Uruguay.

A man of action and letters, Martí worked tirelessly to reorganize the independence struggle. He united the various Cuban exile groups; convinced Cuban cigar workers to donate 10 percent of their wages to the cause; founded the Cuban Revolutionary Party in 1892; accumulated weapons; and formed La Liga de Instrucción to train guerrilla forces.

The short, slender figure with the neatly-clipped, bushy moustache was also a romantic visionary who wed the fight for independence to a campaign for true social justice. He campaigned against despotism and militarism, and—rare for his time— for racial and gender equality. Though enamored of the U.S. Constitution, Martí had also "lived inside the beast" and had little regard for U.S. imperialist policy. He made the fight against Yankee expansionism one of his lifelong passions: "It is my duty … to prevent, through the independence of Cuba, the U.S. from spreading over the West Indies and falling with added weight upon our lands of the Americas." Admired throughout the hemisphere, the undisputed leader of the independence movement was considered an heir to South American liberator and statesman Simón Bolívar.

Martí is almost as well known for his remarkable writing, considered among the finest in the Spanish language. His firebrand essays and simple yet cogent verses fill 73 volumes. Most Cubans know his "Versos sencillos" ("Simple Verses") by heart, and his avant-garde poetry helped initiate the school of modernism in Latin American poetry.

Martí published the *Manifesto de Montecristi* as a blueprint for the second war of independence (1895–1898), which he

The Monumento a José Martí in Havana's Plaza de la Revolución is the preeminent monument to Cuba's national hero.

planned and launched. He was named major general of the Armies of Liberation and, accompanied by Gen. Máximo Gómez, supreme commander of the revolutionary forces, set history in motion.

On the stormy night of April 11, 1895, Martí pulled ashore in a rowboat on a beach at Cajobabo, in eastern Cuba (see p. 224). He kissed the soil he had last seen 16 years before. After an arduous trek through the mountains, the two leaders and four other prominent exiles linked up with the rebel army of 6,000 troops under Col. Antonio Maceo. On May 19, in his first skirmish at Dos Ríos, José Martí was shot through the neck and killed—the first casualty of the war. The gaunt, unlikely soldier in his trademark black frock coat, collared shirt, and bowtie had rushed forward to meet the enemy, committing martyrdom for the cause to which he had dedicated his life. ■

Sierra Maestra

THE SIERRA MAESTRA, THE HIGHEST AND MOST DAUNTING terrain in Cuba, run along the southern shore in a serried spine rising to 6,430 feet (1,960 m). Sparsely inhabited, deeply incised with precipitous ravines, and thickly forested, they are a hiker's delight—and ideal guerrilla terrain: Castro set up his rebel headquarters here and the sierra became the main battlefront in the war to topple Batista. You can visit the former command center and climb to the summit of Pico Turquino—Cuba's highest peak (6,475 feet/1,974 m).

The brooding mountains rise from Cabo Cruz in the west and run in an unbroken chain to the city of Santiago de Cuba, 100 miles (161 km) to the east. From below, they look like an impenetrable wall, and these mountains are so steep that in places grooves are etched across the concrete road for added traction. Most people living here lead a simple lifestyle, raising coffee and traversing narrow trails that link remote hamlets. Many houses have bare-earth floors and no running water.

In the east, access to the Sierra Maestra is via **Cruce de los Baños.** From here a badly potholed road winds up to **El Saltón** *(tel 225/6326),* a popular ecoresort and spa that originally served the communist elite. Trails lead to waterfalls and pools for swimming; you can also rent horses. To the west, the main gateway is the sugar-processing town of **Bartolomé Masó,** where a road begins to climb to the village of **Providencia,** set in an exquisite valley. From here, a left turn at the T-junction leads you to the hamlet of Santo Domingo, nestled above the Río Yara at the base of Pico Turquino. **Santo Domingo**—accessed by a log bridge spanning the river—was the setting for a fierce battle between Batista and rebel forces in June and July 1958. The tale is told in the rustic **Museo Santo Domingo** *($),* exhibiting small arms and a relief map showing the ebb and flow of the battle. Trails lead to the battle sites. Refreshments and cabin accommodations are available at **Villa Santo Domingo** *(tel LP-375; call the operator),* where guides and permits can be arranged for visits to Pico Turquino National Park. Horseback rides are also offered.

PARQUE NACIONAL PICO TURQUINO

This national park encompasses 43,625 acres (17,450 ha) centered around **Pico Real del Turquino,** known colloquially as "el Pico." A permit *($)* and guide are required. The park is frequently off-limits to visitors for long spells. Scientists are sometimes granted access; check in advance with the Academia de Ciencias de Cuba *(tel 7/57-0599)* or the Centro de Inspección y Control Ambiental *(tel 7/204-2676)* in Havana. Visitors are required to have a permit and a guide *($ for each).*

From Santo Domingo, the road winds uphill in a dizzying spiral, with spectacular views through the plunging ravines. After a breathtakingly steep final ascent, you arrive at **Belvedere Alto del Naranjo,** where the view from a small parking lot lays the isle at your feet. From here, a challenging 2-mile-long (3 km) trail climbs westward to **Comandancia De La Plata** *(tel 23/376, permit required),* Castro's guerrilla headquarters,

located atop a ridge in a forest clearing. Here, a series of wooden huts are preserved as a museum, including a dental office and infirmary run by Che Guevara. In Castro's hut is a bedroom with double bed, office, kitchen, and deck. A transmitter from which Radio Rebelde dispatched the rebel's messages to the masses is still here. Cameras are not permitted and passports are required.

Trails also lead to the summit of **Pico Turquino,** which is best attained at dawn for stupendous vistas before the clouds set in. En route you'll pass through a number of ecosystems replete with wildlife. The forests are rich in bromeliads, ferns, and orchids. Near the summit, mists swirl overhead and the crisp alpine weather is a constant interplay of drizzle and warming sunshine. At the summit

is a bust of José Martí, placed here in 1952.

The northerly **Sendero Pico Turquino trail** begins at Alto del Naranjo and leads 8 miles (13 km) via the remote mountain communities of La Platica and Palma Mocha. Most hikers overnight at **Aguada de Joaquín,** a tent camp 2.5 miles (4 km) below the summit.

A second, extremely steep, trail leads north from the **Estación Biológica Las Cuevas,** on the Santiago de Cuba–Marea del Portillo coast road. It's a stiff 8-mile (13 km) hike. The fit can hike round-trip in one day, or you can camp at 5,445 feet (1,660 m) on Pico Cuba (6,177 feet/1,883 m). The ascent is rigorous and the weather fickle; take warm, waterproof clothing. You'll need two sets of guides to hike between Alto del Naranjo and Las Cuevas. ■

View over the Sierra Maestra, where Castro once headquartered the rebel army

West coast

CUBA'S REMOTE SOUTHWESTERN SHORE IS OFF THE BEATEN tourist path, but nonetheless offers a few intriguing sites. Manzanillo boasts beautiful ceramic murals and a museum paying homage to a revolutionary heroine, and nearby are remains of an original sugar mill.

The highway from Bayamo meets the Gulf of Guacanayabo at Manzanillo and runs south a short distance inland of the shore. The local economy is fueled by sugarcane, and during the harvest, smoke-smudged fieldhands slash at the charred stalks, and black plumes swirl over the fields. **Media Luna,** 32 miles (52 km) southwest of Manzanillo, a sugar-dependent town, is also the hometown of revolutionary heroine Celia Sánchez Manduley, who was born in a green-and-white gingerbread house on the main street. Visit the **Museo Celia Sánchez** in what is now a community center. Farther south, **Niquero** is distinct for its wooden architecture in French Caribbean style.

The Gulf of Guacanayabo at sunset

MANZANILLO

This fishing town, 40 miles (64 km) southwest of Bayamo, is known as a sugar port and a center for lobster and shrimp. It also has a major ship repair yard and a tradition of making mechanical organs (introduced by French settlers), which are still played on the streets.

The historic core of the city is centered on **Parque Máximo Gómez,** highlighted by a *glorieta* (bandstand), with cupola, arches, and *azulejos*—delicate tilework in Andalusian style. The park is ringed by wrought-iron lampposts and royal palms, with small stone sphinxes at each corner. Many of the nearby buildings also bear Moorish influences, notably the

23/54158). A crocodile farm 3 miles (5 km) south of town *(tel 23/42-4741, closed Sat.–Sun.)* welcomes visitors on weekdays.

LA DEMAJAGUA

Eight miles (13 km) south of Manzanillo, leave the highway and head west to La Demajagua *($),* the former estate of Carlos Manuel de Céspedes, who sparked the first war of independence when he freed his slaves on October 10, 1868 (see p. 186). A week later his home was destroyed, but a small structure erected in 1968 displays weaponry, edicts, and *banderas* (flags) associated with the estate, Céspedes, and the war. A stone path leads to the sugar mill ruins. Here, *calderos*—large cauldrons used to boil sugarcane—cogwheels, and a steam-operated *trapiche*—sugar press—are encircled by a stone amphitheater inset with the **La Demajagua bell**—Cuba's equivalent of the Liberty Bell, rung by Céspedes when he freed his slaves. ∎

A woman's touch

Celia Sánchez Manduley was born May 9, 1920, in the town of Media Luna. The daughter of a local doctor, she met Castro on February 16, 1957, and was integrated in the 26th of July Movement leadership in October. She organized and ran the Manzanillo-based network that supplied the rebel army. She also became Castro's right hand—and, some say, his lover. This intelligent woman was one of only a handful of people who could challenge his views. Her death from cancer in 1980 severely shook Castro and, it is said, removed the compass from his life. She is called the "most beautiful flower of the revolution." ∎

Edificio Quirch and the **Casa de la Cultura** *(Calle Masó #82, tel 23/54210).* In the courtyard of the latter, see the azulejo mosaics of Don Quixote and of Columbus coming ashore. Stop by the **Museo Histórico,** on the square's east side, to read about regional history, and visit the **Iglesia de la Purísima Concepción,** on the west side, to see its gilded altar.

Walk south along Calle Martí to Calle Caridad, where you should ascend the staircase lined with azulejos of sunflowers and doves, which pay homage to Celia Sánchez (see sidebar right). **Monumento Celia,** featuring a visage of the revolutionary heroine, stands at the top, with an adjacent art gallery *(closed Sun.)* dedicated to her. Immediately south is **Barrio de Oro,** where cobbled streets are lined with wooden houses, each with a cactus planted on the red-tile roof for good luck. You can tipple local rums at the **Fábrica de Ron Pinilla** *(Avenida Rosales, tel*

Tide pooling at
Cabo Cruz

Parque Nacional
Desembarcado del Granma

**Parque Nacional
Desembarcado
del Granma**
Ⓐ 168 A1
Ⓢ $

TUCKED INTO THE ISLAND'S SOUTHWEST CORNER, THIS
little-visited national park is named for the "disembarkation of the
Granma"—the boat that brought Castro and his rebel band to the
island in 1956 to launch the revolution. Today, trails access wetland
and semiarid ecosystems that shelter 170 species of birds.

Lying in the rain shadow of mountains that rise from the arrowhead
point of Cabo Cruz, this area is
notably dry. Cactuses punctuate the
woodlands that cover 80 percent of
the 62,500-acre (25,0000 ha) park,
which harbors such exquisite endemics as the Cuban Amazon butterfly and the blue-headed quail
dove. The mostly limestone terrain
is pocked by caverns, such as **Hoyo
del Morlotte** and **Cueva Fustete.** Hike to them from the highway via the **Sendero Morlotte-
Fustete** trail. Another trail, the
**Sendero Arqueológico Natural
El Guafe,** passes sites of pre-
Columbian antiquity (including a
cavern with stalagmites carved into
Indian totems). It leads from the
highway (look for signs) into coast
mangroves, where you can visit a
crocodile nursery. Bring adequate

water, supplies, and a passport.

To visit a reproduction of the
Granma, head a mile (2 km) south
of **Playa Las Coloradas,** where
**Campismo Villas Las Colo-
radas** *(tel LD-105; call the operator)*
rents simple cabins. Walk a mile (2
km) along the raised boardwalk,
through the mangroves, to a wharf
erected at the spot where the boat
ran aground. The **Museo Las
Coloradas** *($)* provides a map of
battles fought by the rebels as they
sought refuge in the mountains.

Southward, the coast road curls
around **Laguna Guafes,** full of
wading birds, and deposits you at
Cabo Cruz, where a quaint fishing village is marked by an 1877
lighthouse. The snorkeling is excellent amid reefs close to shore.
Watch for white-tailed and red-
billed tropic birds. ■

Pilón & Marea del Portillo

NORTHERN SNOWBIRDS FLOCK TO THIS ISOLATED, SUN-drenched pocket of far southwestern Cuba. Though the beaches aren't the most beautiful Cuba offers, the reclusivity and stunning mountain backdrops offer a unique appeal, best enjoyed by forays along the coast and into the Sierra Maestra.

To the west, the broad coastal plain occupies a basin carpeted in sugar-cane and centered on the small town of **Pilón.** Embraced by sea and mountains, Pilón is defined by tumbledown wooden houses and unpaved, potholed streets. One such house is now the **Museo Celia Sánchez Manduley,** dedicated to the revolutionary heroine (see sidebar p. 195) who ran a secret supply route from here to Castro's army. Additional displays detail the rural literacy campaign and regional history. You can negotiate with a local fisherman to take you out to offshore cays, with coral reefs good for snorkeling.

Farther east, the landscape changes abruptly. The mountains wring the rain from the clouds so that the narrow shore is a virtual desert. You'll pass hardy Brahman cattle and goats munching in cactus-studded, stony pastures. The sierra clamber down to a broad bay that shelters a tourist resort at **Marea del Portillo.** The golden beach is of modest appeal, though its setting in the lee of the Sierra Maestra is fabulous. A white-sand beach, **Cayo Blanco,** lies offshore. Schedule scuba diving at the **Albacora Dive Center** *(tel 23/59-734).* The resort tour desks can book guided horseback trips to the **El Salto waterfall,** as well as excursion tours as far afield as Bayamo and Santiago de Cuba. ■

Pilón & Marea del Portillo

🅰 168 A1, B1

Museo Celia Sánchez Manduley

✉ Calle Benitez #20, Pilón

☎ 23/59-4107

🕐 Closed Mon.

💲 $

Tropical paradise at Marea del Portillo (top). Getting a haircut in Pilón (left)

African zebras get a new lease on life at Cayo Saetía, a former hunting reserve.

More places to visit in Western Oriente

CAYO SAETÍA

This 16-square-mile (26 sq km) cay lies off the north shore of Holguín province and occupies the east side of Bahía de Nipes. It is billed as an ecotour destination, although prior to the collapse of the Soviet Union it served as a hunting reserve for communist sportsmen in pursuit of zebras, antelope, and other beasts imported from Africa. Don't be surprised to see zebra grazing, ostrich bounding across the grasslands, or water buffalo wallowing amid the mangroves. Jeep safaris and horseback rides are offered from **Villa Cayo Saetía** *(tel 24/96901)*, which has a bar, restaurant, and rental cabins, plus trails leading to sugar-fine beaches. ▲ 169 D2

FINCA MANACAS

The country estate where Fidel Castro Ruz was born on August 13, 1926, is at Birán, 38 miles (61 km) southeast of Holguín, at the foot of the Altiplanices de Nipe. The complex of several buildings includes the main, two-story wooden house set in the midst of a small wood; it has a view westward over a lake surrounded by pasture and sugarcane fields. The *finca* was part of a 65,000 acre (26,000 ha) domain owned by Castro's father, Angel Castro y Ariz. Castro's father and mother (the family maid, Lina Ruz González) are buried here. Finca Manacas was closed at press time, but preparations are being made to open the

facility to the public. Permission to visit can sometimes be obtained in advance from the Communist Party headquarters in Holguín *(tel 24/42-2224)*. Be aware that the roads to Birán are full of potholes. ▲ 168 C2

MUSEO INDOCUBANO

Cuba's most important collection of pre-Columbian relics is displayed at this museum, in Banes (see p. 179). The museum exhibits artifacts, pottery, statues, and a notable trove of exquisite jewelry, most dug up locally at the nearby **Chorro de Maita** indigenous site. The prize item is a unique gold idol adorned with a feather headdress. Murals depict the Taino Indian way of life. ▲ 169 C2 ✉ Calle Gen. Marrero #305 ☎ 24/8-2487 🕒 Closed Mon. 🅂 $

VELASCO

This small town, 15 miles (24 km) northwest of Holguín, offers a fascinating cultural center—the **Casa de la Cultura Félix Varona Cecilia** *(tel 24/24214)*. The center was begun in 1964 by New York-raised Cuban-American architect Walter Betancourt (1932–1978) and completed in 1991 by Gilberto Seguí Divinó. Betancourt, a protégé of Frank Lloyd Wright, settled in Cuba in 1961 to show his support for the revolutionary cause. He left Oriente with at least 15 brick buildings of radical design. ▲ 168 C3 ■

Rugged and remote, the eastern portion of the former Oriente province offers diversity: from offbeat Baracoa, Cuba's oldest settlement, to Santiago de Cuba, "cradle of the revolution," infused with an Afro-Caribbean flair.

Eastern Oriente

Monumento Antonio Maceo, Santiago de Cuba

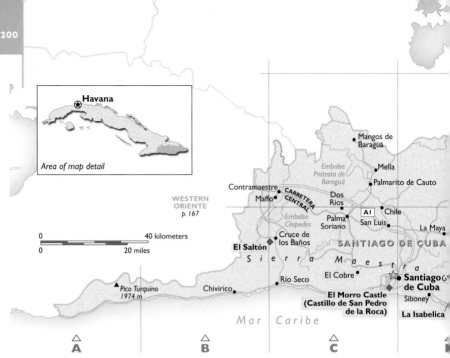

Eastern Oriente

IN FAR EAST CUBA, IN THE EASTERN PART OF THE REGION CALLED ORIENTE, the sun burns down with crushing intensity. The three major cities—Santiago de Cuba, Guantánamo, and Baracoa—each occupy a bowl encusped by mountain topography that has played a key role in Cuban history. The appeals of city life, and their varied histories and cultural influences, combine with those of some of the island's wildest terrain.

Santiago de Cuba, Cuba's second largest city, predates Havana and, though lacking the latter's stature and grandeur, offers notable monuments and attractions befitting its notable history as "birthplace of the revolution." The Cuartel Moncada, for example, is a de rigueur stop on the revolutionary trail. The city is wholly distinct in character—lent an infusion of French-Caribbean influences following the 1791 rebellion in Haiti, notably in its tradition of music and dance. The region has a distinctive folk culture, and it is considered the cradle of *son,* a mixture of old Spanish songs and African choruses. Santiago de Cuba is known for its cabarets and for its Carnival, held in July.

Beyond the city lie a fortified castle; the pilgrimage site of El Cobre; and Parque Baconao, a UNESCO biosphere reserve thus far undeveloped for ecotourism. The latter

hosts a bevy of one-off attractions, not least a classic car museum and a kitschy take on Jurassic Park. Beaches allayed along the narrow coast prove popular with Santiagueros escaping the city, and a half-dozen international resorts of modest standing are sprinkled along shores that deliver one of Cuba's preeminent drives.

In contrast, the city of Guantánamo can safely be skipped, despite its provincial capital status. However, a "stone zoo" in the nearby foothills is worth the excursion. (The famous U.S. naval base cannot be seen.) Most appealing is Baracoa, Cuba's oldest city, with its enchanting setting and sense of otherworldly remove. Baracoa languishes in the lee of mountains that are being developed for ecotourism: There's a heart-catching loveliness to the rainforest-covered heights of the Cuchillas del Toa, drawing birders and hikers to their cobalt green heights.

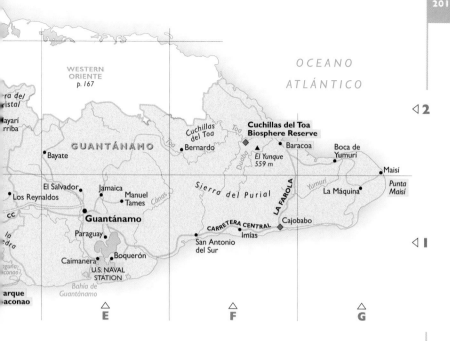

WESTERN
ORIENTE
p. 167

OCEANO
ATLÁNTICO

◁ 2

ra del
ristal

layarí
rriba

GUANTÁNAMO

Bayate

Cuchillas
del Toa

Bernardo

Cuchillas del Toa
Biosphere Reserve

Baracoa

Boca de
Yumurí

Maisí

El Yunque
559 m

El Salvador

Jamaica

Manuel
Tames

Sierra del Purial

LA FAROLA

La Máquina

Punta
Maisí

Los Reynaldos

cc

Guantánamo

Paraguay

Cajobabo

la
dra

Caimanera

Boquerón

CARRETERA CENTRAL

Imías

San Antonio
del Sur

◁ 1

guna
conao

U.S. NAVAL
STATION

arque
aconao

Bahía de
Guantánamo

△
E

△
F

△
G

Cuba's extreme Oriente is a mountainous region. The Sierra Maestra in the west, and the Sierra del Cristal and Sierra del Purial eastward, rise in an immense chain stretching across Santiago de Cuba and Guantánamo provinces. The vegetation grows lusher eastward: The northeast coast around Baracoa faces the prevailing trade winds and is lavished with Cuba's heaviest rainfall. Note, however, that Santiago de Cuba and Guantánamo cities lie in hot rain shadows whose lowland temperatures are markedly higher than elsewhere in Cuba. ■

Rushing the ice home before it melts beneath Oriente's fierce sun

Santiago de Cuba

Cuba's second largest city (population 443,000) boasts a beguilingly enigmatic appeal, wholly unique on the island. The architecture is the city's own, and the people have evolved their own regional expressions of music and dance. Varied museums, imposing monuments, and a compelling cemetery are among the sites that hold visitors spellbound. Santiago de Cuba is also where Castro launched his revolution in July 1953 with an ill-fated assault on the Moncada barracks.

After Diego Velázquez founded the original settlement in 1515, it was named Cuba's capital and thrived on the port trade and on copper mined at nearby El Cobre. In 1553, however, the capital was transferred to blossoming Havana. In 1639 Santiago de Cuba was fortified and in time became a major African slave port. The city became the center of intense fighting during the wars of independence; it was here, on July 1, 1898, that U.S. and Mambí forces ended 400 years of Spanish rule with the destruction of the Spanish fleet and the charge up San Juan Hill.

This city of broad boulevards and intimate plazas has its share of museums. The main

draw is its old town, laid out in a grid tilting down to the harbor. History echoes down the narrow streets graced by timeworn buildings painted in sun-bleached pastels.

In many ways, Santiago de Cuba—a major port and industrial city—is more Caribbean than Havana. The city's proximity to Santo Domingo and Jamaica fostered close historical links with both islands, and thousands of English- and French-speaking immigrants arrived during three centuries to stitch their customs into the city's cultural quilt. Even the lilting tongue of the Santiagueros and the sensuality of their music and dance hint at a Caribbean potpourri. ■

Parque Céspedes

GROUND ZERO IN SANTIAGO DE CUBA'S ANTIQUITY, THE former Plaza de Armas, or military parade ground, lies at the heart of the bustling historic city center. The cosmopolitan square is named for Carlos M. Céspedes (1819–1874), who launched the wars of independence with his *Grito de Yara* in 1868 (see p. 186) and who casts a glance over the square from atop a pedestal shaded by palms.

Parque Céspedes emanates flavorful evocations of history. The boot-steps of Hernán Cortés and Diego Velázquez echo across the square. Velázquez' home—dating from 1516 and thereby said to be the oldest structure still extant in Cuba—stands on the northwest corner. Beautifully maintained, the Andalusian-style Casa de Don Diego Velázquez today houses the **Museo de Ambiente Histórico Cubano** (Museum of Historic Cuban Ambience), full of period

furnishings, armor, and, to the rear, a small gold foundry. Moorish-style *rejas* and wood shutters hang dark and heavy on its somber facade. French influences predominate in a 19th-century house, attached.

To the north is the white-and-blue **Ayuntamiento,** or town hall, with a tiny balcony from which Castro gave the victory speech on January 2, 1959, following Batista's flight from Cuba. The building was erected in the 1950s in neocolonial style, after its antecedent was toppled by an earthquake.

The plaza is dominated to the south by the domed, ocher-colored **Catedral de Nuestra Señora de la Asunción,** dating from 1922 (with interior naves circa 1810) and the fourth cathedral to occupy the site. The remains of Diego Velázquez are supposedly interred in the floor. A statue of the Angel of the Annunciation, complete with trumpet, stands between the twin towers of the neoclassic facade. Note the exquisitely carved choir stalls. The **Museo Arquidio-cesano,** entered on the east side, exhibits religious art and statuary.

The place to savor the square's ambience is from the **Hotel Casa Granda,** rising over the east side. Its first-floor terrace bar overhangs the plaza and makes for a tremendous vantage beneath the shade of Parisian-style awnings. Ascend to the rooftop bar, which affords splendid views down over the old city. ■

Santiago de Cuba

🅐 200 D1

Visitor information

✉ Agenica de Viajes Rumbos #701, bet. Calles Heredia & General Lacret

☎ 22/62-2222

Museo de Ambiente Histórico Cubano

✉ Calle Felix Peña #612

☎ 22/65-2652

💲 $

Musical notes

For a good place to hear traditional *son* music, stop by the Patio Dos Abuelos, Calle Pérez Carbo #5, Plaza de Marte, tel 22/62-3302.

Overview of Parque Céspedes

Plaza de Dolores

Museo Municipal Emilio Bacardí Moreau
✉ Calle Pío Rosado, Aguilera
☎ 22/62-8402
🕐 Closed Sun.
💲 $

Colegio Jesuit Dolores concert hall
☎ 22/62-4623

SMALLER AND MORE INTIMATE THAN PARQUE CÉSPEDES, the former market square called Plaza de Dolores is shaded by tamarinds and ablaze with bougainvillea spilling their tropical hues into the square. It is named for the Iglesia Nuestra Señora de los Dolores, commanding the hill to the east side; the church adjoins the old Colegio Jesuit Dolores, the once prestigious school that Fidel Castro attended between 1935 and 1941; today it is a concert hall.

The square is graced by wrought-iron seats, buildings with original wrought-iron balconies, and a column supporting a statue of Francisco Vicente Aguilera (1821–1877), who wrote Cuba's national anthem. Among its many restaurants is **La Isabelica,** on the southwest corner, a 17th-century bodega where troubadours entertain with traditional music.

One block west, Calle Aguilera opens to a quaint *plazuela* lorded over by a neoclassic structure fronted by Corinthian columns. The **Museo Municipal Emilio Bacardí Moreau**—Cuba's oldest museum—was founded in 1899 by Emilio Bacardí y Moreau (1844–1922), city mayor, son of the founder of the Bacardí rum distillery, and revolutionary. The eclectic collection is on three floors: Colonial artifacts and weapons relating to the wars of independence grace the first (and include personal effects of Antonio Maceo, Carlos Manuel de Céspedes, and José Martí); upstairs, an art gallery spans colonial to contemporary works; and the basement (enter via Calle Aguilera) features Bacardí's personal collection of pre-Columbian artifacts such as shrunken heads, and Peruvian and Egyptian mummies. ■

A *comparsa*—musical group—competes during Carnival.

Carnival!

Santiago de Cuba's famed Carnival dates from the 18th century, when slaves were permitted a carousal. Today's "Festival of Caribbean Culture," held in July, takes its form from the parades of secret societies of ancient Africa, transformed in Cuba into neighborhood *comparsas*—competitive musical groups that parade through the streets in musical melées full of sinister and sensual content. Revelers dress as *orishas* (gods) and clowns with huge papier-mâché heads; others adopt period colonial costume or strip down to sequined, befeathered bikinis. The blare of Chinese cornets and the pounding of *bata* drums echoes through the streets as conga lines and parade floats march down Avenida Jesús Menéndez and the entire city indulges in no-holds-barred carousal. ■

North of Parque Céspedes

THE STREETS IMMEDIATELY NORTH OF PARQUE CÉSPEDES offer a medley of modest attractions for visitors with an ecclesiastical or historical bent. The area boasts four 18th-century churches within a 20-minute walk of the plaza.

Head up Calle Félix Peña two blocks to **Iglesia de Nuestra Señora del Carmen** *(Calle Félix Peña #505, at Tamayo Freites)*, known for its statuary. Two blocks farther north on Félix Peña, turn left for the 18th-century **Iglesia de San Francisco** *(Calle Juan Bautista Sagarra #121, tel 22/62-2812)*.

Félix Peña also leads to another 18th-century church, **Iglesia de Santo Tomás** *(Calle Félix Peña #308, tel 22/62-4389)*, at the junction with Calle General Portoundo. Five blocks east on Portoundo is **Iglesia de la Santísima Trinidad** *(Calle General Portuondo #661, bet. Gral Moncada & Porfirio Valiente, tel 226/62-2820)*, a worthy stop for its decorated ceiling and splendid neoclassic features.

History buffs might call in at **Museo Frank País,** where exhibits pay homage to brothers Frank and José País, the revolutionary heroes who were born in this house. Frank (1935–1958) became Fidel Castro's most trusted provincial leader and commanded the revolutionary M-26-7 movement in Oriente. On November 30, 1956, Frank led the ill-fated assault on the police headquarters in Santiago de Cuba timed to coincide with Castro's arrival in Cuba aboard the *Granma*. Frank was assassinated in July 1957, one month after his brother was also gunned down, inspiring mass demonstrations against the Batista regime.

Tales of the struggle for independence are regaled at the **Museo Casa Natal de Antonio Maceo,** where the brilliant tactician was born on June 14, 1845. The mulatto rose to become second in command of the Mambí forces during the wars of independence. He refused to accept surrender in 1878 and sought exile in Costa Rica after further combat. He returned from exile on April 1, 1895, and was killed in the

Dance moves

Numerous *comparsas* (folklore associations) welcome visitors to their year-round workshops, where they practice routines for the year's coming Carnival. You'll witness performances of *conga oriental, tumba francesa,* and *carabali obulo,* and perhaps be invited to learn a few slick moves yourself. The choreography is based on the black Haitian tradition, heavily influenced by the French quadrille. Among the world-famous Afro-Cuban troupes that host rumbas are **La Tumba Francesa** *(Calles Los Maceos & General Bandera),* **Ballet Folklórico Cutumba** *(Calle L #101, tel 22/62-2441),* and **Foco Cultural El Tivoli** *(Calle Desiderio Mesnier #208).* ∎

skirmish at San Pedro, near Havana, on December 7, 1896. The museum contains period furniture and many of Maceo's personal effects, including the flag used during his invasion on western Cuba and the printing press that published *Cubano Libre,* the newspaper known as the artillery of the revolution. ∎

Museo Frank País

 Avenida General Banderas #266, bet. Trinidad & Habana

☎ 22/65-2710

🕐 Closed Sun.

💲 $

Museo Casa Natal de Antonio Maceo

✉ Calle Maceo #207, bet. Corona & Rastro

☎ 22/62-3750

🕐 Closed Sun.

💲 $

Waiting for the bus in colonial Santiago de Cuba

Walk: Historic Santiago de Cuba

This walk, sloping downhill the entire way, takes in Santiago de Cuba's most colorful street, passing a bevy of attractions that define Santiago's culture, including the once fashionable enclave of Tivoli and ending with a fine vista that puts your walk in perspective.

Begin in **Plaza de Marte ❶**, at the junction of Calle Aguilera and Avenida Victoriana Garzón, which leads to Reparto Vista Alegre. The park itself, which was known during the wars of independence as an execution ground for nationalists, is of modest interest. Note the bust of José Martí at the southern end. The old city falls away as you stroll westward along Aguilera, once the city's foremost commercial thoroughfare; it still bears 1950s-era signs.

After three blocks, you'll enter **Plaza de Dolores ❷** (see p. 204), where you should peek inside the **Iglesia Nuestra Señora de los Dolores.** After a brief perusal, proceed west

two blocks on Aguilera to Pío Rosado, where you should pop in the **Museo Emilio Bacardí Moreau ❸** (see p. 204), with broad-ranging displays and an impressive art gallery. Exiting, turn south and follow Pío Rosado 50 yards (45 m) to **Calle Heredia,** a lively street that reverberates to the clack of the *claves* and beat of the African drum. A cultural fair is hosted on weekend evenings, when traffic is barred and troubadours and other street performers entertain.

The house at the corner of Heredia and Pío Rosaro is adorned with typical 19th-century balconies. The brick stairs lead up to the **Museo del Carnaval** (*Calle Heredia #304, tel*

22/62-6955, *closed Mon.*), exhibiting lavish costumes and other paraphernalia tracing the past and celebrating the present of Santiago de Cuba's famed Carnival.

Turn right and call in at **Casa José María Heredia** ❹ (*Calle Heredia #304, closed Mon.*), an 18th-century town house where the independence fighter and romantic poet, José María Heredia (1803–1839), was born. Heredia paid tribute to the beauty of the Americas in verse, most famously in his "Ode to Niagara." Today, his house is a museum honoring him; it's also a cultural center and meeting point for local poets.

🗺 See area map pages 200–201

▶ Plaza de Marte

↔ 1.3 miles

🕐 2 hours (one way)

▶ Museo de la Lucha Clandestina

NOT TO BE MISSED

- Museo Emilio Bacardí Moreau
- Casa de la Trova
- Catedral de Nuestra Señora de la Asunción
- Museo de Ambiente Histórico Cubano

Everyone dances at Casa de los Tradiciones.

Continue west on Heredia and push through the doors of the **Casa de la Trova** *(Calle Heredia #208),* formerly the home of revered composer Rafael Salcedo (1844–1917), who founded a troubadour tradition carried through to today. An ascetic renovation in 1995 diminished the physical setting, but the walls are still festooned with portraits of famous performers, such as Compay Segundo, who have graced the establishment.

Afternoons and evenings you can still swing your hips to *son,* plaintive boleros, and other classic sounds from such groups as the Trio Matamoros. A similarly heady atmosphere can be enjoyed nighttimes at nearby **UNEAC** *(Calle Heredia #266),* and on Saturday evenings at **Casa de los Estudiantes** *(Calle Heredia #204),* which showcases sensual Afro-Cuban rhythms. **Casa de las Tradiciones** *(Calle Jesus Rabi #154, bet. Santa Rosa & Princesa, tel 65/3892, $),* near Bario Tivoli, is also popular, especially among Cubans. It's an old house turned into a club featuring live traditional music and dance.

After exploring the sites of nearby **Parque Céspedes** ❺ (see p. 203), including the **Catedral de Nuestra Señora de la Asunción** and the **Museo de Ambiente**

Histórico Cubano, follow Calle Félix Peña one block south to Calle Bartolomé Masó. Turn right. After one block, you arrive at **Balcón de Velázquez,** an open area atop an old Spanish fort at the corner of Calle Mariano Corona. Savor the fine views over the historic quarter of Tivoli.

Continue one block west to Calle Padre Pico and turn left. Ahead you will see a broad flight of stairs that you may recognize from many a tourist poster. The stairs are a popular gathering spot for old wags known for offering solicitous compliments to passing females.

Ascend the stairs and follow the crenelated wall as you climb 50 yards (46 m) up Calle Rabi to the **Museo de la Lucha Clandestina** ❻ (Museum of the Clandestine Struggle; *tel 22/62-4689, closed Mon.),* dedicated to the tale of the 26th of July movement and the fight to topple Batista. It is housed in the former police barracks that was attacked on November 30, 1956, by a group of revolutionaries led by Frank País. Three members died as they fled down Padre Pico. Exhibits on two floors revolve around País. Lovingly restored, the bright yellow building has a courtyard and good views of the city.

Your walk ends here. ∎

Reparto Sueño

YOU MIGHT DO A DOUBLE-TAKE AT FIRST SIGHT OF THE
Cuartel Moncada, its crenelated walls and turrets an incongruous
vision of beau geste in the midst of the leafy Sueño suburb. The opening shots of the revolution were fired here in 1953, when 26-year-old
Fidel Castro led lightly armed coconspirators in an assault on the military barracks, as bullet holes in the exterior walls attest (Batista had
the walls repaired, but the holes were faithfully reconstructed once
Castro took power).

Established as a Spanish fortress, the
former barracks of Moncada are now
a school, Ciudad Escolar 26 de Julio.
Three rooms have metamorphosed
as the **Museo de la Revolución**
*(Calle General Portuondo & Avenida
Moncada, tel 22/62-0157, closed
Mon., $),* with maps, bloodstained
uniforms, and other memorabilia
from that fateful day. English-
speaking guides are on hand.

Moncada is bounded to the west
by **Avenida de los Libertadores,**
lined with bronze busts of revolutionary heroes. Facing Moncada,
across the boulevard, is **Parque
Abel Santamaría,** a barren park
of interest for the column topped by
a large granite cube carved in bas-
relief with images of Abel Santamaría and José Martí. A fountain
makes it appear as if the cube is held
aloft by gushing water.

The Sueño district is graced by
many creaky wooden houses in
Caribbean vernacular style—a car-
ryover from the influx of French
Creole immigrants dating back to
1791. In counterpoint, and dominating the skyline, the **Hotel
Santiago,** on Avenida de las
Américas, is a 15-story modernist
structure, gaudily painted and
appearing more cubist than Cuban.
The **Bosque de los Mártires de
Bolivia,** opposite the hotel, is a bas-
relief monument that honors Che
Guevara and his band of Cuban
guerrillas who died in the Bolivian
campaign (see pp. 122–123). ■

Revolutionary attack

Castro launched his revolution to topple Batista at
dawn on July 26, 1953. Lightly
armed, his corevolutionaries
struck during the Carnival celebration. The alarm was raised
and the rebels were caught in a
crossfire, eight of whom were
killed. Fifty-nine others were
captured and tortured to death.
Castro was caught a week later
and sentenced to 15 years in
prison. Photos of the tortured
Fidelistas unleashed a wave of
disgust and lent legitimacy to
Castro's 26th of July Movement
(M-26-7), the revolutionary
group that evolved in subse-
quent years as the preeminent
opposition body. ■

Children at
Ciudad Escolar 26
de Julio celebrate
the anniversary
of the attack on
Moncada.

Plaza de la Revolución

Museo de la Imagen
✉ Calle 8 #106, bet. 3ra & 5ta
☎ 22/64-2234
🕐 Closed Sun.
💲 $

THIS SPRAWLING PLAZA, CAPABLE OF HOLDING A CROWD of 200,000, sits at the junction of Avenida de las Américas and Avenida de los Libertadores.

On the plaza's north side towers the **Monumento a Antonio Maceo,** paying homage to the mulatto general (1845–1896) who rose to become second-in-command of the rebel Mambí forces. Considered the godfather of Santiago de Cuba, the "Bronze Titan" is depicted on a rearing charger. Ascend the marble plinth for a dramatic view. Lending drama are a series of 23 soaring metal girders rising obliquely from the ground. Representing machetes, supposedly they're an allusion to the Protesta de Baraguá, Maceo's refusal to accept the peace treaty of March 23, 1878.

The bowels of the monument contain the **Sala de Exposición de Holgrafía** *($)*. Maceo's role in the wars of independence is regaled using holograms and an illuminated bas-relief model depicting the various battles.

REPARTO VISTA ALEGRE

Take a stroll in the eastern suburb of Vista Alegre, boasting grand houses ranging in style from neoclassic villas to Caribbean vernacular clapboards to mid-20th-century Miami-style houses. Most are in sad disrepair, alas, since their owners departed after the revolution. Vista Alegre is split down the center by Avenida Manduley, lined with some of the more grandiose houses. **La Maison** *(Avenida Manduley #52, tel 22/64-1117)* is superbly maintained and today hosts boutiques and a nightly fashion show. Note the pink, baroque **Casa de Don Pepe Bosch** *(Avenida Manduley, bet. Calles 9 & 11),* now a school for Young Pioneers, with a Soviet MiG fighter jet in the playground.

Nearby, the **Casa de la Cultura Africana Fernando Ortíz** *(Avenida Manduley #106, bet. Calles 3 & 5, tel 22/64-2487)* celebrates Cuba's African heritage with masks, musical instruments, and more. Mysteries of Santería are revealed at the **Museo de las Religiónes Populares** *(Calle 13 #206, closed weekends).* And the **Casa del Caribe** *(Calle 13 #154, tel 22/64-2285),* which studies Caribbean cultures, features minimal exhibits from the region; it also organizes the Festival of the Caribbean Culture. Be sure to stop off at the **Museo de la Imagen,** whose collection of some 500 cameras includes CIA espionage cameras.

Avenida Raúl Pujol borders Vista Alegre to the south. Follow Calle 11 and you'll emerge opposite the entrance to the **Parque Zoológico,** Santiago's meagre zoo.

SAN JUAN HILL

More appealing, and immediately east, is Loma de San Juan, the famous San Juan Hill where, on July 1, 1898, a charge ostensibly led by Theodore Roosevelt's Rough Riders sealed the Spanish-American War and Cuba's fate with it. Today the knoll is a park studded with cannon and monuments dedicated to Cuban revolutionaries and, charitably, to individual U.S. battalions and "the generous American soldiers who sealed a covenant of liberty and fraternity between the two nations." The peace treaty ending the war was signed on July 16, 1898, beneath the **Arbol de la Paz** (Peace Tree)—a ceiba surrounded by cannon—between the zoo and San Juan Hill. ■

Cementerio de Santa Ifigenia

SANTIAGO DE CUBA'S VAST AND FASCINATING CEMETERY IS laid out in a grid and graced by scores of important tombs, many of Carrara marble adorned with angels. Two luminaries in Cuban history are here: Carlos M. de Céspedes (1819–1874), the Father of the Nation, whose tomb is topped by an eternal flame; and José Martí.

Cementerio de Santa Ifigenia
📧 Calzada Crombet
☎ 22/63-2723
💲 $

José Martí slumbers in the **Mausoleo de Martí.** His tomb is draped with the Cuban flag beneath a crenelated hexagonal tower designed so that, during the day, sunlight always shines on him. Other notables buried here include Emilio Bacardí (1844–1922), in the pyramid-shaped tomb to the right of the entrance; and Tomás Estrada Palma (1835–1908), Cuba's first president. Note the many graves marked by red-and-black flags. They denote members of Castro's revolutionary M-26-7 movement who died for the cause, including Frank and José País (see p. 205). The grandiose entrance gate contains remains of Cuban troops who died fighting in Angola and Ethiopia.

To get there, hop in a horse-drawn carriage on Avenida Jesús Menéndez. En route, opposite the glitzy new railway station, you'll pass the **Fábrica Ron Caney** *(Avenida Peralejo #103, tel 22/62-5575),* the former Bacardí rum factory; dating from 1868, it is Cuba's oldest extant rum factory. It was seized by the Castro regime in 1959, when the Bacardí family was forced into exile. It is not open to view, but you can tipple *tragos* (shots) of the various rums made here in a tasting room. Four blocks north, your horse will draw past the **Fortín de Yarayó,** an ocher-colored hexagonal fort at the junction of Avenida Crombet and Avenida Juan Gualberto Gómez. The diminutive encasement is one of 116 such

fortresses (most long-since demolished) that formed a cordon around Santiago de Cuba.

Returning via Avenida Jesús Menéndez, note the colorful revolutionary mural on the factory wall facing the railway station and, farther south, the 656-foot-long (200 m) fresco that traces Cuba's history in 30 wall panels. ■

José Martí's mausoleum

Rum nation

Cuba's national drink is *ron,* rum. It infuses island culture. Rum is made from the fermented juice of sugarcane or a mix of cane-juice and molasses, the dark brown residue left after crystallized sugar has been processed from cane. The basis for almost every island cocktail, rum is amazingly versatile and comes in a broad range of colors and flavors.

We can thank Christopher Columbus for Cuba's fine rums; he first brought sugarcane from the Canary Islands on his second voyage in 1493. Soon, rudimentary ox-powered mills (*trapiches*) were producing sugarcane juice (*guarapo*) and molasses that 16th-century Spanish settlers turned into a crude type of

"molasses wine." In 1838 the introduction of steam power and of distilleries in the manufacturing process led to an increase in sugar production while dramatically improving rum quality. By the mid-19th century, the cities of Havana, Matanzas, Cárdenas, and Santiago de Cuba produced large quantities of export quality rums, sold under such world-famous labels as Bacardí, Bocoy, Havana Club, and Matusalem. The most important company by far was Bacardí, founded by Don Facundo Bacardí, a Catalan migrant, who established his first rum factory in Santiago de Cuba in 1868.

After the 1959 revolution, the state took over the rum industry (the Bacardí family fled the island and took their name with them).

Which rum today (above)? Rum family patriarch Emilio Bacardí Moreau was also an avid art collector; he created Santiago's Museo Bacardí (left) in 1899.

1 to 15 years in oak barrels, in which slow-acting chemical reactions imbue a unique character. All distilled rums are clear. Darker rums attain their distinct flavor and color from the tannins of the oak barrels in which they are stored, and, in some rums, from the addition of caramel during the aging process. The resulting rum is then diluted to reduce the rum to commercial strength before it is bottled.

Cuban rums are traditionally light in flavor. The cheapest—and strongest—is *aguardiente* (firewater), a clear, raw, unaged rum. It is produced exclusively for local consumption and typically drunk in shots *(tragos)*. Of export-quality rums, the title *carta blanca* denotes a clear "white rum" aged for three years, with little body and an alcohol content of 40–60 proof. It is used in most cocktails, including the *cuba libre* (rum and cola), daiquiri (rum, lime juice, sugar, and maraschino blended with crushed ice), and *mojito* (rum with lime juice, sugar, soda water, mint leaves). Dorado rums, aged for five years, are fuller bodied and have an amber color. They form the basis for cocktails such as the *mulatta,* with lime and cocoa liqueur. Premium rums are darker and smoother *añejos,* aged for seven years (or longer) and usually distilled in copper tanks to bring out more aroma and flavor. Usually enjoyed "on the rocks," añejos are as distinct and noteworthy as single-malt whiskeys; the best—such as the 15-year-old Havana Club Gran Reserva—rank with fine cognacs. ∎

Today, some one dozen distilleries throughout Cuba produce about 60 brands of rum. The most notable label is Havana Club, produced today at Santa Cruz del Norte, a town heady with the sweet smell of fermentation.

THE PROCESS

There are four stages in the production of rum: fermentation, distillation, aging, and blending. First, molasses is fermented with yeast (present in the raw material), which transforms the sugar into ethanol. Compressed vapor then heats the fermented brew, which is diluted with distilled water and fed into a copper distillation vat, where the alcohol concentration is increased to about 75 proof; the pleasant flavors are separated out and the unpleasant ones eliminated. The distillate is then aged from

El Morro

El Morro

 200 C1

✉ Carretera del Morro,
6 miles S of
Santiago de Cuba

☎ 22/69-1569

💲 $

THE EASTERN HEIGHTS OVERLOOKING THE BOTTLENECK
entrance to Santiago bay are guarded by this clifftop colossus in stone,
more formally known as the Castillo de San Pedro de la Roca. The
imposing castle, a striking embodiment of Spanish military architecture, dates back to 1643, though much of its current bulk was added
in ensuing decades following depredations by pirates. Cannon point
menacingly from massive batteries, and the powder magazines are
still full of cannonballs.

You are free to roam at leisure,
although guides are on hand to
make sense of the befuddling maze
of dark passageways. From the bastions, magnificent vistas open up
westward along the coast, where the
sunken relics of Spanish vessels
have lain submerged since the
fleet's destruction during the
Spanish-American War. A splendid
exposition regales the tale of the
naval engagements, displayed on a
relief map. Another room houses
the **Museo de la Piratería**

(Museum of Piracy), containing blunderbusses, cutlasses, and other relics that testify to the age when the Caribbean was infested with pirates. U.S. efforts to destabilize the Castro regime are given prominence as a form of latter-day piracy. Note, too, the simple chapel with a large wooden statue of Christ.

CAYO GRANMA

Sheltered within the neck of the harbor, this small, picturesque island makes for a pleasant excursion when combined with a visit to El Morro. The isle, which you can circumperambulate in 30 minutes via the island's sole road, is fringed by red-tile-roofed houses overhanging the water. Be sure to ascend to the hilltop **Iglesia de San Rafael,** offering a fine vantage over the bay. The island is most famous for the **Restaurante El Cayo** (tel 22/69-0109), a waterfront seafood eatery on the cay's northeast side.

To reach Cayo Granma, pick up the passenger ferry from Parque Alameda, on Avenida Jesús Menéndez in Santiago de Cuba; or from Ciudamar, a wharf on Carretera Turística a short distance north of El Morro. Get off at La Socapa, on the isle's western headland. A battery above the ferry berth still bears cannon and offers a grandstand view of El Morro across the channel. ■

In age-old tradition, a cannon is fired nightly at El Morro castle.

El Cobre

CUBA'S MOST IMPORTANT PILGRIMAGE SITE AND THE island's only basilica makes for a fulfilling excursion from Santiago de Cuba. Dramatic in its setting and fascinating for its historical associations twined in legend, El Cobre traces a lineage back to the 1530s, when the Spanish established a copper *(cobre)* mine here.

Thousands of pilgrims flock annually to El Cobre (above) to worship the statue of the miracle-giver Virgen del Cobre (inset).

El Cobre
🅼 200 C1

The slaves who worked the mine were granted freedom in 1801, some 75 years before their brethren in the canefields. The small town their descendants occupy today is backed by the thickly forested Sierra del Cobre, 17 miles (27 km) northwest of Santiago de Cuba. It is dominated by the **Basílica de Nuestra Señora del Cobre,** erected in 1927 and dedicated to the miracle-worker Virgen de la Caridad del Cobre, officially named Cuba's patron saint in 1916.

Enter from the rear, via the **Salon of Miracles,** which contains a baroque silver altar. This side chapel is filled with offerings spanning 200 years, including *milagros* (adornments in the shape of limbs) left in bequest of healing. A staircase accesses the **shrine to the Virgen de la Caridad del Cobre.** She is displayed in a glass case above the altar, her yellow robes the same color as those of Ochún, the Santería goddess. Try to visit on September 8, when thousands of pilgrims descend on El Cobre and the Virgin is carried in a procession. ∎

Virgen del Cobre

In 1606, legend dictates, two *indio* men and a black boy were caught in a storm in the Bay of Nipes. Just as their boat nearly capsized, a plank appeared bearing a statue of a *mulatta* Virgin holding a baby Jesus and bearing the inscription, "Yo soy la Virgen de la Caridad— I am the Virgin of Charity." The waves subsided, and the men declared it a miracle. The figure was taken to El Cobre mine, where a hermitage was built. Miracles were ascribed to the Virgin, who soon came to occupy a pivotal role in the Cuban psyche. The cult of worship is strengthened by the Virgin's associations with Ochún, the Santería goddess of love, femininity, riches, and sweet water. She is usually shown standing atop the waves, with the men at her feet. ∎

Parque Baconao

THIS 80,060-ACRE (32,400 HA) PARK EXTENDS FROM THE
eastern suburbs of Santiago de Cuba to the border with Guantánamo
province. Part of Baconao has been named a UNESCO biosphere
reserve for its biodiversity, including more than 6,000 species of higher plants. A popular weekend getaway for Santiagueros, the park
offers beaches, a valley with prehistoric re-creations, and museums.

Baconao is accessed from Santiago de Cuba via Carretera de Siboney, the same route taken by invading U.S. forces in 1898, and later by Castro and his revolutionaries en route to the Moncada barracks in 1953. Twenty-six monuments honoring the revolutionaries who died in the Moncada assault line the road.

About 8 miles (13 km) east of Santiago de Cuba, a spur road climbs 9 miles (15 km) through shifting ecosystems into the **Sierra de la Gran Piedra.** It's a magnificent drive, with the views growing more dramatic as you ascend to the ridge-crest. At the top, a 454-step staircase delves through exotic vegetation to **La Gran Piedra** (4,006 feet/1,221 m), a mammoth boulder that can be scaled. Refreshments can be had at **Villa Gran Piedra** (tel 226/68-6393), with bungalows for rent.

Back on the main road, at **Granjita Siboney,** Fidel Castro & Co. set out in 26 vehicles on July 26, 1953, to attack Cuartel Moncada. Their small farmhouse is now a museum with weapons and other mementoes from that fateful day. A stone's throw away, the splendid **Museo de la Guerra Hispano-cubano-norteamericana de Baconao** has photos, exhibits, and maps regaling events of the Spanish-American War.

The beach at the village of **Siboney** is a favorite with Santiagueros. A war memorial recalls the landing of U.S. troops here on June 24, 1898.

Continuing on, in a couple of miles you'll spot **El Oasis,** an artists' community. Just north is the **Finca Guajira Rodeo,** a restaurant and bar that sometimes hosts rodeos.

Several more miles brings you to the **Valle de la Prehistoria** ($), a valley laid out Fred Flintstone-style with dozens of life-size dinosaurs; a small **Museo de Ciencias Naturales** ($) offers exhibits of local fauna. Farther on, the **Museo Nacional del Transporte** features 39 classic cars, plus 2,700 toy cars.

Farther east, you pass a **cactus garden;** and a display of Meso-american sculptures—**Museo Mesoamericano.** Several modest hotels are served by a string of mediocre beaches, and by **Acuario Baconao,** a dispiriting aquatic park with dolphin shows.

Finally, reaching the border with Guantánamo province, the road ends at **Laguna Baconao,** a large lake with pedal boats for rent and a small crocodile breeding center. ∎

Parque Baconao
🅰 201 D1

Granjita Siboney
✉ Carretera de Siboney Km 3.5, just before Siboney town
☎ 22/39168
💲 $

Museo de la Guerra Hispano-cubano-norte-americana de Baconao
✉ Carretera de Siboney
💲 $

Museo Nacional del Transporte
✉ Carretera de Baconao
☎ 22/39197
💲 $

Acuario Baconao
✉ Carretera de Baconao
☎ 22/35-6156
🕐 Closed Mon.
💲 $

At the Valle de la Prehistoria

A beach near **Chivirico**; the beauty only increases as you drive westward.

Drive: Santiago to Marea del Portillo

One of Cuba's preeminent drives, this supremely scenic and lonesome road hugs the shore beneath the lee of the Sierra Maestra. The terrain is a kaleidoscope that grows more dramatic westward. The beauty of the looming mountains and the stark low-desert country and teal-blue sea make for a picture-perfect day's outing.

Exit Santiago de Cuba westward along Paseo de Martí, which leads past a slew of dockside factories and, after about 9 miles (15 km), meets the coast at **Playa Mar Verde ❶,** a beach that draws Santiagueros on weekends. The main road, in reasonable condition, slices ruler-straight 13 miles (21 km) west to **Aserradero,** one of a dozen tiny communi-

ties along the route. Here, watch for a gun turret of the Spanish warship *Viscaya* poking above the surf; it was sunk by U.S. warships on July 3, 1898, in the fateful attempt by the Spanish fleet to break out of Santiago harbor (the barrels of another Spanish cruiser, the *Almirante Oquendo,* can be seen just 50 yards/45 m offshore at Ensenada Juan González,

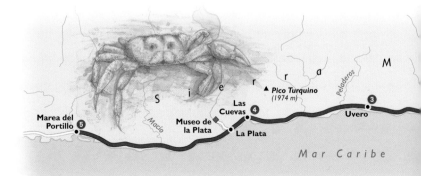

5 miles/8 km west of Playa Mar Verde).

Mountains to the north ascend prominently above the broad coastal plain. About 8 miles (12 km) west of Aserradero, at the Río Seco, you'll pass a turn-off to the right that leads over the mountains to **Cruce de los Baños;** four-wheel-drive is recommended. Continue straight, with the road now rising and dipping between headlands that grow with the miles. You'll pass beaches of variegated colors, including **Playa Blanca** and **Playa Sevilla Guamá,** about 40 miles (64 km) west of Santiago de Cuba and dominated by the clifftop **Hotel Serramar,** an all-inclusive hotel atop Punta Tabacal. Six miles (10 km) farther, you'll pass through **Chivirico ❷,** the only town along the entire route. There is little to inspire a stop.

Now the scenery begins to stagger. Copper-colored cliffs loom massively out of the sea as the mountains close in on the shore. Settlements whittle down to a few rustic rural communities, notably at **Uvero ❸,** 14 miles (22 km) west of Chivirico. This is the site of the first battle won by Fidel Castro's rebel army, on May 28, 1957, when a military outpost was captured and weapons seized. A glade of royal palms leads to a monument honoring the event. Ahead, **Pico Turquino,** Cuba's highest peak at 6,477 feet (1,974 m), lies seemingly within fingertip reach, dipping down to the dancing blue waters. Though the cloud-draped peaks that rise from the shore are lushly forested, the narrow coastal littoral hereabouts receives little rain. Cactuses begin to appear on penurious hillsides nibbled by goats.

At **Las Cuevas ❹,** 16 miles (25 km) beyond Uvero, you'll pass the trailhead to Pico Turquino and, 2 miles (3 km) beyond, **La Plata.** A dirt road leads north to the tiny **Museo de la Plata,** which celebrates events here on January 17, 1957, when Castro's then-tiny band of rebels made its first strike against Batista's troops since Moncada in 1953.

From here westward, it's just you and the buzzards and goats as the road wrinkles up into sharp curves, claws its way over great headlands, and hangs suspended in air before cascading steeply to the next valley. Eventually, you arrive at **Marea del Portillo ❺,** with its resort hotels and welcome refreshments.

In springtime, crabs migrate en masse and attempt to scale the bluffs that rise in places several hundred feet above the shore. Crushed by passing vehicles, they form a treasure of crabmeat for vultures. The road is subject to closure due to occasional landslides.

You'll have to retrace your steps to return to Santiago de Cuba. ∎

🄜 See area map pages 200–201
▶ Santiago de Cuba
↔ 100 miles (160 km)
🕒 Four hours (one way)
▶ Marea del Portillo

NOT TO BE MISSED
- Uvero
- Pico Turquino
- Marea del Portillo

Guantánamo

KNOWN FOR THE SONG "GUANTANAMERA" AND AS THE setting for the contentious U.S. naval base, Guantánamo lies about 20 miles inland of the coast, at the head of a deep bay from which the city and naval base take their names. The sprawling city, laid out in a near-perfect grid, occupies a barren plain and functions primarily as a military town of limited touristic appeal.

Playing chess in Guantánamo

Revolución, to the northwest, boasts a monument to Cuba's war heroes and a dynamic frieze honoring Karl Marx.

Some 16 miles northeast of Guantánamo, in the lush forests of the Sierra del Cristal foothills, **Zoolólogica Piedra** (stone zoo; $) tempts visitors with a whimsical menagerie of nearly 400 life-size lions, elephants, and other beasts, hewn in situ from giant rocks by farmer Angel Iñigo Blanco. Trails wend throughout the site. ■

Guantánamo

🅰 201 E1

Visitor information

✉ Dirección Provincial de Cultura Guantánamo, Calle Calixto García #806

☎ 21/32-2296

Museo Municipal

✉ Calle Martí #804

☎ 21/32-5872

🕐 Closed Sun.

💲 $

The town got a late start in life, boosted in 1791 by the slave rebellion in nearby Santo Domingo, when French settlers and their slaves washed ashore. Early in the 20th century, migrant workers from English-speaking Caribbean islands also arrived. The French- and English-speaking cultures remain strong, nurtured by the British West Indian Welfare Center *(Calle Serafín Sánchez #663, tel 21/325297)* and Tumba Francesa *(Calle Serafín Sánchez #715),* which promote their mother tongues and regional forms of music and dance.

The town's few sites are found around **Parque Martí,** a small square graced by the 1863 **Iglesia Parroquial de Santa Catalina.** Nearby, the rose-pink, neoclassic market—**Plaza del Mercado** *(Calles Antonio Maceo & Prado)*—is Guantánamo's architectural gem. To learn something of the town's history, head to the **Museo Municipal.** The dour **Plaza de la**

The U.S. presence

Since 1903, the U.S. has held an indefinite lease on 45 square miles (116 sq km) of headland at the entrance to Guantánamo Bay. The property comprises a naval station and naval air station, served by 3,300 military and civil service personnel, plus dependents and contractors. The self-contained facility includes a movie house, a golf course, and the only MacDonald's in Cuba. Castro refuses to cash the annual $4,000 lease check and demands that the U.S. vacate the base, which was granted via the Platt Amendment to the Cuban Constitution in 1903. Recently, captured Taliban members have been brought here. Needless to say, the base is off-limits. ■

Baracoa

CUBA'S OLDEST AND EASTERNMOST SETTLEMENT, BARACOA
counts also among the island's most charming cities. Small and compact, it claims a magnificent setting—embraced by mountains and
surrounded by rain forest. Brought into the national fold only within
recent decades, it clings fast to a sense of lifestyle steeped in the past.

Baracoa

🅰 201 F2

**Museo Municipal
de Historia**

✉ Fuerte Matachín

💲 $

Diego Velázquez founded this picturesque town in 1512, making it the
oldest colonial city in the Americas.
Baracoa's remote location did little to
favor the settlement. Cut off from
the rest of the island, it stumbled
along on smuggling and the meager
cocoa trade.

Baracoa feels its age. Its narrow
streets are lined by red-tile-roofed
wooden houses fronted by eaves
supported by creaking timbers. The
town's setting, too, seems fitting for
a Hollywood epic: It spreadeagles
below a dramatic flat-topped formation—**El Yunque,** the anvil—
hovering above the surrounding
hills that form an amphitheater
flowing down to the Bahía de Miel
(Bay of Honey), where fishing boats
bob at anchor. There's no shortage of
things to see and do.

In the 18th century, three

fortresses went up to guard against
predation by pirates. Rising over
Baracoa from atop a soaring out-
crop is **Fuerte de Seboruco,**
built in the 1730s and recently converted into a fine hotel that offers a
bird's-eye view over town. Guarding
the eastern entrance to town is the
well-preserved **Fuerte Matachín,**
dating from 1802. Today it houses
the **Museo Municipal de
Historia,** tracing the region's history since pre-Columbian days. From
here, you can follow the **Malecón,**
a decrepit wave-washed promenade
extending westward to the semicir-
cular **Fortaleza de la Punta,**
guarding the harbor entrance; it's
now a restaurant. En route, call in
at **Hotel La Rusa,** a former restaurant once owned by Magdalena
Rovenskaya, a Russian princess who
fled the Bolshevik Revolution and

**Wooden houses
bespeak
Baracoa's
antiquity.**

Columbus conundrum

Locals are highly partisan about claims that Columbus landed at Baracoa. Although evidence suggests Columbus actually landed farther west, near Gibara, most Baracoans point to their Cruz de la Parra (Cross of the Vine) as proof that the Genoese explorer came ashore here in 1492. In the 1980s, Belgian scientists analyzed samples of the wooden cross. Carbon dating confirmed the relic's antiquity, although tests show that it is hewn of a local hardwood—*Coccoloba diversifolia*—abundant around Baracoa. Thus, doubt was cast on the legend. The venerable relic is tipped with silver, added over ensuing centuries. ∎

settled here, where it is claimed, she went around dressed as if still attending court.

The center of affairs is leafy, triangular **Plaza Independencia,** on Calle Antonio Maceo, dominated by the simple, ocher-colored **Parroquia Nuestra Señora de la Asunción** *(tel 21/43352).* A church has occupied the site since the town's inception. This one, however, dates only from 1833 and was recently restored. Step inside to marvel at the silver-trimmed, 3-foot-tall (1 m) **Cruz de la Parra** (see sidebar left), which locals claim was left on the beach here by Christopher Columbus in 1492 and later found by Diego Velázquez and used to convert the Indians. Local resistance to the Spanish arrival was led by the Dominican-born Taino chieftain Hatuey ("the first Cuban rebel"), burned at the stake in 1512; his noble visage is honored in bronze in Plaza Independencia.

To gain a real taste of the local flavor, check out the **Casa de Chocolate** *(Calle Maceo #121),* which sells chocolate bars made from local cocoa at the **Fábrica de Chocolate** *(1 mile W of town, at Carretera Mabuajbo, tel 21/42646).*

At night, stop by **Plaza Martí,** where townsfolk gather to watch TV alfresco, sitting in neat rows facing the television that by day is kept locked inside its case atop a stand. ∎

Playing ball on Playa de Barigua

Cuchillas del Toa Biosphere Reserve

BARACOA IS HEMMED BY VERDANT MOUNTAINS. THIS WILD northeast corner—Cuba's wettest region—is deluged by rains and cloaked in virgin rain forest that smothers the Cuchillas del Toa, a rugged coastal mountain chain whose dramatic formations are among the least explored terrains in Cuba. The region's unique flora and fauna have evolved in isolation—a godsend for birders and hikers. Some 315,000 acres (127,500 ha) of these glorious lands are protected as the Reserva Biosfera de Cuchillas.

Cuchillas del Toa Biosphere Reserve
🗺 201 F2
✉ Parques Naturales de Baracoa, Calle Martí #207, Baracoa
☎ 21/43665

The reserve was officially created to protect the only known habitat of the ivory-billed woodpecker, a mainland native considered extinct since the 1940s. Then, in the mid-1980s, the bird was sighted in these mountains, prompting the Cuban government to declare the region a protected area. The reserve is subdivided into an amalgam of nature reserves and national parks that are still being developed. Facilities for ecotourists are as yet minimal.

Parque Nacional Duaba includes **El Yunque** (1,887 feet/575 m), the flat-topped mountain that seems to float above Baracoa and which locals claim is "the anvil" described by Columbus in 1492. You can hike or drive to the summit with a guide from Finca Duaba, where a restaurant serves *criollo* dishes.

The park also incorporates the mouth of the **Río Duaba;** a monument here marks the site where mulatto general Antonio Maceo came ashore on April 1, 1895, to relaunch the wars of independence. Nearby, the white-sand beach at **Playa Maguana,** 14 miles (22 km) west of Baracoa, shelves into sheltered teal waters.

Parque Nacional Cuchillas del Toa protects the interior mountains, whose inhabitants still bear the physical features of Indian forebears. The **Río Toa** is being promoted for white-water rafting and kayaking. Farther west, the 187,720-acre (76,000 ha) **Parque Nacional Alejandro Von Humboldt,** named for the German explorer, is Cuba's largest national park and a World Heritage site. ■

On the road between Guantánamo and Baracoa

More places to visit in Eastern Oriente

CAJOBABO

This lonesome beach, 28 miles (48 km) east of Guantánamo, is hallowed ground to Cubans. Here, on April 11, 1895, nationalist hero José Martí returned from exile, accompanied by Gen. Máximo Gómez, to incite the second war of independence (see pp. 190–191). A tiny museum honors Martí and tells the tale. The shingly beach lies about a mile farther east and is unmarked. 201 F1

EL SALTÓN

Billed as an ecoresort, this mountain retreat, 47 miles west of Santiago de Cuba, is tucked into a valley in the Sierra Maestra, about 5 miles (8 km) west of the village of Cruce de los Baños. The **Villa el Saltón mountain lodge** *(tel 225/6326)* was originally built for the communist elite. Today it offers stress treatments plus hikes, horseback rides, and even Jeep tours. Trails lead to a waterfall with natural pools good for refreshing dips, and farther afield to cocoa and coffee plantations. With an appropriate 4WD you can even tackle the rough mountain road that descends to the **Río Seco,** on the south coast. 200 C1

LA FAROLA

Unequaled for drama in Cuba, this 30-mile-long (48 km) mountain road is called "Cuba's roller coaster" for good reason. The road, which links the towns of Baracoa and Guantánamo, claws its way over the **Sierra del Purial** in a dizzying ascent that features numerous bridges suspended magically upon the mountainside. The marvelous piece of engineering was initiated in the 1950s and completed in 1964. Lower down, the road twists through the valley of the **Río Ojo,** whose banks are lined with palms. Higher up, you pass into pine forest. 201 F1

LA ISABELICA

High up on the plains of the Sierra de la Gran Piedra (see p. 217), coffee was farmed a century ago. La Isabelica, established in 1792 by French-Haitian Victor Constantin Couson, exists today in name only. The two-story stone estate house is now a meager **museum** *(closed Mon., $)* with period furnishings and exhibits of farm implements. Part of the former estate is graced by a series of cascading gardens—**Jardín Ave de Paraíso**—where anthuriums, bloodred dahlias, begonias, and other species bloom, including the garden's namesake bird of paradise. 200 D1

PUNTA MAISÍ

An 1862 lighthouse marks Cuba's easternmost accessible point, 800 miles east of Havana. Ascend the 144 steps for a bird's-eye view over the beach and along the cactus-studded coast. You can visit on flight-seeing excursions by biplane from Baracoa. If driving, Punta Maisí is accessed by a dirt road from the mountain village of **La Máquina,** which thrives on the local coffee harvest. 201 G1 ∎

Along string of tiny isles stretching across western Cuba's underbelly, this archipelago exemplifies a paradise escape: Sand, sea, and sun is what it's all about—and plenty of diving, too.

Archipiélago de los Canarreos

Preparing to set sail at Playa Rojas

Archipiélago de los Canarreos

WEARING A NECKLACE OF CORAL, THESE ISLANDS CLAIM SOME OF CUBA'S finest beaches and diving venues. One major island anchors the rest—1,180-square-mile (3,056 sq km) Isla de la Juventud. To the east, a string of 350 coral cays scatter across the sparkling blue Caribbean Sea. The latter are uninhabited but for Cayo Largo, catering to beach-minded package vacationers. The archipelago was struck forcefully by Hurricane Michelle in November 2001; renovations may still be underway.

The Golfo de Batabanó separates the archipelago from the mainland; ferries link Isla de la Juventud to Batabanó, in Havana province.

Isla de la Juventud's earliest inhabitants, the Siboney, left their mark in petroglyphs on the walls of Cuevas Puntas del Este. Christopher Columbus, who landed on June 13, 1494, called the isle Evangelista. Pirates taking refuge here gave it the name Parrot Island for the vast flocks of birds that today exist in lesser numbers. Beginning in the 19th century, the Spanish used the remote island they called Isle of Pines as a prison for Cuban nationalists, including José Martí. A 20th-century prison—Presidio Modelo—has associations with Fidel Castro.

The island's present name, which translates as "isle of youth," recognizes its role as a special municipality for Third World students whom socialist Cuba hosted and educated for free. In exchange, the students helped bring in the citrus harvest. The program, initiated in 1971, has been discontinued, though about 61,750 acres (25,000 ha) are still planted in ill-tended citrus.

Juventud's entire southern half is a wilderness region of scrub and swamp—a precious habitat for Cuban crocodile, and for endangered sandhill cranes and Cuban parrots. This southern half is a military zone, although you can visit by permit (c/o Puertosol, *tel 7/204-5923*).

The archipelago's waters are littered with shipwrecks; dive boats depart for outlying cays, each of which offers its own appeal: flamingoes in the waters surrounding Cayo Pasaje, for example, and iguanas on Cayo Iguana. Most international visitors head to Cayo Largo, offering some of Cuba's finest beaches—perfect for day-trip and overnight packages from Havana. ■

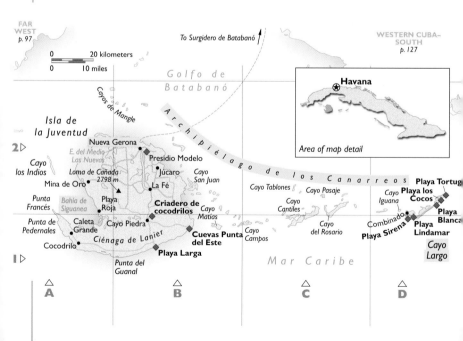

Nueva Gerona

STEEPED IN HISTORICAL CHARM, ISLA DE LA JUVENTUD'S
sleepy capital moves at a yesteryear pace. The few sites can be seen in
half a day's browsing.

Founded in 1830, this port town
exists primarily on the export of
citrus and marble. Recently
restored, the historic core's main
artery is **Calle Martí** (Calle 39).
Anchoring the main square—
Parque Julio Antonio Mella—is
the **Iglesia Nuestra Señora de
los Dolores,** an ocher-colored
church built in 1929. The **Museo
Provincial,** on the square's south
side, traces the region's history, with
a focus on piracy. Calle 28 slopes
east two blocks to the Río Las Casas
and *El Pinero* (tel 61/24162), the
ferry that carried Fidel Castro to
freedom in 1955.

Three other museums are worth
a look. The **Museo de la Lucha
Clandestina** (Museum of the
Underground Fight) regales the
town's history of underground
warfare against Batista during the
1950s. At the town's south end, the
Museo de Ciencias Naturales y
Planetario has simple archaeological and natural history exhibits.
Continue strolling south and, after a
mile, you'll arrive at the **Museo
Finca El Abra** (closed Mon., $). A
farmhouse doubles as a museum
honoring José Martí, who lived here
under house arrest for three months
during his six-year-term for sedition.

Hikers might head west of town
(take Calle 24) to ascend **Loma de
Cañada** (1,020 feet/2,798 m), the
highest point of the Sierra de las
Casas. At its base, three caves contain
pre-Columbian petroglyphs.

The island's main site of interest
is **Presidio Modelo,** 3 miles east of
town. Completed in 1931, it served
as a prison until 1967. Its most illustrious occupant was Castro himself,
incarcerated after the 1953 attack on
the Moncada barracks. The hospital
block in which he was housed is
now the **Museo Presidio Modelo**
(tel 61/25112, closed Mon.). ■

Nueva Gerona
◮ 226 B2
Visitor information
✉ Rumbosa, Calle José
Martí at Calle 22
☎ 61/23947

Museo Provincial
✉ Calle 30 at 37
☎ 61/23791
🕐 Closed Mon.
💲 $

**Museo de la
Lucha
Clandestina**
✉ Calles 24 & 43, at
Calle 45
☎ 61/24582
🕐 Closed Mon.

**Museo de
Ciencias
Naturales**
✉ Calles 41 & 46
☎ 61/23143
🕐 Closed Mon.
💲 $

Bahía de Siguanea & nearby

THE COUNTRY'S PREMIER DIVING IS A KEY DRAW TO THE translucent waters of the Bay of Siguanea, off the coast of Isla de la Juventud, where pirate ships and Spanish galleons can be explored a few fathoms down. Much of the shore backing Siguanea is a precious wildlife habitat of particular appeal to birders.

Siguanea & nearby

⚠ 226 A2

The glassy waters of the Bay of Siguanea, enclosed to the south by a long spit that ends at Punta Francés, have been declared a marine reserve served by the Hotel Colony *(tel 61/98181)*, on Playa Roja, about 20 miles (32 km)

Harvesting oranges at La Granja Patria, a plantation near Siguanea

southwest of Nueva Gerona. Day visitors are welcome *($)*. Today the hotel, which began life in 1959 as a Hilton, operates primarily as a scuba resort; it is served by the adjoining International Scuba Diving Center *(tel 61/98181)*, which

offers scuba certification courses. No diving within the reserve is permitted without an official guide, and call-in visitors wishing to dive must sign up for an organized program.

Divers are spoiled for choice. The zone between Punta Francés and Punta Pedernales is called the **Costa de los Piratas**—Pirate Coast—where the remains of several Spanish galleons and pirate vessels are preserved in pellucid waters teeming with sealife. Three well-preserved galleons at **Cayo Los Indios,** a small cay about 25 miles northwest of Siguanea, are particularly worth exploration. Divers can hand-feed stingrays at a site called **Stingray Paradise.** And the wall off the Pirate Coast is beset with canyons and caves and coral parapets, including the **Caribbean Cathedral—** claimed to be the tallest coral column in the underwater world. The beach of **Playa Francés,** sparkling like dusted diamonds, is indubitably the island's finest.

Trails lead north from the Colony Hotel into the **Refugio de Fauna los Indios,** a 9,880-acre (4,000 ha) reserve that extends along the shore of the Bay of Siguanea and protects an amalgam of ecosystems, among them mangroves, grasslands, and palm forest. Los Indios harbors at least six species of endemic reptiles. Its 153 bird species include the *tocororo*—the national bird—plus two highly endangered endemics: the Cuban sandhill crane and the Cuban parrot, found here in greater numbers than anywhere else in Cuba. ■

Juventud's southern zone

ALTHOUGH SMOTHERED IN ENTIRETY BY INHOSPITABLE terrain, the remote southern half of Isla de la Juventud claims glorious white-sand beaches, a turtle farm, and a cave known for its Indian petroglyphs. Access is via a military post at Cayo Piedra, 24 miles south of Nueva Gerona. A guide is compulsory.

The isle's southern half comprises the **ciénaga de Lanier**—the Lanier Swamp—a vast swath of sedge wetlands and paperbark swamps that shelters wild pigs, deer, and *jutías* (large rodents). Although ostensibly a nature reserve, the area has long been popular with Cuban hunters. You can hire the compulsory guide via Havanautos *(Calle 32 at 39, Nueva Gerona, tel 61/24432)* or the Hotel Colony *(Playa Roja, tel 61/98181)*, which offers tours that include the **criadero de cocodrilos,** 19 miles (30 km) south of Nueva Gerona. Here, hundreds of the reptiles are bred for release into the wild. You can get close to scores of crocs sunning themselves on the mudbanks, motionless as logs. Time your visit for midmorning to watch the savage beasts being fed hacked-up cattle. There are no facilities.

A dirt road leads east from Cayo Piedra to **Cuevas Punta del Este,** 37 miles (59 km) southeast of Nueva Gerona. Here, seven caves of historic and archaeological import back a white-sand beach *(no facilities)*. The series of caves contains pre-Columbian petroglyphs dating from about 800 and representing concentric circles and parallel lines thought to constitute a primitive celestial plan. Some 238 have been identified. Alas, many have been damaged and need conservation.

The main road runs south from Cayo Piedra to **Playa Larga,** whence it parallels the shore westward to the community of **Cocodrilo,** populated by the descendants of English-speaking Cayman Islanders. Nearby, at **Caleta Grande,** you can visit a marine science station where green and hawksbill turtles are bred. ■

Juventud's southern zone
 226 A1, B1

Crocodiles

The endemic and endangered Cuban crocodile—*Crocodylus rhombifer*—was hunted to near extinction during four centuries of colonial rule. The *lagarto criollo* is found today in the wild only in Ciénaga de Zapata and Ciénaga de Lanier—the most restricted geographical range of any crocodile species in the world. The species, with its truncated snout and yellow-and-black mottled skin, is highly aggressive (its cousin, the American crocodile, is comparatively timid) and is genetically coded to strike at anything that moves. Seven *criaderos* throughout Cuba breed crocodiles for reintroduction into the wild, and commercially for skins. ■

One of the bunch at the *criadero de cocodrilos,* Cayo Potrero

Cayo Largo

Cayo Largo

🗺 226 D1, D2

Visitor information

✉ Buró de Turismo Rumbos Cuba

☎ 45/48327

Michelle's wrath
The cay sustained significant damage in Nov. 2001 when Hurricane Michelle passed overhead; it will take time to rebuild the tourist infrastructure.

A scuba diver ascends Devil's Hole off Cayo Largo.

CAYO LARGO IS GIRDED BY SPARKLING SUGAR-WHITE beaches shelving into jade-colored waters. The boomerang-shaped isle is the only cay in the archipelago accessible by air from the mainland, and the only one developed for tourism. Visitors are cast adrift from the cares of the outside world, but you are also as divorced from the "real Cuba" as you would be on Mars.

This 15-mile-long (24 km) sliver of coral and powder-fine beaches, 125 miles (200 km) southeast of Havana and 70 miles (112 km) east of Isla de la Juventud, is the easternmost of the low-lying coral cays that make up the Archipiélago de los Canarreos. The island is entirely dedicated to international package vacationers, some of whom fly in for the day from Havana or other points in Cuba aboard rickety Russian biplanes.

You are greeted with a stupendous view. Limpid, warm waters of impossible Maxfield Parrish blues lap at dazzling white beaches. **Playa Sirena,** the westernmost and most spectacular beach, is reached by ferry from Marina Puerto Sol (*tel 45/48212*), where the isle's meager facilities are concentrated. Eastward, four beaches meld one into the other. Most of the hotel development concentrates along **Playa Lindamar** and **Playa Blanca,** which operates as a nudist beach. Farther east, **Playa los Cocos** appeals to divers for its shallow corals and shipwreck offshore. The easternmost beach, **Playa Tortuga,** derives its name from the marine turtles that waddle ashore to nest in the warm sands. Together, these beaches span 17 miles (27 km) running the length of the seaward side (the leeward side comprises mangrove lagoons).

All told, Cayo Largo's waters shelter more than 30 dive sites, served from a dive center at Marina Puerto Sol. Other activities include sportfishing, snorkeling, and trips to neighboring deserted cays.

The only organized natural site to visit is a turtle farm—**Granja de Tortuga**—in Combinado.

The Cuban government is beginning to promote Cayo Largo as an ecotourism destination. Birding is especially rewarding, with frigate birds, Caspian terns, and parakeets just some of the birds to add to life lists. ■

Travelwise

Old Yankee *cacharros*

TRAVELWISE INFORMATION.

PLANNING YOUR TRIP

WHEN TO GO

Cuba has a warm and humid tropical climate year-round. In general, dry season is Nov.–April, when temperatures average a balmy 22–25°C (72–77°F). Occasional cold fronts sweep down from the north during this period, bringing cool, sometimes stormy, weather. The hottest months are May–Oct., when the temperatures in Havana average 24–26°C (75–79°F), and extreme humidity has visitors breaking out in sweats. This is also the "wet" season, when almost daily showers and prolonged downpours occur, often causing wide flooding. Hurricanes are a rare possibility during this period.

Regional variations are pronounced. Temperatures increase eastward—Santiago de Cuba in the Oriente region, for example, is significantly warmer than Havana, especially in summer. Then, Oriente sizzles in heat, with Santiago de Cuba baking in a stifling basin; while Havana is caressed by near constant breezes.

Higher elevations are somewhat cooler—notably so in the Sierra del Escambray and Sierra Maestra. These heights also receive more moisture than lowland areas; those of far northeast Cuba are comparatively drenched and, hence, blessed with lush rain forests. The predominant winds are from the east, so that the lee of the mountains lie in relatively dry "rain shadows." The southeast coast is fringed by cactus-studded semidesert.

Most tourists visit in winter, when many of the most popular hotels in Havana are booked solid—elsewhere rooms are generally available year-round. Almost all hotels have low and high season rate fluctuations. Festivals occur year-round.

WHAT TO BRING

Cuba has a tropical climate, so dress accordingly. Lightweight, loose-fitting cotton and synthetic clothes are best. Shorts and T-shirts prove comfortable and are acceptable everywhere, including Havana, although you'll want some more elegant wear for nighttime, especially for ritzier restaurants and nightclubs such as Tropicana. Avoid tight-fitting clothes, which are uncomfortable and promote fungal growth in the hot, humid climate. A sweater and/or lightweight jacket are useful for the heavily air-conditioned restaurants and during Nov.–April, when cold fronts moving south from North America may bring cool, rainy weather. A poncho works well against warm season downpours, and a fold-up umbrella is recommended for city slicking. Bring swimwear if you plan on heading to the beach.

You'll want a comfortable pair of walking shoes for exploring Havana and other cities; sneakers work fine. Hiking shoes will prove useful if you plan on exploring mountain trails (often muddy) or wilderness areas. And dress shoes are not out of place for restaurants and nightclubs.

You'll need insect repellent, particularly for coastal areas and during the wet season, even in cities. Mosquitoes can be ferocious (notably around mangrove ecosystems), although other biting insects are few and rarely are mosquitoes a problem in upland or breezeswept areas.

Sunglasses are a necessity, as the tropical light is intense. And a sunhat or baseball cap and sunscreen are mandatory, even for brief periods outdoors. Do not underestimate the strength of the tropical sun.

Medicines are in very short supply, so you should bring a basic first-aid kit that includes aspirins, Lomotil, antiseptic lotions, band-aids, and other essential medications. Bring a spare pair of spectacles or contact lenses rather than a prescription, as replacements are virtually unobtainable. Similarly, bring all the photographic film and equipment you'll need, as these are in short supply and extremely expensive. Birders should also bring binoculars.

INSURANCE

Travel insurance is a wise investment. Companies that provide coverage for Cuba include American Express (800-234-0375) and TravelGuard International (800-782-5151). Assistcard (305-381-9959), based in Florida, has a regional assistance center in Cuba.

ENTRY FORMALITIES

Foreign visitors require a valid passport to enter Cuba (U.S. citizens of Cuban origin need a Cuban passport, issued by the Cuban Interests Section, 2630 16th St., N.W., Washington, D.C., 20009, tel 202-797-8518, fax 202-797-8512). No visas are necessary for tourists. Tourist cards for entry into the country are issued by approved travel agencies, or upon check-in for flights to Cuba; immigration officials stamp the tourist card rather than your passport. Foreigners are limited to a 30-day stay, plus an additional 30 days (prórroga) upon request ($25) from the Inmigración y Extranjería department in the Ministry of Interior: MININT, Calle Factor y Final, Nuevo Vedado, Havana.

U.S. law prohibits spending U.S. dollars in Cuba; all financial transactions involving travel in Cuba are banned. Exceptions are permitted for journalists, professionals and students conducting academic research, Cuban-Americans visiting family, and individuals participating in group tour and study programs arranged by a licensed organization. In reality, most U.S. citizens can participate in such group study tours (see How to get to Cuba, below). Contact the U.S. Treasury Dept., 202-622-2000, http://travel.state .gov/cuba.html, for details. Cuba has no such restrictions and welcomes visitors arriving with or without official U.S. sanction.

HOW TO GET TO CUBA

BY PLANE

The majority of flights arrive at José Martí International Airport, tel 7/33-5777, 15 miles (25 km) southwest of downtown Havana. Other flights arrive at Antonio Maceo International Airport, tel 226/91014, 8 miles (12 km) south of Santiago de Cuba, and at international airports at Camagüey, Cayo Largo, Cienfuegos, Holguín, and Varadero.

Licensed charter flights operate to Havana from Miami, New York, and Los Angeles, and between Miami and Santiago, Cienfuegos, Camagüey, and Holguín. Flights from the U.S. are restricted to passengers legally permitted to spend U.S. dollars in Cuba.

No such restrictions apply to international carriers who operate direct flights to Cuba from Cancún, Nassau, Montego Bay, Toronto, and Montreal, including:
Air Canada, tel 800-268-0024, www.aircanada.ca
Air Jamaica, tel 800-523-5585, www.airjamaica.com
Cubana, www.cubana.cu
Mexicana, tel 800-531-7921, www.mexicana.com.mx

In addition, British Airways, tel 800-247-9297, www.british airways.com, serves Cuba from the U.K.

BY BOAT

Private vessels berth at Marina Hemingway (tel 204-1150), 10 miles (16 km) west of Havana. U.S. skippers must be licensed by the Treasury Dept. (see Entry Formalities, p. 232) in order to legally pay for berthing and other services. Foreign cruise ships departing the Dominican Republic include Havana and Santiago de Cuba in their itineraries. U.S. cruise ships do not.

BY TOUR

Many U.S. organizations offer group study tours to Cuba that include airfare, hotels, and an established itinerary. The Center for Cuban Studies, tel 212-242-0559, www.cubaupdate.org, Last Frontier Expeditions, tel 303-530-9275, e-mail bob@cubatra velexperts.com, and National Geographic Society Expeditions, tel 888-966-8687, www .nationalgeographic.com, all offer tours, from general to special interest programs.

GETTING AROUND

Taxis provide transport from the major international airports to the city centers. Public transport is restricted to overcrowded buses that are best avoided.

BY PUBLIC TRANSPORTATION

IN HAVANA

BY BUS
Guaguas (buses) serve most parts of the city, but are overcrowded and uncomfortable. Large, 300-passenger Metrobuses (called *camellos*, camels, for their hump) link outlying districts with Parque de la Fraternidad, downtown. Beware of pickpockets.

BY TAXI
Havana's taxi service is fast and efficient. Panataxi, tel 55-5555, e-mail panataxi@transnet.cu; Taxis OK, tel 204-9518; and Transtur, tel 208-6666, operate radio-dispatched taxis. Tourist taxis also wait outside major hotels; rates are $0.40–0.70 per km. *Colectivos*—old Yankee jalopies—serve Cubans, charge in pesos, and follow fixed routes. You can rent a classic car through Gran Car, tel 33-5647, from $15 hourly. Bicitaxis (pedal-powered tricycles) ply Habana Vieja and the Malecón ($3). Cocotaxis (motorized tricycles) can be hired outside major hotels.

BY TRAIN
Commuter trains depart Estación de 19 Noviembre, tel 81-4431, for ExpoCuba; and Estación Cristina, tel 78-4971, for Santiago de las Vegas and Parque Lenin.

AROUND CUBA

BY AIR
Major destinations are linked to each other, and to José Martí International Airport. Three domestic carriers—AeroCaribbean, tel 7/33-4543, fax 33-5016; AeroGaviota, tel 7/203-0668, fax 7/204-2621; and Cubana, tel 7/33-4949—serve regional airports with a network of scheduled flights using Soviet-built aircraft. AeroTaxi, tel 33-4064, also offers transportation. Typical fares between Havana and Santiago de Cuba are $80 one way.

BY TRAIN
A central railway line links major cities to each other and to Havana. Interprovincial trains depart Havana's Estación de Ferrocarril, Calle Egido at Arsenal, Habana Vieja, tel 7/61-3509. An overnight *especial* service operates between Havana and Santiago de Cuba (15 hours, $72), stopping in 2 major cities en route; a *regular* train is much slower and makes

more stops. Foreigners get reserved seats and book through Ladis, tel 7/62-4259, or Infotur offices (see Visitor Information, p. 236).

Local train service is sporadic.

BY BUS
Travel by bus is fast and efficient between major tourist destinations. Víazul, Ave. 26 y Zoológico, Plaza de la Revolución, Havana, tel 7/81-5652, fax 7/66-6092, e-mail viazul@transnet.cu, provides express service using modern, air-conditioned buses ($10–67).

Travel by public bus is less reliable. Local demand far exceeds supply, timetables are not strictly adhered to, and many buses are mechanically unsound. Foreigners, however, can reserve seats ($7–53). Buses depart Havana from the Terminal Nacional, Ave. Independencia #109, Plaza de la Revolución, tel 7/70-3397. Guard against pickpockets and luggage theft. Travel light, as space is limited. Most Cubans travel by *camiones*—trucks converted as crude buses.

BY CAR
To rent a car, you should be over 21 and hold a passport and a valid driver's license (a U.S. license is fine). You will need to leave a deposit (usually $200–500).

Rates vary from about $35 daily for the smallest vehicles, and $50 for mid-size cars, to between $90 and $110 for top-line cars. Insurance costs $8–20 extra daily. You should not need a four-wheel-drive vehicle. Thoroughly check your vehicle for damage and missing items before setting out. And refuse any vehicle that does not have a full tank of gas —one of the many scams common among rental staff. Beware additional charges that might appear on your bill when you return the car.

No international car companies are represented. The following Cuban state entities rent cars:

Havanautos, tel 7/203-9805, fax 7/204-1416, email reshautos@cimex.com.cu
Horizontes, tel 7/66-2160, e-mail crh@horizontes.hor.cma.net. Offers a Flexi Fly & Drive package that includes car rental plus prepaid vouchers valid at more than 70 hotels islandwide.
Micar, tel 7/204-2444, email micar@columbus.cu
Panautos, tel 7/55-3298, fax 7/55-5657, e-mail panautos@transnet.cu
Rex, tel 7/33-9160, fax 7/33-9159, e-mail reservas@rex .transnet.cu. Rents Audis and accepts payment with U.S. MasterCard and Visa.
Transtur, tel 7/62-2686
Vía Rent a Car, tel 7/33-9781, e-mail com_rc@gaviota.gav .tur.cu
Campertour, tel 7/833-7558. Rents fully-equipped Mercedes campervans.

These agencies ostensibly provide 24-hour breakdown assistance, but this can take hours to reach you away from major cities. Gasoline is sold at Servi-Cupet and Oro Negro stations nationwide ($0.90 per liter).

See p. 237 for what to do in case of an accident.

Roads everywhere are potholed, and badly deteriorated in places. Drive slowly and be on your guard for wayward bicyclists, stray cattle, and pedestrians in the road.

BY FERRY
Ferries and hydrofoils serve Isla de la Juventud from Suridero de Batabanó, in Havana province, tel 62/83845; in Havana tel 878-1841.

PRACTICAL ADVICE

COMMUNICATIONS

The Cuban state controls all media and keeps a tight-rein on what may be published.

NEWSPAPERS
Granma, the daily newspaper, is an eight-page, self-congratulatory publication with a consistently anti-U.S. slant. An English-language edition is published for tourists. *Juventud Rebelde,* the evening paper of the Communist Youth League, is a mirror image. A number of special-interest magazines offer more in-depth reporting, such as *Bohemia* and *Prisma,* covering the arts and general topics, respectively. A limited number of international publications, such as *Newsweek, Time,* and *National Geographic,* are sold at major tourist hotel gift stores. Western-style news agents do not exist.

TELEPHONES
Etecsa (the state telephone company) operates glass-enclosed telephone kiosks— *centros telefónicos* (or Telecorreos combined with postal services)—on major streets throughout Cuba. They utilize coins and phone cards (which can be purchased either at the kiosks or at most tourist hotels), but not credit cards. Service is generally efficient, but public phones are slightly more complicated to use than North American equivalents; have a stack of coins ready.

Telephone numbers change frequently. Numbers throughout Cuba are gradually being changed to seven-digits as digital exchanges are installed.

For direct-dial international calls, dial 119, then the country code and area code, then the number. Few hotels permit direct-dial international calls. For operator-assisted calls to the U.S., dial 66-1212. For directory inquiries, call 113. Direct dial calls to the U.S. are $2.71 per minute; $2.00 per minute from a kiosk; $2.00 with a calling card 6 a.m.–6 p.m., $1.55 6 p.m.–6 a.m.

Calling from the U.S., dial 011, plus Cuba's country code 53, then the city code and number.

For calls between provinces, add a 0 before dialing the city code.

TELEVISION & RADIO

Television reaches everyone (even the most remote rural community is linked to the national grid) and has been a key tool in spreading the revolution. There are only two major national networks: Cubavision and TeleRebelde, which carry limited international programming (notably select news clips from CNN Español, and telenovelas—soap operas—from other Latin American countries). Most tourist hotels also offer some cable TV U.S. programs.

Cuba has only seven national radio stations. In addition, local radio stations serve regional communities. Reception is intermittent, and there are large areas of the country without any reception. Most international broadcasts are jammed by Cuban authorities, although the BBC World Service can be received in places.

E-MAIL & INTERNET

Access to the Internet is severely proscribed for Cubans, although Cubans are permitted to send and receive e-mails (correos electrónicos) at designated Telecorreos. In Havana, foreigners are granted Internet access in the business centers of most hotels, and in the Capitolio and Centro de Prensa Internacional. Access costs $2–5 for 15 minutes, $6–10 per hour. Most towns on the tourist trail have at least one Internet outlet (bring your passport).

POST OFFICES

It costs $0.50 to mail a postcard to North America and $0.65 for a letter. Never include politically sensitive comments, as mail is generally read by censors; and never mail anything of value, as theft is endemic within the postal service (Correos de Cuba). Allow six weeks for mail between Cuba and North America. Most settlements have a post office, usually open Mon.–Fri., 10 a.m. to 5 p.m., and Sat. 8 a.m. to noon. Many gift stores and hotels sell postage-prepaid letters and postcards.

DHL, tel 7/204-1578, fax 7/204-0999, has offices throughout Cuba and offers express international and domestic service.

CONVERSIONS

Cuba uses the metric system for measurement. Useful conversions are:

1 mile = 1.61 kilometers
1 kilometer = 0.62 miles
1 meter = 39.37 inches
1 liter = 0.264 U.S. gallons
1 U.S. gallon = 3.78 liters
1 kilogram = 2.2 pounds
1 pound = 0.45 kilograms

Weather reports use Celsius. To convert quickly (but roughly) from Fahrenheit to Celsius, subtract 32 and divide by two. From Celsius to Fahrenheit, multiply by two and add 32.

0°C = 32°F
10°C = 50°F
20°C = 68°F
30°C = 86°F
100°C = 212°F

ELECTRICITY

Cuba operates on 110-volt AC (60 cycles) nationwide, although 220-volt is found in places. Most outlets use U.S. flat, two- or three-pin plugs.

ETIQUETTE & LOCAL CUSTOMS

Cuban society is extremely informal and egalitarian, especially compared to most other Latin nations. Cubans typically address each other by their first names, regardless of political or social standing. They often use the informal tu for "you," rather than the formal usted, even with strangers.

Cubans are extremely open with their family and personal life and readily extend invitations into their homes. Cubans of different colors also intermingle with ease, and black visitors will experience little, if any, aloofness. Although institutional racism has been eradicated, subtle racism still exists.

Cubans are highly suspicious of tattle-tales, government agents, and police spies. They are loath to offer negative commentary regarding domestic politics in public or in the company of those they do not implicitly trust. You should avoid drawing Cubans into such conversations against their will.

Dress is relatively conservative for men and provocative for women, who display a preference for minimalist, tight-fitting clothes. Both men and women can be flirtatious, and laxity in sexual relations is an accepted societal norm.

Outside the main tourist areas you may not be understood in English, so it is advisable to learn a few Spanish phrases. Most restaurants in tourist areas have menus in English.

NATIONAL HOLIDAYS

Cuba observes the following national holidays:

January 1, Liberation Day
May 1, Labor Day
July 25–27, National Revolution Day
October 10, Anniversary of Céspedes's Declaration of Independence
December 25, Christmas

Most tourist sites and services stay open for these holidays, but banks and government offices close. Major international religious holidays, such as Easter, are not officially observed in Cuba.

MONEY MATTERS

CURRENCY

The national currency is the peso. However, all tourist trans-actions are enacted in U.S. dollars, and there are very few items that can be paid for in pesos. The currencies trade at "black market" rate; at press time, the exchange rate was 26 pesos to one dollar. You will need to show your passport (or other I.D.) when presenting $50 or $100 bills. Occasionally, you may receive change in *pesos convertibles*, notes on a par with dollar denominations. Excess notes can be exchanged for dollars at the airport when departing.

Banks in major towns usually offer currency exchange services.

American Express travelers checks or any travelers checks issued by U.S. banks are not generally accepted and cannot be used as cash. Travelers checks issued by non-U.S. banks can be cashed at a few specific banks.

CREDIT CARDS

No U.S.-issued credit cards are accepted in Cuba (for an exception, see Getting around by car, p. 234). MasterCard and Visa issued elsewhere (e.g. Canada or Europe) are accepted at most tourist entities. Major banks offer cash advances against non-U.S. credit cards. Cash advances can be drawn on U.S.-issued MasterCard and Visa at Calle 24 #408 (3rd floor), 23/25, Vedado, Havana, tel 7/55-3788, fax 7/55-3789, e-mail quickccash@cuba web.cu.

OPENING TIMES

Most stores are open Mon.–Sun. 10:00 a.m.–6:30 p.m. Most banks are open Mon.–Fri. 8:30 a.m.–3 p.m. Government offices are generally open Mon.–Fri. 8:30 a.m.–4:00 p.m., usually with a one-hour lunch break.

PLACES OF WORSHIP

Most communities have at least one Roman Catholic church. Synagogues, Baptist, Pentecostal, Evangelical, and Anglican churches also exist in some communities, but are not as widespread.

SMOKING

A large percentage of Cubans smoke, and smoking in public places is neither frowned upon nor forbidden. Few restaurants have no-smoking facilities, and "No Smoking" signs are regularly disobeyed.

Cigarettes, including rough, locally made brands and popular U.S. brands, are sold at bars and gift stores. Cigars are not sold at bars; they can be bought at Casas de Tabaco and gift stores in tourist hotels.

TIME DIFFERENCES

Cuban time is the same as U.S. Eastern Standard Time (EST), five hours behind Greenwich Mean Time (GMT). Cuba operates daylight savings time, May–Oct.

TIPPING

Tipping is not a fact of life in Cuba, except in places frequented by tourists, where staff in service jobs are paid in worthless pesos and rely on dollar tips to make ends meet. However, a tip is an acknowledgment of good service—one of Cuba's weak links. If the service is not satisfactory, do not tip.

A 10- to 15-percent service charge is often added onto restaurant bills, although you should ascertain from staff whether they actually receive the tip. Tour guides should be tipped about $1 per person per day for group tours, and more for personalized services. Hotel porters should be given 50 cents per bag, and room service staff $1 per day. Taxi drivers do not expect tips, although a 5- to 10-percent tip is usually appreciated.

TOILETS

Toilets frequently lack toilet seats and tissue paper. Many toilets in restaurants and hotels have attendants who distribute tissue paper in exchange for a tip. Public street toilets are virtually non-existent, and those that exist are to be avoided.

TRAVELERS WITH DISABILITIES

Although paying lip-service to the theme, Cuba does not display great sensitivity to the needs of visitors with disabilities. Few buildings have wheelchair access or provide special toilets. Buses are not adapted for wheelchairs, and few curbs are dropped at corners. In fact, most sidewalks are major obstacle courses, with deep fissures, open gutters, etc.

Some modern, upscale hotels have wheelchair access and a few provide special suites. Older accommodations and restaurants usually present difficulties.

The following agencies provide information on aspects of traveling abroad for visitors with disabilities:
Asociación Cubana de
    Calle 6 #106, bet. Calles 1ra
    & 3ra, Miramar, Havana, tel
    209-3049, fax 204-8787
    e-mail aclifim@infomed.sld.cu
Society for Accessibile Travel
    and Hospitality, 347 5th Ave.,
    Ste. 610, New York, NY
    10016, tel 212-447-7284,
    e-mail sathtravel@aol.com

VISITOR INFORMATION

Cuba's Ministry of Tourism maintains a website: www.cubatra vel.cu. Cuba's tourist information offices abroad are represented by state tourism corporations.

In Canada, Cubanacán has offices in Montreal: tel 514-875-8004, fax 514-875-8006, e-mail mintur@ generation.net; and Toronto: tel 416-362-0700, fax 416-362-6799, email cuba.tbtor@sympatico.ca. In the United Kingdom, the Cuba Tourist Board has an office at 161 High Holborn, London WC1V 6PA, tel 171/240-6655, fax 171/836-9265, e-mail cuba touristboard.london@virgin.net.

The Havana Office of Tourism, tel 204-0624, fax 204-8164, e-mail oficturi@ofitur.mit.cma.net, operates "Infotur" tourist information offices throughout Havana, including at José Martí International Airport: Terminal 2, tel 55-8733; Terminal 3, 66-6101; or 66-6112. Call tel 33-3333 for general information.

EMERGENCIES & HEALTH CARE

CRIME & POLICE

Cuba is relatively free of violent crime. However, petty theft is endemic and far more prevalent than in most North American cities. Caution should be exercised at all times, especially if approached by jineteros or jineteras—hustlers and prostitutes. In towns, there is a danger of pickpockets and snatch-and-grab theft, so be especially wary in crowded areas, such as buses and markets. Scams are common, especially in private street transactions; never take your eyes off any items you purchase. And keep your possessions in a hotel safe or a locked suitcase, as theft by cleaning staff is common.

Avoid leaving luggage of valuables in cars, do not carry large quantities of cash or wear expensive-looking jewelry, and keep passports and credit cards out of sight. If anything is stolen, report it immediately to the police and/or your hotel.

Report crimes to the Policía Nacional Revolucionaria (PNR), tel

867-7777. If you are charged with a crime, request that your deposition be made in front of an independent witness (testigo). Visitors from the U.S. can request a representative of the U.S. Interests Section be present.

Asistur, Paseo del Prado #212, Havana, tel 7/33-8527, fax 7/33-8087, e-mail asisten@asisten .get.tur.cu, exists to provide assistance to tourists in trouble.

EMBASSIES/ CONSULATES

United States Interests Section, Calzada & L/M, Vedado, Havana, tel 7/33-3551, fax 7/66-2095
British Embassy, Calle 34 #702 at 7ma Ave., Miramar, Havana, tel 7/204-1771, fax 7/204-9214
Canadian Embassy, Calle 30 #518 at 7ma Ave., Miramar, Havana, tel 7/204-2516, fax 7/204-2044

EMERGENCY NUMBERS

Ambulance, 55-1584
Fire, 67-5555
Police, 867-7777

HEALTH

Medical services for foreigners are provided by: Clínica Internacional Cira García, Calles 20 & 41, Miramar, Havana, tel 7/204-0330, fax 7/204-2640, e-mail ciragcu@infomed.sld.cu. Be prepared to pay U.S. dollars.

The following international pharmacies serve foreigners:

Farmácia Internacional, Calles 41 & 20, Miramar, Havana, tel 7/204-2051
Farmácia Internacional, Ave. 7ma & Calle 78, Villa Panamericana, Havana, tel 7/95-1157
Farmácia Internacional Camilo Cienfuegos, Calles 13 & L, Vedado, Havana, tel 7/33-3538
Ópticas Miramar, Ave. 7ma at Calle 24, Havana, tel 204-2990, provides optician services. It has

branches in major cities nationwide.

Most tourist centers also have Clínica Internacional and Óptica Miramar outlets. International Farmacies have recently opened in the Hotel Habana Libre and Hotel Comodoro in Havana.

Avoid drinking tap water.

WHAT TO DO IN CASE OF A CAR ACCIDENT

In the event of an accident, do not move the vehicle or permit the other vehicle to be moved. Take down the license plate number and the name, address, and id number from the carnet de identidad (legal identification) of any witnesses. Call the transit police: tel 82-0116 in Havana.

If someone is seriously injured or killed, contact your embassy.

FURTHER READING

Cuba (David Alan Harvey and Elizabeth Newhouse, 2000) Spectacular photos and absorbing text provide a colorful portrait of this beautiful tropical island.
Dirty Havana Trilogy (Pedro Juan Gutiérrez, 2001) A powerful novel exposing the torment and squalor of life in contemporary Cuba through the misadventures of a former journalist.
Fidel: A Critical Portrait (Tad Szulc, 1986) This definitive biography reveals the human being behind one of the most charismatic and misunderstood revolutionary icons of our time.
Mi Moto Fidel: Motorcycling Through Castro's Cuba (Christopher P. Baker, 2001) A lively account of the author's three-month, 7,000-mile journey through Cuba.
On Becoming Cuban: Identity, Nationality, & Culture (Louis A. Pérez, Jr., 1999) A fascinating compendium of Cuban-American relations between the 1860s and the 1950s.

HOTELS & RESTAURANTS

Accommodations in Cuba run the spectrum, although standards vary widely and most hotels are overpriced. With few exceptions, Cubans are not permitted in tourist hotels. There are great differences between the types of facilities available, and it will help you to understand these differences when deciding where to stay. In general, there is no shortage of hotel rooms, although the more popular hotels often fill up at Christmas and New Year—peak season.

Eating out is one of the biggest challenges. Havana offers a wide variety of possibilities, but only a handful of places offer excitement. Elsewhere menus are repetitive and unimaginative, and usually restricted to fried chicken and perhaps a pork or fish dish, and rice and beans. Tourist hotels usually fare better, with more cosmopolitan options. Meals are usually overpriced.

MAKING RESERVATIONS

Although we have tried to give comprehensive information, please check details before booking—particularly the availability of facilities for disabled guests or nonsmoking rooms, acceptance of credit cards, and rates (U.S. credit cards cannot be used). Do not rely on booking by mail; fax or e-mail your reservation, and take your written confirmation with you. Telephone numbers often change.

ACCOMMODATIONS

The Cuban state owns all hotels and applies an overly generous star rating system.

Havana is blessed with charming historic properties, and most other major tourist destinations now boast at least one restored historic hotel. Most resort hotels (and top-of-the-line hotels in Havana) offer international standards, although large sections of the country are still served only by drab hotels dating back to the Soviet era. Mid-range hotels are the norm, offering minimal service, few frills, and often dowdy furniture. Recently built and/or renovated hotels usually feature state-of-the-art air-conditioning, safes, cable TV, and modern furniture.

A handful of hotels aim at an ecosensitive market, but few live up to their billing, and there are no wilderness or mountain lodges. The same is true for spa facilities, which remain basic. Most resort hotels operate as all-inclusive properties under foreign management.

Private room rentals—*casas particulares*—offer good bargains, although standards vary markedly. Most offer the intimacy of a family environment and the option of home-cooked meals. Showers are often cold; warm (tepid) water may be provided by an electric element above the shower. Cuban guests are permitted. Look for postings in home windows. Officially, visitors are required to show reservations for at least two nights' accommodation upon arrival in country; immigration officials may refuse to accept *casas particulares*.

Cubans are not permitted in hotels except those operated by Islazul, a state agency that runs budget hotels accepting both foreigners and locals.

In all but top-end hotels, sink plugs and toilet seats may be missing. Only top-end hotels provide toiletries. Ensure windows and doors are secure.

Avoid "motels" and *posadas,* usually used for short-term sexual trysts.

Unless otherwise stated, all hotels have dining rooms and private bathrooms, and are open year-round.

The following competing state entities operate hotels:

Cubanacán
  tel 7/204-7649, fax 7/208-9080, e-mail comercial@hoteles .cyt.cu; www.cubanacan.cu

Gaviota
  tel 7/66-6777, fax 7/33-2780, e-mail gaviota@gaviota.gav .tur.cu; www.gaviota-grupo.com

Gran Caribe
  tel 7/204-0575, fax 7/204-0565, www.grancaribe.cu

Habaguanex
  tel 7/33-8693, fax 7/33-8697, e-mail gerencia.comercial@ habaguanex.ohch.cu

Horizontes
  tel 7/33-4042, fax 7/33-3161, www.horizontes.cu

Islazul
  tel 7/32-0571, fax 7/33-3458, e-mail comazul@teleda.get.cma. net; www.islazul.cubaweb.cu

RESTAURANTS

The vast majority of restaurants are state-run and serve *comida criollo*. For a sampling of Cuban dishes, see pages 24–25. Menus vary little, reflecting the degree to which bureaucrats run the show, and standards are wanting. Divorced from the international scene for four decades, Cuban chefs are starting from scratch.

"No hay!"—"There is none!"—is a ubiquitous mantra. In the provinces, *bocaditos* (sandwiches) of ham and cheese are often all that's available. Most tourist hotels and restaurants are cocooned from the worst privations, though even there, most meals—usually continental fare—are bland by international standards. Away from major tourist resorts, service is usually slow and sometimes surly. Certain towns, such as Guantánamo, are culinary wastelands.

Lean times have been eased since 1993 by the legalization of farmers' markets, and by private restaurants *(paladares)*, which are relegated to rooms in private homes but where the Cubans' inventiveness shines. The government barely tolerates *paladares*, which are forbidden to sell lobster or shrimp (although most do so) and operate under other burdensome restrictions.

Watch for extra charges for bread and butter.

Cuba's homegrown Burguí (hamburgers) and El Rápido (fried chicken) fast-food chains do not live up to their U.S. equivalents.

A selection of the best restaurants is given below. These include traditional criollo and more continental cuisine, with noted local associations wherever possible.

ORGANIZATION & ABBREVIATIONS
Hotels and restaurants are listed by price, then in alphabetical order.

The key at the bottom of each page explains the icons found after each listing.

D = Dinner
L = Lunch
B = Breakfast

MC = MasterCard
V = Visa

HAVANA

HOTELS

🏨 MELIÁ COHIBA
$$$$$
PASEO, 1RA/3RA, VEDADO
TEL 7/33-3636
FAX 7/33-4555
E-MAIL melia.cohiba@cohiba1
.solmelia.cma.net
A modern European-style high rise at the foot of Paseo, this 22-story hotel is known for its gracious contemporary appointments. Spacious bathrooms gleam. A choice of fine restaurants includes Italian. An upscale shopping arcade and cabaret are highlights.
🛈 462 🅿 🔄 🚭 ❄ 🏊 🏊
🍸 🚫 MC, V

🏨 NOVOTEL CORALIA MIRAMAR
$$$$$
AVE. 5TA, BET. 72 & 76, MIRAMAR
TEL 7/204-3584
FAX 7/204-3583
E-MAIL reserva@miramar.gav
.tur.cu
Swank contemporary design sets this deluxe hotel apart from the competition. Spacious rooms boast lively decor. Five rooms are handicapped accessible. Three restaurants offer international cuisine, and facilities include tennis, squash, and volleyball.
🛈 427 🅿 🔄 🚭 ❄ 🏊 🏊
🍸 🚫 MC, V

🏨 HOTEL GOLDEN TULIP PARQUE CENTRAL
$$$$
NEPTUNO & PASEO DEL PRADO (ZULUETA), HABANA VIEJA
TEL 7/66-6627
FAX 7/60-6630
E-MAIL reservations@gtpc
.cha.cyt.cu
A gracious conversion of a 19th-century mansion retains colonial hints in this thoroughly modern hotel overlooking Parque Central. Foreign managed; efficient service. Choice of elegant eateries. Upscale boutiques.

Cigar lounge.
🛈 279 🅿 🔄 🚭 ❄ 🏊 🍸
🚫 MC, V

🏨 HOTEL NACIONAL
$$$$
CALLES O & 21, VEDADO
TEL 7/33-3564
FAX 7/33-5054
E-MAIL reserva@gcnacio.gca
.tur.cu
Havana's flagship hotel commands a headland overlooking the Malecón. Period style and furnishings combine with modern amenities and complete services, including business center. Cabaret and atmospheric bars.
🛈 450 🅿 🔄 🚭 ❄ 🏊
🍸 🚫 MC, V

🏨 HOTEL PRESIDENTE
$$$$
CALZADA & AVE. DE LOS PRESIDENTES, VEDADO
TEL 7/55-1801
FAX 7/33-5753
E-MAIL reservas@hpdte.gca
.tur.cu
Recently reopened after a complete restoration, this art deco high rise near the Malecón boasts sumptuous classical French decor with modern furnishings and amenities. However, its location offers few advantages.
🛈 160 🅿 🔄 🚭 ❄ 🏊
🚫 MC, V

🏨 HOTEL RIVIERA
$$$$
PASEO & MALECÓN. VEDADO
TEL 7/33-4051
FAX 7/33-3739
E-MAIL reserva@gcrivie.gca
.tur,cu
Mafia associations lend fame to this high-rise 1950s grande dame boasting a handsome lobby bar and top-class cabaret. Rooms remain dowdy despite a recent renovation, and dining options fail to inspire. Overpriced.
🛈 354 🅿 🔄 🚭 ❄ 🏊 🏊
🍸 🚫 MC, V

🏨 HOTEL SANTA ISABEL

Stately elegance and refine
ment are watchwords at this
gracious three-story hotel that
was once the palace of the Count
of Santovenia. Steeped in ambience and offering an unrivaled
location in the heart of Old
Havana, it also boasts modern
appointments. Antiques and
works of art abound, as do regal
colonial touches. Some of the
suites have canopied wrought-
iron beds.
$$$$
CALLE BARATILLO #9, PLAZA
DE ARMAS, HABANA VIEJA
TEL 7/60-8201
FAX 7/862-4127
E-MAIL comercial@habaguan
exhisabel.co.cu
🛏 27 rooms, 10 suites
🅿 ⬍ 🚫 🔂 📶 MC, V

🏨 HOSTAL DEL TEJADILLO
$$$
CALLE TEJADILLO #12 AT SAN
IGNACIO, HABANA VIEJA
TEL 7/63-7283
FAX 7/63-8830
E-MAIL comercial@habaguan
exhtejadillo.co.cu
Three adjoining colonial
buildings have been converted
to form this gracious hotel. An
elegant lobby opens to court-
yards with fountains. Modern
rooms feature lofty ceilings,
safes, and period touches.
🛏 32 🚫 🔂 MC, V

🏨 HOTEL FLORIDA
$$$
CALLES OBISPO & CUBA,
HABANA VIEJA
TEL 7/862-4127
FAX 7/862-4117
E-MAIL comercial@habaguan
exhflorida.co.cu
A stately 18th-century
mansion tucked into Old
Havana's liveliest thorough-
fare, a short distance from the
main plazas. Elegant appoint-
ments recall the graciousness
of yesteryear. Bedrooms

feature modern appointments
and period decor. Chic
restaurant and piano bar.
🛏 25 🅿 🚫 🔂 📶 MC, V

🏨 HOTEL HABANA LIBRE
$$$
CALLES L & 23, VEDADO
TEL 7/33-4011
FAX 7/33-3141
E-MAIL reservathl@solmelia
cuba.com
Landmark high-rise hotel
dating from the 1950s.
Recently renovated rooms
are up-to-date, if a bit frumpy.
Complete services include a
bank, business center, shops,
tour services, cabaret, and
restaurants. Popular with tour
groups. Superb Vedado
location.
🛏 572 🅿 ⬍ 🚫 🔂 📶 📺 MC, V

🏨 HOTEL INGLATERRA
$$$
PRADO #416 AT SAN RAFAEL,
HABANA VIEJA
TEL 7/60-8593
FAX 7/60-8254
E-MAIL reserva@gcingla.gca
.tur.cu
Splendid location overlooking
Parque Central. Extravagant
Moorish lobby and restaurant.
Recently renovated guest
rooms feature intricately
worked ceilings and Belle
Epoque charm, but remain
overpriced.
🛏 83 🅿 ⬍ 🚫 🔂 MC, V

🏨 HOTEL PLAZA
$$$
CALLES ZULUETA & NEPTUNO,
HABANA VIEJA
TEL 7/60-8583
FAX 7/860-8591
E-MAIL reserva@plaza.gca
.tur.cu
This centenary, mid-range
option offers venerable archi-
tecture and atmospheric
though lackluster rooms. Gra-
cious lobby bar and upscale
restaurant. Overpriced,
despite its fine location.
🛏 188 🅿 ⬍ 🚫 🔂 MC, V

🏨 SOFITEL SEVILLA
$$$
TROCADERO #55 AT PRADO,
HABANA VIEJA
TEL 7/60-8560
FAX 7/60-8582
E-MAIL reserva@sevilla.gca
.tur.cu
Built in 1980, this French-
managed hotel boasts a
Moorish motif. Newly renovated rooms boast gracious
appointments; others remain
drab and overpriced, however.
Also on hand: Internet access,
a dazzling rooftop restaurant,
and a fine pool complex.
🛏 188 🅿 ⬍ 🚫 📶 📺 MC, V

🏨 HOSTAL EL COMENDADOR
$$
OBRAPÍA #55 AT BARATILLO,
HABANA VIEJA
TEL 7/67-1037
FAX 7/860-5628
E-MAIL reserva@habaguanex
hvalencia.co.cu
A charming restoration of
a colonial home, this small
hostel is an adjunct to Hostal
Valencia. Marble gleams un-
derfoot. Antique reproduc-
tions and iron-frame beds
highlight graciously appointed
bedrooms, while bathrooms
boast claw-foot tubs. The res-
taurant specializes in tapas.
🛏 14 🚫 MC, V

🏨 HOSTAL CONDE DE VILLANUEVA
$$
MERCADERES #202 AT
LAMPARILLA, HABANA VIEJA
TEL 7/62-9294
FAX 7/62-9682
E-MAIL gerencia.comer
cial@habaguanex.ohch.cu
The former home of Count
Claudio Martínez Pinillo
(1789–1853) has metamor-
phosed into this delightful
small inn with mezzanine
humidor and sumptuous cigar
lounge. Rooms on two levels
surround a peaceful courtyard
with rockers and feature
beamed ceilings, terra-cotta
tile floors, and tasteful mo-

dern appointments. A suite has a Jacuzzi.

🛈 9 🚭 🅰 MC, V

🏨 HOSTAL LOS FRAILES
$$

TENIENTE REY, BET. OFICIOS & MERCADERES, HABANA VIEJA
TEL 7/62-9510
FAX 7/862-9718
E-MAIL comercial@habaguan
exhfrailes.co.cu

An intimate option conjured from a former colonial mansion and playing on a monastic theme. Staff dress in monks' habits (*habitos*) and decor includes life-size monks in bronze. Wrought-iron and earth tones abound in small, somewhat dark but tastefully appointed rooms.

🛈 22 🚭 🅰 MC, V

🏨 HOSTAL SAN MIGUEL
$$

CALLE CUBA #52, PEYA POBRE, HABANA VIEJA
TEL 7/62-7656
FAX 7/63-4088
E-MAIL reserva@sanmiguel
.co.cu

Restored colonial mansion looking toward El Morro. Elegant rooms accessed by marble staircase boast antiques and antique reproductions. The upstairs terrace offers harbor views and is an agreeable place to enjoy cocktails from the downstairs bar.

🛈 10 🚭 🅰 MC, V

🏨 HOSTAL VALENCIA
$$

CALLE OFICIOS #53 AT OBRAPÍA, HABANA VIEJA
TEL 7/67-1037
FAX 7/60-5628
E-MAIL reserva@habaguanex
hvalencia.co.cu

A gracious budget property in the heart of the old town, this 18th-century town house recalls a Spanish *posada*, with wrought-iron balconies and period details. Furnishings are drab, but the inn makes up in its atmospheric paella restaurant, bar, and cigar store.

🛈 12 🚭 🅰 MC, V

🏨 HOTEL AMBOS MUNDOS
$$

CALLE OBISPO #153 AT MERCADERES, HABANA VIEJA
TEL 7/60-9530
FAX 7/60-9532
E-MAIL diana@amundo.cu

A 1920s eye-catcher favored by Ernest Hemingway (his Room 511 is now a museum). Rooms are small and modestly furnished, but offer the essentials. Lively piano bar. Rickety antique elevator. Superb location.

🛈 52 🅿 🚭 🅰 🚭 🅰 MC, V

🏨 HOTEL ST JOHN'S
$$

CALLE O, BET. 23 & 25, VEDADO
TEL 7/33-3740
FAX 7/33-3561
E-MAIL crh@s1.hor.cma.net

A popular option for tour groups, this recently restored mid-price high rise offers a handy location. Rooms have no frills, but come with essential amenities. A rooftop swimming pool and lively disco are highlights.

🛈 78 🅿 🚭 🅰 🏊 🎾 🅰 MC, V

🏨 HOTEL VICTORIA
$$

CALLES 19 & M, VEDADO
TEL 7/33-3510
FAX 7/33-3109
E-MAIL reserva@gcvicto.gca
.tur.cu

This boutique hotel draws business travelers for its gracious appointments, personal staff, and warm ambience. Guest rooms have minibars and safes. An elegant restaurant is a plus, and there's a small boutique.

🛈 31 🅿 🚭 🅰 🏊 🅰 MC, V

🏨 CASA PARTICULAR GISELA MARTÍNEZ
$

AVENIDA 26 #1002, BET. 32 & KOHLY, NUEVO VEDADO
TEL 7/ 81-0101
E-MAIL gisela@foxhiker
.cjb.net

Spacious and elegantly

furnished middle-class home. Tropical garden. Clean, modern bathroom. Bedroom has a minibar, TV, and cassette player. Out-of-the-way location is a hindrance to sightseeing but close to Víazul bus station—good for exploring beyond Havana.

🛈 15 🅿 🚭 🏊

🏨 CASA PARTICULAR JORGE COALLA POTTS

This private room rental— one of Havana's finest— enjoys a splendid location in the heart of Vedado, close to the major hotels, shops, and entertainment centers. The impeccably clean bedroom is spacious, well-lit, and airy, with fans and air-conditioning; and the roomy, tiled bathroom offers hot water (and toilet seat). The hosts are helpful and courteous.

$

CALLE I #456, BET. 21 & 23, VEDADO
TEL 7/32-9032
E-MAIL jorgepotts@isla
grande.cu

🛈 1 🚭 🅰

🏨 CASA PARTICULAR RENE PÉREZ
$

MALECÓN #51, BET. GENIOS & CARCEL, CENTRO HABANA
TEL 7/61-8108

A spacious private room rental close to Habana Vieja. A vast lounge with TV/VCR offers views over the Malecón. Two spacious though dimly lit bedrooms boast genuine antiques.

🛈 2 🅿 🚭

RESTAURANTS

🍴 COMEDOR DE AGUIAR
$$$$$

HOTEL NACIONAL, CALLES O & 21
TEL 7/33-3564

As elite as it comes in Cuba, this spiffy place boasts

immaculately liveried waiters and a creative continental menu. Food quality and service are well above average. Try the butterfly lobster.

🅿 🔣 🕒 Closed B 🖲 MC, V

🍴 TOCORORO
$$$$$
CALLE 18 #302 AT AVE. 3ᴿᴬ, MIRAMAR
TEL 7/204-2209
An elitist criollo-cum-continental restaurant with fabulous decor and a Who's Who list of patrons. The overpriced menu features seafood brochette, grilled lamb chops, and sushi. A jazz ensemble entertains.

🅿 🔣 🕒 Closed B 🖲 MC, V

🍴 DON CANGREJO
$$$$
AVE. Iᴿᴬ, BET. CALLES 16 & 18, MIRAMAR
TEL 7/204-4169
This seafront mansion specializes in seafood and draws Cuba's elite. Crab claws, garlic shrimp cocktail, and paella are on the menu, which is backed by a large wine list. Fair weather permits patio dining.

🅿 🔣 🕒 Closed B 🖲 MC, V

🍴 EL FLORIDITA
$$$$
CALLE OBISPO #557 AT MONSERRATE, HABANA VIEJA
TEL 7/863-1300 (FOR RESERVATIONS 7/863-1299)
This famous Hemingway haunt specializes in lobster and seafood, but offers frog's-leg soufflé and other French-inspired fare. Overbearing classical decor, including lively mural. Avoid overly ambitious dishes. A sugarless double daiquiri—"Papa Special"—is de rigueur, despite the prices. Bring a sweater.

🅿 🔣 🕒 Closed B 🖲 MC, V

SOMETHING SPECIAL

🍴 LA GUARIDA
Havana's hip showcase *paladar* is patronized by glamorous models, foreign diplomats, and others among the elite. The operatic setting of the decrepit three-story town house may be familiar from the movie *Fresa y chocolate*, parts of which were filmed here. The inventively French-criollo menu changes frequently, but eggplant caviar with red pepper coulis, and fillet of snapper in white wine sauce are typical. A large wine list spans the globe. Reservations recommended.

$$$$
CALLE CONCORDIA #418, BET. GERVASIO & ESCOBAR, CENTRO HABANA
TEL 7/62-4940
🅿 🕒 D only

🍴 ROOF GARDEN RESTAURANT
$$$$
SOFITEL SEVILLA, TROCADERO #55, HABANA VIEJA
TEL 7/60-8560
Stupendous neoclassic decor and elegant place settings in this regal rooftop eatery with views over the city. Inspired French cuisine with savory sauces from a French chef. Note the Florentine paneled ceiling.

🅿 🔣 🕒 D only 🖲 MC, V

🍴 LA TORRE
$$$$
EDIFICIO FOCSA AT CALLES 17 & M, VEDADO
TEL 7/55-3089
Visit this French restaurant atop the Focsa Building for the superb view from the 36th floor, though the fare is among Havana's finest. The French chef who brought La Torre up to par recently left, but his influence remains in the creative menu featuring foie gras, shrimp in honey, and imported meats. A large wine list.

🅿 🔣 🕒 Closed B 🖲 MC, V

🍴 EL ALJIBE
$$$
AVE. 7ᴹᴬ, BET. 24 & 26, MIRAMAR

TEL 204-1584 OR 204-7231
Open-air dining in an expansive thatched eatery popular with monied Cubans, tour groups, and businessfolk. The house dish—a consistently flavorful and succulent roast chicken in orange sauce—comes with all-you-can-eat rice and beans, fried plantains, French fries, and salad. The menu is criollo and includes coconut pie and other worthy desserts. Service is surprisingly swift and efficient for a state-run restaurant.

🅿 🕒 Closed B 🖲 MC, V

🍴 LA COCINA DE LILIAM
$$$
CALLE 48 #1311, BET. 13 & 15, MIRAMAR
TEL 7/209-6514
This exclusive *paladar* combines a splendid aesthetic with a creative continental-inspired *criollo* menu featuring chicken breast with pineapple, and a delicious stew of lamb simmered with onions and peppers. You dine on comfy wrought-iron chairs in the romantic garden patio, or inside if inclement. Popular with expatriates. Go early.

🚭 ❄ D only; closed Sat. & Dec. 💳 MC, V

🍴 LA ESPERANZA
$$$
CALLE 16 #105, BET. IRA & 3RA, MIRAMAR
TEL 7/202-4361
Art nouveau decor in this well-run paladar, in a large home in a quiet corner of Miramar. Aperitifs can be enjoyed in a lounge stuffed with period knickknacks, and a small garden patio is at hand for postprandial pleasure. The food is exquisite. One of the most creative menus in Cuba by a self-taught, French-influenced chef.
🅿 ❄ Closed Thurs.

🍴 LA GIRALDILLA
$$$
CALLES 222 & 37, LA LISA
TEL 7/33-0568
Consistently superior upscale restaurant, thanks to foreign management. Dining options include a tapas bar; the open-air El Patio los Naranjos; a noteworthy subterranean Spanish restaurant and wine cellar, La Bodega del Vino; and the Bistro Gourmet, boasting a beamed ceiling and lavish arts and antiques. Creamy vegetable soup, sautéed prawns in garlic, and grilled lobster in Ricard sauce are typical. A lively cabaret and the city's trendiest disco follow (free to restaurant guests).
🅿 🚭 ❄ Closed B 💳 MC, V

🍴 LA PAELLA
$$$
CALLE OFICIOS & OBRAPÍA, HABANA VIEJA
TEL 7/67-1037
Heart of Havana location. Exudes charm lent by its traditional Spanish decor and wooden rejas. The menu features a filling caldo (soup) plus tasty paellas (minimum two people); otherwise the menu is criollo. Service is aloof yet efficient.
❄ Closed B 💳 MC, V

🍴 LA PIAZZA RISTORANTE
$$$
MELIÁ COHIBA, AVENIDA DEL PASEO, VEDADO
TEL 7/33-3636
Clean, attractive ambience for this upscale eatery serving Italian fare. The menu includes 12 types of pizza, plus seafood, gnocchi, and other pasta. Bring a sweater.
🅿 🚭 ❄ Closed B 💳 MC, V

🍴 RESTAURANTE SANTO ANGEL
$$$
CALLE TENIENTE REY & SAN IGNACIO, PLAZA VIEJA, HABANA VIEJA
TEL 7/861-1626
This elegant restaurant offers gracious appointments and views over Plaza Vieja. The nouvelle criollo menu includes gazpacho, mushrooms in garlic, and pork chops in mustard. Service can be slow, but food quality makes amends. Musicians play day and night.
💳 MC, V

🍴 RESTAURANTE 1830
$$$
MALECÓN #1252 AT CALLE 20, VEDADO
TEL 7/55-3091
Standards at this colonial mansion have been raised since a French chef took over the helm, though service remains unsure. Classy decor. An inventive international menu includes roast leg of lamb with garlic.
🅿 🚭 ❄ Closed B 💳 MC, V

🍴 LA ROCA
$$$
CALLES 21 & M, VEDADO
TEL 7/33-4501
1950s redux in this elegant restaurant with stained-glass windows in the heart of Vedado. The continental menu offers a variety of lobster and seafood dishes of varying quality. Service is swift. A pianist entertains. Pop into the

adjoining bar for postprandial pleasure. Bring a sweater.
🅿 🚭 ❄ Closed B 💳 MC, V

🍴 LAS RUINAS
$$$
PARQUE LENIN, CALLE 100 & CORTINA DE LA PRESA, BOYEROS
TEL 7/44-3026
The unique ambience of this outskirts-of-Havana eatery blends colonial ruins into a modern concrete structure featuring stained glass. The expansive **criollo**-cum-continental menu includes lobster Bellevue and shrimp enchilada.
🅿 🚭 ❄ Closed B & Mon. 💳 MC, V

SOMETHING SPECIAL

🍴 LA BODEGUITA DEL MEDIO
A de rigueur treat for any visitor to Havana, this venerable *taberna* offers mouth-watering criollo dishes such as *ajiaco* (meat and vegetable stew) and roast pork with garlic yucca and fried plantain steeped in rum. Intimate bohemian setting is enhanced by troubadours and graffiti-covered walls. Lunch tends to be fresher than dinner. Alas, the *mojitos* are insipid; stick to beer, or buy a bottle of rum.
$$
CALLE EMPREDADO #206, BET. SAN IGNACIO & CUBA, HABANA VIEJA
TEL 7/867-1375
🚭 ❄ Closed B 💳 MC, V

🍴 CAFÉ TABERNA BENY MORÉ
$$
CALLE MERCADERES #531 AT TENIENTE REY, HABANA VIEJA
TEL 7/861-1637
Creative criollo fare with flair enjoyed in a stylish and popular restaurant honoring singer Beny Moré. Tremendous atmosphere enhanced by a nine-piece band. Lively bar. Check your bill carefully

for phantom charges.
🔆 ⊕ Closed B 🏧 MC, V

🍴 LE CHANSONNIER
$$
CALLE J #259, BET. CALLES 15 &
LINEA, VEDADO
TEL 7/32-1576
An antique-filled mansion and
sophisticated, soft music
provide a pleasant back-
ground for French-inspired
cuisine featuring well-
prepared sauces. Filling
portions and personable and
efficient staff at this *paladar.*
🅿 🔆 ⊕ Closed B 🏧 MC, V

🍴 LA MEDINA
$$
CALLE OFICIOS, BET. OBISPO &
OBRAPÍA, HABANA VIEJA
TEL 7/67-1041
A taste of the Orient, with
couscous and lamb dishes,
plus kebab and hummus
highlighting the Arabian menu,
though items aren't always
available. A troupe of female
troubadours entertains in the
patio, lush with planters and
palms.
⊕ Closed B 🏧 MC, V

🍴 LA TERRAZA
$$
CALLE REAL #161, COJÍMAR
TEL 7/65-3471
Famous seafood restaurant
that plays on its Ernest
Hemingway associations. Try
the paella, washed down by
the house cocktail, named in
honor of the late patron
Gregorio Fuentes. Fish soups,
shrimp cocktails, and lobster
dishes are offered.
🅿 🔆 ⊕ Closed B 🏧 MC, V

🍴 BAMBÚ
$
JARDÍN BOTÁNICO, BOYEROS
TEL 7/54-7278
Havana's only true vegetarian
restaurant is set in a Japanese
garden in the Botanical Gar-
dens. It's open for lunch only
and serves a filling buffet for
under $12. The set lunch
buffet features *fufú* (mashed
boiled banana with garlic),

eggplant cooked in cheese
sauce, and about 25 other
creative dishes using organic
produce grown in the
Botanical Gardens.
🅿 ⊕ Closed B &
Mon.–Tues. 🏧 MC, V

🍴 COPPELIA
$
CALLE 23 AT CALLE L, VEDADO
TEL 7/32-6149
Reputedly the world's largest
ice-cream parlor. The ice
cream is worth the long wait,
which is part of the experi-
ence. Seating is communal in
any of half a dozen indoor
and outdoor areas. Avoid the
touristy dollar section (unless
you want to skip the line) and
bring pesos—15 cents' equiv-
alent buys a full bowl.
⊕ Closed Mon.

🍴 HANOI
$
CALLE TENIENTE REY &
BERNAZA, HABANA VIEJA
TEL 7/67-1029
Filling quasi-Oriental dishes
enjoyed in a colonial home
with Oriental motif. The
attempt to re-create a
Vietnamese-Chinese menu
suffers from lack of ingre-
dients, and most dishes are
criollo. A grapevine graces the
patio. A budget bargain with
ambience.
⊕ Closed B

CAYO LEVISA

🏨 VILLA CAYO LEVISA
$$
CAYO LEVISA, PINAR DEL RÍO
TEL 8/66-6075
FAX 8/33-3161
E-MAIL crh@horizontes.hor
.cma.net
Known as a dive resort, this
tranquil facility makes for a
good beach break. Simple yet
adequately appointed
thatched cabins sprawl along a
scintillating beach. Water
sports are offered.
🔢 20 🔆 🏧 MC, V

JIBACOA

🏨 BREEZES JIBACOA
$$$
VIA BLANCA KM 60, JIBACOA,
HAVANA
TEL 692/85122
FAX 692/85150
A sprawling all-inclusive resort
in contemporary Spanish
style. Guest rooms are
spacious and appealingly
furnished and feature a full
array of amenities, including
safes. Suites have minibars.
Five bars, plus four eateries
serving above-average fare. All
activities and entertainment
are "on the house."
🔢 250 (including 10 suites)
🅿 🔆 🔆 🏊 🔆 🏧 MC, V

LAS TERRAZAS

🏨 HOTEL LA MOKA
$$
AUTOPISTA NACIONAL KM 51,
CANDELARIA
TEL 85/2996 OR 82/78600
FAX 85/2921 OR 7/78605
E-MAIL comercial@terraz.get
.cma.net
Charming neocolonial
architecture and a woodsy
hilltop location overlooking a
lake and Las Terrazas village.
Abundant Spanish tile, terra-
cotta floors, and wood beams
grace guest rooms. Billed as
an "eco-resort."
🔢 26 🅿 🔆 🔆 🏊 🏧 MC, V

PINAR DEL RÍO

🏨 CASA PARTICULAR LAS DELICIAS
$
CALLE DELICIAS 206, JUSTO
HIDALGO/MARINA
TEL 53/82/771678
Simple, back-to-basics *casa
particular* run by friendly
hosts, who prepare meals on
request. Clean but modest
furnishings in self-contained
apartment rental with hot
water (but no toilet seat).
Secure parking.
🔢 2 🅿 🔆

🏨 HOTEL PINAR DEL RÍO
$
CALLE MARTÍ & AUTOPISTA NACIONAL
TEL 82/5070
E-MAIL comazul@teleda.get.cma.net
Ho-hum cement structure catering to Cubans and tourists. Modest furnishings and uninspired decor are mitigated by the availability of tourist services. The swimming pool is a noisy weekend gathering spot for locals.
ℹ️ 136 P 🔁 🚭 🏊
🔲 MC, V

🏨 VILLAS TURÍSTICA SOROA
$$
CARRETERA DE SOROA KM 8, CANDELARIA, PINAR DEL RÍO
TEL 85/78218 OR 2122
Mountain hotel. Simple cabins with modern appointments set around a landscaped pool, with a forest at hand for hikes and horseback rides. A restaurant serves criollo dishes.
ℹ️ 49 P 🔲 🏊 🔲 MC, V

🍴 RUMAYOR RESTAURANTE-CABARET
$
CARRETERA A VIYALES KM 1
TEL 82/63007 OR 82/63051
The South Pacific decor appeals at this rustic, thatched eatery known for its smoked chicken; otherwise the criollo fare is moribund. Stick around for the nightly cabaret.
P

SAN DIEGO DE LOS BAÑOS

🏨 HOTEL EL MIRADOR
$
CALLE 23
TEL 82/78338
Handsome neocolonial property a stone's throw from the mineral spa. Recent refurbishment has blessed rooms with lively modern decor. An elegant restaurant serves criollo and continental fare.
ℹ️ 30 P 🔲 🏊 🔲 MC, V

VIÑALES

🏨 HOTEL LA ERMITA
$$
CARRETERA A LA ERMITA KM 1.5
TEL 8/93-6250
FAX 8/93-6069
E-MAIL laermita@laermita.co.cu
A spectacular setting overlooking Viñales Valley is the main draw for this expansive open-plan property with pool set amid lawns. Rooms offer simple decor and columned balconies, but the restaurant is lackluster.
ℹ️ 62 P 🔲 🏊 🔲 MC, V

🍴 CASA DE DON TOMÁS
$$
CALLE SALVADOR CISNERO #140
TEL 8/93-6300
Hearty criollo fare in a mellowed 1822 wooden mansion with balcony dining. Popular with tour groups. Troubadours entertain.
P

WESTERN CUBA–NORTH

CAYO SANTA MARIA

🏨 SOL CAYO SANTA MARÍA
$$$
TEL 42/35-1500
FAX 42/35-1505
E-MAIL cayostamaria@tpeninsula.solmelia.cu
Opened in 2002, this all-inclusive, Spanish-run resort caters to a predominantly European crowd. Lively contemporary decor. Three restaurants, plus a bevy of bars, tennis courts, water sports, and entertainment.
ℹ️ 300 P 🔲 🚭 🏊 🔲 MC, V

🏨 VILLAS LAS BRUJAS
$$
CAYO LAS BRUJAS
TEL 42/35-0199
FAX 42/35-0599
This rustic enclave of wood-and-stone cabins sits atop craggy Punta Periquillo. A thatched restaurant offers views over a spectacular beach and sheltered cove. Away-from-it-all setting good for birders and anglers.
ℹ️ 24 P 🔲 🚭 🔲 MC, V

REMEDIOS

🏨 HOTEL MASCOTTE
$$
CALLE MÁXIMO GÓMEZ
TEL 42/39-5467
FAX 42/39-5144
E-MAIL mascotte@cyvc.inf.cu
Charming, recently restored small historic hotel in the Islazul chain. Modest yet gracious furnishings and modern appliances. On the main plaza.
ℹ️ 10 🔲 🔲 MC, V

SANTA CLARA

🏨 CASA PARTICULAR ELIAR & MARÍA LEZCANO
$
CALLE SAN PABLO #19, CAROLINA/MAXIMO GOMEZ
TEL 422/5175
Splendid, quiet location on Plaza del Carmen, a short walk from downtown. Spacious, simply appointed room and clean, modern bathroom. Filling meals upon request. Gracious hosts.
ℹ️ 15 P 🔲

🍴 BODEGUITA DEL CENTRO
$
CALLE VILLUENDAS #264, SAN MIGUEL/NAZARENO
TEL 422/20-4356
This *paladar* serves the usual criollo fare in generous portions. Walls are covered with graffiti and eclectic decor in a take on Havana's Bodeguita del Medio. (see p. 243)
🔲 🔲 Closed B

HOTELS & RESTAURANTS

VARADERO

HOTELS

🏨 SOL PARADISUS VARADERO
$$$$$
CARRETERA LAS MORLAS
TEL 5/66-8700
FAX 5/66-8705
E-MAIL sec_com_div@melia
.solmelia.cma.net
This beautifully conceived
hotel in French classical style
opened in 2001 as a deluxe
all-inclusive. Its bright tropical
motif and hip, contemporary
decor appeal. Attractive
landscaping, atmospheric
restaurants, and a full array of
water sports and entertainment add to the draw.
🛈 421 🅿 ⬚ ⬚ ⬚ ⬚
⬚ MC, V

🏨 BEACHES VARADERO
$$$$
CARRETERA LAS MORLAS KM
14
TEL 5/66-8470
FAX 5/66-8335
E-MAIL varadero@beaches
.var.cyt.cu
Top-notch, all-suite all-inclusive
under Jamaican management.
Complete services, lively,
contemporary decor. King-size
beds standard. Creative fare
and high standards in four
restaurants.
🛈 350 🅿 ⬚ ⬚ ⬚ ⬚
⬚ MC, V

🏨 HOTEL & VILLAS KAWAMA
$$$$
AVENIDA KAWAMA
TEL 5/61-4416
FAX 5/66-7334
E-MAIL reserva@kawama.gca
.cma.net
Reclusive stone villas dis-
persed along the Kawama
headland. Eye-pleasing mo-
dern decor. Maid service.
Choice of restaurants, water
sports, and touristic services.
🛈 204 🅿 ⬚ ⬚ ⬚ ⬚
⬚ MC, V

🏨 HOTEL VARADERO INTERNACIONAL
$$$
AVENIDA LAS AMÉRICAS
TEL 5/66-7038
FAX 5/66-7246
E-MAIL reserva@gcinter.gca
.cma.net
Venerable 1970s hotel set in
well-groomed gardens front-
ing an attractive section of
beach. Full complement of
ancillary services, including
Varadero's liveliest cabaret..
Within walking distance of
the village.
🛈 163 🅿 ⬚ ⬚ ⬚ ⬚
⬚ MC, V

🏨 IBEROSTAR BARLOVENTO
$$$
AVENIDA 1RA, BET CALLES 10 &
12
TEL 5/66-7140
FAX 5/66-7218
E-MAIL reserva@ibero.gca
.tur.cu
Spanish-run hotel with a
gracious contemporary
Mediterranean aesthetic.
Guest rooms in rich pastels
offer pleasing decor and
modern amenities; louvered
windows and stained glass
evoke a colonial theme. Villas
are an option.
🛈 276 🅿 ⬚ ⬚ ⬚ ⬚
⬚ MC, V

SOMETHING SPECIAL

🏨 MANSION XANADU
Varadero's most exclusive
address. Exquisite 1930s
period decor recalls the days
when Iréneé du Pont lived here.
Marble floors, wrought-iron
beds, and throw rugs for furnishings, plus modern accoutrements
such as minibars and cable TV.
Marble bathrooms boast walk-in
showers. A superb restaurant and
bar, plus unrivaled coastal views.
Guests get privileges at Meliá Las
Américas hotel. The mansion
doubles as the clubhouse for
Varadero Golf Club.
$$$
AUTOPISTA SUR KM 8.5

TEL 5/66-8482
FAX 5/66-8481
E-MAIL varaderogolfclub@ip
.etecsa.cu
🛈 6 🅿 ⬚ ⬚ ⬚ MC, V

🏨 MERCURE CORALIA CUATRO PALMAS
$$$
AVENIDA 1RA, BET. CALLES 60 &
64
TEL 5/66-7040
FAX 5/66-7208
E-MAIL reserva@gcpalho.gca
.cma.net
Steadfast mid-range favorite
of tour groups. A recent
renovation has added modern
decor and livelier ambience
while retaining a Spanish
colonial touch. Central
location and French
management are pluses.
🛈 312 🅿 ⬚ ⬚ ⬚ ⬚
⬚ MC, V

🏨 HOTEL DOS MARES
$
AVENIDA 1RA & CALLE 53
TEL 45/61-2702
FAX 45/66-7499
E-MAIL recepcion@dmares
.hor.tur.cu
Training hotel in the heart of
Varadero. Decor is simple and

PRICES

HOTELS
An indication of the cost
of a double room without
breakfast is given by $ signs.

$$$$$	Over $200
$$$$	$150–200
$$$	$100–150
$$	$50–100
$	Under $50

RESTAURANTS
An indication of the cost of a
three-course dinner without
drinks is given by $ signs.

$$$$$	Over $50
$$$$	$35–50
$$$	$20–35
$$	$10–20
$	Under $10

rooms are small, but keen staff and pleasant restaurant and bar make amends. It admits Cuban workers as guests.

🚹 34 🅿 🔆 ⬚ ⬚ MC, V

🏨 HOTEL PULLMAN
$
AVENIDA 1RA & CALLE 49, VARADERO
TEL 5/66-7161
FAX 45/66-7499
E-MAIL recepcion@dmares
.hor.tur.cu
This converted mansion is a no-frills favorite of budget travelers. Modest, colonial-style decor; TVs, telephones, and safes are standard.

🚹 15 🅿 🔆 ⬚ MC, V

RESTAURANTS

🍴 ESQUINA CUBA
$$
AVENIDA 1RA & CALLE 36
TEL 5/61-4019
Sibling to the famous Havana eatery, this smaller version offers El Aljibe's trademark all-you-can-eat roast chicken. You dine under thatch.

🅿 ⬚ Closed B ⬚ MC, V

🍴 EL BODEGÓN CRIOLLO
$$
AVENIDA DE LA PLAYA & CALLE 40
TEL 5/66-7784
Tasty criollo fare enjoyed indoors or on a shady patio. The menu is heavy on pork and chicken. Seeks to emulate the decor in Havana's Bodeguita del Medio (see p. 243).

🅿 ⬚ Closed B ⬚ MC, V

🍴 EL MESÓN DEL QUIJOTE
$$
AVENIDA DE LAS AMERICAS
TEL 5/66-7796
Exquisite rustic decor in this charming hilltop restaurant serving continental and criollo fare. Seafoods are a specialty.

🅿 🔆 ⬚ Closed B ⬚ MC, V

🍴 RESTAURANTE ANTIGUEDADES
$$
AVENIDA 1RA & 59
TEL 5/66-7329
If you wish to dress up, this is the place. Stuffed full of antiques and Hollywood bric-a-brac. Elegant place settings. Menu is weighted toward surf-and-turf.

🅿 🔆 ⬚ Closed B ⬚ MC, V

WESTERN CUBA–SOUTH

CIENFUEGOS

🏨 HOTEL LA JAGUA
$$
CALLE 37, 0/2
TEL 432/545-1003
FAX 432/545-1245
E-MAIL reserva@jagua.gca
.cma.net
Recent restoration has blessed this high rise with modern decor and amenities. Service has improved under new French management. Top-floor rooms offer fine views. Nightly cabaret, plus shops and touristic services.

🚹 145 🅿 🔆 🔆 ⬚ 📺
⬚ MC, V

🏨 HOTEL LA UNION
$$
AVENIDA 54, CALLE 31
TEL 432/545-1020
FAX 432/545-1685
E-MAIL comercial@union.cfg
.cyt.cu
A recently restored colonial-era hotel one block from main plaza. This charmer combines exquisite traditional ambience with modern amenities, including a gym and sauna. Bedrooms are appointed with antique reproductions. The restaurant—serving continental and criollo dishes —is perhaps the best in town.

🚹 49 🅿 🔆 🔆 ⬚ 📺
⬚ MC, V

🏨 FINCA LOS COLORADOS B&B
A *casa particular* exceptional for its European sophistication. Guest rooms feature metal-frame antique beds, plus antiques and modern fittings. There's a Roman motif throughout. Exquisite meals are prepared in a state-of-the-art kitchen and eaten in an elegant dining area or outside on a patio with arbor. Splendid breeze-swept clifftop locale outside town, on the road to Pasacabello. There's a playground for children. Gracious hosts speak English.

$
CARRETERA DE PASACABELLO KM 18, PLAYA RANCHO LUNA
TEL 432/51-3808

🚹 3 🅿 🔆 ⬚ MC, V

🍴 BODEGÓN DEL PALACIO DE VALLE
$$
CALLES 37 & 0
TEL 432/545-1226
The effusive Mughal decor is reason enough to visit. The seafood menu promotes lobster in various guises. A pianist entertains.

🅿 ⬚ Closed B ⬚ Cash only

PENÍNSULA DE ANCÓN

🍴 BRISAS TRINIDAD DEL MAR
$$$
PENÍNSULA ANCÓN
TEL 419/6500
FAX 419/6565
E-MAIL reservas@brisastdad
.co.cu
A pleasing contemporary motif adds charm to this modern, low-rise beach resort centered on a sprawling, free-form pool. Rooms boast a panoply of modern amenities. Water sports are offered.

🚹 241 🅿 🔆 🔆 ⬚ 📺
⬚ MC, V

🔆 Nonsmoking 🔆 Air-conditioning ⬚ Indoor/⬚ Outdoor swimming pool 📺 Health club ⬚ Credit cards **KEY**

PLAYA GIRÓN

🍴 RESTAURANT COLIBRI
$$
CARRETERA DE LA CIENAGA
KM 16, LA BOCA DE GUAMA
NO TEL
Crocodile features on the menu of this African-style thatched restaurant overhanging the lagoon at La Boca. The menu is wholeheartedly criollo. Splendid ambience. It sustained significant hurricane damage in November 2001, however.
🅿 🚫 🔲 L only

SANCTI SPÍRITUS

HOTELS

🏨 CASA PARTICULAR JOSÉ LUIS DIAZ TOUZEF
$
CALLE MÁXIMO GÓMEZ #51, CALDERÓN/TIRSO MARÍN
NO TEL
Self-contained apartment one block from the main plaza. Roomy, simply furnished, with a commodious kitchen and small bathroom. Hospitable owner. Street noise, however, is a factor in this *casa particular*.
🚹 1 🚫

🏨 HOSPEDAJE LAS PALMERAS
$
CALLE BARTOLOMÉ MASÓ #161, CUBA/CUARTELO
TEL 41/22169
Clean, well-kept *casa particular* in a middle-class home handily close to the bus station. Breezes and air-conditioning keep the place cool. Shared bathroom. Friendly hostess.
🚹 2

🏨 HOSTAL EL RIJO
$$
CALLE MÁXIMO GÓMEZ, PLAZA HONORATO
Opened in 2002, this restored colonial mansion-turned-hostelry is entered via grand carriage doors. Terra-cotta

tiles, wrought-iron lamps, and beamed ceilings hark back in time. Modern amenities include cable TV and period-themed art.
🚹 16

🏨 VILLA RANCHO HATUEY
$$
CARRETERA CENTRAL KM 383
TEL 41/28315
FAX 41/28350
E-MAIL gerente@rhatuey .vcl.cyc.cu
Mediterranean-style two-story bungalows on the city outskirts. Nightly cabaret, plus squash court and elegant restaurant. Popular with tour groups.
🚹 76 🅿 🚫 🚫 🔲 🍷 🍴 MC, V

RESTAURANTS

🍴 LA QUINTA SANTA ELENA
$
CALLE EL LLANO
TEL 41/29167
Stately colonial mansion overlooking the river. Expansive *criollo* menu, but the real reason to come here is the atmosphere. A cabaret is hosted on Saturday nights.
🅿 🔲 B on request
🍴 MC, V

🍴 MESÓN DE LA PLAZA
$
CALLE MÁXIMO GÓMEZ #34
TEL 41/28546
A recently opened Spanish bodega serving classic Cuban-Iberian fare such as *pollo asado* and garbanzos with pork and sausage washed down by sangría. Charming, rough-hewn ambience.
🚫 🔲 Closed B 🍴 MC, V

TRINIDAD

🏨 HOTEL HORIZONTES LAS CUEVAS
$$
CALLE GENERAL LINO PÉREZ (FINAL)
TEL 419/6133 OR 419/6402

FAX 419/6161
E-MAIL crh@horizontes .hor.tur.cu
Splendid location on a hillside overlooking the old town. The bungalow and split-level accommodations are minimal, however, and meal quality is wanting. Tennis courts. Car rental and excursions offered.
🚹 112 🅿 🚫 🚫 🔲
🍴 MC, V

SOMETHING SPECIAL

🏨 HOSTAL CASA MUNOZ
Dating back to 1800, this private *casa particular* is one of Trinidad's treasures, replete with antiques that draw tour groups. Modern bathrooms dispense piping-hot water, and a patio provides a calm spot for reading and sunning. The owner —an accomplished photographer and authority on local history— speaks English and can act as tour guide. Good for families.
$
CALLE JESÚS MARÍA #401, BET. OLVIDO & ANGARILLA
TEL/FAX 419/3673
E-MAIL juliotrinidad@Latin Mail.com
🚹 25 🅿 🚫 🚫 🍴 MC, V

🏨 CASA PARTICULAR CARLOS SOTOLONGO
$
CALLES SIMÓN BOLÍVAR & FRANCISCO JAVIER
TEL 419/4169
Located directly overlooking Plaza Mayor, this exquisite colonial home is filled with antiques and fine art. The two rooms vary: One is modern and air-conditioned, whereas the second is colonial and features a metal-frame bed.
🚹 25

🍴 PALADAR ESTELA
$
CALLE SIMÓN BOLÍVAR #557
TEL 419/4329
Though simple, this is perhaps Trinidad's finest *paladar*. Criollo dishes are served on a

tree-shaded patio or in a *sala* filled with antiquities. In a colonial home, one block north of Plaza Mayor.
🅿 🅢 🅔 D only

CENTRAL CUBA

CAMAGÜEY

HOTELS

🏨 **CASA PARTICULAR TERESA SANTANA**
$
CALLE SANTA RITA #37, SAN RAMÓN/SANTA ROSA
TEL 322/95145
Spacious, simple colonial home with modest furnishings yet congenial host and handily close to the historic core. TV lounge. Meals, by request, can be served on a patio.
ⓘ 2 🅿 🅢

🏨 **GRAN HOTEL**
$
CALLE MACEO #67, IGNACIO AGRAMONTE/GENERAL GÓMEZ
TEL 32/29-2093
E-MAIL comazul@teleda. get.cma.net
Caringly restored 18th-century hotel in the heart of the historic city. Antiques and a period aesthetic abound. Piano bar. The elegant rooftop restaurant is the best in town and serves continental buffets, plus a creative criollo menu featuring lobster enchiladas. Caters to both Cubans and foreigners.
ⓘ 72 🅿 🅢 🅢 🌊 🅢 MC, V

RESTAURANTS

🍴 **CAMPAÑA DE TOLEDO**
$
PLAZA SAN JUAN DE DÍOS
TEL 322/95888
Mellow tile-roofed colonial inn with rustic decor and views over the historic plaza. Criollo menu. Terra-cotta wall murals.
🕐 Closed B

🍴 **EL OVEJITO**
$
CALLE HERMANO AGUERO #280
TEL 322/29-2524
Restored colonial bodega known for its lamb dishes highlighting a broader criollo menu. Atmospheric decor features terra-cotta wall murals.
🕐 Closed B

CAYOS COCO & GUILLERMO

🏨 **MELÍA CAYO COCO**
$$$$$
CAYO COCO
TEL 33/30-1180
FAX 33/30-1195
E-MAIL melia.cayo.coco@ solmelia.com
Sprawling all-inclusive resort under Spanish management. Exquisite landscaping makes good use of the lagoon-and-beach setting. Decor plays on a classical Iberian theme. Full complement of services and sports facilities includes water sports, boutiques, and nightly entertainment.
ⓘ 250 🅿 🅢 🅢 🌊 🌊 🅢 MC, V

🏨 **SOL CLUB CAYO GUILLERMO**
$$$$
CAYO GUILLERMO
TEL 33/30-1760
FAX 33/30-1748
E-MAIL jefederecepcion.scg@ solmelia.com
Lively tropical colors abound at this mid-range all-inclusive resort. King-size beds and elegant furnishings. Choice of restaurants and complete range of water sports and activities, including theme parties.
ⓘ 264 🅿 🅢 🅢 🌊 🌊 🅢 MC, V

🏨 **TRYP CAYO COCO**
$$$$
CAYO COCO
TEL 33/30-1300
FAX 33/30-1386

E-MAIL jefe.reservas.tcc@sol meliacuba.com
Stretching along 2 miles of beachfront, this international standard resort offers a variety of accommodations, all graciously appointed and with oversize bathrooms. Services comprise water sports, tennis courts, entertainment, and excursions. Four pools, including a saltwater pool.
ⓘ 972 🅢 MC, V

🏨 **IBEROSTAR DAIQUIRI**
$$$$
CAYO GUILLERMO
TEL 33/30-1650
FAX 33/30-1645
E-MAIL comercia@ibsdaiq .gca.tur.cu
Foreign-managed all-inclusive on a scintillating beach. Contemporary Spanish-style public areas feature marble. Lively furnishings blend with modern appointments, including bathrooms with colonial tiles. A full range of activities includes water sports.
ⓘ 312 🅿 🅢 🅢 🌊 🌊 🅢 MC, V

CAYO SABINAL

SOMETHING SPECIAL

🏨 **RUMBOS PLAYAS LOS PINOS**
Five utterly rustic wooden beach huts atop sugar-white sands, with a jade lagoon a stone's throw away. Appeals to the barefoot and button-down crowd with minimal furnishings and cold-water showers. A bucolic beach bar-cum-restaurant serves seafood, including lobster, often delivered fresh by boat. There are no other facilities— but the reclusiveness and simplicity are part of the magic.
$
PLAYA LOS PINOS
NO TEL
ⓘ 5 🅿

SANTA LUCÍA

🏨 HOTEL CUATRO VIENTOS
$$$
PLAYA SANTA LUCÍA
TEL 32/36-5120
FAX 32/36-5142
E-MAIL comerc@cvientos
.slt.cyt.cu
Under Spanish management, this three-star beachfront resort draws budget package groups yet remains the best of Santa Lucía's offerings. Rooms have the essentials—TV, minibar, and telephone. Handsome swimming pool. Nightly entertainment.
🛏 400 P 🅿 🚫 ♿ 🔁
🚭 MC, V

🏨 CLUB SANTA LUCIA
$$$
PLAYA SANTA LUCIA
TEL 32/33-6428 OR 32/33-6109
FAX 32/36-5147
E-MAIL aloja@coral.stl.cyt.cu
Newly rehashed yet still uninspired (as are all hotels in Santa Lucía) three-star resort popular with Italian package groups. Safes, minibars, and TVs are standard. Beach volleyball, water sports, car rental, and excursions.
🛏 252 P 🅿 🚫 ♿ 🔁
🚭 MC, V

WESTERN ORIENTE

BARTOLOMÉ MASÓ

🏨 VILLA SANTO DOMINGO
$
SANTO DOMINGO
TEL LARGA DISTANCIA 375 (VIA THE OPERATOR) OR 23/42-5321
E-MAIL comazul@teleda.get
.cma.net
Sitting over the Río Yara at the base of Pico Turquino, this rustic complex is a good base for hikers. Simple rooms are meagerly furnished but have safes and refrigerators. A video room, game room, and

bar are on hand.
🛏 20 P 🅿 🔁

BAYAMO

🏨 HOTEL ROYALTON
$
CALLE MACEO #53, PLAZA CÉSPEDES
TEL 23/42-2224
FAX 23/42-4792
A recently restored hotel of antiquity. A marble staircase leads to the small, modestly furnished rooms (one room is handicapped accessible). Cable TV and telephones are standard. Cuban guests accepted. A small nightclub is popular with locals.
🛏 31 P 🅿 🔁

CAYO SAETÍA

🏨 VILLA CAYO SAETÍA
$$
CAYO SAETÍA, MAYARÍ
TEL 24/96901
FAX 24/96903
E-MAIL vsaetia@ip.etecsa.cu
Small, secluded resort on an island sheltering African game (both game-viewing and hunting safaris are offered). Rustic accommodations feature TVs, refrigerators, and telephones. Jeep and horseback excursions are offered. Beaches lie at hand. Animals shot on "safari" stare down in the restaurant, where antelope is on the menu.
🛏 12 P 🅿 🔁 ♿ 🔁 MC, V

GUARDALAVACA

🏨 MELÍA RÍO DE ORO
$$$$$
PLAYA ESMERALDA, CARRETERA GUARDALAVACA
TEL 24/30090 OR 24/30072
FAX 24/30095
E-MAIL meila.rioro@oro.sol
melia.cma.net
Colorful contemporary decor and a full roster of amenities to this modern, upscale all-inclusive managed by the Spanish Meliá group. Accommodation is in junior suites, some with king-size

beds. Cable TV, safes, and minibars are standard. Beach volleyball and scuba diving. Car rental and excursions. Internet access.
🛏 300 P 🅿 🚫 ♿ 🔁
🚭 MC, V

🏨 LAS BRISAS CLUB RESORT
$$$$
GUARDALAVACA
TEL 24/30218
FAX 24/30418
E-MAIL reserv@brisa.gcv
.cyt.cu
Well-run all-inclusive serving a predominantly Canadian clientele. Choice of accommodations, including suites and villas, all in a neoclassic theme. Beauty salon, shops, tennis, water sports center, and a choice of restaurants.
🛏 231 P 🅿 🚫 ♿ 🔁
🚭 MC, V

🏨 ATLÁNTICO BUNGALOWS
$$$
GUARDALAVACA
TEL 24/3180
FAX 24/30200
E-MAIL recep@hatlant.gvc
.cyt.cu
Contemporary styling enhances this all-inclusive

---

complex 200 meters inland of the beach. Rooms in two-story villas overlook a handsome free-form pool. Elegant restaurant. Car rental and excursions. Guests get privileges at the less appealing Hotel Atlántico, which has scuba diving and water sports.
🏨 136 P 🄢 🄢 🌊 🄫 MC, V

LTI COSTA VERDE BEACH
$$$
PLAYA PESQUERO
TEL 24/30510
FAX 24/30515
E-MAIL sales@ltihog.co.cu
Handsome all-inclusive opened in 2001 with full amenities, including five restaurants, four bars, tennis courts, volleyball, scuba diving, and entertainment. Gracious contemporary decor in guest rooms. Children's camp. Car and scooter rental.
🏨 309 P 🄢 🄢 🌊 🄫 🄫 MC, V

HOLGUÍN

VILLA PALOMA
$
CALLE MACEO #8
TEL 24/42-2579
Once-elegant 1950s home with a huge lounge and dining room graced by period furnishings. The gracious hosts of this casa particular are devout. The rear patio has a fruit orchard. Quiet neighborhood, within walking distance of the historic center.
🏨 2 P 🄢

VILLA LIBA
$
CALLE MACEO #46
TEL 24/42-3823
This casa particular retains its original sumptuous (if slightly jaded) 1950s decor and furnishings. The middle-class home is one of Cuba's finest private room rentals. Some rooms share bathrooms. A vine arbor graces the patio.
🏨 3 P 🄢

VILLA MIRADOR DE MAYABE
$
ALTURAS DE MAYABE
TEL 24/42-2160
FAX 24/42-5498
Fabulous hilltop location with valley views. Bungalows are basically furnished. A self-contained, fully staffed villa is more elegantly decorated with modern furniture and offers TV plus private bathrooms in each of four rooms. A thatched restaurant specializes in criollo fare. Islazul.
🏨 24 (including 5 suites) P 🄢 🌊 🄫 MC, V

LAS TUNAS

LA VILLA
$
CALLE FRANCISCO VERONA #266, LORA/HEREDIA
TEL 31/42260
A middle-class home provides a pleasing environment for this casa particular featuring pleasant, though dated, furnishings. Shared bathrooms. TV lounge.
🏨 4 P 🄢

MAREA DEL PORTILLO

HOTEL FARALLON DEL CARIBE
$$
CARRETERA DE PILÓN KM 12.5, PILÓN
TEL 23/59-7081
FAX 23/59-7080
E-MAIL dsk@hfarcar.ma.grm.cyt.cu
Most upscale of four hotels locally, this hilltop all-inclusive offers modern decor and amenities. Expansive pool terrace with swim-up bar. Boutiques, car rental, excursions, and cabaret. Attracts a Canadian clientele.
🏨 140 P 🄢 🄢 🌊 🄫 MC, V

NIQUERO

HOTEL NIQUERO
$
CALLE MARTÍ & CÉSPEDES
TEL 23/59-2498
This recently opened hotel offers clean, up-to-date, yet fundamentally modest accommodations in the heart of this historic town. A rooftop bar draws locals on weekends.
🏨 26 P 🄢

PINARES DE MAYARÍ

VILLA PINARES DE MAYARÍ
$
PARQUE LA MENSURA, MAYARÍ
TEL 24/53308
FAX 24/30126
E-MAIL gaviota@gaviota.gav.tur.cu
No-frills mountain lodge with rustic wooden cottages and rooms, now fitted with hot showers. Operates as an eco-resort offering hiking, horseback rides, and spa treatments. Tennis court. Communal meals.
🏨 28 P 🄢 🌊 🄫 MC, V

SANTIAGO DE CUBA

HOTELS

HOTEL CASA GRANDA
$$$$
CALLE HEREDIA #201, BET. SAN FÉLIX & SAN PEDRO
TEL 226/86600
FAX 226/86035
E-MAIL director@casagran.gca.cyt.cu
Superb location overlooking Parque Céspedes. Newly restored and now French-managed, this grande dame offers modern conveniences. Suites boast antiques. Parisian-style patio lobby bar good for watching events in the plaza; it also serves inexpensive, filling meals. The elegant Restaurante Casa Grande offers a touch of class, plus continen-

HOTELS & RESTAURANTS

tal and **criollo** dishes and good-value breakfasts.
🛈 58 🅿 🔲 🔲 🔲 MC, V

🏨 MELÍA HOTEL SANTIAGO
$$$$
AVENIDA LAS AMÉRICAS & CALLE M, REPARTO SUEÑO
TEL 22/68-7070
FAX 22/68-7170
E-MAIL melia.santiago@santiago.solmelia.cma.net
Santiago's showcase hotel, this modern high rise offers spacious rooms with a contemporary aesthetic and oversize bathrooms. Amenities include a cigar store, beauty parlor, business center, sauna, and a rooftop bar with cabaret. Choice of four restaurants. Spanish managed.
🛈 302 🅿 🔲 🔲 🔲
🔲 MC, V

🏨 HOTEL SAN JUAN
$$
CARRETERA SIBONEY KM 1.5, LOMA SAN JUAN
TEL 226/87200
FAX 226/87137
E-MAIL crh@horizontes.hor.tur.cu
Suburban hotel adjacent to San Juan Hill. Modestly furnished in contemporary decor. Upper-level rooms are preferred for their lofty ceilings. Tour desk and car rental. The elegant La Ceiba Restaurant is one of the finest eateries in town, serving nouvelle criollo cuisine such as snapper with fruit sauce. A cabaret is hosted. Horizontes.
🛈 112 🅿 🔲 🔲 🔲
🔲 MC, V

🏨 CASA PARTICULAR ESMERALDA GONZÁLEZ
$
AVENIDA PUJOL #107 & 5TA, REPARTO VISTA ALEGRE
TEL 22/64-6341
Pleasant middle-class 1950s home with a well-lit guest room with period furnishings and a gleaming bathroom

with plentiful hot water. Separate entrance. Leafy suburban location.
🛈 I 🅿 🔲

🏨 CASA PARTICULAR FLORINDA CHAVIANO
$
CALLE I #58, 2DA/3RA, REPARTO SUEÑO
TEL 226/53660
Modern, nicely furnished home with a TV lounge, and rear patio with arbor good for enjoying home-cooked meals. Well-lit guest room features a clean, modern bathroom. Quiet neighborhood, close to Moncada.
🛈 I 🅿 🔲

🏨 CASA PARTICULAR MR. ASENSIO
$
CALLE J #306, AVENIDA LAS AMÉRICAS/6TA, REPARTO SUEÑO
TEL 226/24660
Lively 1950s decor in this nicely renovated, self-contained upstairs apartment. The owner lives part-time in Italy, and brings an Italianate aesthetic. Burglar alarm and rooftop patio.
🛈 I 🅿 🔲

RESTAURANTS

🍴 RESTAURANTE EL CAYO
$$
CAYO GRANMA
TEL 22/69-0109
Overhanging the waters on the east side of Cayo Granma, with fabulous views across the bay toward El Morro. Seafood menu features lobster, shrimp, and seafood paella.
🔲 Closed B

🍴 RESTAURANTE EL MORRO
$$
CARRETERA AL MORRO
TEL 22/69-0109
Spectacular clifftop setting with magnificent coastal vistas. Rustic bodega-style decor, with terra-cotta tiles, wood

beams, and goat-hide chairs. The patio with arbor is preferred. Creative international menu includes bean soup, and baked fish with shrimp. Musicians entertain.
🅿 🔲 Closed B

🍴 SANTIAGO 1900
$$
CALLE SAN BASILIO #354, BET. SAN FÉLIX & CARNICERÍA
TEL 22/62 3507
Former colonial mansion of the Bacardí family, still stocked with antiques. Dine indoors or on the airy patio with fountain and arbor to the rear. The continental-cum-criollo menu offers the usual run-of-the-mill fare. The *mojitos* make amends.

🍴 PALADAR SALÓN TROPICAL
$
CALLE FERNANDEZ MARCANE #310, 9/10, REPARTO SANTO BARBARA
One of the few *paladares* in town providing both ambience and value. You dine beneath an arbor on a rooftop patio. The criollo menu includes garbanzo stew and a barbecue chicken special.
🅿 🔲 Closed B

BACONAO

🏨 CORALIA CLUB BUCANERO
$$$$
CARRETERA DE BACONAO KM 4, ARROYO LA COSTA
TEL 22/68-6367
FAX 22/68-6073
E-MAIL bucanero@hbucanero.co.cu
French-managed all-inclusive enjoying a reclusive setting backed by cliffs. Fieldstone and timber structures. A restaurant sits on stilts above the exquisite pocket-size beach, with water sports, including scuba diving Popular with Canadian and European charter groups.
🛈 200 🅿 🔲 🔲 🔲
🔲 MC, V

CHIVIRICO

🏨 HOTEL LOS GALEONES
$$$$
CARRETERA DE CHIVIRICO KM 72
TEL 22/26160
FAX 22/29116
E-MAIL sierrmar@smar.scu
.cyt.cu
Small, intimate, Spanish-style hilltop property with guest privileges to Sierra Mar. Spacious rooms have king-size beds. Sauna and scuba diving facilities. Romantic poolside restaurant. The beach is accessed by a long staircase.
🛈 34 🅿 🅢 🌊 🖥 🅢 MC, V

🏨 SIERRA MAR
$$$
CARRETERA DE CHIVIRICO KM 60
TEL 22/29110
FAX 22/26116
E-MAIL sierrmar@smar.scu
.cyt.cu
All-inclusive hilltop property overlooking Playa Sevilla Guamá. Expansive views from the lively pool terrace with water-slide. Complete amenities include entertainment, water sports, choice of bars, and excursions. Popular with Canadian charter groups.
🛈 200 🅿 🅢 🌊 🖥
🅢 MC, V

GUANTÁNAMO

🏨 VILLA REVE'S
$
CALLE PEDRO PÉREZ #670A,
PASEO/NARCISO LÓPEZ
TEL 21/32-2159
This modest *casa particular* offers modern rooms at the rear of a colonial home in the heart of the historic center. Avoid the gloomy interior rooms. Meals by request in an airy patio.
🛈 5 🅢

BARACOA

🏨 HOTEL EL CASTILLO
$$
CALLE GALIXTO GARCÍA,
LOMA EL PARAÍSO
TEL 21/42125
FAX 21/35-5519
E-MAIL castillo@ip.etecsa.cu
A handsome and respectful conversion of an ancient castle, with grand views over town and toward El Yunque. Terra-cotta tiles, plentiful hardwoods, and modern appointments in guest rooms. A small swimming pool studs the forecourt. Car rental and tour desk. A bodega-style restaurant serves regional criollo meals, such as shellfish in coconut sauce with coriander, onion, and oregano.
🛈 35 🅿 🅢 🌊 🅢 MC, V

🏨 CASA PARTICULAR EL CASTILLITO
$
CALLE MARIAN GRAJALES #9-A, BET. CALIXTO GARCIA & JULIA MELLA
TEL 21/43625
Self-contained apartment with a spacious though meagerly outfitted kitchen with dining room. Simply furnished bedroom. Clean, modern bathroom with hot water.
🛈 1 🅢

🏨 CASA PARTICULAR EL MIRADOR
$
CALLE MACEO #86, 24 DE FEBRERO/10 DE OCTUBRE
TEL 21/43592
Colonial mansion with breeze-swept rooms upstairs. A balcony has rockers, and a rear veranda offers views of El Yunque. Shared bathroom. Gracious hostess.
🛈 2 🅢

🍴 PALADAR LA COLONIAL
$
CALLE MARTÍ #123, BET. MARTÍ & FRANK PAÍS
TEL 21/43161
Exquisite colonial decor in this historic home-turned-private restaurant. Filling portions and efficient service. The menu is heavy on seafood, including swordfish. Dine early, as many items sell out early.
🅢

ARCHIPIÉLAGO DE CANARREOS

CAYO LARGO

🏨 HOTEL PELICANO
$$$$
PLAYA LINDAMAR, 3 MILES FROM THE AIRPORT
TEL 5/48333
FAX 5/48160
E-MAIL reserva@pelicano
.gca.cma.net
Low-rise, sprawling resort in Spanish colonial style. Functions as the node of touristic activity. Guest rooms face the ocean: Deluxe rooms feature TVs and minibars. Water sports. A piano bar, nightclub, and cabaret draw guests from other hotels. Severely damaged in November 2001 hurricane.
🛈 307 🅿 🅢 🌊 🖥
🅢 MC, V

🏨 VILLA CAPRICHO
$$$$
PLAYA BLANCA, 4.5 MILES FROM THE AIRPORT
TEL 5/48111
FAX 5/48160
E-MAIL reserva@pelicano
.gca.cma.net
Rustic thatched wood-and-fieldstone saddle-roof bungalows boast porches with hammocks. Some have kitchens and loft bedrooms. Exquisite location overlooking Playa Blanca. Few facilities, but guests have access to adjacent resorts. Severely damaged in November 2001 hurricane.
🛈 75 🅿 🅢 🌊 🅢 MC, V

🏨 SOL CLUB CAYO LARGO
$$$$
PLAYA LINDAMAR, 3 MILES FROM THE AIRPORT
TEL 45/48260
FAX 45/48265
E-MAIL sol.club.cayo.largo
@solmelia.com

HOTELS & RESTAURANTS

Opened in 2001, this beautiful all-inclusive property has upped the ante and offers Cayo Largo's first quality hotel living up to its star rating. Sponge-washed walls and tropical color schemes add vitality. Guest rooms feature contemporary vogue. Full resort services, including shops. Tennis courts.

🛈 290 (including 7 junior suites and 52 with sea views) 🅿 ⛁ 🏊 📺 🏠 MC, V

ISLA DE LA JUVENTUD

🏨 HOTEL EL COLONY
$$
CARRETERA SIGUANEA KM 41
TEL 61/98181
FAX 61/98420
E-MAIL reservas@colony
.gerona.inf.cu
Former 1950s mobster hotel now catering to scuba divers and package vacationers. Modestly decorated rooms feature TVs. Water sports, scooter rental, and excursions are offered. Out-on-a-limb location good for nature hikes.

🛈 77 (including 24 bunga-lows) 🅿 ⛁ 🏊 🏠 MC, V

🏨 CASA PARTICULAR RAFAEL CÉSPEDES
$
CALLE 32 #4701A, 47/49
TEL 61/23167
One of the better private room rentals in town. Rooms are modestly furnished and each has its own clean bathroom. TV lounge. The congenial hosts have a classic car for touring.

🛈 2 🅿 ⛁

🏨 VILLA ISLA DE LA JUVENTUD
$
AUTOPISTA GERONA-LA FÉ KM 1.5
TEL 61/23290
FAX 61/24486
E-MAIL comazul@teleda.get
.cma.net
The best place in town. Modestly furnished bungalows

with marble floors surround a small swimming pool. Entertainers perform for guests, which include Cubans. The few facilities include a restaurant. On the outskirts of Nueva Gerona.

🛈 20 🅿 ⛁ 🏊 🏠 MC, V

🍴 RESTAURANT DRAGON
$
CALLE 39 & 26
TEL 61/24479
Authentic Chinese decor and staff—a rare find in Cuba! The menu offers familiar dishes, such as a chop suey special. Ingredients are often wanting. Romantic ambience.

⛁

SHOPPING IN CUBA

The tourist boom has spawned a great deal of kitsch but also an outpouring of quality crafts, from wooden carvings, papier-mâché figurines, and knitted lace to jewelry, leatherwork, and vibrant paintings of landscapes, sensual *mulattas,* and street scenes that capture the surrealism of Cuban life. Havana has numerous crafts markets and state-run art galleries, the latter reflecting the tremendous vitality and often explicitly erotic experimentalism of Cuban art.

Model classic cars are a favorite subject, crafted from copper wire, papier mâché, or recycled soda cans. Typically, jewelry sold at crafts markets makes use of recycled silverware. Unfortunately, much jewelry uses endangered black coral—refrain from buying. Bargaining is the norm at markets, but prices are usually already discounted substantially.

Cuban cigars, unavailable in the United States, are of renowned quality and a tremendous bargain. Buy at state-run Casas del Habano, and avoid *jineteros*—street hustlers—passing off fake or inferior stogies as the real McCoy. Street scams are common. Buy premium export-grade coffee, sold pre-packaged; domestic coffee is notably inferior. When buying rums, stick with the quality—albeit more expensive—brands, such as Havana Club and Matusalem. Music CDs and cassettes are no bargains, but the choice is wide and includes rare sounds of danzón, cha-cha-cha, and son.

Most upscale tourist hotels have gift stores selling cigars, coffee, CDs, and arts and crafts. The **Fondo Cubano de Bienes Culturales,** Calle 36 #4702, Havana, tel 7/203-8144 and 7/203-6523, e-mail fcbc@cubarte .cult.cu, is another good source and has outlets nationwide. The Feria Internacional de Artesanía, held at Pabexpo in Jan./Feb., is Cuba's annual international handicrafts fair.

Cuba suffers from a dearth of shops or markets outside the main tourist centers.

Licensed travelers can bring back up to $100 of "commercial" goods and are limited to two boxes of cigars and two liters of alcohol, as well as unlimited "educational" items that include, but is not limited to, art, crafts, books, and CDs. Items purchased by non-licensed travelers are subject to seizure by U.S. Customs.

HAVANA

The capital city is blessed with shopping opportunities. Most arts and crafts outlets concentrate in Habana Vieja; Calle Obispo is lined with *expoventas*—private art galleries. The largest is the artisans' market on Calle Tacón. Crocheted clothing can be found in the main plazas; skirts, shawls, blouses, and crocheted bikinis and *tangas* are popular items.

ARTS & ANTIQUES

Casa de Antigüedades, "Dos Leones," Calle Galiano, Centro Habana, opposite the Hotel Lincoln. Vast array of antiques, from art deco lamps to crystal chandeliers.
Colección Habana, Calle Mercaderes #13, O'Reilly/ Empedrado, Habana Vieja, tel 7/861-3388. Antique reproductions and decorative pieces.
Galería Haydeé Santamaría, Calle G, 3ra/5ta, Vedado, tel 7/55-2706. This premier gallery sells art of the Americas, featuring premier Cuban artists.
Taller Experimental de Gráfica, Callejón de Chorro, Plaza de La Catedral, Habana Vieja, tel 7/862-0979. Lithographic workshop selling original lithos from up-and-coming artists.

BOOKS & MAPS

Instituto Cubano de Libro, Calle O'Reilly #4, Plaza de Armas, Habana Vieja, tel 7/62-8091. The Cuban Book Institute sells English-language novels and guidebooks, plus Cuban editions.
Librería La Internacional, Calle Obispo & Bernaza, Habana Vieja, tel 7/62-3283. Modest offering of English-language titles spanning literature to natural history.
Librería Fernando Ortíz, Calles L & 27, Vedado, tel 7/32-9653. Mostly Spanish titles, but some works in English.
Mercado de Libros, Plaza de Armas, Habana Vieja. Secondhand book market selling political works by Castro & Co., plus atlases, 19th-century illustrated books, and first edition novels.
El Navegante, Calle Mercaderes #115, bet. Obispo & Obrapía, Habana Vieja, tel 7/861-3625. An Aladdin's Cave of tourist maps and nautical charts.

CIGARS

Casa del Habano, Fábrica Partagas, Calle Industria #520, Barcelona/Dragones, Habana Vieja, tel 7/33-8060. Large walk-in humidor and knowledgeable staff. A private smoking lounge and bar to the rear has its own humidor.
Casa del Habano, Hostal Conde de Villanueva, Calle Mercaderes & Lamparilla, tel 7/862-9294, fax 7/862-9682. Huge range of quality cigars and a sumptuous smoker's lounge.
Casa del Habano, Hotel Nacional, Calles O & 21, Vedado, tel 7/33-3564. Large humidor with complete range of quality cigars.
Casa del Habano, Ave. 5ta & 16, Miramar, tel 7/204-1185. Huge, well-stocked humidor and professional staff. Bar and smoking lounge.
Casa del Tabaco Parque Central, Hotel Parque Central, Calle Neptuno, Prado/Zulueta, Habana Vieja, tel 7/66-6627.

Modern smoking lounge and knowledgeable staff.

Club Havana, Ave. 5ta, 188/190, Miramar, tel 7/204-5700. Complete range of cigars. Expert staff.

El Corojo, Hotel Meliá Cohiba, Paseo, 1ra/3ra, Vedado, tel 7/33-3636. Large stock and personable, professional staff.

Palacio del Tabaco, Fábrica la Corona, Agramonte #106, Colón/Refugio, Habana Vieja, tel 7/33-8389. Large selection includes some rarer smokes. A small bar is attached.

CLOTHES & ACCESSORIES

Exclusividades Verano, Calle 18 #4106, 41/43, Vedado, tel 7/204 1982. Cuban-designed fashion wear for women. Also straw hats.

La Maison, Calle 16 & Ave. 7ma, Miramar, tel 7/204-1543. Series of upscale boutiques, plus jewelry and cosmetics stores. Fashion shows held nightly.

El Quitrín, Calle Obispo #163, bet. San Ignacio & Mercaderes, Habana Vieja, tel 7/862-0810. Handmade *guayaberas* for men. Also skirts, dresses, and blouses, plus embroideries. Items can be made to order.

Le Select, Aves. 5ta & 30, Miramar, tel 7/204-7410. Exquisite mansion housing various upscale men's and women's fashion boutiques, plus jewelry and accessories stores.

Peletería Claudia, Calle 12, 23/25, Vedado, tel 7/66-2438. Expansive range of imported shoes. Also luggage and accessories.

CRAFTS & JEWELRY

Casa del Abanico, Calle Obrapía #107, bet. Oficios & Mercaderes, Habana Vieja, tel 7/863-4452. Traditional decorated Spanish fans made and hand-painted on-site.

Galería Victor Manuel, Plaza de La Catedral, Habana Vieja, tel 7/861-2955. Splendid fine handmade silver (and black

coral) jewelry, creative wood carvings, and quality paintings.

Palacio de la Artesanía, Cuba #64, bet. Cuarteles & Peña Pobre, Habana Vieja, tel 7/33-8072. Several stores selling T-shirts, crafts, and souvenirs.

GIFTS

Casa del Café, Calle Baratillo & Obispo, Habana Vieja, tel 7/33-8061. Export-quality Cuban coffees, roasted and ground. Also coffee sets and accessories.

Farmácia Taquechel, Calle Obispo #155, Mercaderes/San Ignacio, Habana Vieja, tel 7/862-9286. Natural products, including face creams, fortifiers, oils, potions, and sponges.

Habana 1791, Calle Mercaderes #156 at Obrapía, Habana Vieja, tel 7/861-3525. Quality Cuban and imported perfumes, soaps, lotions, colognes, and toiletries.

MARKETS

Fería de Artesanía, Calle Tacón, Habana Vieja, closed Sun., Mon., Tues. This open-air street market offers the largest collection of art and crafts in Cuba. Paintings, wood carvings, cowhorn sculptures, straw hats, musical instruments, dolls, berets and other Che memorabilia, plus crocheted bikinis, dresses, and sexy wraps, etc.

Fería del Malecón, Malecón & D, Vedado. Crafts market offering many original items—particularly jewelry—not represented at the Fería de Artesanía.

MISCELLANEOUS

Bomboneria La Ambrosia, Calle Mercaderes, Obispo/Obrapía. Boxed Cuban chocolates, including "Peter's" brand from Baracoa.

Centro Cultural Cinematográfico, Calle 23 #1155, bet. Calle 10 & 12, Vedado, tel 7/831-1101. The Cuban Film Institute sells Cuban films on video. Also silkscreen prints.

Colección Habana, Calle Mercaderes #13, bet. O'Reilly & Empredrado, Habana Vieja, tel 7/861-3388. Quality home decor and reproduction items, from ceramics to furniture. Also exquisite fabrics and jewelry and accessories.

Galería La Exposición, Calle San Rafael #12, Bélgica/Agramonte, Habana Vieja, tel 7/863-8364. Cramped basement store stuffed with reproduction prints of Cuban artwork and posters.

MUSIC

Casa de la Música Egrem, Calle 20 #3308, bet. Calles 33 & 35, Miramar, tel 7/204-0447. A vast collection of CDs and cassettes spanning the Cuban musical spectrum. Also musical instruments.

Industria de Instrumentos Musicales Fernando Ortíz, Calle Pedroso #102 at Calle Nueva, Cerro, tel 7/79-3151. Worskhop making guitars, drums, claves, and other musical instruments.

Longina, Calle Obispo #360, Habana Vieja, tel 7/62-8371. Large CD collection, plus *bata* drums and other instruments.

RUM

Fábrica de Ron Bocoy, Calzada de Cerro, Patria/Auditor, Cerro, tel 7/870-5642. Rare Bocoy and other rums produced here. Sample the goods in the tasting room, upstairs, as some rums are disappointing.

Fundación Havana Club, Museo del Ron, Ave. San Pedro #262 & Sol, tel 7/862 4108. Well-stocked rum store selling Havana Club brand, plus gift-sets, T-shirts, and other souvenirs.

Taberna del Galeón, Calle Baratillo & Obispo, Habana Vieja, tel 7/33-8476. Colonial mansion now housing a rum store selling a wide range of brands. Free rum-tasting in the upstairs bar.

FAR WEST

The region is not blessed with shopping opportunities. The town of Pinar del Río is an exception.

GIFTS

Fábrica de Bebidas Guayabita, Calle Isabel Rubio #189, Pinar del Río, tel 82/2966. The region's famed brandylike *guayabita* liquor is made here from rum and wild guava. You can take a group tour and sample the drink (which comes in sweet and dry versions).

Fábrica de Tabacos Francisco Donatien, Calle Maceo Oeste #157, Pinar del Río, tel 82/3424. This small cigar factory produces for domestic consumption, but the store sells export brand cigars, including Vequeros, produced on site.

WESTERN CUBA–NORTH

Buying opportunities are concentrated in Varadero, where most upscale hotels feature gift stores. Some even have their own Casa del Habanos, with well-stocked humidors. In Santa Clara, "El Bulevar" (Calle Independencia, between Maceo and Zayas) is lined with boutiques and stores.

CIGARS

Casa del Habano, Calle 63, Aves. 1ra/3ra, Varadero, tel 5/66-7843. A large humidor offers premium cigars. You can enjoy your stogie in the smoking lounge, upstairs.

CRAFTS & JEWELRY

Bazar Varadero Publicigraf, Ave. 1ra, Calle 44, Varadero, tel 45/66 7691. Paintings, prints, ceramics, *muñequitas* (dolls), plus T-shirts and other souvenirs.

Galería de Arte, Ave. 1ra & Calle 59, Varadero, tel 45/66 7691. Quality artwork including erotic hardwood and marble

carvings, and paintings and prints by top Cuban artists.

Joyería Coral Negro, Calle 63 & Ave. 2da, tel 45/61-4870. Expansive collection of name-brand watches (a Swatch with Che Guevara on the *facia* costs $50) and quality local silver and black coral jewelry.

Taller de Cerámica Artística, Ave. 1ra & Calle 59, Varadero, tel 45/66-7554. Magnificent kitchen sets and other hand-painted ceramics produced by leading Cuban artists such as Alfredo Sosabravo and Sergio Roque.

MARKET

Fería de Artesanía, Ave. 1ra, bet. Calles 44 & 46, Varadero. Visit this large crafts market, where dozens of stalls sell arts and crafts from kitschy berets with Che's image to cowhorn sculptures, crocheted bikinis, straw hats, musical instruments, and Santería dolls.

MISCELLANEOUS

Ediciones Vigía, Calle 272, Calles 85/91, Matanzas. This unique institution produces handbound, limited edition books. You can tour the facility before purchasing a collector's first-edition.

MUSIC

Max Music, Calle 63 & Ave. 1ra, Varadero, tel 5/61-4186. Wide selection of CDs and cassettes spanning the spectrum of Cuban music.

WESTERN CUBA–SOUTH

Trinidad is a trove of crafts. Cienfuegos has several boutiques and stores concentrated along Ave. 54, a pedestrian precinct colloquially called "El Bulevar."

CRAFTS & JEWELRY

El Alfarero Cerámica, Calle Andrés Berro Macias #51, Pepito Tey/Abel Santamaría, Trinidad, tel 419/3053. Family-run cooperative producing ceramics.

Cubartesanía, Ave. 54 & Calle 31, Cienfuegos, tel 432/43-5602. Browse this souvenir store for T-shirts and crafts.

Fábrica de Cerámica Guama, La Boca de Guama. The ceramics—bowls, vases, teapots—produced at this workshop are intended for the domestic market, but masks and other fanciful creations might take your fancy.

Fondo Cubano de Bienes Culturales, Calle Independencia #55, Sancti Spíritus, tel 41/22820. Locally produced arts and crafts, plus T-shirts and souvenirs.

Fondo Cubano de Bienes Culturales, Calle Simón Bolívar #418, Trinidad, tel 416/3590. Wide range of mostly quality crafts that includes wickerwork.

Galería de Arte Benito Ortíz, Calle Ruben Mártinez Villena #357, Plaza Mayor, Trinidad. Two-story art gallery displaying contemporary art and classical pieces.

Galería Maroya, Ave. 54 #2506, Parque Martí, Cienfuegos, tel 432/545-1208. Diverse array of arts and crafts that include batiks, carvings, leatherwork, and paintings.

Tienda el Fundador, Ave. 54, Calle 31, Cienfuegos. Wide selection of quality crafts and music cassettes and CDs.

MARKET

Fería de Artesanía, Calle Jesús Menéndez & Fernández Hernández, Trinidad. The largest of several street fairs selling arts and crafts.

MUSIC

Artex El Topacio, Ave. 54 #3510, bet. Calles 35 & 37, Cienfuegos. A broad selection of music CDs and cassettes, plus

musical instruments.
Casa de la Música, Calle Juan Manuel Márquez, bet. Simón Bolívar & J. Menéndez, Trinidad, tel 416/3414. One of the best-stocked music stores in the country.

CENTRAL CUBA

CRAFTS & JEWELRY

Fondo Cubano de Bienes Culturales, Ave. de la Libertad #112, Camagüey, tel 322/28-5382. A small yet well-stocked shop selling arts, crafts, T-shirts, etc. Look for miniature ceramic *tinajones.*
Galería de la Asociación Cubana de Artesanía, Calle Padre Valencia, Plaza de los Tra-bajadores, Camagüey. Intriguingly inventive sculptures and carvings highlight the mostly naïve arts and crafts displayed here.

GIFTS

Fábrica de Instrumentos Musicales, Calle Camilo Cienfuegos, Minas, tel 32/96232. This cooperative produces guitars, violas, cellos, and other musical instruments. The items displayed for sale to tourists are of inferior quality; ask to see the real McCoy.

WESTERN ORIENTE

CRAFTS & JEWELRY

Fondo Cubana de Bienes Culturales, Calle Frexes #196, Parque Calixto García, Holguín, tel 24/42-3783. Beautiful artwork, including impressive ceramics, hardwood lamp shades, Daliesque paintings.
Fondo Cubana de Bienes Cul-turales, Calle Colón #171, Plaza Martí, Las Tunas, tel 31/43469. A selection of straw baskets, leather saddles, paintings and prints plus bas-relief ceramics.

EASTERN ORIENTE

In Santiago de Cuba, most hotels have souvenir stores selling muñecitas (dolls) of the orishas, and music CDs and cassettes—notably of *son,* cha-cha-cha, and other local sounds.

CRAFTS & JEWELRY

Cubartesanía, Calle Carnicería #360 Callejón del Carmen/San Gerónimo, Santiago de Cuba, tel 22/62-2003. A broad range of quality arts and crafts.
Comunidad Artística El Oasis, Carretera de Baconao, Baconao. This community of artists produces quality work—paintings, ceramics, sculptures—sold in open studios.
Comunidad Artística Verraco, Carretera de Baconao, Baconao. Another dedicated artists' community with indivi-dual studios selling experimental paintings, sculptures, and pottery.
Galería de Arte UNEAC, Calle Heredia #266, Hartmann/Pío Rosada, Santiago de Cuba, tel 22/65-3465. A large collection of dynamic art.
Galería las Musas, Calle Maceo, bet. Maraví & Frank País, Baracoa. Studio of noted artists Roel Caboverde and Orlando Piedra.
Taller de Muñequitas, Calle Martí #124, Baracoa. This small workshop, in a former colonial mansion, fashions dolls for sale, including orishas.
Galería Pelay Alvarez López, Calle Félix Ruenes #25, Baracoa. The eponymous artist sculpts hardwoods into precious carvings.

GIFTS

Fábrica de Tabaco César Escalante, Ave. Aguilera & Jesús Menéndez, Santiago de Cuba, tel 226/54207. Well-stocked humidor sells most well-known cigar brands.
Fábrica de Ron Caney, Ave. Peralejo #103, Santiago de Cuba, tel 226/62-5575. Famous rum factory with sampling room

selling locally produced rums, including Ron Paticruzados ("cross-legged rum").

MARKET

Fería de Artesanía, Calle Heredia, Santiago de Cuba. A daily artisans' street market. Look for papier-mâché masks and cars, *maracas,* and carvings of ebony and other hardwoods.

MUSIC

Artex, Calle Heredia #304, bet. Calvario & Carnicería, Santiago de Cuba, tel 22/62-7037. Cultural center with live music daily. Large selection of music cassettes and CDs.
Fábrica de Instrumentos Musicales, Calle Patricio Lumumba #55, Santiago de Cuba, tel 22/62-5256. This workshop makes guitars, drums, and other musical instruments, which can be bought on site.

ARCHIPIÉLAGO DE CANARREOS

CRAFTS & JEWELRY

Centro Experimental de Artes Aplicadas, Calle 40, Calles 37/39, Isla de la Juventud. This experimental workshop has a store selling ceramics.
Fondo Cubano de Bienes Culturales, Calle 39, Calles 24/26, Nueva Gerona, Isla de la Juventud, tel 61/23151. Locally made bas-relief ceramics and wooden reliefs.
Taller de Cerámica Artística, Calle 26 & 37, Nueva Gerona, Isla de la Juventud. Potters produce plates, tea sets, and surrealistic figurines.

GIFTS

Caracol, Playa Larga, Cayo Largo, tel 5/48243. Catering mostly to beach-going vacationers, this store stocks swimwear, T-shirts, sandals, etc., but also has crafts and souvenirs. Avoid the inflated toads, stuffed turtles, and black coral items.

ENTERTAINMENT & ACTIVITIES

Havana befits its role as capital city with everything from classical concerts to hip discos. Events are listed in La Cartelera Juventud Rebelde, La Isla: Catálogo Cultural and Granma. The tourist radio station, Radio Taino (FM 93.3), posts entertainment updates.

Most Cubans are inventive in their entertainment. Cumbanchas—street parties—and pesas (musical gigs) are popular. Most towns have a communal street party on Saturday nights; you'll need your own cup to buy the cheap and rum sold at street stalls. Provincial cities each have their own cultural life, usually centered on the local Casa de la Cultura (House of Culture)—relaxed community venues hosting state-sponsored bolero, Afro-Cuban rumba, and folkloric performances, plus art classes and exhibitions, etc. Times and performances vary daily. Local communities are also served by a Casa de la Trova, where traditional trova music is performed.

The casinos are long gone, but Las Vegas-style cabarets espectáculos, with befeathered, G-stringed mulattas (albeit no longer topless), remain immensely popular with Cubans.

Most regions have their own musical traditions. Festivals enliven the year.

The nation has not yet made the most of its potential for activities, especially regarding nature, although things are changing.

ACTIVITIES

Two state-owned corporations control most commercial outdoor activities:

Cubamar, 3ra and Malecón, Havana, tel 7/66-2423 or 7/95-2309, fax 7/33-3111, e-mail cubamar@cubamar.mit.cma.net.
Rumbos, Calle O #108, 1ra/3ra, Miramar, Havana, tel 7/204-4520, fax 7/204-7167, e-mail director@rumvia.co.cu.

Water sports are well developed; most upscale resorts offer a selection of watercraft, plus scuba diving and snorkeling. In most other regards, Cuba is virtually starting from scratch.

BIRDING

Good primers for birding and nature hikes are: Field Guide to the Birds of Cuba by Orlando H. Garrido and Arturo Kirkconnell, and Natural Cuba by Alfonso Silva Lee.
Cubatur, tel 7/33-4037
Questers, tel 800-468-8668, fax 212-251-0890, e-mail quest1973@aol.com

BICYCLING

Cycling is an increasingly popular way to experience Cuba alongside Cubans. If exploring on your own, bring spare parts. A good resource is the **Federación de Ciclismo,** tel 7/68-3776.

The following offer organized tours:
Club Nacional de Cicloturismo, tel 7/96-9193, fax 7/66-9908, e-mail trans@mail.infocom.etecsa.cu
Global Exchange, tel 415-255-7296, fax 415-255-7498, e-mail info@globalexchange.org
International Bicycle Fund, tel/fax 206-767-0848, e-mail ibike@ibike.org
MacQueen's Adventure Tours, tel 902-894-4547, 800-969-2822, e-mail david@macqueens.com

FISHING

The Gulf Stream—Hemingway's "great blue river"—is flush with feisty billfish and tuna that give anglers rod-bending fights to remember. Sportfishing is available in Havana and major

resorts. Boat charters cost $150–250 a half day (up to four people).

Sportfishing excursions are operated by **Marina Hemingway,** tel 7/204-6848. They also offer boat rides without fishing, boat rides along the coral reef with or without lunch, and scuba diving. All excursions include open bar.

The lagoons of Zapata and the shallow waters of the Jardines de la Reina and Jardines del Rey offer prime fishing for tarpon, bonefish, and other hard-fighting species. And Lake Zaza and Lake Habanilla are among the more popular of several inland lakes where prize-size bass can be landed.
Last Frontier Expeditions, tel 303-530-9275, fax 303-527-3903, e-mail bob@cubatravelexperts.com

GOLFING

Golf courses are found only in Varadero and Havana (see regional entries), although more are planned for Cayo Coco and Holguín province.

TRADITIONAL MUSIC & DANCE

Immerse yourself in Cuba's vibrant music and dance scene and learn sensual hip-swiveling moves.
Plazacuba, tel 510-848-0911, e-mail plazacuba@yahoo.com

SCUBA DIVING

Coral reefs surround Cuba, enchanting divers from far and wide. Whale sharks are often seen in Bahía de Corrientes. Spanish galleons and coral formations highlight diving off Isla de la Juventud, Cayo Largo, and Jardines de la Reina. Visibility is excellent. Temperatures average 27°C to 29°C year-round. Dive centers are found throughout the island. See regional entries.
Scubacan, tel 416-927-1257,

ENTERTAINMENT & ACTIVITIES

888-799-2822, fax 416-927-8595, e-mail scubacan@idirect.com
Scuba Cuba, tel 308-532-4700, e-mail divecuba@aol.com
Scuba in Cuba, tel 310-842-4148, e-mail scuba@cubatravel.co.mx

HAVANA

THE ARTS

Gran Teatro, Paseo de Martí #458, bet. San Rafael & San Martín, Habana Vieja, tel 7/861-3077. Classical and ballet performances; $10 best orchestra seats. Dress code (no shorts).
Teatro Amadeo Roldán, Ave. 7ma & D, Vedado, tel 7/32-1168. Classical performances; occasional jazz.
Teatro Karl Marx, Ave. 1ra & 8, Vedado, tel 7/23-0801. Big name bands such as Los Van Van. Closed Sun.
Teatro Mella, Calles 7 & A, Vedado, tel 7/35651. Contemporary dance, avant-garde theater.
Teatro Nacional, Paseo & 39, Plaza de la Revolución, tel 7/879-6011 and 7/879-3558, e-mail tnc@cubarte.cult.cu. Theater, exhibitions, dance and music performances.

CULTURAL CENTERS

Casa de las Américas, Calle 3ra & Presidentes, Vedado, tel 7/55 2706. Movies, lectures, art exhibitions, and performances.
Casa de la Amistad, Paseo #406, 17/19, tel 7/830 2468. Live open-air performances of son, boleros, and other musical forms. Tues. and Sat.
Casa de la Cultura, Calle Aguilar #509 & Teniente Rey, Habana Vieja, tel 7/863-4860. Closed Mon.
Casa de la Cultura, Ave. Salvador Allende #720, Centro Habana, tel 7/878-4727

FESTIVALS

APRIL
International Percussion Festival, tel 7/203-8808, e-mail lneira@cubarte.cult.cu

MAY
Hemingway International Dialogue, Finca Vigía, tel 7/91-0809, e-mail mushem@cubarte.cult.cu
International Guitar Festival & Contest (biennial), tel 7/31-1234
May Day Parade (May 1), Plaza de la Revolución. Political parade; over one million people show their solidarity with the revolution.

JULY/AUG
Carnaval de La Habana, Paseo de Martí & Malecón. Processions, floats, music, dance.

OCTOBER
International Ballet Festival, (biennial), Gran Teatro and other venues, tel 7/835-2951, fax 7/836-3117, e-mail bnc@cubarte.cult.cu, www.balletcuba.cu. The National Ballet of Cuba highlights this acclaimed festival.

NOVEMBER
Havana Biennale, various venues, tel 7/861-2096. International artists display their works.

DECEMBER
New International Latin-American Film Festival, Hotel Nacional and other venues, tel 7/55-2854.
Procession of the Miracles (Dec. 17), Santuario de San Lázaro, Rincón. Religious procession to request or give thanks for miracles.

NIGHTLIFE

Most nightclubs draw a predominantly expatriate and touristy crowd. Jineteras often attempt to hang on patrons' coattails to gain entry. Drinks in touristy discos are often exorbitant; follow the Cuban example and buy a bottle of rum to share around. Many bars and upscale restaurants feature live musicians.
La Bodeguita del Medio, Calle Empedrado #207, Habana Vieja, tel 7/867-1375. Rustic bar with Hemingway associations.
Cabaret Copa Room, Hotel Riviera, Paseo/Malecón, tel 7/33-4051. Cabaret followed by danc-

ing, Wed.–Mon.
Cabaret Parisién, Hotel Nacional, Calle O/21, tel 7/33-3564. Cabaret, nightly.
Cabaret Tropicana, Calle 72 #4504, Marianao, tel 7/267-1717. Full-on cabaret extravaganza, nightly under the stars. Pricey, but a "must visit." Closed Mon.
Café Concert Gato Tuerto, Calle O, 17/19, Vedado, tel 7/55-2696. Bolero, rap, and "feeling music" draw Cubans and foreigners alike to this tight-packed, smoke-filled club.
Disco Chang, Calle San Nicolás #517, Dragones/Zanza, Centro Habana, tel 7/862-1490. Private disco drawing Cubans.
Habana Café, Hotel Meliá Cohiba, Paseo and 1ra/3ra, Vedado, tel 7/33-3636. Colorful 1950s-style club with cabaret, nightly. Clientele comprises tourists and jineteras.
Jazz Café, Galerías de Paseo, Paseo & 1ra, Vedado, tel 7/55-3475. Top jazz bands, nightly.
Macumba Habana, La Giraldilla, Calle 222, 37/51, La Coronela, tel 7/33-0568. Open-air disco preceded by cabaret nightly. Fashion show, Mon.
La Maison, Calle 16 #701 at 7ma, Miramar, tel 7/204-1543. Open-air fashion show, nightly.
Salón Turquino, Hotel Habana Libre, Calle L, Vedado, tel 7/33-4011. Varying entertainment plus dancing; cabarets.
La Zorra y el Cuervo, Calle 23, N/O, Vedado, tel 7/66-2402. Jazz greats such as Chucho Valdéz draw crowds to this cramped subterranean club.

SPECIAL EVENTS

Ceremonia del Cañonazo, Fortaleza de San Carlos de la Cabaña, tel 7/62-0671. Lighting of cannon by soldiers in period uniform, nightly at 8:45 p.m.
Noche en la Plaza de La Catedral, Plaza de La Catedral, Habana Vieja. Cocktails, dinner, and folkloric espectáculo in the cathedral square, third Sat. monthly. Also at Plaza de San Francisco. Reservations c/o Habaguanex, tel 7/33-8693.

TRADITIONAL MUSIC & DANCE

Casa de la Trova, Calle San Lázaro #661, Centro Habana, tel 7/879-3373. Traditional music and poetry, evenings. Thurs.–Sun. 7–10 p.m.
Caserón del Tango, Calle Justíz #21, Habana Vieja, tel 7/861-0822. Informal tango *peñas,* Wed. and Fri.; shows on Sat. evenings.
Encounter With Cuban Music, Calle San Ignacio #78, Habana Vieja, tel 7/61-0412. Live rumba hosted on a private rooftop overlooking Plaza de La Catedral, Mon. and Fri. eve.
El Gran Palenque, Calle 4 #103, Calzada/5ta, tel 7/33-9075. Afro-Cuban rumba by the Conjunto Folklórico Nacional de Cuba, Sat. 3–5 p.m.
Rumba del Cayo, Callejon de Hamel & Hospital, Centro Habana, tel 7/878-1661. Afro-Cuban rumba and celebration of Santería. Sun. noon (every third Sat. is for kids).
Yola en Familia, Calle Cuba, Brasil/Muralla. Informal, lively street *peña* with musicians; third Sat. each month, 4 p.m.

OTHER ACTIVITIES

BASEBALL
Estadio Lationamericano, Calle Zequeira #312, Cerro, tel 7/870-6526. Cuba's main stadium.

BOXING
Sala Polivalente Kid Chocolate, Prado at Teniente Rey, Habana Vieja, tel 7/867-1547. Hosts boxing matches.

DANCE LESSONS
Cátedra de Danza, Calle 5ta #253, D/E, Vedado, tel 7/832-4625, www.balletcuba.cu. Ballet and modern dance.
Folkcuba, Calle 4 #103, Calzada/5ta, Vedado, tel/fax 7/830-3939. Popular Cuban dance, from rumba to cha-cha-cha.

GOLF
Club de Golf Habana, Calzada de Vento Km 8,

Capdevilla, tel 7/33-8919. 18-hole course.
Club Habana, 5ta Ave., 188/192, Rpto. Flores, tel 7/204-5700. Practice range.

HORSEBACK RIDING
Centro Ecuestre, Parque Lenin, tel 44-3026. $15 per hour for lessons, $10 for riding. Closed Mon., Tues.

SCUBA DIVING
Centro de Buceo La Aguja, Ave. 5ta & Calle 248, Miramar, tel 7/204-6848

SPORTFISHING
Marlin S.A., Marina Hemingway, Ave. 5ta & Calle 248, Miramar, tel 7/204-1150 ext 242
Marina Puertosol Tarará, Via Blanca Km 19, Playa Tarará, tel 7/97-1462

FAR WEST

THE ARTS

Teatro José Jacinto Milanés, Pinar del Río, tel 82/3871

CULTURAL CENTER

Casa de Cultura, Pinar del Río, tel 82/2324. Known for *punta campesina* folkloric dances.

FESTIVAL

Humor Bienal Internacional (March–April), San Antonio de los Baños. Biennial comedy festival.

NIGHTLIFE

Cabaret Rumayor, Pinar del Río, tel 82/63007. Small *espectáculo* Tues.–Sun. evenings.

OTHER ACTIVITIES

BASEBALL
Estadio Capitán San Luís, Pinar del Río

BIRDING
Villas Turística Soroa, tel 82/3534
Centro Ecológico Las

Terrazas, c/o Hotel La Moka, tel 82/78600

GUIDED HIKES
Villas Turística Soroa, tel 82/3534
Hotel La Moka, Las Terrazas, tel 82/78600
Centro Ecológico Península de Guanahacabibes, see
p. 109.

SCUBA DIVING
Cayo Levisa, tel 8/66-6075, e-mail: crh@horizontes.ht.cma.net
María la Gorda International Dive Center, tel 84/78131

TRAIN RIDES
Hershey Train, tel 8/62-4888. Casablanca to Matanzas, daily.

WESTERN CUBA–NORTH

THE ARTS

Teatro Sala José White, Matanzas, tel 45/29-0153. Jazz, classical, and other concerts, nightly (theater closed for renovations at press date).
Teatro Sauto, Matanzas, tel 45/24-2721. Classical concerts, Fri.–Sun.

CULTURAL CENTERS

Casa de la Cultura, Matanzas, tel 45/29-2709 and 45/61-2562
Casa de la Cultura, Remedios, tel 42/39-5581
Casa de la Cultura, Santa Clara, tel 42/21-7181 or 42/21-5592
Casa de la Cultura, Varadero, tel 45/61-2562
UNEAC, Matanzas, tel 45/24-4857. Poetry, musical events.

FESTIVALS

In Rhythm with Caturla (March), Santa Clara, tel 7/57-0210, e-mail ahs@ujc.org.cu National festival of chamber music.
Festival of the Cuban Danzón (Nov., biennial), Matanzas, tel 45/24-3512. Workshops and

ENTERTAINMENT & ACTIVITIES

competitions of danzón and other folk dances.
Festival of Rock (Nov.), Santa Clara. The best of Cuban rock bands perform.
Parranda Remedianas (Dec.), Remedios and neighboring villages. Ferocious fireworks battles.

NIGHTLIFE

La Bamba, Hotel Tuxpán, Varadero, tel 45/66-7560. Western-style disco (open only to hotel guests).
Cabaret Cacique, Santa Clara. Comedy and *espectáculo*.
Cabaret Continental, Hotel Varadero Internacional, Varadero, tel 45/66-7039. Full-on cabaret, Tues.–Sun. evenings.
Cabaret Los Laureles, Sancti Spíritus, tel 41/27016. Cabaret and disco, Fri.-Sun.
Cabaret Tropicana, Matanzas. Sensual *cabaret espectáculo* under the stars.
Cueva del Pirata, Varadero, tel 45/66-7751. *Cabaret espectáculo* in a cave. Closed Sun.
Habana Café, Hotel Sol Palmeras, Varadero, tel 45/66-7009. Western-style disco with small *espectáculo*.
Mambo Club, Gran Hotel, Km 14 Carretera Las Morlas, Varadero, tel 45/66-8565. Western-style disco.
Palacio de la Rumba, Km 4.5 Ave. de las Américas, Varadero, tel 45/66-8385.

SPECIAL EVENTS

Annual International Regatta (May), Varadero
Gregorio Fuentes White Marlin Fishing Tournament (June), Varadero, tel 45/66-8060

OTHER ACTIVITIES

CRUISES
Jolly Roger Catamaran Cruises, tel 45/66-7565. Seafari to Cayo Blanco.

FISHING
Cayo Santa María, see p. 126.
Last Frontier Expeditions, see p. 259.

GOLF
Varadero Golf Club, Varadero, tel 45/66-7788, fax 45/66-8481. Cuba's only 18-hole championship course.

GUIDED HIKES
Parque Ecológico Varadero, see p. 119.

SCUBA DIVING
Acua Diving Center, Varadero, tel 45/61-2818
Barracuda Scuba Cuba, Varadero, tel 45/66-7072 or 45/61-3481

SKYDIVING
Centro Internacional de Paracaidismo, Varadero, tel 45/66-7256, fax 45/61-0660

SPORTFISHING
Marina Chapelín, Varadero, tel 45/66-7550, fax 45/66-7093

WAVERUNNERS
Jungle Tour, Varadero, tel 45/66-8440, e-mail jungle@ip.ete csa.cu

YACHT RENTAL
Marina Varadero, Varadero, tel 45/66-7755, fax 45/66-7756

WESTERN CUBA–SOUTH

THE ARTS

Teatro Tomás Terry, Cienfuegos, tel 432/51-3361. Performances from classical to salsa.

CULTURAL CENTERS

Casa de la Cultura, Sancti Spíritus, tel 41/23772.
Casa de la Cultura, Trinidad, tel 419/4308.

FESTIVAL

International Popular Music Festival (Sept.), Cienfuegos. Biennial celebrating Beny Moré.

NIGHTLIFE

Club Beny Moré, Cienfuegos,

tel 432/545-1105. Cabaret theater and disco.

TRADITIONAL MUSIC & DANCE

Look for performances by Conjunto Folklórico de Trinidad and Cocoró y su Aché. The latter is an Afro-Cuban troupe.

Casa de la Trova, Sancti Spíritus, tel 41/26802. Traditional music, Thurs.–Sun.
Casa de la Trova, Trinidad, tel 419/6445. Traditional music and dance.

OTHER ACTIVITIES

BIRDING
Parque Nacional Ciénaga de Zapata, Playa Larga, tel 59/7249. Fantastic birding.

FISHING
Fishing is spectacular in the Laguna de las Salinas, Ciénaga de Zapata. Freshwater fishing in Embalse Habanilla, see p. 149; and Presa Zaza, see p. 150. Also contact Rombos S.A., see p. 259.

GUIDED HIKES
The Sierra del Escambray offer mountain forests and rich birdlife; see p. 136.
Complejo Turístico Topes de Collantes, Corporación Gaviota, Trinidad, tel 42/540228, fax 42/540117, e-mail topescom@ip.etecsa.cu

SCUBA DIVING
Hotel Ancón, Playa Ancón, tel 419/6120, fax 419/6151
Club Octopus International Dive Center, Playa Larga, tel 459/7294, 459/7241, or 459/7206
Puertosol Marina Trinidad, Playa Ancón, tel 419/6205

CENTRAL CUBA

THE ARTS

Teatro Principal, Camagüey, tel 322/93048. Performances of the world-class Camagüey Ballet.

CULTURAL CENTERS

Casa de la Cultura, Camagüey, tel 322/29-3366
Casa de la Cultura, Ciego de Ávila, tel 33/23974.
Casa de la Cultura, Morón, tel 335/4309

FESTIVAL

National Folk Arts Fair (Nov.), Ciego de Ávila, tel 33/22386 or 33/23624

NIGHTLIFE

Tourist hotels on Cayos Coco and Guillermo have bars and offer in-house entertainment.
Gran Hotel, Camagüey, tel 322/92314. Lively piano bar.
Hotel Horizontes Camagüey, Camagüey, tel 322/87267. *Cabaret espectáculo,* Tues.–Sun. evenings.

TRADITIONAL MUSIC & DANCE

Casa de la Trova, Camagüey, tel 322/91357. Traditional music.
Casa de la Trova, Morón, tel 335/4158. Traditional music. Closed Tues.

OTHER ACTIVITIES

BIRDING
Flamingoes parade the lagoons of Cayos Coco, Guillermo, and Sabinal.

FISHING
Lago de la Redonda, Morón. Excellent bass fishing.
La Casona de Morón, tel 335/2236, fax 335/2125

HORSERIDING
King Ranch, Playa Santa Lucía, c/o Rumbos, see p. 259.
Sitio la Güira, Cayo Coco, tel 33/30-1208

SCUBA DIVING
Coral reefs at Jardines del Rey and Jardines de la Reina. Most tourist hotels on Cayos Coco and Guillermo offer scuba diving.
Blue Diving, Cayo Coco, tel

33/30-1323
Puertosol, tel 7/204-5923, fax 7/204-5928, e-mail reserva@ psol.mit.tur.cu

SPORTFISHING
Marina Aguas Tranquilas, Cayo Coco, tel 33/30-1221 or 33/30-8152
Marina Cayo Guillermo, Cayo Guillermo, tel 33/30-1738, fax 33/30-1737

WESTERN ORIENTE

THE ARTS
Teatro Comandante Eddy Suñol, Holguín, tel 24/46-3161

CULTURAL CENTERS
Casa de la Cultura, Bayamo, tel 23/42-5917
Casa de la Cultura, Holguín, tel 24/35241
Casa de la Cultura, Las Tunas, tel 31/45401
Casa de la Cultura, Manzanillo, tel 23/54210

FESTIVALS
May Festival (May), Holguín. Art exhibits, traditional music and dance performances.
El Cucalambé Festival (June, biennial), Las Tunas, tel 31/47770. Renditions of *decimas.*
Festival of the Cuban Essence (Oct.), Bayamo. Celebrates the roots and development of the national identity.
Festival of Iberian-American Culture (Oct.), Holguín, tel 24/46-1673. Honors the Spanish heritage in Cuban culture.

NIGHTLIFE
Most tourist hotels in Guardalavaca and Playas Esmeralda and Pesquero have bars and in-house entertainment.
Cabaret Bayamo, Bayamo, tel 23/48-1698, Fri.–Sun. evenings.
Cabaret Taíno, Las Tunas, tel 31/43823. *Cabaret espectáculo,* Thurs.–Sun. evenings.
Centro Nocturno, Holguín, tel 24/42-5185. *Cabaret espectáculo.*

Closed Tues.
Disco Luanda, Las Tunas, tel 31/46259. Western-style disco.
Disco la Roca, Guardalavaca, tel 24/30167. Popular open-air disco overlooking the sea.
Escuela de Música, tel 24/36-5642. Jazz concerts, Sat. eve.

OTHER ACTIVITIES

BASEBALL
Estadio Calixto García, Holguín, tel 24/46-2014

GUIDED HIKES
Parque Nacional Desembarco del Granma, see p. 196.
Parque Nacional La Mensura, see p. 185.
Parque Nacional Pico Turquino, see p. 192.
Reserva Ecológica Las Guanas, Playa Esmeralda, see p. 180.

SCUBA DIVING
Hotels at Playa Esmeralda have on-site dive facilities; see p. 180.
Eagle Ray Dive Center, Guardalavaca, tel 24/30-7741
Marlin Watersports Base, Guardalavaca, tel 24/30185

TRAIN RIDES
Transnico, tel 7/66-9954, fax 7/66-9908, e-mail trans@ip .etecsa.cu. Steam train rides in the Grupo Montañoso Maniabón mountains.

EASTERN ORIENTE

THE ARTS

Teatro Heredia, Santiago, tel 226/64-1124. Classical and other musical concerts.

CULTURAL CENTERS

Casa de la Cultura, Baracoa, tel 21/42364
Casa de la Cultura, Guantánamo, tel 21/32-6391
Casa de la Cultura, Santiago, tel 226/25710

FESTIVALS

Bolero Festival (June), Santiago de Cuba
Festival of the Caribbean (July), Santiago de Cuba, tel 22/62-3569. Carnival celebrating Caribbean folk cultures.
International Chorus Festival (Nov.–Dec.), Santiago de Cuba. Week-long biennial with Cuban and foreign choral singers.
Guantanamera Festival (Dec.), Guantánamo, tel 21/32-2296. Country dances, concerts, samples of French-Haitian folklore.

NIGHTLIFE

Cabaret San Pedro del Mar, Santiago, tel 22/69-1287. Small but colorful cabaret espectáculo, Wed.–Sun. evenings.
La Maison, Santiago, tel 22/64-1117. Fashion show followed by disco, nightly.
Noches de Praga, Baracoa, tel 21/43446. Earthy Western-style disco.
Pico Real Bar, Hotel Meliá Santiago, tel 22/68-7070. Rooftop bar hosting cabaret espectáculo and disco.
Tropicana Santiago, Santiago de Cuba, tel 22/64-1031, fax 22/68-6573. Sensational cabaret espectáculo, Wed.-Sun. evenings.

TRADITIONAL MUSIC & DANCE

Watch for traditional performances by Ballet Folklórica Cutumba, see p. 205; and Conjunto Folklórico de Oriente.

Alianza Francesca, Santiago, tel 22/64-1503. Tumba francesa.
Museo del Carnaval, see p. 206. Afro-Cuban rumba, Sun. evenings.

OTHER ACTIVITIES

BASEBALL
Estadio Guillermón Moncada, Santiago de Cuba. Tues.–Thurs. evenings, and Sat.–Sun. evenings Nov.–March.

BIRDING
Cuchillas del Toa Biosphere Reserve, see p. 223.

DANCE LESSONS
Center for Creative Education, tel in U.S. 845-687-4590. www.CCEdrums.org

GUIDED HIKES
Gaviotatours, tel 21/45103
Parques Naturales de Baracoa, Baracoa, tel 21/43665

WHITE-WATER RAFTING
Parques Naturales de Baracoa, Baracoa, tel 21/43665. Runs on the Río Toa offer short rapids in the midst of rain forest.

ARCHIPIÉLAGO DE CANARREOS

CULTURAL CENTER

Casa de la Cultura, Nueva Gerona, tel 61/23591

FESTIVAL

Grapefruit Festival (March), Nueva Gerona. Carnival celebrating the toronja harvest.

NIGHTLIFE

Cabaret el Patio, Nueva Gerona, tel 61/22346. Small cabaret espectáculo followed by dancing. Tues.–Sun. evenings.

OTHER ACTIVITIES

BIRDING
Hotel Colony, see p. 228.

SCUBA DIVING
"Colony" International Scuba Diving Center, Siguanea, tel 61/98181
Marina Puertosol Cayo Largo, Cayo Largo, tel 45/48213, fax 45/48212, e-mail gcom@psol.cls.tur.cu

SPORTFISHING
Marina Puertosol Cayo Largo, Cayo Largo, tel 45/48213, fax 45/48212, e-mail gcom@psol.cls.tur.cu

USEFUL WORDS & PHRASES

Excuse me *Perdón*
Hello *Hola*
Goodbye *Adiós*
Please *Por favor*
Thank you *Gracias*
You're welcome *De nada*
Good morning *Buenas días*
Good afternoon/evening *Buenas tardes*
Good night *Buenos noches*
today *hoy*
yesterday *ayer*
tomorrow *mañana*
now *ahora*
later *más tarde*
this morning *esta mañana*
this afternoon/this evening *esta tarde*
Do you speak English? *¿Hablas inglés?*
I am American *Yo soy americano/americana*
I don't understand *No entiendo*
Where is ... ? *¿Dónde esta ... ?*
I don't know *No lo sé*
At what time? *¿A que hora?*
When? *¿Quando?*

Do you have ... ? *¿Tienes un ...*
a single room *una habitación sencilla?*
a double room (double bed)? *una habitación matrimonio?*
a double room (twin beds) *una habitación con dos camas?*
for one night? *para una noche?*

I need a doctor/dentist *Necesito un médico/dentista*
Can you help me out? *¿Me puedes ayudar?*
hospital *hospital*
police station *comisaría de policia*

I'd like *Me gustaría*
How much is it? *¿Cuánto es?*
Do you accept credit cards? *¿Puedo pagar con tarajeta de crédito?*
cheap *barato*
expensive *caro*
post office *el correo*
visitor information center *la oficina de turismo*
open *abierto*
closed *cerrado*
every day *todos los día*

ILLUSTRATIONS CREDITS

Cover: David Alan Harvey Cover (all)

The photographs were taken by:
Pablo Corral Vega: 4, 9, 10-11, 21, 22-23, 24-25 (both), 28-29, 46-47 (all),
50&51, 52-53, 54-55, 56-57, 58, 59, 62, 64, 66, 68&69, 70, 72&73, 77, 80-
81, 82-83 (all), 84-85, 86&87, 90&91, 92, 93, 94&95, 138&139, 141
(both), 142, 144&145, 148, 150, 151, 154&155, 156-157, 160, 162, 167,
170&171, 180, 191, 197 (both), 199, 201, 202-203, 208, 211, 213, 214-215,
218, 231; AP/Wide World Photo 172.

Cristobal Corral Vega: 1, 2-3, 14-15, 18-19, 42-43, 45, 48&49, 63, 76,
88&89, 97, 98, 100&101, 102-103 (all), 104&105, 106-107 (all), 108&109,
110, 112, 113, 115, 116&117, 118&119, 120-121, 122&123, 124&125, 126,
127, 129, 130&131, 132, 134-135, 136 (both), 140-141, 146-147, 161,
164&165, 166, 169, 173 (both), 174-175, 177, 178&179, 181, 182-183,
184&185, 187 (both), 188-189, 193, 194-195, 196, 198, 204, 206-207, 209,
212-213, 216-217 (all), 220, 222&223, 224, 225, 227, 228&229.

Photographs also by:
Christopher P. Baker 96; David Alan Harvey 12-13, 16-17, 20, 38-39, 40-
41, 137, 152, 221; Hulton/Archive by Getty Images 27, 32, 34, 35, 36-37;
Corbis 30-31, Sygma/Sven Creutzmann/Corbis 39, Hulton-Getty/Corbis
133, Bettmann/Corbis 190.

Cutaway illustrations on pp. 74–75 and 158–159 by Maltings
Partnership, Derby, England.

One of the world's largest non-profit scientific and educational organizations, the National Geographic Society was founded in 1888 "for the increase and diffusion of geographic knowledge." Fulfilling this mission, the Society educates and inspires millions every day through its magazines, books, television programs, videos, maps and atlases, research grants, the National Geographic Bee, teacher workshops, and innovative classroom materials. The Society is supported through membership dues, charitable gifts, and income from the sale of its educational products. This support is vital to National Geographic's mission to increase global understanding and promote conservation of our planet through exploration, research, and education.

For more information, please call 1-800-NGS LINE (647-5463) or write to the following address:

National Geographic Society
1145 17th Street N.W.
Washington, D.C. 20036-4688
U.S.A.

Visit the Society's Web site at www.nationalgeographic.com.

Published by the National Geographic Society
John M. Fahey, Jr., *President and Chief Executive Officer*
Gilbert M. Grosvenor, *Chairman of the Board*
Nina D. Hoffman, *Executive Vice President,*
    President, Books and School Publishing
Kevin Mulroy, *Vice President and Editor-in-Chief*
Elizabeth L. Newhouse, *Director of Travel Publishing*
Charles Kogod, *Director of Photography*
Marianne Koszorus, *Design Director*
Cinda Rose, *Art Director*
Carl Mehler, *Director of Maps*

Staff for this book:
Barbara A. Noe, *Senior Editor and Project Manager*
Kay Hankins, *Designer*
Olivia King Carter, *Editorial Researcher*
Melissa G. Ryan, *Illustrations Editor*
Matt Chwastyk, Joseph F. Ochlak, Gregory Ugiansky, and XNR
    Productions, *Map Edit, Research, and Production*
R. Gary Colbert, *Production Director*
Richard S. Wain, *Production Project Manager*
Sharon Kocsis Berry, *Illustrations Assistant*
James B. Enzinna, *Indexer*
Janet Cave, Sallie Greenwood, Jane Sunderland, *Contributors*

Map art by ChrisOrr.com, Southampton, England
Cutaway illustrations by Maltings Partnership, Derby, England

ISBN 0-7922-6931-4

ISSN 1541-5287

Printed and bound by R.R. Donnelley & Sons, Willard, Ohio
Color separations by Quad Graphics, Alexandria, Virginia
Cover printed by Miken Inc., Cheektowaga, New York

Visit the society's Web site at http://www.nationalgeographic.com

The information in this book has been carefully checked and to the best of our knowledge is accurate. However, details are subject to change, and the National Geographic Society cannot be responsible for such changes, or for errors or omissions. Assessments of sites, hotels, and restaurants are based on the author's subjective opinions, which do not necessarily reflect the publisher's opinion. The publisher cannot be responsible for any consequences arising from the use of this book.

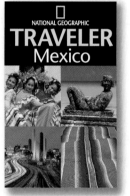